HOW CAPITALISM WAS BUILT

Anders Åslund is known for making bold predictions that initially arouse controversy but become common wisdom a few years later. He foresaw the collapse of the Soviet Union in his book *Gorbachev's Struggle for Economic Reform* (1989). He depicted the success of Russia's market transformation in *How Russia Became a Market Economy* (1995), when others saw little but chaos. After Russia's financial crisis of 1998, Åslund insisted that Russia had no choice but to adjust to the world market (*Building Capitalism*, 2002), although most observers declared the market economic experiment a failure.

- Why did Russia not choose Chinese gradual reforms?
- Why are the former Soviet countries growing much faster than the Central European economies?
- How did the oligarchs arise?
- Where are the postcommunist countries heading?

These are just some of the questions answered in his new book, *How Capitalism Was Built*, which tells the story of how all but three of twenty-one former communist countries were transformed into market economies from 1989 to 2007, but less than half of them became democracies.

Anybody who wants to understand the often confusing dramas unfolding in the region and to obtain an early insight into the future will find this book useful and intellectually stimulating.

Anders Åslund is a leading specialist on postcommunist economic transformation with more than 30 years of experience in the field. The author of seven books, he has also worked as an economic advisor to the Russian government, to the Ukrainian government, and to the president of the Kyrgyz Republic.

Dr. Åslund joined the Peterson Institute for International Economics in Washington, D.C., in January 2006. Before that he was the Director of the Russian and Eurasian Program at the Carnegie Endowment for International Peace. He teaches at Georgetown University.

He was born in Sweden and served as a Swedish diplomat. He earned his PhD from Oxford University.

Other books by Anders Åslund:

Private Enterprise in Eastern Europe, 1985.

Gorbachev's Struggle for Economic Reform, 1989.

Post-Communist Economic Revolutions: How Big a Bang? 1992.

How Russia Became a Market Economy, 1995.

Building Capitalism: The Transformation of the Former Soviet Bloc, 2002.

How Capitalism Was Built

The Transformation of Central and Eastern Europe,
Russia, and Central Asia

ANDERS ÅSLUND

Peterson Institute for International Economics,
Washington, D.C.

CAMBRIDGE UNIVERSITY PRESS

Cambridge, New York, Melbourne, Madrid, Cape Town, Singapore, São Paulo, Delhi

Cambridge University Press
32 Avenue of the Americas, New York, NY 10013-2473, USA

www.cambridge.org
Information on this title: www.cambridge.org/9780521865265

First published 2007

Printed in the United States of America

A catalog record for this publication is available from the British Library.

Library of Congress Cataloging in Publication Data

Åslund, Anders, 1952–
How capitalism was built : the transformation of Central and Eastern
Europe, Russia, and Central Asia / Anders Åslund.
p.   cm.
Includes bibliographical references and index.
ISBN 978-0-521-86526-5 (hardback) – ISBN 978-0-521-68382-1 (pbk.)
1. Former communist countries – Economic policy.   2. Former communist countries –
Economic conditions.   3. Post-communism – Former communist countries.
4. Privatization – Former communist countries.   I. Title.
HC244.A8135   2007
330.9470009′049–dc22   2007010103

ISBN   978-0-521-86526-5 hardback
ISBN   978-0-521-68382-1 paperback

For Anna, Carl, and Marianna

Contents

List of Tables and Figures

TABLES

FIGURES

List of Abbreviations

BEEPS	EBRD – World Bank Business Environment and Enterprise Performance Survey
CBR	Central Bank of Russia
CIS	Commonwealth of Independent States
CMEA	Council of Mutual Economic Assistance
CPSU	Communist Party of the Soviet Union
EBRD	European Bank for Reconstruction and Development
ECE	Economic Commission for Europe (United Nations)
EU	European Union
FIG	Financial-industrial group
GATT	General Agreement on Tariffs and Trade
GDP	Gross domestic product
GDR	German Democratic Republic
GNP	Gross national product
IFI	International financial institution
ILO	International Labor Organization
IMF	International Monetary Fund
IPO	Initial public offering
OECD	Organization for Economic Cooperation and Development
PHARE	EU technical assistance program for EU accession countries
TACIS	Technical Assistance for the CIS (EU program)
UNDP	United Nations Development Program
USAID	United States Agency for International Development
VAT	Value-added tax
WTO	World Trade Organization

Acknowledgments

This book is partly a sequel, partly an updating and revision of my book *Building Capitalism: The Transformation of the Former Soviet Bloc* (Cambridge University Press, 2002). At that time, the implications of the Russian financial crash of 1998 were still hazy. Today the perspectives on how capitalism was built are so much clearer, allowing me to paint the picture in stronger colors and focus on its main features.

The Peter G. Peterson Institute for International Economics and its director, C. Fred Bergsten, has graciously permitted me to write this book in the course of 2006. Julija Remeikaite has offered me wonderful research assistance. Matthew Gibson and Christian Grabas have provided me with additional assistance. Discussions at the Peterson Institute have been most stimulating, and I am grateful to many colleagues, especially Simon Johnson, Michael Mussa, and John Williamson.

Victor Pinchuk, Hans and Märit Rausing, as well as Adolf and Eva Lundin have provided generous financial support. I am deeply indebted to them also for their intellectual input.

This is the fourth book I am doing with Cambridge University Press, and I want once again to thank Scott Parris for his expedience and kindheartedness.

To understand what is going on in this wide region, reading is never sufficient. One also needs to travel extensively and talk to many people. I am grateful to a great many interlocutors. The gratitude that I expressed to many people in *Building Capitalism* remains valid also for this book. In addition, I thank a large number of people for their oral contribution to my understanding of the transformation of this large region (in alphabetical order): Aivaras Abromavicius, Askar Akaev, Irina Akmova, Leon Aron, Ewa and Leszek Balcerowicz, Carl Bildt, Peter Boone, Al Breach, Per Brilioth, Olexander Chalyi, Anatoly Chubais, Keith Crane, Marek Dąbrowski, Pavel

Daneiko, Dennis De Tray, Mikhail Dmitriev, Peter Elam Håkansson, Boris
G. Fedorov, Bohdan Futey, Clifford Gaddy, Yegor Gaidar, Ardo Hansson,
Andrei Illarionov, Bruce Jackson, Albert Jaeger, Nazgul Jenish, Andrzej
Kozlowski, Andrius Kubilius, Andrew Kuchins, Mart Laar, Nancy Lee,
Johannes Linn, Michael McFaul, Tatyana Maleva, Michael Marrese, Mark
Medish, Branko Milanovic, Vladimir Milov, Kalman Mizsei, Alexei Mozhin,
Boris Nemtsov, John Odling-Smee, Djoomart Otorbaev, Irina Paliashvili,
Vladimir Papava, Carlos Pascual, Alexander Paskhaver, Steven Pifer, Andrei
Piontkovsky, Olena Prytula, Nathaniel Rothschild, Charles Ryan, Stephen
Sestanovich, Lilya Shevtsova, Ben Slay, Eva Srejber, Mats Staffansson, Angela
Stent, Carl Sturén, Fredrik Svinhufvud, Vito Tanzi, David Tarr, Marat
Tazabekov, Dmitri Trenin, Dmitri Vasiliev, Valentina Vedeneeva, Yevgeny
Yasin, Yuriy Yekhanurov, and Ksenia Yudaeva.

I have greatly benefited from comments on draft chapters by Simon
Johnson, John Williamson, John Odling-Smee, Johannes Linn, Albert Jaeger,
Andrea Schaechter, Julija Remeikaite, Mathew Gibson, Anna Åslund, and
an anonymous reviewer.

Most of all I thank my understanding and supportive family, who have
helped me to write this book in more ways than I can mention here.

The responsibility for any remaining faults rests with me.

Anders Åslund
Washington, D.C.
November 2006

Introduction: A World Transformed

In 1989, the Soviet bloc – from Berlin to Vladivostok – was struck by one of the greatest liberal revolutions of all times. Since then, society has changed profoundly. A complete ideological, political, economic, and social system passed away, and some 400 million people had to choose a new system. The rejection of socialism was unequivocal. A broad consensus aspired to build democracy and a market economy based on private ownership and the rule of law, and opposition to these goals was concealed in disagreement on how to accomplish them.

At the collapse of communism, liberal revolutionaries seized the political initiative. They aspired to build a "normal society" and to "return to Europe." The petrified communist dictatorships had to give way to democracy and individual freedom, the state-controlled economy to markets, and public ownership to private property. Communism had rejected the rule of law, which should now be established. A total transformation was needed, and nobody thought it would be easy.

Communists always feared the return of capitalism. They planted many poison pills to secure the destruction of capitalism, such as the comprehensive nationalization of property, the annihilation of civil society, the elimination of markets, and the suppression of law. Communism was dead as an ideology, unable to resist the liberal revolution, but its poison pills were alive. They bred a rent-seeking state that was actually the alternative to free market capitalism. The main struggle of postcommunist transformation stood between radical market reformers, who desired a swift and complete transition, and rent seekers, whose desire was to make money on a prolonged period of market distortions.

The building of capitalism was widely seen as comprising four key steps. The first and most fundamental step was to deregulate prices and trade so that a market could be formed. Second, when prices were freed, they

1

inevitably rose because of shortages caused by excess demand, and inflation had to be brought under control by many means. Third, the nominally public enterprises lacked real masters, and the only plausible principals to be were private owners, which required large-scale privatization. Fourth, everybody understood that postcommunist transformation would involve massive social dislocation, and all acknowledged the need for a new social safety net. Democracy and the rule of law were, of course, desirable.

Perspectives change over time. As often happens during revolutions, people's expectations become exaggerated and then people become disappointed. The institutional changes have been immense, but even so the legacies of the old society remain palpable, as Alexis de Tocqueville (1856/1955) noted so accurately in *The Old Regime and the French Revolution*. Some institutions have been much more successfully reformed than others.

Postcommunist transformation has been an intense battle. On one side of the barricades stood radical reformers, who wanted to build a normal society. Their main opponents were rent seekers, not old communists. The rent seekers' goal was plain: to make as much money as possible on transitional market distortions. Their endeavors led to a great misallocation of resources and slumping output. Their hunger for state subsidies and subsidized credits boosted inflation, disorganizing the whole economy. All their successes skewed income and wealth distribution in their favor.

Despite all hardship, most socialist economies have swiftly become ordinary market economies. Of the twenty-one countries studied in this book,[1] all but three – Belarus, Turkmenistan, and Uzbekistan – have been successfully transformed. Transactions are monetary, reasonably free, and carried out on markets. In almost all of these countries, inflation has fallen to single digits, and nearly two-thirds of the national output is produced in privately owned enterprises. The international community knew how to build a market economy. Predominantly, it advocated a radical market economic reform with deregulation, macroeconomic stabilization, privatization, and the formation of a new social safety net. To a reasonable degree, this policy was implemented, but mostly with delays. To build a market economy was a political choice that most, but not all, governments made. The three CIS

---

[1] They once formed the Soviet bloc in East-Central Europe and the Soviet Union. I call Poland, the Czech Republic, Slovakia, and Hungary "Central Europe," and Bulgaria and Romania "Southeast Europe." Estonia, Latvia, and Lithuania are the Baltic states. Together, I call these three subregions "East-Central Europe." The rest of the region consists of the twelve countries belonging to the Commonwealth of Independent States (CIS), Russia, Belarus, Ukraine, Moldova, Armenia, Azerbaijan, Georgia, Kazakhstan, Kyrgyzstan, Tajikistan, Turkmenistan, and Uzbekistan.

nonreformers showed that the success of the market economy was not a given.

The building of democracy and the establishment of the rule of law have been much less successful. Frequent complaints are that too much attention and resources were devoted to economic reform and too little to political and legal reforms. This may be true, but more striking is that in these spheres no viable theory predominated and the policy advice was often too vague and diverse to be helpful. National leaders had no clear idea or program to follow. As a consequence, only the European Union (EU) accession countries, which adopted all the EU institutions, were successful in building democracy. The promotion of the rule of law has been even more unsatisfactory.

The outcomes of postcommunist transition have been remarkably diverse. The results have depended on early policy choices, which were influenced by the conditions prevailing in each country. The Central Europeans swiftly shifted to normal market economies and privatized. They adopted West European social welfare systems with high taxes, large social transfers, and excessive labor market regulation, which have impeded their economic dynamism, but they have also become impeccable democracies, and corruption is relatively limited.

Nine Commonwealth of Independent States (CIS) reformers also developed market economies, but of a more East Asian type with low taxes, limited social transfers, and liberal labor markets. The low taxes are a major cause of their recent high growth rates. Low flat income taxes, decreasing corporate profit taxes, and the liberalization of labor markets are proliferating from the East into the EU. Alas, they are at best semidemocratic and mostly authoritarian states, with pervasive corruption.

The Baltics cleverly chose the best of both of these worlds, adopting full-fledged market economies with limited public sectors and high economic growth. They also enjoy democracy and limited corruption. Southeast Europe straddles a middle ground between the social democratic Central European model and the liberal Baltic model. It is still too early to say what eventual choice it will make.

Three CIS countries are completely nonreformed, Belarus, Turkmenistan, and Uzbekistan. They are true tyrannies, and they maintain a state-dominated, Soviet-style system.

Overview of the Arguments of this Book

Postcommunist transition has aroused many debates. Often the discussion has been heated, because the issues involved have been of great importance to numerous people. To offer the reader an overview of the arguments of this book, some of the most common, as well as contentious, questions are posed here with brief answers summarizing what the reader will find in this book.

Why Didn't Russia Follow the Successful Chinese Model of Economic Reform?

Secretary General Mikhail Gorbachev attempted gradual economic reforms for two years until he realized that the omnipotent party bureaucracy blocked all his efforts. He responded by launching glasnost and partial democratization to undermine the apparatchiks. In China, the bureaucracy had been disciplined by the Cultural Revolution and still obeyed the Center. The Soviet Union had experimented with gradual reforms in the 1920s, 1950s, 1960s, and 1980s, but all these reforms had been reversed. The dominant reformist conclusion was that reforms had to be more radical to become irreversible. China had successfully started with reforms in agriculture, but that sector was not very large in the Soviet economy, so any success would have had limited impact on the economy as a whole. Moreover, Soviet collective farms were large-scale and industrialized, rendering their reform far more complex than in the manual Chinese agriculture. Gradual price deregulation seemed to work in China, but in Russia it was a major source of disruptive rent seeking. The Soviet Union collapsed in hyperinflation, whereas the Chinese leaders never lost control over macroeconomic stability. In the end, surprisingly little can be compared in China and Russia, because their preconditions differed greatly. So it would be surprising if the same model would generate similar results or even be applicable.

Why Was Postcommunist Transition So Arduous?

The postcommunist transition was replete with hardship. The initial conditions were truly awful. Most countries entered transition amid serious economic crisis with high inflation and output nearly in free fall. The combination of excessive foreign debt, large budget deficits, and prevalent shortages necessitated price liberalization. But when prices were freed, they skyrocketed. The overarching early task was to defeat inflation because as long as inflation stayed high, output plummeted. A whole new system had to be built, and the knowledge of how to do so was limited.

Another reason for enduring hardship was that many rent seekers, who were prominent members of the old and new elite, could make fortunes on market distortions. They favored low regulated prices and restricted trade to make money on privileged foreign trade arbitrage. They insisted on low state interest rates because they benefited from ample access to state credits. As conditions altered, they swiftly found new means of extracting rents until the construction of a market economy had been completed. They did what they could to prolong the transition period because it was a window of opportunity for them. Meanwhile, the rent-seeking elite ignored the negative impact on output, not to mention on the well being of the population, of their shenanigans. All measures indicate that as radical and early a transition as possible yielded the best economic and social results.

Has Output Really Fallen More than During the Great Depression?

The decline in output can hardly be compared to the degree of decline experienced during the Great Depression, but we shall never possess an exact answer because the problems of measurement and definition are immense. All official statistics exaggerate the decline in output, and the multiple biases point in one direction. In the Soviet system, managers wanted to exaggerate their output to reach their plan targets, whereas private businessmen prefer to understate their production to alleviate taxation. Statistical systems could not survey the many new private enterprises, and the unregistered economy grew. Much of the socialist product was unusable and unsaleable – sheer value detraction that should never have been recorded as value added. Under socialism, consumers suffered from shortages, massive queuing, awful quality, limited choice, and forced substitution because more often than not they could not find what they wanted. Military production accounted for about one-quarter of the Soviet gross domestic product (GDP) in the late 1980s. This production was real, but demand for it plummeted with the end of the Cold War. The energy and raw material producers in the former Soviet Union gave large implicit subsidies to the energy-poor states in the west and south, and the Central Asian republics received large annual budget subsidies from Moscow. Because we shall never be able to agree on the value of the Soviet GDP, we cannot agree on how much it has fallen. All told, the "real" output fall might have been about half as much as official statistics suggest.

Hadn't a More Gradual Dissolution of the Soviet Union Been Better?

A gradual dissolution would not have been better; the greatest disaster at the dissolution was the maintenance of the ruble zone for one and a half years, which led to hyperinflation (more than 50 percent of inflation in the course of one month) in ten of the twelve CIS countries because of competitive issue of money by multiple central banks. The Baltic countries were the most successful both in their building of market economies and democracy thanks to their early and clean break with the rest of the Union. The Soviet Union had stopped functioning as a fiscal and monetary entity by late 1990 because the Union republics no longer passed on their fiscal revenues to the Union treasury while irresponsibly boosting their expenditures beyond their means. Because Russia had democratized more and earlier than the Soviet Union, Russia enjoyed more political legitimacy than the Union. Finally, no empire has succumbed with as little bloodshed as the Soviet Union. The dissolution of the Soviet Union in December 1991 stands out as a wise and heroic deed of great foresight.

Has Privatization Been Overdone?

Privatization has not been overdone. The predominance of private enterprise has been a precondition of both market economy and democracy. Private enterprises have generated virtually all economic growth. The price paid for an enterprise at its privatization was not very important because successful privatized firms often pay annual taxes exceeding the highest price imaginable of the original asset. Because private companies generally do better than public enterprises, it is more important that enterprises are privatized early than how they are privatized. The later the privatization, the greater the destruction of both physical and human capital was. But it does matter that a privatization be perceived as legitimate, so that the resulting property rights are politically recognized. Restitution, mass privatization, and sales to insiders have been more easily accepted than initial sales to outsiders, although the latter have been economically successful.

Are Oligarchs Pure Parasites?

Oligarchs are not parasites per se. In the early transition, the oligarchs were the most outstanding rent seekers, but as normal market economies obtained, the oligarchs adjusted and have been highly productive since 1999. In Russia, Ukraine, and Kazakhstan, young, able, local businessmen have revived and restructured many a Soviet mastodon, especially in energy and metals. In these industries, existing enterprises were large and so were the economies of scale. Foreign investors have mostly proved helpless in the early restructuring of large Soviet factories. Local businessmen have excelled in these tasks: managing relations with both regional and central governments, defeating pervasive criminality at plants, and handling the complex social rules while slashing the work force, utilizing the existing physical capital rationally, and securing both property rights and contracts. Because of the weak legislation and judicial system, which resulted in poor corporate governance, concentrated ownership has been superior to widespread ownership. As a consequence of their concentrated ownership of large successful corporations, the oligarchs have become very wealthy. By contrast, because of unwillingness to sell cheaply to local businessmen, large plants have mostly died in Central Europe either in the hands of inept foreign investors or, more often, in protracted, unproductive state ownership.

Has Western Aid Been Excessive?

Western assistance to the postcommunist countries has been small by any standard. The total grant assistance to the region was a couple of billion dollars a year, which is tiny. By contrast, the U.S. peace dividend, that is, the reduction in U.S. military expenditures that became possible because of the end of the Cold War amounted to a stunning $1.4 trillion in the 1990s, or as much as 3 percent of the U.S. GDP in 1999. Amazingly, Western governments received more in debt service on old communist loans than they gave in both loans and grants to the postcommunist countries from 1993 to 1996. The Western negligence to make a serious effort at assistance in the early transition is disturbing.

East Germany has suffered from the opposite problem. Since 1990, West Germany has poured over $80 billion a year into its new *Laender* – about half its GDP and twice the global assistance to developing countries – which has greatly exceeded that region's absorption capacity. East Germany has been priced out of the market by this giant financial flow that has formed an insurmountable social welfare trap. Strangely, this harmful wastage of public resources is continuing unabated.

Is the European Union the Best Solution?

The European Union has made impressive contributions to the transformation of the EU accession countries. It provided the standard of a normal society. Both through its demands and its transfer of institutions, it helped to reinforce democracy in the accession countries. From an early stage, the EU opened its vast market to them. In the accession process, the EU compelled the new members to adopt 80,000 pages of legal texts in the *acquis communautaire*. The great advantage was that the new members were forced to adopt a standard Western market economic and legal system. The shortfall was that they were induced to accept a West European social welfare model with high taxes, large social transfers, and various forms of overregulation, notably of labor markets and agriculture. That model is not conducive to high economic growth, which is one of these countries' greatest needs.

Have the Postcommunist Countries Achieved Sustainable Economic Growth?

Sustainable growth has probably been achieved. The Russian financial crash turned out to be the catharsis Russia needed to accomplish a full-fledged market economy with a critical mass of markets, macroeconomic stability, and private enterprises. Its impact was felt throughout the post-Soviet region. Growth returned with a vengeance. It has been driven by sound macroeconomic policies, structural reforms, sharp cuts in public expenditures, low exchange rates, and a commodity boom. Since 2000, the huge former Soviet region from the Baltics to Kazakhstan has recorded an average growth of more than 8 percent a year.[2] The former Soviet Union has joined the growth belt that started in East Asia a few decades ago and has proliferated through China and India. Common features of all these economies are sound macroeconomic policies, low taxes, small social transfers, and relatively liberal labor markets. In 2003, Goldman Sachs stunned the world with a paper about the BRICs (Brazil, Russia, India, and China), predicting that in 2028, Russia would be the fifth biggest economy in the world after the United States, China, Japan, and India (Wilson and Purushothaman 2003). If sustained high oil prices are added, Russia could become the fifth biggest economy in the world before 2020 (Westin 2005). Most of the former Soviet Union is growing even faster than Russia. Will this growth survive the current commodity boom? It probably will in the star performers – the Baltics, Armenia, Azerbaijan, and Kazakhstan because they have undertaken considerable reforms. The main question mark is Russia, which has seriously aggravated its structural policies and reverted to renationalization.

Alas, approaching the European Union, this dynamism fades away. Central Europe (Poland, the Czech Republic, Slovakia, and Hungary) got stuck with a growth rate of only 4 percent a year from 2000 to 2005. Admittedly, that is more than twice the EU rate, but these still-poor countries need much faster growth, and at this rate, they will not converge with the rest of the EU.

Latin America is a natural yardstick for achievements in the postcommunist region. Both before and after the collapse of communism, their economic level was similar. The postcommunist countries have caught up with Latin America by establishing a market economy and privatization. Latin America has been more successful in democratization, whereas the postcommunist region has achieved much higher growth rates because

---

[2] Throughout this book, all averages are unweighted because we are interested in the relative performance of different countries. In economic weight, Russia and Poland dominate.

its structural economic reforms are proceeding. At present, the economic future of Eurasia looks brighter, but the combination of authoritarian rule and the energy curse might take major countries in this region astray.

This book is a history of the economic development of this postcommunist region from 1989 until 2006. It is devoted to the postcommunist economic transformation of the twenty-one countries in the former Soviet bloc in Eurasia, including Poland, the Czech Republic, Slovakia, Hungary, Romania, Bulgaria, and all the fifteen former Soviet Republics,[3] while excluding all the former Yugoslav republics – Albania, China, Mongolia, and Vietnam. All these twenty-one countries had much in common: the hierarchical and bureaucratic communist dictatorship, the socialist economic system, and closely connected foreign trade system. Although reforms in Hungary and Poland had altered their systems, the socialist principles remained, whereas the economic and political systems of Yugoslavia and China were profoundly different.

The structure of this book is systematic with one chapter for each major topic. Chapter 1 discusses what communism was and how it collapsed. Chapter 2 presents the main discussion with arguments for a radical or more gradual market economic reform. Chapter 3 examines what actually happened to output and how that can be explained. Chapter 4 focuses on deregulation, Chapter 5 on macroeconomic stabilization, and Chapter 6 on privatization. Chapter 7 deals with social developments and Chapter 8 with the politics of transition. Chapter 9 considers the problems of establishing the rule of law. The newly emerged oligarchs deserve Chapter 10 for themselves. Chapter 11 is devoted to the role of international assistance, after which conclusions follow.

I published *Building Capitalism: The Transformation of the Former Soviet Bloc* in early 2002. This book is not a second edition but partly a sequel and partly a slimmed revision of that volume. Most of this book is newly written. My ambition is to streamline the argument and concentrate on the dominant trends, which have become more evident over time. I have reduced technical details and statistics, replacing many tables with summary graphs in the hope of providing a better overview. Today we can say that the building of capitalism has been successful, and it is time to take stock of how this was accomplished. The academic literature on postcommunist

---

[3] Estonia, Latvia, Lithuania, Russia, Belarus, Ukraine, Moldova, Armenia, Azerbaijan, Georgia, Kazakhstan, Kyrgyzstan, Tajikistan, Turkmenistan, and Uzbekistan.

transition is immense, and I have tried to limit the references to the most essential to make the book readable. I hope that this book will serve not only as a standard for the academic community and as a textbook for students but also as a source of inspiration to a broader public, notably investors who want to benefit from these growing economies.

1

Communism and Its Demise

All happy families are similar, but every unhappy family is unhappy in its own way.

Lev Tolstoy, *Anna Karenina*

Today, the case for socialism is no longer persuasive, but this was not always so. Once, many intelligent people considered socialism not only morally but also economically superior to capitalism and democracy. They thought a benign state would pursue higher ideals than a petty democracy and execute them more effectively. Marxist-Leninist ideas and socialist institutions conditioned the postcommunist transition. To provide some background, I review the essence of the Soviet-type system.[1] As communism broke down, countries faced very different political and economic preconditions, and their collapses proceeded in sharply contrasting ways.

Real Socialism

Karl Marx, Friedrich Engels, Vladimir Lenin, and other communist theoreticians left many ideas on how to develop a socialist state, but Josef Stalin was the one who formed the classical communist economic system with the first five-year plan of 1929–33. This system remained intact until his death in March 1953, and he imposed it on all countries in the Soviet bloc. Despite many reform attempts, the lasting changes were remarkably small. This system was the least common denominator of all the countries discussed in this book.[2] The institutional barriers built to reform it were formidable.

---

[1] I use "socialist" and "communist" interchangeably as synonyms for Soviet-type communism.

[2] This account draws primarily on Kornai (1992a), arguably the best account of the communist economic system, Hewett (1988), and Nove (1969, 1977).

The communist system was the most thoroughly politicized system the world has seen. As János Kornai (1992a, p. 360) stated: "The key to explaining the classical socialist system is . . . the political structure. The starting point is the undivided political power of the ruling party, the interpenetration of the party and the state, and the suppression of all forces that depart from or oppose the party's policy." The essence of communism became the dictatorship of a hierarchical Communist Party. Its elitist Nomenklatura system was reminiscent of the hierarchical tsarist civil service (Voslenskii 1984). Everything was politics and had to be imbued with Marxism-Leninism. Political obedience became more important than work performance. Patron-client networks were the hallmark of the communist system.

Nationalization of the means of production was carried out zealously. Industry, trade, transportation, infrastructure, and banks were usually nationalized. Agriculture, handicrafts, and some services were initially collectivized and gradually nationalized. The collectivization of small farmers was brutal. Hardly any legal entrepreneurs persisted. The main exception was the German Democratic Republic (GDR), where Stalin delayed sovietization of the economy because of uncertainty about the German question. As late as 1972, one-third of the urban labor force in the GDR was employed in the private sector (Åslund 1985). The other exception was Polish agriculture, 70 percent of which remained private until the end of communism because of ferocious popular resistance. Elsewhere, odd remnants of private enterprise persisted in housing, private agricultural plots, and craftsmanship. The nearly complete nationalization of the means of production was supposed to make communist domination over society eternal and to render the restoration of capitalism impossible.

Centralized bureaucratic allocation replaced market allocation. The communist state set physical production targets for all major goods and enterprises through thousands of "material balances" compiled by the State Planning Committee (Gosplan). These "plans" were central commands that were constantly altered at will by the political leaders, so the system has often been called a "command economy." With the growing complexity of a modern economy with millions of products, the system became increasingly dysfunctional, leading to persistent shortages.

Economic policy making was strictly hierarchical. The Politburo of the Communist Party made the key decisions, which had been prepared by the Central Committee of the Party. The government or Council of Ministers was subordinate to the Party and not very important. Within the government, the State Planning Committee dominated policy making, while the Central Bank and the Ministry of Finance were little but bookkeeping organs. Operative state control over enterprises was delegated to scores of branch ministries. To simplify their administration and supervision, the ministries gradually reduced the number of enterprises through mergers. The political organization determined the size of enterprises, limiting the size of the big companies but minimizing the number of small firms. As a consequence, the Soviet Union had no less than thirteen companies producing tractors, whereas the capitalist optimum might have been two or three. As markets functioned poorly, enterprises preferred autarky, avoiding subcontractors and incorporating most subordinate production, which limited their specialization and efficiency. This system left a problematic legacy, such as the extreme centralization of decision making and the actual supervision by the Party, which was an extralegal body.

Prices were subordinate because physical output was the central objective. Prices of major products, such as raw materials and staple foods, were fixed, and most prices were set as cost plus a regulated markup; higher prices were allowed for new products. As a result, the prices of raw materials were largely constant, whereas more complex products were subject to rising hidden inflation. This pricing system encouraged intentional lowering of quality. Because prices were not checked by market forces, they became increasingly distorted.

There was no real money. The national currency was several separate currencies because different people and enterprises had access to separate market outlets with varying prices and supplies. The big divide was between enterprise money or bank transfers and cash that was reserved for transactions with ordinary citizens – wages and retail purchases. A bank ruble and a cash ruble had different values, and they were arbitraged in black markets. Most communist countries experienced one or more confiscatory currency reforms, which undermined the confidence in the domestic currency. It was not perceived as a sound store of value despite low inflation. Goods and hard currency were frequent objects of savings.

Mobilization of resources. The socialist state tried to mobilize all resources for the sake of long-term economic development. It organized jobs for the unemployed and women and labeled unemployment "parasitism." Public savings were sharply increased to boost investment in heavy industry while limiting private consumption, and gigantic construction projects became a Soviet fetish.

The building of a strong military industry. Stalin's economic policy did not aim at economic welfare but at military strength, and Stalinism implied the far-reaching militarization of the whole society. It embraced the idea of unbalanced growth, allocating disproportionate resources to strategic industries to speed up economic development. Heavy industry, particularly steel and heavy-machine building, was favored, whereas agriculture was deemed backward and reactionary; most services were considered of little value. Price regulation boosted industrial prices relative to agricultural prices, forcing agriculture to finance investment in industry. Stalin minimized investment in transportation, housing, and services as well.

Wages and private consumption were held back to the benefit of investment and military expenditures, and the standard of living stagnated. A saying developed: "They pretend to pay us, and we pretend to work." Shoddy work, poor quality, low efficiency, and demoralization became hallmarks of the command economies. Soviet people who had never traveled abroad considered stories of capitalist shops without shortages ludicrous, rendering any trip to the West a devastating disillusion with the communist system.

Investment in human capital was the most positive aspect of socialism. Communism provided good education, ensuring general literacy, much mathematics, and good engineering. However, three academic disciplines were intentionally neglected for ideological reasons: ordinary economics, because market economics was considered ideologically wrong; law, which unduly restricted communist power; and foreign languages, because socialist citizens were discouraged from corrupting international influences.

Each communist country had a national economic system aiming at autarky. Foreign trade was accepted, but it was supposed to be isolated from the domestic economy. The government maintained state monopoly over foreign trade to prevent opportunities for arbitrage. In the classical socialist system, no exchange rate existed. The Ministry for Foreign Trade purchased abroad according to instructions from the State Planning Committee and sold as much as was necessary to pay for imports, separating foreign trade prices from domestic prices. The Soviet Union was littered with expensive uninstalled imported equipment because the customers did not know how to install it, and they were prohibited from contacting the supplier for advice! After World War II, the Soviet Union tried to develop a *socialist foreign trade system* for its new satellites. The Council of Mutual Economic Assistance (CMEA) was set up in 1949 as a Soviet bloc trade organization for eventually ten member states. Even by Soviet standards, it was considered overly bureaucratic with prices and trade more distorted than domestically. Prices of manufactured goods rose disproportionately in relation to raw materials in CMEA trade, boosting implicit Soviet subsidies to all the other members of the CMEA (Hewett 1974). Much of the CMEA trade was worthless, and the extraordinary distortion of foreign trade was one of the greatest poison pills communism left behind.

Shortages. The outstanding characteristic of the communist economic system was persistent shortages of goods and services. At the macro level, the volume of money exceeded the volume of goods at given prices, and at the micro level people demanded other goods than those supplied. János Kornai (1980) labeled this "economics of shortage." To enterprises, money was not scarce, which meant that they suffered from "soft budget constraints," in János Kornai's terminology. The state subsidies available to state enterprises were not fixed but subject to bargaining (Kornai 1992a, p. 140). Such negotiations also involved taxation, soft bank credits, and administrative pricing. A state enterprise could hardly go bankrupt because the state would always bail it out. Naturally, personal and political relations with superiors were more important than economic performance in such an environment. Rationally, state enterprise managers concentrated on lobbying among government and party officials, ignoring efficiency of production.

High growth rates. The great pride of the communists was double-digit growth rates, especially in the early 1930s, when the capitalist world was suffering from the Great Depression. In the first half of the 1950s, the new communist economies boasted growth rates of about 10 percent a year. This was accomplished by a mobilization of all available resources: high savings, directed to investments in machinery and new factories; high employment; and comprehensive public education. Soviet growth rates were greatly exaggerated, however, and the real rates are still open to dispute.[3] This falsification was so extraordinary that the late Soviet authorities refrained from publishing any exact growth rates for the period prior to 1960. The iconoclastic Russian economists Vasili Selyunin and Grigori Khanin (1987) assessed that the real Soviet growth rate was an average of 3.2 to 3.5 percent a year from 1928 to 1985 – high but not extraordinary.

Decline and Fall of Socialism

The decline of communism was as protracted as its collapse was sudden. Many dates can be regarded as the beginning of the end, and each date indicates one particular cause of the demise. In 1919, Ludwig von Mises (1920) declared that the economic principles of socialism could never work. The terror of Stalinism and the fear it had imbued in the population ended with the death of Josef Stalin in March 1953. In June 1953, a first major workers' protest against dictators ruling in their name occurred in Berlin.

---

[3] The main downward revision was Bergson (1961). In the late Soviet period, Russians went much further in degrading historical Soviet growth rates (Selyunin and Khanin 1987).

The Hungarian revolt of October 1956 was the first open challenge to both communism and the Soviet empire. The Warsaw Pact invasion of Czechoslovakia in August 1968 discredited the notion that Soviet-type socialism could be reformed to attain a "human face." Repeated Polish worker uprisings in 1956, 1970, 1976, and 1980 forewarned of socialism's collapse. The sixteen months in 1980–1 when the Solidarity trade union existed legally indicated that communism persisted on borrowed time. Communism's problems were as multiple as its tenacity was impressive. Strong centralized control kept communism alive for many years, but the system's petrification made its collapse inevitable (Bunce 1999b).

By the 1980s, the collapse of communism was both overdetermined and long overdue. The fundamental problem with communism was its institutions. The overcentralized system could not handle challenges demanding decentralized initiative, such as craftsmanship, agriculture and information technology. Economic distortions of prices and industrial structure grew worse over time. The Soviet Union could mobilize neither the technology nor the financial strength to keep up the arms race with the United States. Economic reforms were attempted, but they did not improve growth. Instead, they delegitimized the socialist system both politically and economically. In the end, most countries were hit by fiscal emergencies, accompanied by external shocks.[4]

Falling growth rates. In the early 1960s, growth rates started declining sharply in the most developed socialist countries. In 1963, Czechoslovakia was the first communist country to register an official decrease in national income during peacetime – a shattering event. By the early 1980s, general stagnation had taken hold, and the long reign of Soviet Secretary General Leonid Brezhnev from 1964 to 1982 later became known as the period of stagnation. From 1985 to 1989, growth rates fell in most of the region. In Romania, output dropped by almost 8 percent in 1989 because of Nicolae Ceauşescu's draconian endeavors to pay back the entire national debt. The Soviet Union suffered a complete breakdown in 1991.

Challenges from the arms race and information technology. Incredibly, in the late 1980s the Soviet Union still harbored illusions of keeping up with the United States in a modern arms race. Until 1988, the Soviet Union steadily increased its defense expenditures every year, until they reached about one-quarter of GDP, whereas the United States spent only 6 percent of its GDP on defense (Åslund 1990). When U.S. President Ronald Reagan

---

[4] My preferred source on the demise of communism and the Soviet Union is Dobbs (1997); see also Dunlop (1993) for a detailed account of the Soviet collapse.

challenged the Soviet Union with his high-tech "Star Wars" initiative, he exposed Soviet technological and economic weakness. Mikhail Gorbachev singled out the arms race as the rationale for his "perestroika" (economic reforms) just before he was elected secretary general of the Communist Party of the Soviet Union (CPSU) in December 1984:

Only an intensive, highly developed economy can safeguard a reinforcement of [our] country's position on the international stage and allow it to enter the next millennium with dignity as a great and flourishing power. (Gorbachev 1987a, p. 86)

The rigid communist system was helpless when facing new challenges from the rise of information technology, because its incentive structure resisted technological change and innovations. Its hierarchical command structure could not handle small enterprises or entrepreneurship, which new technology required. The communist police mentality opposed the free transmission of information, facilitated by personal computers and modern telecommunications. Even the use of photocopiers was restricted until the downfall of the Soviet Union. The Soviet system could hardly have survived the Internet, and it collapsed before the information revolution.

Delegitimization of communist ideology. Declining growth rates inspired economic reforms in most communist countries. In the mid-1950s, Poland pioneered market socialist reforms. Czechoslovakia and Hungary followed in 1968, and the Hungarian reforms survived. Poland attempted market economic reforms again in 1982. In the Soviet Union of the late 1980s, Gorbachev tried some market reforms, but the old Stalinist system continued with little change in East Germany, Czechoslovakia, Bulgaria, and Romania. These reforms were too partial to generate the desired economic growth and welfare, but they broke down many ideological dogmas. They augured a social democratic welfare society, thus legitimizing social democracy, the old foe of communism. Unemployment was legalized, and Poland, Hungary, and the Soviet Union introduced unemployment benefits. These capitalist reforms annihilated socialism's claim to moral superiority over capitalism, and social democracy was widely accepted in the communist elite as the ideal form of socialism.

Deconcentration of power. The nature of Soviet political power changed slowly but steadily. Under Stalin, Soviet power was truly totalitarian. As the secretary general of the Communist Party, Stalin did whatever he cared to do. With the end of terror, however, the communist elite or Nomenklatura of less than 1 percent of the population arose as the collective dictator (Voslenskii 1984; Murrell and Olson 1991). Under Nikita Khrushchev, the Politburo was the ruling body. Leonid Brezhnev succeeded in holding power from

1964 to 1982 by obliging the collective will of the Nomenklatura. Power was deconcentrated to lower levels of the Party and state hierarchy, rendering the Soviet Union a dictatorship of industrial ministers and regional first Party secretaries. The real distribution of power became evident when Mikhail Gorbachev was appointed secretary general of the CPSU. His endeavors at reform of the system were foiled by the bureaucrats. As a Swedish diplomat in Moscow, I visited a senior official at the USSR Ministry of Agriculture soon after Gorbachev's elevation to power to ask about his first decree on agricultural reform. To my great surprise, this official told me that he could not care less about a decree signed by the secretary general of the CPSU. This decree would have limited the power of the Ministry of Agriculture, so its officials openly defied it. Evidently, Gorbachev was not a dictator to this official.

Many have blamed Gorbachev for not having been sufficiently reformist during his early years (Goldman 1991), but he had little choice because of political resistance posed by the communist elite. Too little power remained at the top to make a top-down reform possible against the interest of the bureaucracy. Gorbachev drew the logical conclusions that he had to check the power of the conservative Party establishment. First, he opted for substantial freedom of the media ("glasnost") and, from January 1987, for partial democratization. As a consequence of his considerable political skills and stubbornness, Gorbachev succeeded in breaking down the CPSU and the state economic administration, but that left economic power vested in state enterprise managers, who were not accountable to anybody. They had all incentives to steal "their" state enterprises bare (Åslund 1991).

Aggravated political illegitimacy. No country had chosen communism voluntarily, and the communist system did not appeal to popular support but relied on a loyal, privileged elite, the Nomenklatura. Nikita Khrushchev ended the Stalinist terror with his secret speech to the Twentieth Congress of the CPSU in 1956, and gradually society thawed. Rather than being grateful, people began perceiving communist dictatorship as illegitimate, all the more so as the external capitalist threat dwindled away. The political emancipation of Soviet bloc peoples occurred in fits and starts through reform movements and popular uprisings – in 1956 in Poland and Hungary, in 1968 in Czechoslovakia, and in Poland in 1970 and 1980. After the Polish communist regime's standoff against the anticommunist trade union Solidarity for 16 months, the regime crushed this attempt at real democratization with a military clampdown in December 1981.[5] Even so, Solidarity had dealt a

---

[5] The story is eminently told by Ash (1983).

death blow to communism. It was only a matter of time before Soviet communism would falter. Thanks to greater international openness, millions of Poles and Hungarians could travel abroad and see the West for themselves, and they liked it.

Rising Soviet fiscal deficits. Fiscal discipline varied greatly. The Soviet Union had a large budget deficit exceeding 6 percent of GDP from 1986, and as the deficit expanded, the country was heading toward hyperinflation from late 1990. This was a direct result of the financial negligence characteristic of perestroika (Åslund 1991). Poland and Hungary had small deficits of 3 percent of GDP in 1989, whereas the communist stalwarts Bulgaria, Czechoslovakia, and the GDR had no official fiscal deficits until the bitter end. Absurdly, Romania had a huge budget surplus of 7.5 percent of GDP in 1989 because of Ceauşescu's idiosyncratic decision to repay Romania's foreign debt (United Nations Economic Commission for Europe [UNECE] 1991, p. 58).

Shortages and inflation. Because of the absence of financial instruments, even a small budget deficit could cause great harm. Apart from foreign loans, the only available financing was monetary emission, which led to shortages, inflation, or both. By 1989, Poland had lost control over nominal wage increases, as the Soviet Union did in 1991, while Hungary experienced substantial wage inflation. The other countries proved the strength of their dictatorships, controlling nominal incomes. Real incomes rose sharply only in Poland because the Polish government could neither hold back wage increases nor raise prices sufficiently. Before the collapse of communism, open inflation was problematic only in Poland and the Soviet Union, which both had inflation exceeding 100 percent a year. Poland experienced a minor incident of hyperinflation in the fall of 1989, although its budget deficit was officially only 3 percent of GDP. Incredibly, Czechoslovakia, the GDR, and Romania reported inflation below 3 percent a year even in the revolutionary year of 1989, and Bulgaria had a moderate inflation of 6 percent that year (UNECE 1991, 1992).

Excessive foreign debt. The communist countries could do little to alleviate a fiscal crunch but to borrow from abroad. In the early 1970s, Poland borrowed heavily to increase both investment and consumption, but its return on investment was poor because of its inefficient economic system. As a result, Poland faced external default and remained a basket case throughout the 1980s. Hungary drew more cautiously on foreign credits than Poland, but it also came close to its limit. The GDR was also badly indebted, but it was bankrolled by West Germany. Less conspicuously, poor Bulgaria had accumulated excessive debts in the 1980s. The Soviet Union's foreign debt was comparatively limited, but its overall financial crisis was all the deeper, depleting its international reserves in 1991. All these five countries suffered from serious foreign debt problems. Ironically, the two hard-line communist countries, Czechoslovakia and Romania, had little foreign debt because nobody wanted to lend to Czechoslovakia, and Romania had repaid its debt.

Falling oil prices. At the end of the 1980s, when the creditworthiness of the Soviet bloc was poor, Soviet oil production started to plunge, and the world oil price fell as well. The combination of an excessive debt burden, falling oil output, and low oil prices was just too much. The Soviet financial crisis was beyond salvation.

In the end, the depth of crisis varied considerably. The Soviet Union was in a profound macroeconomic crisis. It had lost control over its budget in 1986 and had run out of international financing. Tremendous shortages caused a dramatic fall in output, and hyperinflation was a near certainty. The Polish crisis was similar but not as deep. The other countries faced much less severe financial concerns. Bulgaria's problem was limited to its excessive foreign debt, and Romania suffered from an idiosyncratic austerity crisis, making the population outraged over their drastically falling standards of living. East Germany lacked national legitimacy. Hungary had succeeded in reforming itself into a socialist market economy while managing its macroeconomic strains. Czechoslovakia, finally, maintained an amazingly well-functioning Brezhnevian economy with little dynamism but good balance.

The Demise of Communism in Central Europe

Each country experienced its own unique demise of communism. In the fall of 1989, the communist governments fell in one country after the other. Revolution spread like wildfire, reminiscent of the great liberal revolution of 1849. Timothy Garton Ash (1990, p. 78) quipped: "In Poland it took ten years, in Hungary ten months, in East Germany ten weeks: Perhaps in Czechoslovakia it will take ten days!" (It actually took 24 days.)[6]

For Central Europe, the monumental event was the end of the Brezhnev doctrine. After the Soviet-led invasion of Czechoslovakia in 1968, the Soviet Union had officially declared that it had the right and duty to intervene to "defend socialism" in any part of the socialist commonwealth, which became known as the "Brezhnev doctrine" (Brown 1996, p. 240). However, after the failed Soviet war in Afghanistan, Gorbachev declared in a major speech to

---

[6] The outstanding account of these epic events is Ash (1990).

the United Nations in December 1988 that all countries had freedom of choice:

For us the necessity of the principle of freedom of choice is clear. Denying that right of peoples, no matter what the pretext for doing so, no matter what words are used to conceal it, means infringing even that unstable balance that it has been possible to achieve. Freedom of choice is a universal principle and there should be no exceptions. (Brown 1996, p. 225)

This speech ended the Brezhnev doctrine, because socialist rule in Central Europe had been established and maintained by Soviet troops. The demise of these Soviet-controlled regimes was only a matter of time.

Negotiated transition: Poland and Hungary. Because of prior democratic and market economic developments, Poland and Hungary were ready for early democratization. In Poland, the communist government could barely rule because of strong opposition from the Solidarity trade union and the Catholic Church. It started roundtable negotiations with Solidarity in early 1989, and the parties agreed to hold partially democratic parliamentary elections on June 4, 1989. The elections were a landslide victory for Solidarity and resulted in a predominantly anticommunist coalition government in September 1989, with the liberal professor of economics Leszek Balcerowicz as minister of finance. This peaceful and negotiated transfer of power forced democrats to substantial compromises, which caused lasting cracks within their ranks.

The Hungarian Socialist Workers' Party was the most liberal ruling communist party, and Hungary had undertaken more reforms than any other socialist country. Following the Polish lead, the Hungarian communist government negotiated with the opposition at a roundtable from June to September 1989. The parties agreed to full democratization, with free parliamentary elections on March 25, 1990. The opposition Hungarian Democratic Forum won these elections and formed a government. It was a conservative, Christian democratic party with rural roots. Although it was committed to a market economy, it was more interested in national themes. The Hungarian Socialist Party transformed itself into a social democratic party, which brought benefits in later elections. The smooth Hungarian transfer of power immediately led to full democracy, but economic policy was left without firm leadership (Stark and Bruszt 1998).

Popular revolt: East Germany and Czechoslovakia. The GDR and Czechoslovakia remained repressive dictatorships until 1989. Reforms in the Soviet Union, Poland, and Hungary caused internal pressures in the GDR, but East Germans responded by increasingly fleeing to the West. The catalyst of change was the Hungarian government's decision to open its border to Austria on August 23, 1989, allowing thousands of young East Germans to cross that border to move on to West Germany, where they automatically obtained citizenship. In the wake of this mass escape, large demonstrations erupted in the GDR, primarily in Leipzig, under the slogan: "We are the people!" Finally, unrest spread to Berlin, and on November 9, 1989, the communist leaders agreed to open the wall to West Berlin. The illegitimate regime crumbled in no time. On March 18, 1990, the Christian Democratic Union (CDU), under the leadership of West German Federal Chancellor Helmut Kohl, won the parliamentary elections with the slogan "Nobody will be worse off and many will be better off." On July 1, 1990, East Germany adopted the West German deutsche mark on favorable conditions. By October 1990, it reunited with the Federal Republic after having adopted its legislation.

Despite its proud interwar democratic traditions, Czechoslovakia was late in its democratic transition because of its profound petrification after the Warsaw Pact invasion of 1968 and the ensuing severe dictatorship. Yet in late 1989, Czechoslovakia was a tinder box. On November 17, 1989, students staged a minor demonstration for freedom, and the police lashed out at them with truncheons, igniting the spark that set Czechoslovakia alight and caused its "Velvet Revolution." Large mass demonstrations erupted, and opposition groups united in the Civic Forum, a broad popular front led by Václav Havel, which demanded the ouster of leading communists, freedom, and democracy. By December 10, President Gustáv Husák resigned. A government was formed with a majority of Civic Forum members but a communist prime minister. The leading Czech economic reformers entered the government and Václav Klaus became minister of finance. On December 29, 1989, Václav Havel was elected president by the parliament (Ash 1990). Parliamentary elections were held in June 1990, and parties arising out of the Civic Forum were victorious. The Velvet Revolution had an air of a fairy tale. The old evil surrendered without bloodshed. After years of suffering, well-educated dissidents came to power to serve their country, eminently directed by the country's greatest playwright, Václav Havel. It appeared too good to be true.

Communist coups: Bulgaria and Romania. Before the fall of communism, Bulgaria had undertaken little reform and Romania none. On November 10, 1989, the day after the fall of the Berlin wall, Todor Zhivkov, Bulgaria's communist dictator since 1954, was ousted in an internal coup. This putsch started the country's democratization, but it was carried out under tutelage of reform communists. A roundtable negotiation in early 1990 led to democratic elections to a Grand National Assembly on June 10, 1990. Politically, Bulgarians were almost equally divided between socialists and democrats, with a small Turkish minority party straddling the middle. The first democratic elections led to a narrow communist victory, now renamed socialists (Bell 1997). The Bulgarian transition to democracy was peaceful, but the political parties and democratic institutions were formed in haste, and the communists maintained a strong hold.

By December 1989, only diehard Romania was left. It was relatively independent from the Soviet Union, but Communist leader Ceaușescu pursued a ruthless dictatorship. Because of Ceaușescu's nepotism, his rule was characterized as "socialism in one family." Unrest started with a demonstration on December 16, 1989, after police attempted to evict a Hungarian protestant pastor from his house in a provincial town, resulting in carnage. On December 21, a real revolution erupted. In freezing cold weather, Ceaușescu spoke to tens of thousands of people ordered out into the Palace Square. Suddenly, the crowd started booing, and the dictator fled by helicopter. Rebellious masses stormed the Central Committee building, and wild shooting started. A few days later, the fleeing Ceaușescu was caught and summarily executed. The power vacuum was swiftly filled by disgruntled representatives of the Communist Party, who formed the National Salvation Front, led by an old communist functionary, Ion Iliescu. The Front won 66 percent of the votes in democratic parliamentary elections in May 1990, and Iliescu was elected president. The communist establishment managed to legitimize its leadership by executing Ceaușescu and maintained a strong hold on power (Tismaneanu 1997).

The Collapse of the Soviet Union

Although the Soviet Union used to be one country, the fifteen countries that arose out of its ruins harbored even greater differences than Central and Southeast Europe in culture, history, politics, and economic development. Six countries drew on Muslim traditions and nine on different Christian denominations. Communism's duration was much shorter in the Baltics, Moldova, and Western Ukraine, which had been annexed during World War II. The Baltics, Georgia, and Armenia could claim to be old nationstates, but the others had less sense of national identity.

National causes became increasingly divisive. The Balts and West Ukrainians had never reconciled with the Soviet annexation, and they were prepared to exploit any opportunity for their national cause. Unwittingly, Gorbachev contributed to the destruction of the Union, apparently believing that the

Soviet Union had solved all national questions. In his book *Perestroika*, Gorbachev (1987b, p. 118) stated: "If the nationality question had not been solved in principle, the Soviet Union would never have had the social, cultural, economic and defense potential it has now. Our state would not have survived if the republics had not formed a community based on brotherhood and cooperation, respect and mutual assistance." He allowed forbidden questions about national repression to be raised, but he had no good answers. Why, for instance, had one-quarter of the Ukrainians and Kazakhs been killed in an artificial famine in the 1930s? The old conflict between the Armenians and Azerbaijanis erupted again in 1988.

Juan Linz and Alfred Stepan (1992) argued that the sequence of democratization sealed the fate of the Soviet Union. Democratization proceeded faster at the national level than at the union level. Some elections to national parliaments in early 1990 were more democratic and thus more legitimate than the Union parliament elected in March 1989. Soviet President Gorbachev never contested a democratic vote, which deprived the Soviet presidency of legitimacy, and Boris Yeltsin was democratically elected Russian president on June 12, 1991. The national crisis led to a "war of laws" between the Union and the republics, and the republican laws became more legitimate than the Union laws in 1990 and 1991, because key republics were more democratic. The republican parliaments legislated huge, populist social expenditures but refused to send their tax revenues to Moscow, starving the Union treasury. The result was a ballooning Soviet budget deficit of some 20 percent of GDP by the end of 1991, guaranteeing hyperinflation.

A farcical abortive putsch by hardliners from the Communist Party, the Soviet government, the KGB, and the military on August 18–21, 1991, served the death knell to the Soviet Union. In its aftermath, President Yeltsin's Russian administration emerged as the only legitimate power in Moscow. In a democratic breakthrough in Russia, he quickly abolished the Communist Party of the Soviet Union and most Soviet institutions. President Gorbachev discredited himself for good by citing Lenin and claiming: "I am convinced that socialism is correct" (Dunlop 1993, p. 259). The other republics had no choice but to opt for independence. The Baltics made themselves fully independent in August 1991, while the others waited until December 1991.

The collapse of an empire is usually very bloody. World War I finished off the Habsburg, German, Russian, and Ottoman Empires. By comparison, the end and dissection of the Soviet Empire was remarkably peaceful, although the civil war in Tajikistan and the war in Chechnya each claimed tens of thousands of lives (Lieven 2000). The Commonwealth of the Independent

States (CIS) was created in December 1991 to replace the Soviet Union for twelve countries, all of the former Soviet republics but the Baltics; it was, however, little but a conference organization. Ensuing developments in the various former Soviet republics became remarkably different.

Russia: Attempt at democracy and radical economic reform. Russia set out as a democracy after the abortive August 1991 coup under President Boris Yeltsin. Rather than completing the democratic reforms, Yeltsin focused on economic reform and appointed a reform government under the leadership of Yegor Gaidar in November 1991. It attempted a radical reform in January 1992, but the unfinished democratic reforms caught up with the new government. It was severely constrained by resistance from the quasi-democratic old parliament, which had been elected without political parties in March 1990. Its deputies were accidental, disorganized, unaccountable, and predominantly communist. Russia's two first years of transition were consumed by a constitutional crisis that ended in a failed armed uprising by the old parliament in October 1993 (Aron 2000).

The Baltic states (Estonia, Latvia, and Lithuania): Determined democracy and radical reform. The Balts had been independent in the interwar period, and they knew they wanted to be so again. In all three countries, broad anticommunist popular fronts were established in 1988 with the aim to restore their countries' independence. The Lithuanian and Estonian Communist Parties tried to keep up with the nationalists as the communists in Poland and Hungary, while the Latvian Communist Party split in the middle. In parliamentary elections in February–March 1990, the popular fronts won more than two-thirds majorities in all three parliaments and assumed executive power. They declared independence, which was finally recognized by the Soviet Union after the abortive August 1991 coup in Moscow. These countries were ripe for full democracy and radical economic reform. Their national objectives were firmly set: to turn their backs on Russia, to reintegrate with the West, and to establish ordinary Western systems (Lieven 1993).

Ukraine and Moldova: Communists stayed in power as nationalists. The situation in Ukraine and Moldova was quite similar. Both had rather strong nationalist popular fronts, but they were not sufficiently potent to win democratic majorities, and their eastern parts were less nationalist. Agile communist leaders embraced national independence when they realized that the communists were about to lose power in Moscow. As a result, communist leaders were elected presidents with nationalist support in both countries, and the old Nomenklatura stayed in power. National independence and unity were the prime considerations. Economic reform barely entered the political agenda. As Ilya Prizel (1997, p. 344) put it: "Ukraine lacked both an elite committed to democratic reforms and liberal economics and a fully developed, capable democratic alternative."[7] The same could be said of Moldova. Its situation was complicated by Russian separatists having declared a large part of the country, Transnistria an independent Soviet Socialist Republic, and it remains under the control of the separatists to this day (Crowther 1997). The preoccupation with security and nation building left little time for economic reform, and the politics were semidemocratic.

The war-torn Caucasus. The Caucasus inherited ancient minorities, national disputes, and political violence. The three Caucasian countries were ready to leave the Soviet Union early, but all were drawn into armed conflicts before its demise. The threat of warfare permitted little thought or energy to economics. In *Georgia*, the hard-line communist leaders were ousted after the Soviet military opened fire on a peaceful demonstration, killing twenty people on April 9, 1989. The Communist Party dwindled away, and a prominent dissident, Zviad Gamsakhurdia, won both parliamentary and presidential elections. Yet his rule foundered in his struggle for more control over two autonomous national regions, South Ossetia and Abkhazia, which tried to break away by force. A brief but bloody civil war raged in December 1991 and January 1992, leading to Gamsakhurdia's overthrow. Three years of chaos and economic collapse followed. Former First Party Secretary of Georgia and Minister for Foreign Affairs of the Soviet Union Eduard Shevardnadze returned to take control of Georgia in March 1992, but he was elected president only in 1995 (Slider 1997). Shevardnadze was ousted in the Rose Revolution in November 2003.

Armenia and Azerbaijan were clinched in mutual strife. In February 1988, the regional authorities in Nagorny Karabakh, an ethnically Armenian autonomous region belonging to Azerbaijan, demanded its transfer to Armenia. This Armenian-Azerbaijani conflict escalated into a full-scale war in February 1992, and it has defined the politics in both countries. In *Armenia*, the Soviet leaders and the Communist Party were discredited for their inability to defend Armenian interests against Azerbaijan. A coalition of noncommunist Armenian parties won the parliamentary elections in 1990, and nationalist dissident Levon Ter-Petrossian was elected chairman

---

[7] I spent the week before the August 1991 coup in Kiev talking to economic policy makers. I was shocked by the predominance of hard-line communists in economic policy making, while the rising nationalists had little clue about economic affairs. When I was in Kiev in 1985, I met a Soviet Academician, Aleksandr Emelianov, who struck me as the most ideological Marxist-Leninist I ever encountered. In August 1991, he was Kravchuk's economic advisor.

of Parliament and later president. The Armenian government presented a market economic program and launched the first land reform in the Soviet Union in 1991, but this small, landlocked country suffered badly from an embargo by Azerbaijan and Turkey, putting reform in jeopardy (Dudwick 1997).

In *Azerbaijan*, the Communist Party of Azerbaijan maintained a harsh dictatorship, and opposition was weak. In 1989, an Azerbaijani Popular Front had been formed, and it called for democratization, but the communist authorities blamed it for a mysterious pogrom of Armenians in Baku in January 1990. Soviet troops killed hundreds of people, and the anticommunist resistance had been quashed. After some tumult in the early 1990s, Azerbaijan's old Soviet leader Heidar Aliyev took over as a mild dictator with neither democracy nor market economic reform on his agenda (Altstadt 1997). The economy is run like a family corporation.

Belarus and Central Asia: Continued authoritarian rule. Belarus can be described as the Prussia of the Soviet Union, being the most militarized, sovietized, russified, and disciplined Soviet Republic. Dissent was weak, repression harsh, and the Communist Party was solidly hard line. Nowhere in the Soviet Union did the command economy work as well as in Belarus. Nonetheless, Gorbachev's liberalization reached Belarus as well. Inspired by Lithuania, nationalists established the Belarusian Popular Front in 1988, but it went over the top and became more radical than Belarusian popular sentiment. Independence came to Belarus as an accident in December 1991. The Belarusian communists stayed in power until the elections in 1994 (Mihalisko 1997). Their moribund rule prompted the victory of the populist Aleksandr Lukashenko in the presidential elections in July 1994, and he finished off Belarusian democracy by 1996. Market economic reform was never an issue.

Kazakhstan, Turkmenistan, and Uzbekistan saw no real democratization, and their communist leaders stayed in power. Although they dismissed the communist parties, they ruled through old Nomenklatura and clan networks. Turkmenistan's Saparmurat Niyazov was appointed first party secretary in 1985 to impose central Soviet control. Kazakhstan's President Nursultan Nazarbayev and Uzbekistan's President Islam Karimov were selected Party leaders in June 1989 by Moscow to conciliate their republics' interests. In Kazakhstan, the authoritarian rule softened somewhat, whereas Turkmenistan and Uzbekistan maintained severe dictatorships. Niyazov called himself Turkmen-bashi, the father of Turkmens, and introduced his own cult of personality which lasted until his death in December 2006 (Olcott 1996).

Kyrgyzstan's communist elite was jolted by bloody ethnic riots between Uzbeks and Kyrgyz in the south of the republic in the summer of 1990, which resulted in the ouster of the communist leader. The parliament elected Askar Akaev, a prominent liberal communist and physicist, as its chairman. Akaev was also elected president. Although democracy faded, its civil society and independent press were quite strong, rendering the country politically open to market economic transformation. Akaev was ousted in the Tulip Revolution in March 2005.

Tajikistan was the poorest of the Soviet republics, and it has remained so. Bordering on Afghanistan, Tajikistan got trapped in a full-fledged civil war in 1992 between communists and Islamists. A Russia-led force intervened and brought a communist, Emomali Rahmonov, to power after much bloodshed. Rahmonov has managed to stay in power, but his leadership is weak, and political stability remains evasive (Olcott 1996). All the Central Asian countries are ruled like family corporations.

As communism finally broke down, countries faced very different political preconditions, and their collapses proceeded in contrasting ways. A first group of countries, consisting of Central Europe, the Baltics, Russia, and Kyrgyzstan, were reasonably democratic, with liberal regimes and strong civil societies. Democratization there had brewed for a couple of years before the democratic breakthrough. Most of them opted for successful radical reform. A second group consisted of Bulgaria, Romania, Moldova, and Ukraine. They were about as democratic as the first group, but the old communist elites stayed in power. Their choice was gradual market economic reform, generating poor results. A third group encompassed Belarus, Kazakhstan, Uzbekistan, and Turkmenistan, which were never democratized and where the old communist elite simply continued to rule. Of these countries, Kazakhstan chose gradual market reforms, whereas the others have maintained Soviet-style economic systems. Finally, Armenia, Azerbaijan, Georgia, and Tajikistan (and to a lesser extent, Moldova) were caught in military conflicts and could neither democratize nor pursue much of an economic policy in the early transition. With delays, they have undertaken market reforms, which with necessity have been gradual.

2

Shock Therapy versus Gradualism

The end of communism in Europe was the event of a lifetime. Suddenly twenty-eight countries with 400 million people had to choose their political and economic systems anew. Where should they begin? What was most important? What was possible? What theory should be applied? What policy corresponded to their interests? A frequent point was that no book prescribed how to transition from socialism to capitalism, whereas hundreds elaborated on the opposite, no longer desired, direction. A popular joke compared the transition from communism to capitalism to making an aquarium out of a fish soup.

The discussion became heated from the outset because so much was at stake. The fate of a large part of the world was up in the air. Could and should the former Soviet bloc be embraced by the Western world, or should it be shunned? Could armed conflicts be avoided? How much economic and social hardship would people in these countries have to suffer? Which ideology would win?

Intellectuals of all disciplines and convictions, governments, and international organizations geared up to answer the many questions. Although no clear goal was defined, a strong sense of direction prevailed. The popular battle cry was, "We want a 'normal' society!" By "normal," people in the Soviet bloc meant an ordinary Western society – a democracy with a market economy, predominant private property, and the rule of law. Because all these countries had far to go, the final destination did not appear very relevant at the outset of the march, and any specification of the goal could be politically divisive. In the havoc of a collapsing socialist system, East and Central Europeans cared little whether their society would be a West European social welfare state or a freer American market economy, both being evidently superior to their socialist ruins. These distinctions were left for later.

For Central Europe, Southeast Europe, and the Baltics, the urge for a normal society was complemented by another battle cry for a "return to Europe," meaning their integration in West European economic and political organizations, notably membership in the European Union (EU) and the North Atlantic Treaty Organization (NATO).

This was a time of liberal triumph. In many ways, the Central European revolutions of 1989 most resembled the European revolutions of 1848 (Ash, 1990; Dahrendorf 1990) because late Communist society was reminiscent of feudal society, with its hierarchic rule and delegation of partial property rights to vassals, with detailed regulation but no rule of law. The instincts were the same. Many saw the state as evil in the tradition of the great liberal thinkers of the mid–nineteenth century, such as John Stuart Mill (1859/1975). The natural response was a demand for the same kind of far-reaching liberalization that occurred in the 1840s and focus on the creation of checks and balances to state power.

Many socialist ideas just died, whereas others reemerged later. "Market socialism," workers' self-management or a "third way" between capitalism and Soviet-style socialism, were no longer discussed. The central issue was instead the strategy of transition to a market economy. How fast and in what order? The dominant intellectual debate over postcommunist transition was between radical and gradual reformers, while the outright enemies of market reform kept quiet. The focus of the debate lay on speed. The issue was whether the possible reforms – liberalization, macroeconomic stabilization, and privatization – should be undertaken as fast as possible or deliberately more slowly. The purported objective of all reformers was the same – namely, to establish a market economy, leading to higher economic efficiency, economic growth, and improving the average standard of living, but other agendas were concealed.

At the outset of transition, a broad and cohesive group of economists and policymakers called for an early and radical economic reform, which is outlined in section one. The gradual reform proposals of the early transition were much more diverse. They are presented in the long section two. Section three leaps out from the intellectual debate to the conditions that had been created during the Gorbachev reforms for rent seeking and how rent seeking was carried out in the early transition. Initially, the dominance of the radical program was reinforced, but problems in the East, especially in Russia, led to new criticism against radical reform, which culminated around Russia's financial crash in 1998, which is discussed in the final section.

The Radical Reform Program: A Big Bang

The radical program for market economic reforms was supported by three powerful groups. The first group consisted of leading mainstream Western, primarily American, macroeconomists, such as Jeffrey Sachs, Stanley Fischer, Lawrence Summers, and David Lipton. Harvard University, the Massachusetts Institute of Technology, and the London School of Economics were focal points of radical reform thinking. A second important set was the best economists in the East, notably Leszek Balcerowicz in Poland, Václav Klaus in Czechoslovakia, and Yegor Gaidar in Russia. They were few but bright, and they knew what they wanted. They were later joined by politicians with economic insights, such as Mart Laar in Estonia and Einars Repše in Latvia. Most of them became leading policy makers. The third group supporting radical reform was the international financial institutions, primarily the International Monetary Fund (IMF) and the World Bank, and the major Western governments, primarily their ministries of finance and central banks.

For American macroeconomists, the IMF, the World Bank, and the U.S. government the Latin American experience with macroeconomic stabilization in the 1980s showed them the way. Their view was that a radical and comprehensive reform program was the best cure (Bruno et al. 1988). This program had been named the "Washington Consensus" by John Williamson (1990). It can be summarized as "prudent macroeconomic policies, outward orientation, and free-market capitalism," and it drew on neoclassical mainstream economic theory. The choice of name was somewhat unfortunate because it seemed as if Washington dictated economic policies for the world, but the fundamental ten points of this program were pretty obvious in that they were not very detailed and avoided ideological controversy:

1. Fiscal discipline is needed.
2. Among public expenditures, discretionary subsidies should be minimized, and education, health, and public investment should be priorities.
3. The tax base should be broad, and marginal tax rates ought to be moderate.
4. Interest rates should be market-determined and real interest rates positive.
5. Exchange rates should be competitive.
6. Foreign trade policy should be rather liberal.
7. Foreign direct investment is beneficial but not a high priority.

8. Privatization is beneficial because private industry is managed more efficiently than state enterprises.
9. Deregulation is a useful means to promote competition.
10. Property rights need to be made secure.

Many economists simultaneously presented similar ideas about the need for radical economic reform.[1] The intellectual development in the East was very sudden. Even the most radical reformers in the Soviet bloc did not think of a full-fledged market economic transformation as a real possibility until the late 1980s. The breakthrough occurred in Moscow in early 1987, as the literary journal *Novy mir* published a couple of articles with devastating criticism of the Soviet economic system (Selyunin and Khanin 1987; Shmelev 1987).

The first truly market economic program to propose large-scale privatization was presented in Poland in 1988 (Dąbrowski et al. 1989). Leszek Balcerowicz (1992) has detailed how the radical economic reform program emerged. It was the result of an economic reform group that he led in Warsaw throughout the late 1980s. Prominent members of his group were Marek Dąbrowski and Stefan Kawalec, later deputy ministers of finance. These Polish liberals were tired of gradual reforms that were reversed. They wanted to break out of market socialism and accomplish a real market economy. Their fundamental insight was that the market reforms had to be truly radical as well as comprehensive. Therefore, they were more radical than others. In May 1989, Balcerowicz wrote a summary reform program, which included privatization, liberalization of foreign trade, currency convertibility, and an open economy.

Before the Polish reform government was formed in September 1989, the last communist government had liberalized food prices, which led to an inflation of some 40 percent in the month of September. An effective financial stabilization program had to be added to the radical structural reform, which Balcerowicz's advisors Harvard Professor Jeffrey Sachs and his collaborator David Lipton did with their experience of how to defeat high inflation in Latin America. They also assisted by propagating the Polish radical reform program in the West, gaining Western sympathy.

The radical reform program for postcommunist countries followed the Washington Consensus closely, but it went further and was more specific. It is incorrect, as is often done, to equalize the two. The original radical

---

[1] Notably Blanchard et al. (1991); Boycko (1991); Brada (1993); Fischer and Gelb (1991); Kornai (1990); and World Bank (1996a). My own contribution to this discussion is Åslund (1992).

reform program was adjusted to the prevailing Polish conditions. Moreover Balcerowicz had not read the Washington Consensus when he drafted his original reform program. Many issues had to be added or reinforced because they had already been done in Latin America – notably, deregulation to create a market and privatization to establish private property. The Balcerowicz program became the standard for a radical, comprehensive reform. Its prescriptions applied also to other countries in similar predicaments. This program was lucid and is easy to summarize:[2]

1. *Macroeconomic stabilization.* Their immediate concern was to halt hyperinflation, which required a swift reduction of a large budget deficit. Fiscal policy had to be centralized and brought under control by a reinforced ministry of finance. Monetary policies should be tightened, and positive real interest rates were necessary. The Central Bank had to be independent and focus on low inflation. The exchange rate should be unified and the currency needed to be convertible on current account to be freely available for foreign trade.
2. *Deregulation.* Prices had to be deregulated and price subsidies eliminated to let demand and supply determine prices. Domestic trade should be liberalized and monopolies broken up to avoid monopolistic pricing. A regime of relatively free foreign trade had to be established, eliminating rents in both exports and imports. A realistic price structure would be imported. Free trade would alleviate the rampant shortages, facilitate production, and boost living standards.
3. *Privatization.* Restrictions on the private sector had to be abolished and new private entrepreneurs offered a maximum of freedom. Small-scale privatization was to be initiated early on. The privatization of large and medium-sized enterprises had to be started as soon as possible, but everybody understood that it would take time, and no agreement existed on how to do it.
4. *Reinforcing the Social Safety Net.* The ardors of restructuring required the introduction of a social safety net targeted at new groups in need, especially the unemployed, and an increase of pensions.

Key government functions – notably, centralized fiscal and monetary control – did not exist. Radical reformers wanted to minimize the role of the old state apparatus, eliminating its harmful parts, while building a new democratic government. Any social engineering was out of the question.

---

[2] See Lipton and Sachs (1990a), Sachs and Lipton (1990), and Sachs (1990, 1991, and 1993), and Balcerowicz (1992, 1994, and 1995).

Jeffrey Sachs (1994, p. 510) summarized the radicals' view of the state in transition:

A government facing political and economic collapse (the case at hand) must give up responsibility for market prices in order to focus on the core functions of government that are not being met: law and order, public security, a stable monetary system, and basic social welfare. Governments that have reached hyperinflation cannot, *self-evidently*, be expected to develop complex industrial policies or structural policies. After all, they aren't even carrying out their most fundamental tasks.

The state had an important role to play, but it would be very different from what the socialist state had played. Many state functions had to be strengthened – notably, the rule of law, the registration and defense of private property rights, the fiscal system, central banking, regulation of banking and financial markets, and targeted social support.

Radical reformers supported unemployment insurance and higher pensions, as they aspired to stimulate and facilitate structural change (Fischer and Gelb 1991). The later, so frequent accusations that radical reformers had "forgotten" about institutions and social policy had no base in reality. Indeed, the successful radical reformers undertook the greatest institutional reforms and spent greatly on social assistance.

On all these measures the radical reformers agreed, but their views varied on some other measures, including exchange rate policy, wage controls, international assistance, and privatization.

- Poland, Czechoslovakia, and Estonia pegged exchange rates early on as nominal anchors for their financial stabilization, whereas others opted for floating exchange rates.
- Poland and Czechoslovakia introduced strict wage controls as an important part of their initial stabilization policy, whereas others had little wage control.
- The role and size of international financial assistance and debt relief varied. Jeffrey Sachs took an international lead as a proponent of aid, whereas others opposed nearly all financial support.
- There were as many views on privatization as there were economists, although the radical reformers considered speedy privatization important.

The differences over exchange rates and wage controls were of a technical nature, while the differences over international assistance and especially privatization were profoundly ideological.

The Importance of Speed And Comprehensiveness
The common conviction of the radical reformers was that these major market reforms had to be undertaken as comprehensively and swiftly as possible (Åslund 1992). The protagonists of radical reform had a clear understanding that many measures could not be undertaken instantly and that transition would take at least a decade (notably, Fischer and Gelb 1991). "*Different processes of economic reform have different maximum possible speeds*" (Balcerowicz 1994, p. 82, emphasis in original). Everybody realized that privatization of large enterprises would take years, as would complex reforms, ranging from tax reform, social reforms, civil service reform, and legal reforms to the development of a financial sector. The radical reformers were all convinced that a radical and comprehensive reform was needed to bring about a real breakthrough, which would minimize the social costs and render the economic upswing earlier and sharper. This was their prime bone of contention with the gradualists.

First, liberal economists in the Soviet bloc had bitter memories of failed and reversed reforms. They concluded "that the economic reforms failed because they were not radical enough, that is, they did not reach a certain threshold of necessary changes rapidly" via "critical mass" of market reforms (Balcerowicz 1995). If the system did not achieve a certain degree of cohesion and consistency, it could theoretically be even more inefficient than the old command economy (Kornai 1990; Boycko 1991; Winiecki 1991a).

Second, the radical reformers were acutely aware of the prevalence of both state and market failure, but they were more fearful of state failure. A new market would be imperfect, but the communist state was even more imperfect, so it could not be entrusted with much intervention. The reforms had to deliver a "shock" that could break the hold of the old system to introduce a viable new market economy (Gomułka 1989).

Third, people's expectations had to be changed to render the systemic changes credible and irreversible. Balcerowicz (1995, p. 342) derived from Leon Festinger's theory of cognitive dissonance in social psychology "that people are more likely to change their attitudes and their behaviour if they are faced with radical changes in their environment, which they consider irreversible, than if those changes are only gradual." Otherwise, people would suspect a rollback toward communism and refuse to adjust their behavior.

Fourth, because of the severity of the crisis and the new hope of freedom, the public was prepared to make short-term sacrifices for long-term benefits of society out of sheer idealism. Balcerowicz (1994) emphasized the importance of utilizing this period of "extraordinary politics" to get a full package of reform laws adopted by the parliament, while radical economic reforms remained popular.

Fifth, quick systemic change also transforms the intellectual paradigm. In Central Europe and the Baltics, comprehensive reforms soon changed the intellectual paradigm, while slower reforms kept rather parochial economic ideas alive in the Commonwealth of the Independent States (CIS) countries.

Sixth, standard theories agreed that macroeconomic stabilization had to be done fast to break inflationary expectations.

Seventh, liberalization of prices and trade had to go far enough to generate a critical mass of markets and provide credible incentives. Because the old prices were hopelessly distorted, any gradual adjustment would send inaccurate signals about costs, demand, and supply. Inflationary expectations would be maintained, and entrepreneurs would be unwilling to invest. The profitability of an enterprise would be determined by price regulation, which would render bankruptcies socially unacceptable. Liberalized imports were vital to activate the market and end shortages (Sachs and Lipton 1990).

Eighth, the hardest task was to convince enterprise managers to alter their behavior. Their incentives had to be changed through the introduction of hard budget constraints or a "demand barrier." If they were not convinced that the rules had changed for good, they would not adjust (Sachs and Lipton 1990).

Ninth, corruption, misappropriation of public funds, and rent seeking were ballooning amid the breakdown of communism. Partial liberalization facilitated arbitrage between regulated prices and free prices, but a quick and comprehensive reform could mitigate these distortions.

Tenth, extremely little accurate information was available during the early transition, as everything was changing fast and radically, and new statistics were often completely flawed. If little could be measured and few relevant facts could be established, it would have been both pretentious and foolish to attempt anything but a policy based on principle (Balcerowicz 1995).

Finally, the state bureaucracy had numerous reasons to oppose a radical reform program. Under reform, it would lose its prior power, and most of its human capital would become obsolete because the old socialist micromanagement of enterprises no longer existed. Bureaucrats easily colluded with abundant secret service officers, state enterprise managers, and Communist Party officials. "Populist politicians will try to hook up with coalitions of workers, managers and bureaucrats in hard-hit sectors to slow or reverse the adjustment" (Sachs 1990). It was vital for the sustenance of democracy to disarm the old elite through radical reform. The abortive coup in August 1991 in Moscow and the armed uprising by the predemocratic Russian parliament in October 1993 illustrated the threat of a bureaucratic counter-revolution.

Gradual Reform Programs

The opponents of radical reform did not form one school but proposed more gradual reform in one or several regards, so no full conceptualization of a gradual reform was apparent. In 1990, the discussion was dominated by contrasts between the just-launched reforms in Poland and Hungary. Gradualists defended the Hungarian methods against the Polish shock therapy with little regard for diverse preconditions. Another source of inspiration was the successful Chinese reform. Then there was ignorance, nostalgia for the old, and rent seeking.

The fundamental difference between gradualists and radical reformers was their view of market failure and state failure. First, gradualists thought the old communist economy and state more viable than radical reformers did. Second, gradualists downplayed the economic crisis after communism, looking at the mild predicament of Hungary rather than the collapse of the Soviet Union. Third, gradualists refused to accept that the communist state was highly corrupt or even kleptocratic, being more concerned about market failures, such as possible monopoly effects. They favored state intervention and retained a strong belief in social engineering. Fourth, while radical reformers considered the transition a risky task that could fail, gradualists took the success of the market economy for granted because of the strength of the state, suggesting detailed optimal sequencing of reform measures. As a consequence, gradualists wanted to impede the transition process, whereas radical reformers feared it would be stalled. Fifth, gradualists wanted to stimulate output through demand management, whereas radical reformers saw a systemic lack of supply as the prime problem. The overt disputes were limited to the speed and order of reforms, but hardly anybody defended a larger public sector than in Western Europe in the early transition debate. In reality, however, many gradualists retained more socialist views than they wanted to reveal at the moment of liberal triumph.

The dominant argument for a more gradual approach was the evident economic successes of the Chinese model of communist reform, which many people of all kinds of persuasions wanted to apply to the former Soviet bloc.

A broad group of Western social scientists based their opposition on the contention that radical reform would lead to a greater fall in output and be more socially costly than gradual reform. They wanted to make the reforms less radical and argued for trade-offs between reform and social costs. On such premises, they developed theoretical models of political economy. Institutional economists wanted to postpone the introduction of market economy until most institutional reforms had been undertaken.

In the former Soviet Union, reform communists, who had gained considerable authority by calling for market reforms in the early Gorbachev years, now turned against such reforms and refused to accept the reality of a normal market economy.

The Chinese Model

When communism collapsed in the Soviet bloc, East Asia stood out as a shining economic success, and many praised China as a model for the transition countries.[3] One contention was that Mikhail Gorbachev mistakenly started with democratization in January 1987 and that he should have begun with economic reforms instead (Nolan 1995; Goldman 1996). However, the Communist Party of the Soviet Union opposed any market economic reform when Mikhail Gorbachev became its secretary general in March 1985 (Åslund 1991). At that time, Soviet society was utterly petrified and increasingly dysfunctional. After having attempted economic reforms for two years, Gorbachev realized that the omnipotent party bureaucracy blocked everything, which convinced him to launch partial democratization to undermine it. In China, by contrast, reforms were launched after the devastating Cultural Revolution, which had brought economic decline and terrorized the Party apparatus. To argue that democratization should have followed market economic reform amounted to opposition to any change in the Soviet Union.[4] Russian liberal Vladimir Mau (1999) retorted that "the Chinese path entails leaving power in the hands of the old Nomenklatura in order to preserve a one-party system and the ideological purity of the regime. Economic transformations then are to be undertaken gradually under Nomenklatura control. Any attempt to increase the political activity of individuals must be heavily suppressed." The Soviet Nomenklatura was almighty, and the public had no voice.

---

[3] For example, Parkhomenko (1992), Amsden et al. (1994), Nolan (1995), Goldman (1996), and Stiglitz (1999a).

[4] Marshall Goldman (1991, p. 224) presented a more plausible view of the Gorbachev reforms in 1991: "even if Gorbachev had adopted a more rational and coherent policy, it is unlikely that he would have succeeded. The Soviet population . . . was too resistant to evolutionary change. For that reason, the odds are that no one else would have done much better." The problem, though, was the Nomenklatura rather than the population.

Another argument was that experimentation was better than full-scale reforms (e.g., Murrell 1992b; Stiglitz 1999a), but no communist country had experimented as much with economic reforms as the Soviet Union. It carried out reforms and experiments in the 1920s, 1950s, 1960s, and 1980s, but the problem was that they were all reversed. The same was largely true of Central Europe (Balcerowicz 1995). Only in Hungary did significant systemic changes persist, but they did not lead to significant growth, and a broad Hungarian consensus advocated more radical reforms (Kornai 1986, 1990). The question is rather why experimentation succeeded in China and failed in the Soviet bloc.

Third, the champions of Chinese reforms agreed that it was right to start the reform with agriculture and small enterprises and leave the large industrial enterprises in state hands, creating a dual economy with a market economy for the small enterprises and the old state governance for the large state enterprises. The new private or quasi-private sector could generate growth and develop without antagonizing the old state sector (Murrell 1992b; Amsden et al. 1994; Goldman 1996; Nolan 1995). Jeffrey Sachs and Wing Thye Woo (1994) objected that agriculture in China was dominant, whereas it was a small part of the overindustrialized economy in Central Europe and the Soviet Union. Soviet state industry dominated the economy and could not be left aside. Furthermore, Soviet agriculture was industrialized and large scale, too. To break up big state and collective farms was technically difficult. In addition, the huge communist agrarian bureaucracy blocked any progressive economic development for its selfish reasons. Gorbachev tried agricultural reforms in the Soviet Union in the spring of 1985, but he got nowhere. He grandly legalized cooperatives in May 1988, but they became predominantly vehicles of management theft (Åslund 1989, 1991).

Fourth, most proponents of the Chinese model favored gradual price liberalization and opening of the economy (Amsden et al. 1994; Nolan 1995; Goldman 1996). Well, the Soviet Union did so, and the result was truly disastrous: massive rent seeking by prominent members of the Nomenklatura, which is also going on in China (Dąbrowski et al. 2001).

A final argument was that China was right in carrying out a far-reaching decentralization, but the Soviet Union failed to do so. However, Peter Murrell and Mancur Olson (1991) argued convincingly that the decline of the centrally planned economies could be explained by the devolution of power within the party and state hierarchy and the collusion of bureaucrats at lower levels undoing the dictatorship of the secretary general. "The last stage of communism is not the stateless and classless society that Marx forecast, but rule by a rather large aristocracy of upper level bureaucrats" (p. 260). Power was devolved both within the party bureaucracy and to state enterprise managers, but without accountability or responsibility. The Chinese Communist Party maintained some control over its bureaucrats, whereas the Soviet state fell apart. Soviet bureaucrats were relatively more numerous than Chinese bureaucrats and had more flawed incentives, rendering them more harmful. China and Russia are today deemed similarly corrupt, but Russian corruption is perceived as socially more costly (Shleifer and Treisman 2000; Transparency International 2006).

In the end, surprisingly little can be compared. Although both China and the Soviet Union were communist dictatorships with socialized economies, most preconditions differed when they launched market economic reforms in 1978 and 1985, respectively. First, the Soviet state and Party were so petrified that they could no longer reform but only collapse, yet the Chinese state and its Communist Party were still reformable (Åslund 1989). Second, China was dominated by agriculture, but the Soviet Union by large-scale industry (Sachs and Woo 1994). Third, the Soviet Union collapsed in hyperinflation, whereas the Chinese leaders never lost control over macroeconomic stability. China did not need any macroeconomic shock therapy, but the Soviet Union did.

Western Arguments for Gradualism
Four main arguments for gradualism are social democratic political economy, theoretical political economy, the concept of disorganization, and evolutionary or institutional economics.

Przeworski's Political Economy. European social democrats were profoundly uncomfortable during the collapse of communism. Many of them had argued that nothing of the kind could ever happen, and everything was wrong from their point of view. As the postcommunist output collapse started, left-wingers drew parallels with the Great Depression of 1929–33, the worst crisis of capitalism. In a highly acclaimed book on democracy and the market in Eastern Europe, Adam Przeworski (1991), a leading scholar of comparative politics, laid out the argument. His first postulate was that democracy had to justify itself by material achievements: "To evoke compliance and participation, democracy must generate substantive outcomes: it must offer all the relevant political forces real opportunities to improve their material welfare" (p. 32). Implicitly, he assumed that people opted for democracy for the sake of economic welfare, not for political reasons. Przeworski's second postulate was that people demanded quick results. "Can structural economic transformation be sustained under democratic conditions, or must either reforms or democracy be sacrificed?" (p. 138). His underlying thought was this: "Even if the post-reform system would be more efficient...a transient deterioration of material conditions may be sufficient to undermine either democracy or the reform process" (p. 137). Third, Przeworski (1991, p. 163) assumed that "the social cost is higher under the radical strategy, where social cost is defined as the cumulative decline in consumption during the period of transition." "Inflation is likely to flare up again and again under inertial pressures. Unemployment, even if temporary, is difficult to tolerate. Increasing inequality stokes conflicts" (p. 189). Finally, he presumed that the threat to democracy came from a dissatisfied population. In his 1995 book, Przeworski (1995, p. 85) came back with an even harsher judgment: "we have been critical of the standard neoliberal recipes since we believe that they are faulty in three fundamental ways: they induce economic stagnation, they incur unnecessarily large social costs, and they weaken the nascent democratic institutions." Przeworski assumed that "the continuing material deprivation, the technocratic style of policy making, and the ineffectiveness of the representative institutions undermine popular support for democracy" (1991, pp. 189–90). His assumptions were shared by a large number of political scientists.[5]

The problem with these assumptions was that they did not square with reality. Larry Diamond (1999) has debunked Przeworski's first postulate, showing that people see democracy as a value in itself and do not judge it only by economic results. As we shall see, economic reform and democracy were positively correlated, and radical reforms caused less economic decline and social costs. Joel Hellman (1998) made the profound point that the main threat to reforms did not come from the population but from the winning elite. Because of his inaccurate assumptions, Przeworski's conclusions were faulty as well.

Theoretical political economy. A small group of Western economists, primarily Gérard Roland, Mathias Dewatripont, Phillipe Aghion, and Olivier Blanchard, developed an extensive theoretical literature on the political economy of transition.[6] With a cursory look at economic developments in a few transition countries, mostly Poland and Hungary, they made rather heroic assumptions in line with Przeworski's, which were not realistic. The

---

[5] Similar views were expressed by Elster (1990), Offe (1997), Andreas Pickel in Pickel and Wiesenthal (1997), and Stark and Bruszt (1998).

[6] See in particular Dewatripont and Roland (1992a, 1992b), Aghion and Blanchard (1994), and Roland (1993, 1994, 2000).

gist of this literature is the assumption that radical reform leads to a sharper decline in output and greater social costs than gradual reform: "Assume that big bang...has a negative expected outcome" (Roland 1993, pp. 534–5). Another assumption was that the population would not tolerate more than a certain decline in output or a certain degree of unemployment As a trade-off, they suggested slow liberalization and privatization, as well as more social benefits and subsidies, to make reforms politically possible. They also made other unrealistic assumptions, for example, that the key political actor was the majority of the population (Dewatripont and Roland 1992b), implying that the nascent democratic institutions were both representative and effective. Then, "gradualism may allow for 'divide and rule' tactics when compensation for the losers from reform is costly, provided the government has enough agenda-setting power" (Roland 1994, p. 1162). They presumed not only a very democratic but also a strong and effective government, assuming nearly perfect social engineering (Dewatripont and Roland 1992b). They also assumed that a more radical reform would lead to higher taxes and, therefore, to a slower growth of the private sector (Dewatripont and Roland 1992a; Aghion and Blanchard 1994).

Economic models can be relevant, even if a few assumptions are not very realistic. The problem with these models, however, was that all of their major assumptions contradicted reality, as we shall see in the rest of this book, and that their conclusions largely depended on the assumption that more radical reform brought more social hardship. This theoretical literature hangs detached from most empirical research, which has found that radical reform have been less socially costly. Katz and Owen (2000) have shown that if the assumptions in Dewatripont and Roland (1992b) are changed to the real situation, their article "may be viewed as lending strong support to the big-bang strategy" (Havrylyshyn 2006, pp. 23–4).

Disorganization. Olivier Blanchard and Michael Kremer (1997) developed an alternative model to explain the decline in output with disorganization. Under communism, a typical industry had fewer firms than in the West. For many inputs, firms knew of only one supplier, and for many outputs only one buyer. During transition, old trade links were disrupted or became uneconomical. With asymmetric information or incomplete contracts, the initial results of bargaining might have been inefficient, implying that market imperfections caused output to fall with the transition. Blanchard and Kremer noticed that shortages persisted because adjustments took time. Looking at Central Europe, the Baltic countries, and Russia, they found empirical evidence for the decline in output having been more pronounced for goods with more complex production processes. They inquired "whether the need to preserve existing production networks provides a justification for gradualism" and whether "a commitment by the government to subsidize state firms for some time may avoid their immediate collapse" (Blanchard and Kremer 1997, p. 1123). However, the authors cautioned that this was only a limited, theoretical case for gradualism, and they acknowledged that it was valid only in the short term because enterprises could be presumed to solve their contract and bargaining problems relatively soon.

Blanchard and Kremer's empirical proof was a regression, showing that more advanced manufacturing industries experienced greater decline, but because those were also the greatest value detractors, it was desirable that their substandard production plummeted. The systemic disruption prompted every enterprise to review its contracts, which was one of the original arguments for radical reform (Boycko 1991; Murphy et al. 1992). The question is rather which kind of reform minimizes the period of disorganization, and as we shall see, the answer is radical reform.

Institutions first. Nobel laureate Douglass C. North accused radical reformers of having "forgotten" institutions. North (1994, p. 359) saw radical reform ideas as dominated by neoclassical theory, which he argued "is simply an inappropriate tool to analyze and prescribe policies that will induce development." "While the rules may be changed overnight, the informal norms usually change only gradually . . . transferring the formal political and economic rules of successful Western market economies to third-world and Eastern European economies is not a sufficient condition for good economic performance. Privatization is not a panacea for solving poor economic performance." However, he offered no evidence for this alleged forgetfulness of institutions. In reality, all radical reformers were deeply committed to changing the old communist institutions, using Friedrich Hayek (1944/1986, 1960), the leading liberal institutionalist, as the main source of inspiration (Balcerowicz 1992; Klaus 1992; Mau 1999; Akaev 2000).

Peter Murrell (1992a, 1992b, 1992c) tried to develop an *evolutionary theory* for postcommunist economic transition. He observed that in Central Europe "organizations that were expected to change their behavior in response to the new conditions have failed to do so," particularly the dominant large state enterprises (Murrell 1992b, p. 81). He agreed with the radical reformers on the need for a coherent economic environment, but he drew the opposite conclusion: "little in the economic record of the past two years suggests that the radical program of reform can be successful. The old cannot be simply destroyed and therefore the radical reform plans have serious problems of coherence" (Murrell 1992b, p. 82). He concluded: "The information and skills of existing personnel are attuned to the existing set of institutions and lose much of their value when those institutions are destroyed" (Murrell 1992c, p. 50). Hence, gradual reforms would cause less output losses, because the old sector would suffer less, whereas the new private market sector would develop better (Murrell and Wang 1993).

Many gradualists insisted that market institutions should be established before the economy was liberalized to avoid market failures. The UN Economic Commission for Europe (1990, p. 23) pleaded: "legal and financial infrastructures of the market economy must be put in place before markets can perform." Only East Germany did so, because West Germany imposed its commercial legislation, but East Germany stands out as one of the most costly and least successful transitions (see Chapter 11). If nothing was done, market reforms would certainly fail, as Belarus has shown. Oleh Havrylyshyn (2006, p. 272) starkly pointed out: "it is easily seen in the time-path of the transition index that those countries which moved most slowly on liberalization elements moved even more slowly on the institution-building elements. This implies that the proclamations of the political elites in these countries that the society was not ready for the market and a gradual evolution was necessary, were not sincere proclamations but masked a hidden agenda." Obviously, institutions could not be built very fast, but the issue was what kind of reform would lead to a faster and better building of institutions.

Reform Communists Opposing a Normal Market Economy

The starkest antireform opposition came from the old Soviet establishment in Russia, but it resonated throughout the former Soviet Union. As soon as Boris Yeltsin and Yegor Gaidar presented their ideas of radical economic reform in late 1991, reform communists started attacking them viciously with a mixture of vulgar Marxism, populism, and vested interests. Most vocal were Russia's Vice President Aleksandr Rutskoi, Chairman of the Central Bank of Russia Viktor Gerashchenko, and parliamentary Speaker Ruslan Khasbulatov.

The old reform communists regarded "the real economy," production, and investment as important while disregarding finance, money, and inflation because they saw money as a free utility. Because the sharp output fall had caused the high inflation, they wanted to issue more money to support production. Their thinking was so out of line with modern macroeconomics that it needs to be quoted at length. Gerashchenko (1992) wanted the money supply to rise with the price level: "Could the economy manage with the former money supply when the prices were rising ... were the previous monetary resources really sufficient to exist at the present price level, when the wholesale prices have risen 16–18 times? According to my view, they were inadequate." Prominent Soviet economists insisted: "Financial stabilization cannot precede the stabilization of production . . . As long as the fall of production does not turn into sustained growth, it is necessary to abandon any attempt at forming a state budget without deficit. When the volume of production in a country is falling, a budget without a deficit can only be accomplished at the price of hyperinflation . . . there are no state budgets without deficits even in well-to-do countries with market economies" (Fedorenko et al. 1992). The highly respected Director of the Institute of Economics of the Russian Academy of Sciences Leonid Abalkin reckoned: "the budget deficit cannot be diminished by tax increases. Their rise will lead to price hikes and the reduction of production and tax evasion" (Abalkin 1992).

Inflation was seen as structural and unrelated to monetary policy: "Liberalization of prices on energy will indisputably lead the economy to open hyperinflation." The government faced the choice "either to abandon strict monetary policy and satisfy the demand for money to preserve production or to allow mass bankruptcy of commercial banks and completely disorganize monetary circulation" (Yaremenko et al. 1992). At that time, commercial banks were making more money than ever before or after, while high inflation was disorganizing the payment system. The leading communist economist, Academician Dmitri S. Lvov (1996, pp. 181–2), insisted that inflation stimulated production:

Macroeconomic calculations show that a reduction of inflation by one percent results in a fall of output of three–five percent . . . to "cut" inflation from 10 percent a month to zero, it is necessary to reduce production almost to zero. But if we agree to increase inflation to, for instance, 15 percent a month, it is possible, as these calculations evidence, to reach a production level that is 70 percent of the level of 1991.

Although these Soviet economists considered themselves market socialists, they regarded the deregulation of prices and trade as simplistic and unprofessional. The state had to build the market, which could not develop spontaneously. "Only under the conditions of sufficiently strong state regulation can the transition to the market take place; the most important part of this transition must be a state program for the establishment of a market infrastructure" (Petrakov et al. 1992). Russian Vice President Aleksandr Rutskoi (1992) could not imagine the absence of price controls: "The liberalization of prices without the existence of a civilized market requires strict price control. . . . In all civilized countries such strict controls exist."

With their limited belief in the market and knowledge of the outside world, these critics did not think liberalization would abolish shortages. "I suppose that we should not place great hope in the abolition of the multiple shortages and the appearance in the shops of an abundance of goods" (Bogomolov 1992). The state, on the contrary, was considered omnipotent despite its rampant crisis, and the issue was political will. "Is the state really not able to establish control over the prices of monopolized production? Of course it can, if it wants to" (Rutskoi 1992). Whereas the reformers aspired to restructuring of Soviet-era production, the Soviet economists desired the full utilization of the old production capacity, advocating higher export tariffs, state subsidies to the export industry, and more protectionism, which were major causes of corruption in Russia (Glaziev 1996).

Sequencing was another major concern. The Soviet establishment opposed the privatization of large and medium-sized enterprises until 1991, yet now they suddenly argued that it should have been undertaken before price liberalization. As one old Soviet academician put it: "And why was it not possible to start with a fast privatization and the breaking up of monopolies already? [in October 1991]" (Arbatov 1992). Soon, however, after the Russian government had carried out a stunningly fast privatization, the same people complained that privatization had been too fast (Russian Academy of Sciences 1994).

The reform communists' last stand was that Russia was unique. "Our situation is special. It cannot be described by general rules" (Petrakov et al. 1992). "The economic reforms must not be based on abstract and extremely simplified models, but on decisions derived from real life, on considerations of the real situation in the economy, the population of the country, and the experiences of the whole political and socioeconomic history of Russia" (Khasbulatov 1992).

The ultimate feat of these Soviet economists was when five American Nobel Prize laureates in economics joined the whole Soviet economic establishment in what was a campaign effort for the communist presidential candidate Gennady Zyuganov in 1996.[7] Together they claimed: "In spite of the hopes of the reformers for a flourishing private business which supports the economy, their program generated economic collapse, a strengthening of the mafia and growing political instability, which is destructive for the

[7] The five Nobel Prize winners were Kenneth Arrow, Lawrence Klein, Vassily Leontieff, Douglass North, and James Tobin. They were joined by John Kenneth Galbraith and Marshall Goldman (Bogomolov 1996, pp. 21–3; Klein and Pomer 2001). Their joint declaration in apparent support of Zyuganov was published in Nezavisimaya gazeta (July 1, 1996), just before the presidential elections (Mau 1999).

business climate." They demanded a higher progressive income tax, price controls, higher protective customs tariffs and industrial policy, including government subsidies and credits. Their key request was "the necessity to reinforce the role of the government in the process of transformation," but the malfunctioning of the state was ignored. Instead, corruption was presented as a consequence of privatization: "To a considerable extent, privatization, which goes together with the spreading corruption, lowers the existing level of welfare and leads to the impoverishment of most of the population" (Bogomolov 1996, pp. 17–21).

Although Soviet economists and populist politicians took the public lead in the Russian debate, the ultimate beneficiaries of their arguments were the state enterprise managers. They abstained from acrimonious criticism while cautioning that government policy should be "pragmatic." They called for "common sense," "consensus," and "moderation," which all meant minimal and slow reforms, but they did not desire to return to the Soviet system (Parkhomenko 1992).

Such was the gist of the public debate in the CIS countries in 1992 and 1993, of which gradual reform became characteristic. In most of them, the old communist leaders stayed in power, and they wanted a minimum of political and economic change. They were forced to adjust to financial collapse and reform in Russia, but they delayed fiscal stabilization, which threw ten CIS countries in the ruble zone into hyperinflation in 1993. The Russian price liberalization compelled them to liberalize some prices, but they limited it and regulated foreign trade, creating huge price differentials between regulated and free prices. Although central planning had fallen apart, the CIS governments maintained state orders for much production. Privatization was slow, favoring insider privatization by state managers. As the state remained omnipotent, democracy was weak. Eventually, most of these countries became market economies, but a few reverted to socialist economies without ideology.

Rent Seeking: The Scourge of Transition

The most important gradualist group consisted of those who wanted to make money on the very transition to a market economy.[8] They dominated in the former Soviet Union, where they hid their real agenda behind old Soviet reform communist economists and populists, the most ardent critics of radical reform. This politically most influential group consisted of

[8] I first developed this theme in Åslund (1996) and elaborated on it in Åslund (1999).

rent-seeking state enterprise managers and Soviet officials, who benefited from the inconsistencies of the transitional system and wanted to perpetuate them. They did favor a market economy, but their aspiration was to prolong and complicate transition to maximize market distortions, from which these people knew how to make fortunes. In the real policy world, these rent seekers were the main opponents of the radical reformers.

Postcommunist transformation is the history of the war for and against rent seeking. Reformers wanted to establish a normal market economy, but rent seekers desired to make money on both market and state failures. Initially, the prime rent seekers were state enterprise managers and officials, but soon new entrepreneurs surged, and the wealthiest of them became oligarchs.

A useful definition of rents is "profits in excess of the competitive level" (Brealey and Myers 2000). Anne Krueger (1974) introduced the term "rent seeking" in modern economic inquiry in reference to the costs of government regulation. The Western discussion about rent seeking focused on the regulation of foreign trade and domestic prices, which were much smaller than the rents generated at the end of communism.

Liberal reformers won in Central Europe and the Baltics, while rent seekers dominated in the CIS countries. The rent seekers' strategy involved a confusing mixture of freedom and regulation because they aspired to a maximum of economic freedom for themselves but severe regulations for others. Wisely, they avoided pronouncing their strategy openly. At the collapse of communism, the opportunities for rent seeking were probably greater than at any other time in world history. Huge resources lay unguarded. Large rents arose from arbitrage between free market prices and state-controlled prices, aggravated by multiple exchange rates. As inflation mounted, state interest rates remained low while huge interest subsidies became available. Large state enterprise subsidies persisted, and state enterprise managers privatized them through transfer pricing. Rents faded away with time, but successful rent seekers bought politics to impose new rents. A vicious circle of self-reinforcing rent seeking evolved. Finally, the rent seekers privatized the state enterprises, which ironically turned them into profit seekers and caused high economic growth.

In hindsight, the seemingly haphazard economic reforms introduced by Soviet President Mikhail Gorbachev in the late 1980s appear designed to construct a rent-seeking machine. Although most deregulations were minor, some were amazingly liberal. The explanation for why these reforms, later so obviously a result of trial and error, provide such a clear pattern is that certain reforms were accepted because they facilitated rent seeking by Soviet officials, but they refuted other reforms that contradicted their interests. Presumably without understanding it himself, Gorbachev built a hothouse of rent seeking from 1987 to 1991. Seven changes in economic policy provided the preconditions for extraordinary rent seeking.[9]

One of Gorbachev's first significant reforms was a partial liberalization of foreign trade in August 1986, long before the domestic market was liberalized. The prime goal was to break up the monopoly power of the Ministry for Foreign Trade. By 1988, more than 200 corporations had been granted the right to pursue foreign trade, and in 1990, their number approached 20,000. This liberalization was premature, but it allowed powerful state bodies to make money on foreign trade. A privileged few obtained an opportunity to arbitrage between low domestic prices and many times higher world prices.

Second, these early foreign trade reforms also introduced up to 3,000 so-called currency coefficients, effectively one exchange rate for each significant foreign trade good. Their ratio varied from one to twenty, offering extraordinary opportunities for arbitrage. In late 1990, these coefficients were replaced by a unified commercial exchange rate, but even so, the Soviet Union had one official rate, one commercial rate, and a plummeting black market exchange rate, permitting ever greater arbitrage gains.

Third, in January 1988, the Soviet Law on State Enterprises came into force. It was a halfway attempt at economic reform, leaving the economy with neither plan nor market. Compulsory plan targets were abolished, and enterprises were given more freedom in setting prices and wages. As managers preferred to produce less but charge more money, both wages and prices started to skyrocket.

Fourth, with the Law on State Enterprises, the State Planning Committee (Gosplan), and the industrial ministries lost control over state enterprise managers and could no longer dismiss them. State enterprise managers obtained freedom without accountability, becoming quasi-owners of "their" state enterprises, and soon they started "spontaneous privatization" (Åslund 1995).

Fifth, the revolutionary Soviet Law on Cooperatives of May 1988 legalized all kinds of private enterprises with minimal regulation. Predominantly, the new cooperatives were trading companies owned by a state enterprise manager and attached to his state company. State managers started selling the produce of their state companies to their private trading cooperatives at a low

---

[9] The section that follows draws on Åslund (1991). Peter Boettke (1993) analyzes the failure of perestroika from this perspective of rent seeking.

price, and their cooperatives reaped the profit. These trading cooperatives became management theft companies.

Sixth, another form of new "cooperatives" was commercial banks, which mushroomed without regulation. At the time of the collapse of the Soviet Union, Russia already had 1,360 commercial banks. They demanded unlimited access to state credit at minimal nominal interest rates, which was possible because of the competition between the Soviet and Russian Central Banks in 1990 and 1991 (Johnson 2000). Effectively, they usurped the inflation tax of mounting hyperinflation.[10]

Seventh, traditionally the Ministry of Finance and the Central Bank were weak authorities, subordinate to the State Planning Committee and dozens of industrial ministries. As partial markets started operating, the previously passive money assumed real life, and many called for more money to be issued. Because of the lack of fiscal or monetary restraints, money flooded freely. The Soviet budget deficit exploded to at least 20 percent of GDP in 1991, and it was financed with the emission of money. An economic madhouse had been created. By late 1990, the standard assessment of both Soviet and Western economists was that Soviet hyperinflation was virtually inevitable. Then, the country and its political and economic systems collapsed.

As Michael Dobbs (1997, p. 373) wrote, "There was a *fin de régime* atmosphere in Moscow in the spring of 1991, and bureaucrats were lining up to jump ship before it was too late. . . . " "Why drive a Volga when you could be driving a Mercedes?" This division of the elite helps to explain the pathetic abortive August 1991 coup. Pragmatic state enterprise directors opposed the coup because of their rising commercial interests, contributing to the peaceful termination of communism. "The durability of communism and the speed with which it collapsed were two sides of the same coin. There came a point at which the strengths of the system – massive repression, rigid centralization, an all-embracing ideology, the obsession with military power – turned into fatal weaknesses" (Dobbs 1997, p. 440). The extraordinary economic distortions necessitated radical reform, but they had bred overwhelming vested interests that cherished these market distortions.

---

[10] In May 1990, I chaired a seminar in Stockholm with the Moscow Professor of Economics Ruslan Khasbulatov, who later became chairman of the Russian Parliament. Responding to a question about the monetary overhang in the Soviet Union, Khasbulatov exclaimed: "What is the problem? If there is more money, there will be more production!" True to this policy, as chairman of the Russian Supreme Soviet, he commanded the issue of massive cheap credit (Matyukhin 1993).

From 1988, the Soviet Union displayed an incredibly innovative spirit. Soviet citizens made money in every conceivable way. Most people were shocked, because the methods were often objectionable, the damage incurred was huge, and the fortunes accumulated were monumental. The forms of rent were multiple, and the methods of rent seeking shifted swiftly.

The basic method of rent seeking was arbitrage between fixed state prices and private market prices, preferably abroad. The multiple exchange rates had all along fed a corps of black exchange traders, offering tourists six times the official exchange rate. In the late 1980s, foreign trade rents surged. Western computers were imported and sold at high prices on the domestic market, because of extreme shortage and high domestic sales taxes. In 1990, the real bonanza opened up, when some managers of Soviet commodity plants started exporting oil and metals independently through their private trading companies. The domestic oil price plummeted with the Soviet ruble to as little as half a percent of the world market price. In 1992, the state-controlled prices of commodities were at most one-tenth of the world market prices, and more than 70 percent of Russia's exports were commodities subject to export quotas (Aven 1994, p. 84). Total Russian exports outside of the CIS amounted to $42.2 billion. The collected export tariffs amounted to some $2.4 billion, while GDP was only $79 billion in 1992, because of the very low exchange rate (World Bank 1996b). That means that the total export rents were no less than $24 billion, or 30 percent of GDP.

Another major source of rents was subsidized imports. Because of the fear of starvation, Russia maintained special exchange rates for so-called critical imports until 1993. The Russian importers of grain bought hard currency for only 1 percent of the going exchange rate in 1992, allowing them to pay only 1 percent of the world market price for imported grain, while bread was sold at ordinary domestic prices. The IMF (1993, p. 133) calculated total Russian import subsidies at 17.5 percent of GDP that year.

A third source of rents was the emission of subsidized state credits. The Central Bank of Russia issued new credit equivalent to 31.6 percent GDP in 1992 (Granville 1995b, p. 67). Because these loans were largely given at an interest rate of 10 or 25 percent a year while inflation that year was 2,500 percent, they were sheer gifts (Åslund 1995). These gifts rendered the chairman of Russia's Central Bank, Viktor Gerashchenko, very popular in the Russian elite, although the banking sector was impregnated with crime.

Fourth, the state budget provided direct enterprise subsidies, amounting to 10.4 percent of GDP in Russia in 1992 (European Bank for Reconstruction and Development 1997, p. 83). From these four sources, total gross rents amounted to almost 90 percent of Russia's GDP in 1992. Even so, we have left some rents, such as tax exemptions, aside. Presumably rents have never been larger as a ratio of GDP anywhere in the world than they were in the former Soviet Union in 1992. As select citizens transferred these rents and subsidies from state enterprises to their private accounts through transfer pricing or outright theft, they became very wealthy. This took place throughout the CIS. The more partial and slow the reforms were, the greater the distortions and the larger the rents. The most prominent source of rent seeking in the public mind was privatization, but rent seeking peaked in 1992 when privatization had barely started.

Rent seekers were cold-blooded, rational businessmen. They had no ideology but convenience. They engaged in politics mainly to secure their rents. Confusingly, they were reformist and progressive as long as communism lasted, because their profits derived from the market, however distorted, and they wanted to escape the old communist control system. As soon as communism was over, however, the threat to rent seekers came from a truly free market. Logically, they tried to slow down market reforms to preserve market distortions that generated rents while invoking many fine social causes. Later on, many wealthy businessmen became interested in securing their property rights against capricious rulers, which rendered them more liberal again. Now they stood up for the principles of a free society.

Rent seekers were the ultimate gamblers. They knew that a game could not last for long, but if possible, they would try to prolong it. When one game was over, they jumped on another lucrative market distortion, such as barter, to make more money. As a result, macroeconomic stabilization and liberalization often looked hopeless, but suddenly something happened – an economic crisis, a determined political attack, or the emergence of more attractive rents – and a politically impossible policy was instantly carried out. Examples are price liberalization, the abolition of import subsidization or subsidized credits, the deregulation of exports, cuts in enterprise subsidies, and the transition from soft to strict monetary policy in most post-Soviet countries.

Rents could be brought down by many means, but they could not stay that high for long. Arbitrage would inevitably dissipate rents caused by extreme regulation, and the slump of the inflation tax during hyperinflation would devalue inflationary rents. Rents ended with privatization. The course of postcommunist transition was determined by what means policy makers chose to deal with rent seeking, and that choice depended on the political regime. The path selected determined the nature of society after transition.

We can define postcommunist transition as the period of this extraordinary rent seeking. In the former Soviet Union, it started in 1990 and ended on August 17, 1998, the day of the Russian financial crash, which disciplined the prime rent seekers of the day, the Russian oligarchs. In Central Europe and the Baltics, the transition period was much shorter, and its end was not so distinct. Afterward the transformation of postcommunist society has continued in a less dramatic fashion. In the period after 1998, a quite different pattern of more normal development took over.

Criticism of Radical Reform after the Russian Financial Crash

After the aggressive early debate and a nervous start of transition, policies started to bite, and the international community cheered the successes of radical economic reform in Central Europe and the Baltics, and the prevailing sentiment was that Russia and the rest of the CIS countries were eventually getting on the bandwagon.[11] In 1996, the World Bank (1996a) devoted its annual World Development Report to transition. Its main conclusions read as a credo of the radical economic reform (pp. 142–5, *emphasis in original*):

- *Consistent policies, combining liberalization of markets, trade, and new business entry with reasonable price stability, can achieve a great deal – even in countries lacking clear property rights and strong market institutions.*
- *An efficient response to market processes requires clearly defined property rights – and this will eventually require widespread private ownership.*
- *Major changes in social policy must complement the move to the market.*
- *Institutions that support markets arise both by design and from demand.*
- *International integration can help lock in successful reforms.*

As the years passed, however, Russia's economic growth failed to take off, although mass privatization had been carried out. Inflation had abated in 1996, and the new stock market skyrocketed. The loans-for-shares privatization in late 1995, which transferred a dozen of Russia's most valuable

---

[11] A number of quite positive books on the Russian economic transition were published; see Åslund (1995), Granville (1995a), Layard and Parker (1996).

oil and metals companies to a handful of new oligarchs aroused an outcry about "original sin" in both Russia and the West. The view that Russia had lapsed into a morass of organized crime and corruption proliferated in vivid journalism.

As the question marks piled up around Russia's transition, the country approached a financial crash in slow motion. On August 17, 1998, the Russian government defaulted on its domestic debt, let the ruble exchange rate plummet, and froze all bank accounts, and roughly half the Russian bank system went bankrupt. The shock was horrendous. The Russian middle class lost most of its bank savings for the second time. Russian inflation exploded again, and output fell. In an article in the *New York Times*, John Lloyd (1998) famously asked "Who lost Russia?" Had the attempts to build a market economy in Russia failed? In Russia, the main conclusions were that the long-lasting large budget deficit had to be eliminated and the exchange rate be made competitive.

In the West, however, the left-wing criticism of Joseph Stiglitz came to dominate, especially through his best-selling book *Globalization and Its Discontents* (2002).[12] Stiglitz (1999a, 1999b, 2000, 2002) attacked IMF policy on Russia, arguing that the Washington Consensus model did not work there. He reckoned that Russia should have followed China's example, but "the Western advisers, especially from the United States and the IMF . . . marched in so quickly to preach the gospel of the market economy . . . arguing for a new religion – market fundamentalism" (2002, p. 134). Logically, Stiglitz (1999b, p. 4) praised the gradual reforms in truly tyrannical Uzbekistan. In his support of gradualism, Stiglitz lauded Gorbachev's policies: "The Gorbachev-era *perestroika* reforms furnish a good example of incremental institutional reforms" (Stiglitz 1999a, p. 24). The problem was that they had brought about the collapse of the Soviet Union and its economy, a fact on which Stiglitz refrained to comment.

Another criticism was institutional, that the reformers had ignored the importance of the institutional infrastructure of a market economy and dissipated the communist organizational capital. Stiglitz criticized radical reformers for blaming "the failure of the shock therapy on corruption and rent seeking at every turn . . . without recognizing any role of the institutional blitzkrieg in destroying but not replacing the old social norms – and thus in removing the last restraints against society-threatening levels of corruption . . . Once dissipated, organizational capital is hard to reassemble"

---

[12] Similar views were expressed by Cohen (2000), Klein and Pomer (2001), Reddaway and Glinski (2001), and Goldman (2003).

(Stiglitz 1999a, p. 9). Stiglitz defended the postcommunist state: "The state is seen as the primary source of the problems: interfering in state firms and preying on private firms. The emphasis is on government failure, not on market failure" (p. 20), while he called radical reformers "market Bolsheviks." The organizational capital he lauded contained the Communist Party and the secret police, which are rarely considered assets in democratic societies.

Stiglitz's third and greatest concern was the Russian privatization. He condemned the Russian loans-for-shares scheme as the main source of corruption. "Russia's oligarchs stole assets, stripped them leaving their country much poorer" (2002, p. 160). "Russia's kind of ersatz capitalism did not provide the incentives for wealth creation and economic growth but rather for asset stripping" (p. 162). Instead, he wanted to give away state enterprises to the old elite: "Perhaps trying to discipline spontaneous privatization might have offered the greatest hope" (Stiglitz 1999a, p. 6). Stiglitz largely ignored the macroeconomic crisis, simply arguing that "the rapid liberalization at the beginning had led to the burst of inflation" (2002, p. 156), and that "the tight monetary policies also contributed to the use of barter" (p. 157). He concluded: "Prospects for the future are bleak" (p. 133).

Ironically, this criticism dismissed Russia's economic transformation as a failure just when Russia rose from its ashes, accomplishing sound macroeconomic stability and an average GDP growth of nearly 7 percent for at least eight years, while the region as a whole recorded even higher growth rates.[13] A nearly unison choir of macroeconomists argued that the problems with Russia's stabilization was not shock therapy but gradualism: "It was not the shock therapy program but the refusal to stick to it that catalyzed many contradictions in Russia's postcommunist development, including its institutional problems" (Mau 1999). "It is said that institutional reforms and privatization should take place first, and liberalization and stabilization should take place later ... but the experiences of those countries that undertook market reforms does not provide a single case to prove such a concept viable" (Mau 1999). Oleh Havrylyshyn (2006, p. 272) underlined: "those countries which moved most slowly on liberalization elements moved even more slowly on the institution-building elements." Mau (1999) refused to blame the IMF, because a "good part of the 'IMF conditions' were developed in Moscow, not in Washington.... This is a typical way for a weak

---

[13] Two of the sharpest responses were produced by the Russian liberal Vladimir Mau (1999) and the Polish liberals Marek Dąbrowski, Stanisław Gomułka, and Jacek Rostowski (2001). See also Yevstigneev and Yevstigneeva (1999). Havrylyshyn (2006) offers a later and full criticism. My own contribution was Åslund (1999).

government to launch unpopular reforms." With regard to privatization, Mau and other liberal Russians emphasized that the government could not control state property. "Property manipulation is an important feature of weak state power." Therefore, early and fast privatization with some order was the best option to create a stratum of private owners as a base for a market economy.

The most unabashed rebuttal of the criticism of the Russian economic transformation was presented in a much noticed article by Andrei Shleifer and Daniel Treisman (2004) in *Foreign Affairs*. Their thesis was this: "Russia was in 1990, and is today, a middle-income country . . . comparable to Argentina in 1991 and Mexico in 1999. Almost all democracies in this income range are rough around the edges: their governments suffer from corruption, their judiciaries are politicized, and their press is almost never entirely free. They have high income inequality, concentrated corporate ownership, and turbulent macroeconomic performance. In all these regards, Russia is quite normal" (p. 22). "In sum, Russia started the 1990s as a disintegrating, centrally planned economy and ended the decade as a market system in a burst of rapid growth" (p. 30). Boldly, Shleifer and Treisman defended the economic performance of the oligarchs in the loans-for-shares companies. "Have the oligarchs stripped assets from the companies they acquired in privatization, rather than investing in them? The audited financial statements of these companies suggest that their assets have grown dramatically, especially since 1998. . . . And the major oligarchs have been investing hundreds of millions of dollars annually in their companies. . . . In contrast, the greatest asset-stripping scandals occurred in companies that remained under state control" (p. 29).

As growth and macroeconomic stability of the CIS countries have become stellar, the interest of international debate has faded away.

3

Output: Slump and Recovery

A fundamental but poorly understood issue of postcommunist economic transformation is what actually happened to output. There is no agreement on the fundamental facts, and the statistical uncertainties are too great for any consensus to emerge any time soon. Throughout the region, transition started with huge recorded falls in output. Some argued that a unique devastation was taking place; others saw a combination of measurement problems and "creative destruction" in Joseph Schumpeter's (1943/1976) sense.

The universal output slump after communism has been greatly exaggerated. A substantial part of the big recorded decline, probably about half, was not real but can be explained with mismeasurement, an expansion of the unregistered economy, and the elimination of value detraction. In addition, many countries lost substantial subsidies as well as implicit trade subsidies. Output did fall in almost all countries, but not nearly as much as officially recorded. The main real problem was the long delay in economic recovery in many countries, not the initial slump.

The initial development of output was closely correlated with reform policies. Radical reformers soon returned to growth, whereas partial and nonreformers experienced a long period of contraction. The duration of the output decline varied greatly. A strong early supply effect occurred in the radical reform countries, especially Poland, which returned to growth in its third year of transition; Ukraine, by comparison, was a very gradual reformer, and experienced ten years of economic decline. The output fall lasted much longer and was steeper in the former Soviet Union. The covariation between many possible causes makes it impossible to distinguish the decisive reason, but hyperinflation and the general collapse of the state are strong candidates.

The great difficulty of the laggard states to return to economic growth shows that neither establishment of market economy nor economic recovery were automatic and that the initial slump was no cyclical recession. Before recovery could start, inflation had to be brought under control, and monetary and fiscal stimulation was not only ineffective but counterproductive. Structural reforms, primarily liberalization, especially of foreign trade and prices, and privatization, drove economic recovery.

In the transition lasting until 1998, the region could roughly be divided into three groups: successful reformers in a virtuous cycle in Central Europe and the Baltics, which swiftly returned to economic growth; unsuccessful partial reformers in a vicious cycle, including Romania, Bulgaria, and most of the Commonwealth of the Independent States (CIS) countries, which suffered protracted decline; and the three nonreformers, Belarus, Turkmenistan, and Uzbekistan, whose economies contracted less.

The picture changed in 1998, when the laggards in the former Soviet Union turned into leaders in economic growth. The catalyst of this new development was the Russian financial crash of August 1998. It compelled most post-Soviet states to clean up their acts and become real market economies. In particular, they were forced to cut their public expenditures dramatically, which gave them sufficient economic freedom to allow substantial economic growth. In parallel, the global energy boom boosted demand and prices for the region's ample resources of oil and gas, also driving economic growth. The conclusion is that high public expenditures and taxes are bad for economic growth, at least in corrupt postcommunist countries saddled with excessively large governments of poor quality. Unsurprisingly, greater economic freedom promotes economic growth.

The overall picture, as reflected in the official statistics, is shown in Figure 3.1. From 1989, the whole region saw substantial declines in output, which were greater in the former Soviet Union than in Central Europe. Central Europe returned to growth in 1993, the Baltics in 1995, and finally the CIS in 1997. The surprise is that the CIS countries have had roughly twice as high a growth rate as Central Europe from 1999, although the Baltics have almost reached the CIS level.

The first section scrutinizes the official data on output, the total decline, the length of decline, and the potency of the new growth, taking note of the new patterns of growth. The second section queries whether the huge but varied initial declines in recorded output were real. Section three investigates the causes of renewed economic growth, drawing on an extensive literature of cross-country regressions. Finally, I examine the boom and the changed growth pattern since 1999.

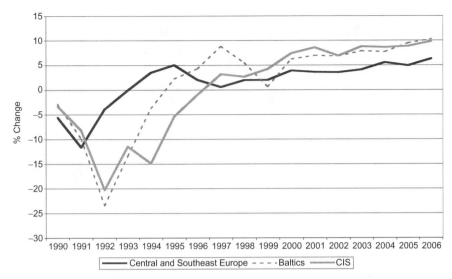

Figure 3.1. Official GDP Growth, 1990–2006. *Sources:* World Bank (2006) and IMF (2007).

Sharp Decline in Recorded Output and Varied Recovery

When the transition to a market economy began, the Soviet economy was already in free fall, and recorded output plummeted in all former Soviet countries. In 1990, only Poland and Hungary launched their transitions. Their relative economic performance set the stage of the early debate. Registered output in both countries fell shockingly, by 11.6 percent in Poland and 3.5 percent in Hungary. Although Poland swiftly caught up, the formative idea of the debate was that Poland's radical reform prompted greater decline in output than Hungary's gradual reform. The farther market transition proceeded, the worse output fared. When other countries in Central and Southeast Europe launched transition in 1991, their registered output plunged by 12–15 percent. In 1992, the former Soviet republics entered transition, with monumental recorded output falls.

The total recorded decrease in output was staggering. Overall, the former Soviet countries, including the Baltics, recorded much greater output declines than the Central Europeans. In Central Europe, the total registered output fall stopped at 18 percent and in South-East Europe at 28 percent.[1] In the former Soviet Union, the collapse was truly stunning. Despite the

---

[1] All averages in this book are unweighted, giving each country equal weight.

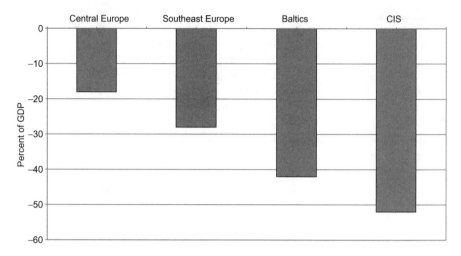

Figure 3.2. Total Official Fall in GDP from 1989 to Nadir. *Note:* Nadir years range 1991–93 for Central Europe; 1992–97 for Southeast Europe; 1994–95 for the Baltics; and 1993–98 for the CIS. *Source:* United Nations Economic Commission for Europe (2004, p. 80).

Baltic countries having launched early and vigorous reforms, their output fell by an average of a staggering 42 percent, compared with 52 percent for the CIS countries, which undertook much less reform (see Figure 3.2). Statistical revision has been considerable. In earlier statistics, the slump was far greater.

Within the former Soviet Union, four of the five war-torn countries – Georgia, Azerbaijan, Tajikistan, and Moldova – suffered the worst total official slumps, ranging from 67 to 77 percent, and Armenia experienced a fall of 56 percent. The two least reformed countries, Uzbekistan and Belarus, saw the smallest drops of "barely" 20 percent and 36 percent, respectively. The economy of the most radical reformer, Estonia, shrank by "only" 36 percent, but other reformers, such as Lithuania, Latvia, and Kyrgyzstan, went through bigger contractions. Terms of trade changes were obviously of great importance; the three big energy exporters – Kazakhstan, Turkmenistan, and Russia – faced comparatively small declines of 39–44 percent (United Nations Economic Commission for Europe [UNECE] 2004, p. 80). It was costly to get rid of socialism, but the cost varied, and it was much greater in the former Soviet Union than in Central Europe.

As substantial declines continued, attention turned to their duration. Poland took an early lead by returning to growth in 1992. Slowly, growth proceeded to the south and the east. The Czech Republic and Romania followed in 1993. By 1994, the whole of Central and Southeast Europe registered growth, and two of the most vigorous reformers in the former Soviet Union had also arrived – Armenia and Latvia. In 1995, they were followed by three other reformers, Estonia, Georgia, and Lithuania. Five countries (Poland, the Czech Republic, Slovakia, Romania, and Armenia) achieved growth rates of 6–7 percent that year. By 1997, Georgia, Estonia, and Kyrgyzstan even reached 10 percent growth. Central Europe, the Baltics, the Caucasus, and Kyrgyzstan appeared to have attained sustainable economic growth. The unreformed countries, Belarus and Uzbekistan, also achieved growth but through recentralization of state control rather than reform.

Still, several CIS countries experienced prolonged decline followed by stagnation, in particular, Russia, Ukraine, Moldova, and Kazakhstan. Their market economic reforms did not suffice for growth. Just as they seemed to have hit the bottom and began recovering, a severe international financial crisis hit the whole region in 1998, most of all Russia. Russia's financial crash in August 1998 reduced growth rates throughout the region as other CIS countries saw both their export markets and borrowing options drying up.

Paradoxically, the Russian financial crisis provided the CIS countries with the necessary catharsis, and the whole postcommunist growth pattern was turned upside down. Whatever was true until 1998 became its opposite afterward. From 1999 to 2005, the CIS countries had excellent average annual growth of 8.2 percent, whereas the four Central European countries recorded mediocre average annual growth of 3.9 percent. The three Baltic countries came closer to the first group with 7.5 percent growth, and Romania and Bulgaria closer to the Central Europeans with 5.0 percent (see Figure 3.3). Sharp devaluations benefited all the CIS countries and rising world market prices of oil helped the four energy exporters Russia, Kazakhstan, Azerbaijan, and Turkmenistan. Most of the difference in growth, however, can be explained by the varying courses of structural reforms in the CIS countries and Central Europe (Åslund and Jenish 2006).

An alternative, less extreme picture is offered by GDP per capita in purchasing power parities, which the World Bank heroically calculates. Figure 3.4 shows these statistics for 1990 (presumably overestimated), 1998, and 2004. By 1998, only Poland had a significantly higher GDP per capita in purchasing power parities (PPP) in 1998 than in 1990 (24 percent higher). From 1998 until 2004, by contrast, all countries in the region went through substantial growth. The disparity in performance varies greatly. Poland is an outstanding success with a growth of 54 percent from 1990 to 2004, and Moldova recorded the greatest decline at 57 percent (World Bank 2006).

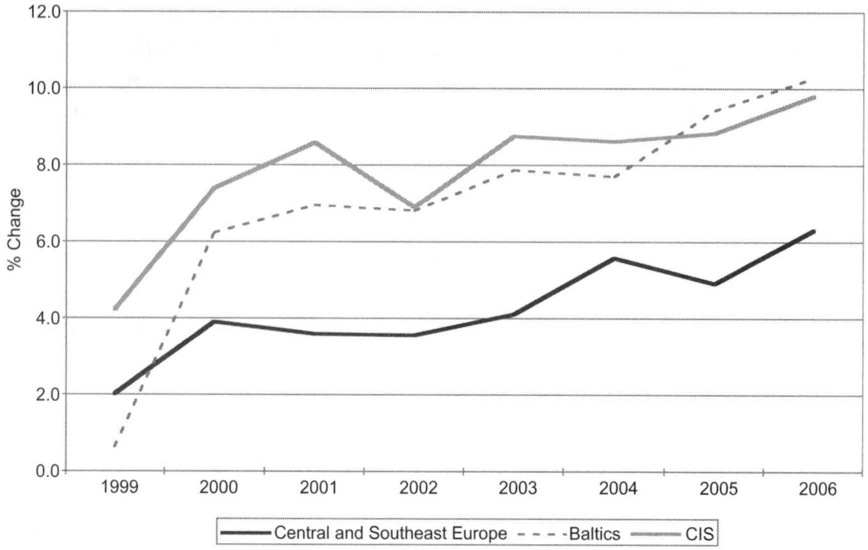

Figure 3.3. Official GDP Growth, 1999–2006. *Sources:* World Bank (2006) and IMF (2007).

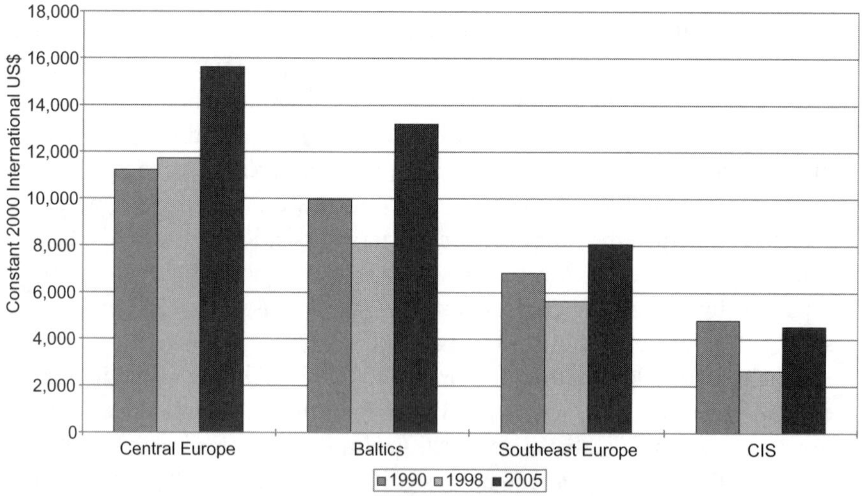

Figure 3.4. GDP per Capita in Purchasing Power Parities, 1990, 1998, and 2005. *Sources:* World Bank (2006) and United Nations Economic Commission for Europe (2003, 2004).

Exaggeration of the Slump

Much of the literature about the postcommunist slump discusses it as a colossal tragedy, exceeding the Great Depression of 1929–33. However, the words "depression" and "recession" evoke the images of a business cycle gone awry, whereas this was a profound systemic change, representing a desired return to a normal market economy. Many perceived costs of transition were purely statistical because most real costs had already been imposed on society by communism. Both communist and postcommunist statistics are deeply flawed, but in different ways. Although all analysts recognize these biases and some authors detail them, all proceed to work with official statistics because no full alternative set exists, leaving the question about the fate of real output unanswered. Especially the Soviet economy had been in far worse shape than understood.

The first statistical confusion concerns the starting point of the transitional slump. Economic chaos prevailed at the end of communism, and Romania and the Soviet Union registered sharp output falls in the last year of communism. East-Central European transition is sensibly measured against the last communist year, but the standard for the former Soviet republics is 1989, although communism ended in late 1991. That correction eliminates an average of 12 percent of 1989 GDP of the decline for the former Soviet republics (UNECE 2006).

Second, notorious socialist overreporting was replaced by capitalist underreporting. Under central planning, all bonuses depended on gross production, which motivated everybody to exaggerate their production and led to persistent overreporting of probably some 5 percent of GDP (Åslund 1990). This incentive disappeared immediately with transition. Under capitalism, on the contrary, people and enterprises often underreport their production to avoid or evade taxes.

Third, with capitalism, the unofficial economy expanded. It was not necessarily illegal, but just not reported to the state statistical office. Statistical agencies were not designed to measure the performance of small and private enterprises and failed to keep up with myriad new enterprises. An underground economy existed also in the Soviet Union, but it was tiny, as evident from the pernicious shortages and interviews with Soviet émigrés (Ofer and Vinokur 1992). The only comparable GDP numbers available for many transition countries are rough estimates based on electricity consumption, assumed to develop broadly in line with GDP (see Figure 3.5; Kaufmann and Kaliberda 1996; Johnson et al. 1997a). The initial underground economy was comparatively large in the liberal socialist economies – Hungary

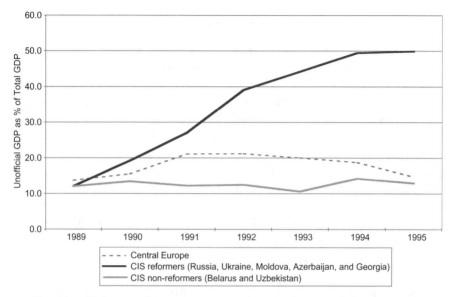

Figure 3.5. Underground Economy, 1989–95. *Source:* Johnson et al. (1997a, p. 183).

and Poland – and small in the strict socialist economies. With transition, the underground economy expanded everywhere, but soon it started to shrink in successful reform countries. In East-Central Europe, the unofficial share of GDP rose from 17 percent in 1989 to 21 percent in 1992 but declined to 19 percent in 1995. The development was similar in the most repressive state-controlled economies, whereas the underground economy continued to grow in partially reformed economies. The average unregistered share of real GDP in former Soviet countries rose from 12 percent in 1989 to 36 percent in 1994. In the extreme cases of Azerbaijan and Georgia, it exceeded 60 percent of total GDP. The unregistered economy peaked approximately when the official GDP hit its nadir. Repeated revisions of official GDP gradually include more of the unregistered economy, boosting output numbers, but statisticians err on the conservative side, and their revisions remain timid.

Fourth, thanks to pervasive shortages and soft budget constraints under socialism, state enterprise managers enjoyed extreme monopoly and could ignore consumer demand and quality. They produced what was easy because anything could be sold in the Soviet Union. As transition ended excess demand, enterprises built up a normal inventory of finished goods, which amounted to a one-for-all reduction of demand (Kornai 1994). People started using up all the consumer goods they had hoarded at home for their security, which reduced their aggregate demand for some time.

Fifth, much of Soviet manufacturing was sheer value detraction or value destruction. For instance, Soviet fishermen caught excellent fresh fish. Rather than selling it on the market, they processed it into often inedible fish conserves, reducing the fish's value to almost zero. Incorrectly, this value detraction was recorded as value added in Soviet national accounts and included in GDP. Value detraction increased throughout the processing chain. Soviet raw materials were excellent. Intermediary goods (such as metals and chemicals) were shoddy, whereas consumer goods and processed foods were substandard. Many unsalable goods disappeared in storage or were quietly scrapped without any statistical recording. Proper national accounts should exclude most of the "production" of consumer goods and processed foods. When transition set in, the decline in manufacturing output was staggering everywhere. Roughly half of consumer output just vanished from the market when exposed to the least import competition, although imports were exorbitantly expensive because of low exchange rates. In Russia from 1991 to 1996, output fell by no less than 84 percent in light industry, 44 percent in food processing, and 57 percent in civilian machine building (Goskomstat 1997, p. 336). As few manufactured goods were worth buying even at extremely low prices, this contraction reflected a desirable reduction of value destruction, although it was recorded as a decrease in GDP.

Unfortunately, we cannot calculate the eliminated value detraction directly because manufacturing's share of GDP is not available. The most relevant available measurement of reduced value detraction is probably reduced overindustrialization, measured as the decline in the industrial sector's share of GDP. Usually, this decline in industrial share – or reduced value detraction in industry – was in the range of 9–20 percent of GDP until 1995 (World Bank 2006). But value was also detracted outside of industry, and state subsidies and regulation maintained it for years. The share of unsalable goods probably amounted to around 20 percent of GDP in the last year of communism.

A sixth statistical conundrum was implicit foreign trade subsidies and interrepublic budgetary subsidies. Socialist states mostly exchanged goods nobody wanted, forcing substandard and overpriced merchandise on one another. The wrong things were traded for the wrong reasons between the wrong people in the wrong places at the wrong prices. The share of unsalable goods in mutual trade was probably even greater than in the domestic economies. Much of the intraregional trade consisted of exports of manufactured goods from the more developed countries to the energy exporters.

Hungarian losses of exports to formerly socialist countries consisted predominantly of machinery and buses, which hardly anybody wanted in
the West (Gács 1995). Raw materials, on the contrary, were valuable, but
their low prices meant that the energy exporters, Russia, Turkmenistan,
Kazakhstan, and Azerbaijan, paid huge implicit export subsidies to other
socialist countries. A lot of these raw materials were wasted and were not
demanded at market prices under capitalism. The decline in mutual trade
between the postcommunist countries resulted from the dissolution of the
Council of Mutual Economic Assistance (CMEA) in 1991, the dissolution
of the Soviet Union in 1992, and the overall systemic change. It combined
the beneficial shake-out of unsalable goods with the elimination of implicit
trade subsidies, but it also contained an element of disorganization (Berg
et al. 1999; European Bank for Reconstruction and Development [EBRD]
1999; Popov 2000).

Economists calculated the "costs" or changes in terms of trade for Southeast and Central Europe from the dissolution of the CMEA from a high of
7.8 percent of GDP for Hungary (Rodrik 1992) to 1.5 percent for Czechoslovakia, and negligent for Romania in 1991 (Rosati 1995, p. 152; cf. Gács 1995,
p. 179). The trade effect was greater on countries that traded more with the
Soviet Union and the CMEA (notably Bulgaria), countries that were more
open (most of all Hungary), and countries that imported a lot of energy
(Bulgaria and Hungary).

Within the Soviet Union, foreign trade distortions were far greater than in
Central Europe because extreme protectionism forced most Soviet republics
to pursue 90 percent of their trade with one another. Lucjan Orlowski (1993)
and David Tarr (1994) calculated implicit trade subsidies for the former
Soviet republics, comparing the prior prices with prevailing world market
prices. In 1990, three countries exporting oil and natural gas provided substantial subsidies as a share of their GDP: Russia (17.7 percent of GDP),
Turkmenistan (19.5 percent), and Kazakhstan (7.4 percent), which benefited greatly from the abolition of implicit trade subsidies. Consequently,
they experienced limited output contraction. Five states enjoyed substantial
implicit trade subsidies: Moldova (16.1 percent of GDP), Estonia (12.7 percent), Latvia (11.3 percent), Lithuania (9.7 percent), and Armenia (7.6 percent). Not surprisingly, these countries, suffered from large falls in recorded
output, although most undertook significant reforms. For the remaining
former Soviet republics, the total effect was less than 5 percent of their
GDP. Because of the very gradual transition in the CIS, implicit transfers
remained significant in 1992–4, complicating any comparisons (Olcott et al.
1999).

Substantial direct budget transfers were limited to Central Asia in Soviet times. In 1989, Kyrgyzstan received 7.8 percent of its GDP in union budget transfers; Tajikistan, 8.2 percent; Turkmenistan, 9.0 percent; Kazakhstan, 9.3 percent; and Uzbekistan, 11.3 percent (Orlowski 1995, p. 66). Naturally, Russia had no reason to maintain such transfers when these countries became independent. Their elimination hurt economic welfare in Central Asia, especially the provision of public services, while the previous donors, primarily Russia, benefited.

A seventh statistical issue is Soviet military expenditures. An old saying runs that the United States had a military-industrial complex, whereas the Soviet Union *was* one. Soviet defense expenditure was a matter of persistent dispute among Western Sovietologists. Gradually, the U.S. Central Intelligence Agency (CIA) raised its assessment of Soviet defense spending to 15–17 percent of GDP in 1986 (Berkowitz et al. 1993), but that was based on the CIA's exaggerated estimate of Soviet GDP. As late as 1990, the CIA considered Soviet GDP per capita 43 percent of the U.S. level in PPP. The European Comparison Program, which cooperated with Soviet statistical authorities, undertook a careful empirical analysis, setting Soviet GDP per capita at 32 percent of that of the United States in 1990 (and Soviet household consumption per capita at only 24 percent of the U.S. level; Bergson 1997).[2] If we use the CIA assessment of Soviet defense expenditures and the European Comparison Program assessment of Soviet GDP, the defense burden would amount to 22 percent of GDP. Even these GDP numbers are likely to be too high because the poor quality of goods and services were not fully accounted for, and shortages and the resulting forced substitution were disregarded. The Soviet Union probably spent about one-quarter of its GDP on military purposes in the late 1980s (Åslund 1990).

The Russian reform government slashed official military spending to an internationally normal level of about 3 percent of GDP, although Western intelligence argues the real number was 5 percent of GDP, because a substantial part of military spending occurs outside of the budget of the Ministry of Defense. Most other postcommunist countries decreased their defense expenses to 1–2 percent of GDP. This reduction in military demand would result in a 20 percent nominal decline in the 1989 GDP in the whole former Soviet Union, and more for Russia, Belarus, and Ukraine, which harbored most of the military-industrial complex. In East-Central Europe, military expenditures were not much higher than in the West, but even there the

---

[2] This tallies well with a World Bank study led by Paul Marer (1985) setting the Soviet GNP per capita at 37 percent of the U.S. level for 1980.

trimming of the military sector probably accounted for a couple percent of the fall in recorded GDP. The military production was real, although its utility may be disputed. When demand for it disappeared, no sensible alternative use could be found for most of the military resources.

An eighth statistical issue is socialist investment. Socialism was a system of waste. A Soviet factory needed about three times more input than a Western factory to produce the same output, because managers were insensitive to costs. Some of these losses represented inefficiency, others theft. With the introduction of hard budget constraints, managers started bothering about costs, reducing domestic demand for inputs, such as steel, metals, and chemicals. Communist regimes prided themselves on huge investment ratios, but the socialist landscape was scarred by unfinished construction projects (Winiecki 1988, 1991b). The high ratios of fixed investment were indications of theft and waste rather than real investment. Because ample capital goods were underutilized, a contraction of investment for a few years was desirable. Conversely, socialist enterprises hoarded large inventories of inputs, such as raw materials, which were labeled investment in national accounts. These inventories continuously accumulated without any cyclical tendency, indicating sheer waste. Poland had the best statistics, showing that "investment" in inventories amounted to 7 percent of GDP or one-quarter of total investment in the mid-1980s (World Bank 2000a).

Already in the early transition, reformers imposed demand barriers in Poland, Czechoslovakia, Estonia, and Latvia. The national demand curve shifted permanently, initially reducing recorded output. Substantial dishoarding of inputs and capital goods started, as desired, and stocks of finished goods rose, reflecting the problems of selling that are characteristic of capitalism. Andrew Berg (1994) calculated that the total reduction in inventory because of dishoarding accounted for two-thirds of the total decline in Poland's GDP in 1990. Scrutinizing statistics on consumption, investment, and exports, Berg and Sachs (1992) found that the decline in Polish GDP from 1989 to 1990 was not 12 percent as stated in the production statistics but 4.9 percent. Heavy manufacturing and mining contracted the least, suggesting that their budget constraints remained relatively soft. Investment that was sheer waste should preferably be deducted from GDP, so the average decline in the investment ratio of 11 percent of GDP makes sense. Most countries undertook large-scale wasteful public investment long after they had returned to growth, and new productive investment started early on.

Summing up all these factors, it is obvious that the official numbers greatly exaggerate the overall decline in output. Every bias led to the exaggeration of the decline of output. East Germany offers an enlightening illustration of the degree of statistical distortion. The German Institute of Economic Research (Deutsches Institut für Wirtschaftsforschung 1977) in West Berlin assessed East German GDP per capita at about 60 percent of the West German level, and East Germany had a higher investment ratio than West Germany. After the Berlin Wall fell, East German productivity turned out to be barely 30 percent of the West German level, only half of the previously estimated level. It also became obvious that the East German fixed capital per capita was only 30 percent of the West German level (Siebert 1992, p. 39).

Alas, too many factors are uncertain to allow any agreement on a reassessment of the actual slump as yet. In a detailed reassessment (Åslund 2002, chapter 4), I argued that roughly half the recorded decline in output appears to have been fictitious, although varying by country, suggesting that Poland did not really see any decline in output (Berg 1994), whereas Moldova faced a drastic drop of perhaps 35 percent in total. A careful overall assessment by Oleh Havrylyshyn (2006) acknowledged all the factors mentioned earlier and consequently argued that official data highly exaggerates the output decline, but rather than provide specific numbers, he offered a wide range of alternative numbers depending on counterfactual assumptions.

Statistics are an important input in economic policy making, and the distorted official statistics were a major cause of bad policies. They did not reveal the strong, early supply effects caused by radical reforms. Consequently, the successful Polish model was not widely adopted, and many started calling for fiscal and monetary stimulation instead. Even if postcommunist people were healthily skeptical of official statistics, they believed in bad news, which led them astray. The distorted official statistics encouraged a march of folly toward bad policies. Given the poverty of statistics, policy makers were better off acting on principles than trying to fine-tune their policies.

Radical Reform: Least Decline and Early Recovery

Initially, all countries suffered from large drops in output, but different trajectories of economic growth developed. Until 1998, the radical reformers in Central Europe and the Baltics performed the best. From 1999, on the contrary, the CIS countries have greatly outperformed the Central European countries while the Baltic countries have continued their stellar growth. Romania and Bulgaria have occupied the middle ground but stayed closer to Central Europe (see Figure 3.3). The dramatic turning point was the Russian financial crash in August 1998.

Table 3.1. *Patterns of GDP Growth, 1995–7 (Average GDP change in percent per year)*

	Central Europe	Baltics	Southeast Europe	CIS
Consistent growth, U-curve	Poland Czech Republic Slovakia Hungary 4.5	Estonia Latvia Lithuania 5.1		Armenia Georgia Kyrgyzstan 5.8
Growth reversals, W-curve or stagnation			Bulgaria Romania −1.3	Belarus Azerbaijan Uzbekistan 0.6
Little growth, L-curve				Russia Ukraine Moldova Kazakhstan −3.5 Tajikistan Turkmenistan −8.8

Sources: This table is adapted from Havrylyshyn and Wolf (2001). Growth rates are calculated from World Bank (2006).

Before 1998, postcommunist countries could roughly be divided into three categories – radical reformers, intermediate reformers, and nonreformers. A first group of highly reformist countries can be described by a healthy U-curve, with an initial decline followed by a steady recovery. They include Central Europe (Poland, the Czech Republic, Slovakia, and Hungary), the Baltics (Estonia, Latvia, and Lithuania), Armenia, Georgia, and Kyrgyzstan (see Table 3.1). Six countries in a second group are marked by a sad L-curve of a sharp decline followed by stagnation. Four were slow CIS reformers: Russia, Ukraine, Moldova, and Kazakhstan; two, Tajikistan and Turkmenistan, undertook minimal reform. Tajikistan was devastated by civil war, and Turkmenistan was the victim of Russia's temporary refusal to let it sell natural gas through Russian pipelines. A third group, Bulgaria and Romania, ended up with a W-curve, a double-dip with a first decline followed by an unsustainable recovery and a new decline, or stagnation. They were intermediate reformers, whose market reforms remained fragile.

Azerbaijan, Belarus, and Uzbekistan experienced stagnation. None of them was a reformer, and they maintained the old socialist economy.

A large number of cross-country regression analyses were undertaken from 1996 through 2000.[3] They investigated the impact on economic growth of a great variety of variables, and this literature displays a great deal of agreement.[4]

Control of inflation: A necessary precondition for growth. All transition countries except Hungary and Czechoslovakia were hit by fiscal calamities, with inflation surging to more than 100 percent a year. Financial stabilization became the natural focus of economists' attention, with macroeconomists and the International Monetary Fund coming to the fore. All the multi-country regressions have found a strong positive correlation between high inflation and falling output. Fischer et al. (1996b, p. 89) concluded: "The simple – but essential – message that emerges... is that real GDP rebounds following inflation stabilization, which in turn appears highly correlated with the improvement in the public finances." The fall in output outlasted high inflation in every single country, and no country returned to economic growth until inflation had fallen below 45 percent a year. The longer high inflation lasted, the greater the total contraction in output (De Melo et al. 1997a). Christoffersen and Doyle (2000, p. 439) observed: "There is no evidence that disinflation necessarily incurs significant output costs, even at moderate inflation rates." Early on, Stanley Fischer (1993) established through cross-country regressions that growth was negatively associated with inflation, large budget deficits, and distorted foreign exchange markets. Bruno and Easterly (1998) suggested that the crucial inflation threshold was as high as 40 percent a year, whereas Christoffersen and Doyle (2000) put it at 13 percent a year.

Macroeconomic stabilization was a necessary, but not sufficient, condition for economic growth (Havrylyshyn and Wolf 2001). In several former

---

[3] The main contributions are as follows: De Melo et al. (1997a) was the pioneering work that provided most of the fundamental answers, and De Melo et al. (1997b) studied the role of initial conditions. Fischer et al. (1996a, 1996b, and 1997), Lougani and Sheets (1997), and Christoffersen and Doyle (2000) focused on the role of macroeconomics. Berg et al. (1999), Havrylyshyn and Wolf (2001), and Campos and Coricelli (2002) provided the current view of the state of affairs. Other relevant papers are Åslund et al. (1996), De Melo and Gelb (1996, 1997), Sachs (1996), Selowsky and Martin (1996), Hernandez-Cata (1997), Krueger and Ciolko (1998), Heybey and Murrell (1999), and Fischer and Sahay (2000). Of all these papers, Berg et al. (1999) is by far the most ambitious, which I see as the most authoritative.

[4] The output data used are by necessity the official data, which means that later studies are based on better data, and countries with large unofficial economies are underrated.

Soviet economies (Russia, Ukraine, Moldova, Kazakhstan, and Belarus), growth did not rebound after stabilization, and over time the direct link between macroeconomic performance and output became more tenuous. Berg et al. (1999, p. 9) concluded: "The impact of macroeconomic variables, while significant, is much smaller than that of either initial conditions and structural reforms." They found that the fiscal balance was more important for growth than the control of inflation. Several countries brought down inflation through very strict monetary policy, with lasting real interest rates of 50–100 percent a year, because their budget deficits remained too large.

This was a stinging empirical rebuke to the Russian economists, who had argued that it was structurally impossible to lower inflation to less than 100 percent a year without hampering growth because of the preponderance of monopolies and state ownership in the Russian economy (Yavlinsky and Braguinsky 1994; Lvov 1996). The evidence also contradicted the advocacy of softer macroeconomic stabilization. Guillermo Calvo and Fabrizio Coricelli (1992, 1993) argued that Polish output had suffered from an excessive credit crunch. Andrew Berg (1994, p. 21) retorted that surveyed enterprise managers complained of a lack of demand for their output, not inability to purchase inputs, and concluded that "there is no evidence that tight credit caused a supply constrained output decline." The conclusion is that the post-communist economies badly needed harder budget constraints or demand barriers, which were very difficult to impose but necessary to unleash supply (Fischer and Sahay 2000).

Liberalization: most important for growth. The first cross-country regressions on transition economies established that "economic growth is positively correlated with reform progress" (Sachs 1996, p. 128), and the evidence has grown ever stronger. The most fundamental structural reform was the deregulation of prices and trade. Liberalization is usually divided into internal and external liberalization. Internal liberalization comprises the freeing of domestic prices and the abolition of state trading monopolies, and external liberalization consists of the unification of the exchange rate, the introduction of currency convertibility, the elimination of export controls and export taxes, and the substitution of moderate import tariffs for import quotas and high import duties (De Melo et al. 1997a). As with macroeconomic stabilization, Central Europe and the Baltics started off with radical liberalization. Bulgaria and Romania did only a little better than the CIS countries, which were generally slow liberalizers.

Initially, liberalization was often seen as a subfactor of financial stabilization, perceived to impose initial costs (Selowsky and Martin 1996; Hernandez-Cata 1997). Over time, however, liberalization has emerged as the most effective growth-stimulating factor in the transition countries. Berg et al. (1999) found that liberalization helped all countries in the later transition and most of them even in the early transition. From the fourth year after the transition, structural reforms were the main determinant of growth, driving economic recovery. External liberalization had a particularly great positive effect on output. Havrylyshyn and Wolf (2001) reckoned that most measures of structural reform were closely correlated with growth, but the only measure they could single out as uniquely effective on its own was price liberalization.

It is easy to understand why liberalization has had such great positive impact on output. The initial output slump was largely attributable to substantial shifts in relative prices and demand, which rendered many old products unsalable. Competition brought about the necessary, dramatic changes in the composition of output, which drove the recovery in output (De Melo et al. 1997a). "For over-industrialized, distorted, and inefficient economies, recovery only comes after some elimination of the wasteful old production" (Havrylyshyn and Wolf 2001, p. 102). Jeffrey Sachs (1996, p. 129) summed up the evidence: "Experience suggests that a quick move on liberalization following the fall of communism was important in achieving comprehensive liberalization, since delays in liberalization gave time for vested interests to form around remaining barriers to trade."

Privatization. Privatization has been heralded both as the key solution (Yavlinsky and Braguinsky 1994) and as of little consequence (Stiglitz 1999a). Regression analyses on the impact of privatization on economic growth show a strong positive correlation between the share of GDP arising from the private sector and output (Åslund et al. 1996; Havrylyshyn and Wolf 2001). However, a lag is evident, because it takes some time for privatized enterprises to shape up. Berg et al. (1999) found that privatization and private sector conditions had significant effects on growth in the ensuing period.

Until 1999, privatization appeared less effective in the former Soviet Union than in Central Europe. A number of studies argued that privatization to insiders had little or no beneficial effect, whereas privatization to outsiders had a pronounced positive effect (Frydman et al. 1998). Newly started enterprises were doing much better than former state enterprises that had been privatized (Johnson and Loveman 1995). Many enterprise surveys in the former Soviet Union showed little difference between large and medium-sized enterprises that were still state-owned or had been privatized. The EBRD (1999) even argued that privatization might be counterproductive if it allowed vested interests to reinforce their hold on the state. Yet with the growth spurt after 1999 in the CIS region, its predominant mass privatization generated higher growth than other forms of privatization (Bennett et al. 2005). Not surprisingly, the positive effects of privatization have become more tangible over time.

The evidence is overwhelming that early, radical, and comprehensive reforms constituted the best option. Almost all the arguments for gradual reforms reported in Chapter 2 have been empirically disproved. Fast and comprehensive stabilization and liberalization proved better for economic growth than slow or partial reforms. More privatization was better than less. Radical reform led to less overall decline in output and accordingly to greater economic welfare than partial reform. The countries that undertook the most radical and comprehensive structural reforms also implemented the most far-reaching institutional reforms (Havrylyshyn 2006). They were also the most democratic (see Chapter 8).

A dichotomy is apparent. Either a country entered a virtuous circle or a vicious circle (De Melo and Gelb 1997). A slow start of reform led to little subsequent reform, whereas a radical start usually brought about ever deeper and more comprehensive reforms and better economic results. The question remains why some countries chose a suboptimal path of delayed and gradual reforms. Initial conditions strongly influenced the choice of policy. Countries with adverse initial conditions were inclined to pursue disadvantageous economic policies. If highly distorted prices and exchange rates persisted, people with privileged access to power made fortunes on rent seeking, arbitraging between regulated and unregulated markets, and extracting money from the state. If the rules of the games were not swiftly changed, the well-placed establishment would reassert its grasp on power. Such passive policies concentrated economic wealth and power in the hands of privileged groups, which later could purchase state power to their continued advantage (EBRD 1999). "These vested interests often began by accumulating wealth through the economic rents resulting from large price distortions in energy and raw materials, and by borrowing from central bank credits during years of inflation.... The potential virtuous circle of reform and growth is replaced by a vicious circle of suspended reforms and stagnation" (Havrylyshyn and Wolf 2001, p. 112). Growth did not occur because it did not enhance the revenues of the privileged few.

Radical reform policies represented a broad public interest, which explains why they were positively correlated with democracy. The virtuous path of reinforcing market economic reforms led to substantial economic growth. The main drama of the early transition was whether a small group of vested interests focused on rent seeking were to dominate society or whether a broader constituency truly interested in the public interest, and thus economic growth, would assume political power.

Late Reformers: Surged after 1998

In the longer term, standard neoclassical growth theory suggests that growth is largely determined by the initial level of income, the investment rate, investment in human capital, and the rate of population growth (Levine and Renelt 1992; Barro and Sala-i-Martin 2004).

Yet postcommunist idiosyncrasies persist. As these countries suffered from overindustrialization and overinvestment, they needed to rationalize and reallocate their physical capital rather than expand it. Total investment includes inventory, which should shrink because of growing efficiency under capitalism. The communist countries had invested more in education than they could benefit from, leaving vast underutilized human capital. The standard measurement of human capital is secondary school enrollment, or, alternatively, the teaching of mathematics. By both measures, the postcommunist region is richly endowed, which could generate growth in the future. The rate of population growth, however, is low or even negative because of low birth rates and emigration, which hampers growth. The key bottlenecks requiring investment appear to be infrastructure and housing.

Another determinant of long-term economic growth is economic policy and institutions, which are often difficult to distinguish from one another. All conceivable variables have been analyzed in multicountry regression analyses (notably Sala-i-Martin 1997). Market distortions, measured as real exchange rate distortions or black market premia, stand out as critical. Another central economic policy is the openness of an economy. Jeffrey Sachs and Andrew Warner (1995) showed that countries that had been open to foreign trade for a number of years do achieve economic growth. The degree of capitalism in the economic organization has also proven of significance (Hall and Jones 1999).

There is also the laggard effect. *Ceteris paribus*, countries with a lower level of development tend to grow faster than more advanced countries. Hence, the CIS countries would be expected to grow faster than the Central Europeans after they had caught up with regard to transition reforms. However, this "laggard effect" would hardly explain a difference of more than 1–2 percent annual growth between these two groups of countries (Åslund and Warner 2004). Until 1998, however, the post-Soviet countries

with lower levels of development grew more slowly than the Central Europeans, because they pursued worse economic policies, constrained by the
dominance of rent-seeking interests on the politics of these states.

Strangely, whatever had been true until 1998 was false from that year
(Åslund and Jenish 2006). All of a sudden, the twelve CIS countries started
growing more than twice as fast as the four Central European countries
year after year (see Figure 3.3). The dividing event was the Russian financial
crash of August 1998, which had repercussions for the whole CIS region.
Several CIS countries underwent similar crises, and they reacted in the same
fashion. They had accumulated large external debts during years of sizable
budget deficits. When they finally approached the verge of external default,
the CIS governments had no choice but to slash their budget deficits because
they could no longer borrow money from abroad or their population, and
tax revenues could not be boosted in haste. Several countries curtailed their
public expenditures by about one-tenth of their GDP in a year or two, often
when their GDP was falling sharply. These cuts amounted to one-quarter
or more of total public expenditures.[5]

Such drastic reductions differ from ordinary budget trimming. As governments fought desperately to avoid disaster, the budget politics changed
completely. Whatever was politically impossible suddenly became accepted
as economically vital. In crisis, most transition countries have drastically
cut enterprise subsidies, which often involved rent-seeking schemes, such
as barter. As a consequence, enterprises' budget constraints were hardened,
and the playing field became more level. Many former state managers, who
had seized their old enterprises but did not know how to run them under
capitalism, feared they would lose everything. They were persuaded to sell
their plants to skillful new entrepreneurs, which helped revive many seemingly moribund factories.

The Russian financial crash was the crucial event that rendered nine CIS
countries full-fledged market economies. Their fiscal systems were put in
order, and budget deficits and inflation have been moderate ever since. A
critical mass of market economy and private enterprise has been achieved,
although the CIS countries continue to lag behind the EU accession countries. The nine CIS reformers derive an average of 64 percent of GDP from
their private sectors. Markets, albeit encumbered, drive their economies.

---

[5] For instance, Bulgaria reduced its public expenditures as a share of GDP by 11 percent in
    1997, Moldova by 10 percent from 1998 to 2000, Kyrgyzstan by 9 percent from 1995 to
    1997, and Russia by 8 percent in 1999 (Åslund 2002, p. 226; EBRD 2005, p. 53).

A regression analysis of the causes of growth (Åslund and Jenish 2006) shows that cuts in government spending explain two-thirds of this difference in economic growth between the CIS countries and Central Europe since 1999. Conspicuously, the CIS countries slashed their public expenditures to about one-fifth less as a share of GDP than in Central Europe. Because the many and high taxes evidently could not be collected, they made little sense, and they have been replaced by low and flat taxes. As tax rates fell, tax administration was simplified, corruption diminished, and tax collection improved. János Kornai (1992b, p. 15) noticed that the "Hungarian welfare state was born 'prematurely'", which was also true of the rest of Central Europe. It has turned out to be a social welfare trap with West European tax rates, social transfers, and labor market regulations. Sachs and Warner (1996b; Sachs 1995b) argued that not even the Central European countries would catch up with the European Union if they did not adopt more aggressive growth policies than those prevalent in the EU. Sachs and Warner were prescient. They warned that the transition countries needed lower rates of marginal taxation, lower levels of current government expenditures as a share of GDP, relatively high levels of government investment expenditures, and pension policies based on individual savings accounts rather than public pay-as-you-go transfers.

The Russian financial crash was followed by several other dramatic developments. Russia devalued the ruble by three-quarters in 1998, and most other CIS countries subsequently devalued their currencies by about 50 percent, which benefited exporters. Soon afterward, a commodity boom started, driven by Chinese imports, allowing the CIS countries to boost their exports despite stagnant EU markets and EU protectionism. Energy exports are the second significant explanation of the differences in growth in the transition countries (Åslund and Jenish 2006). Although only four of twelve CIS economies were significant energy exporters (Russia, Kazakhstan, Azerbaijan, and Turkmenistan), growth rates across the CIS were strong. Commodity-poor Armenia registered one of the highest growth rates (12 percent a year during 2001–5). The export boom was followed by increased investment, which further reinforced the economic growth. Oil-rich Azerbaijan and Kazakhstan have received very large foreign direct investment, motivated by potential oil production. Economic regulation and corruption have moderate impact, whereas the laggard effect and investment play a negligible role.

A substantial literature on economic growth and the size of the state exists, but it contains no agreement. A basic work is Robert Barro (1989), who did cross-country regressions on about 100 countries after World War II. He found that government consumption was inversely related to growth. La Porta et al. (1999b) showed with empirical surveys from 200 countries that bigger governments are usually better, but such a regression does not say anything about causality. The Scandinavian countries had very small states in the 1930s, but because they had minimal corruption, the public sector's role was allowed to increase.

But the postcommunist states were no average states. First of all, the public sector was much larger than in other countries at that level of development regardless of measurement (taxation, public distribution, degree of regulation, or the share of public property). Although severely overstretched, it was subject to fewer checks and balances than in most other states. Second, the postcommunist state was parasitical. It did the wrong things, hindering economic development rather than promoting it while antisocially redistributing from the poor to the rent-seeking elites (Hellman 1998; Milanovic 1998). Third, the postcommunist state was ineffective and inefficient because of a high degree of corruption (Transparency International 2006). Naturally, it would be desirable to reduce corruption swiftly, but that is rarely possible. Corruption is usually sticky, but it falls with rising income and openness (Treisman 2000). Under those preconditions, a sharp reduction in public expenditures is the best, and perhaps the only, way to boost economic growth.

In effect, the CIS countries have adopted the highly successful East Asian growth model lock, stock, and barrel, with low taxes and small social transfers, but an authoritarian and rather corrupt political system. The less dynamic Central European countries have adopted the EU model, which has not been conducive to high economic growth, even if some countries, mainly Ireland and the three Baltic countries have gone against the current.

Growth and democracy were nicely correlated in the 1990s, but the picture was reversed after 1998. The CIS countries, which are by and large authoritarian, have grown faster than the democratic countries in Central Europe (Freedom House 2006). The CIS countries also have de facto freer labor markets than the Central European countries. The old idea of authoritarian advantage has some relevance when the main risks to economic development are popular pressures for high taxes on the rich, large social transfers, and the regulation of labor markets in favor of insiders. The dominant risk during the first decade, by contrast, was rent seeking by elites, which was best checked by democracy (cf. Acemoglu 2003).

A few additional possible explanations of the rising growth rate of the CIS countries should be mentioned. One is recovery growth, drawing on the considerable unused capacity in many post-Soviet economies after an official decline in output of about half of GDP (Gaidar 2005). The McKinsey Global Institute (1999) concluded a study on Russia with the assessment that Russia could reach an economic growth rate of 8 percent a year with the right economic policies without significant increase in investment ratio because the physical capital was in better shape than widely believed. The key problem for this region was economic policies, not resources.

In the longer run, the predominance of the resource sector in the energy exporting countries is likely to play a negative role (Gaddy and Ickes 2005). Sachs and Warner (1996a) showed that the larger the share of a country's exports that consists of raw materials, the slower it will grow, as the presence of raw materials tends to generate rents and poor economic policies.

Renewed growth has been export-led. Foreign trade has driven both systemic change and economic recovery. Invariably, exports have started surging before output, often massively (World Bank 2005a). The restructuring of foreign trade has been truly amazing in both speed and quality, especially in the most fortuitous reform countries. All the former communist countries reoriented their trade from one another to the West, and until 1999, postcommunist growth depended on access to Western markets. Christoffersen and Doyle (2000) found that output growth was strongly associated with the expansion of export markets, and the most reformist countries saw an impressive and steady increase of their exports (Havrylyshyn and Wolf 2001). For most CIS countries, Russia remains the main export market, as it should according to the gravity model, which means that Russia's economic recovery was vital to growth in many transition economies (Christoffersen and Doyle 2000). This leaves open the question whether reforms were more successful in some countries because of their access to Western markets or whether they accessed these markets because they had been successfully reformed (Åslund and Warner 2004). Figure 3.6 shows how exports took off even before output expansion in 1992 in Central Europe. The Baltics followed in 1994, and the CIS countries only in 1996. From 2000, the whole region has seen a very similar export expansion, with exports increasing impressively by about 10 percent a year.

With growing exports, the successful exporters have received more foreign earnings, allowing them to increase their imports. Most countries went from current account crisis to trade surplus. As they obtained access to foreign finance, they could import more than they exported, allowing the East-Central Europeans to finance significant current account deficits.

A major macroeconomic distortion under socialism was underconsumption and overinvestment. As anticipated, consumption has increased – from

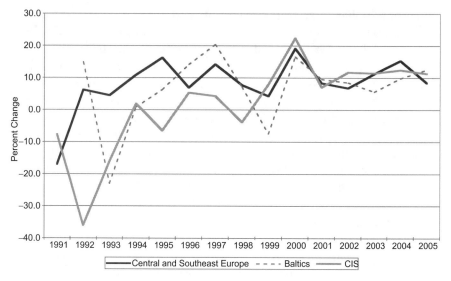

Figure 3.6. Expansion of Exports, 1991–2005. *Source:* World Bank (2006).

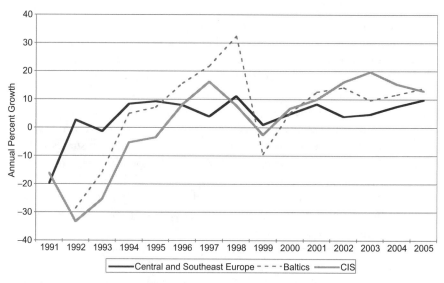

Figure 3.7. Gross Fixed Investment, 1991–2005. *Sources:* World Bank (2006) and United Nations Economic Commission for Europe (2006).

an average of 73 percent of GDP before the transition to 84 percent around 1997. As superfluous inputs and underutilized real assets were sold off, the overall investment ratio contracted from an average of 28 percent of GDP in 1989 to 21 percent of GDP in 1997, which is still quite respectable. Yet differentiation increased. Three groups of countries were spending a larger share of their GDP on investment in 1997 than before the transition – namely, the most advanced reformers in Central Europe; the conservative states Belarus and Uzbekistan, which continued the Soviet practice of wasteful public investments; and Azerbaijan, buoyed by oil-related foreign investment. Most countries, however, saw sharp declines in their investment shares because of limited need, poverty, and poor investment climate. Rather than being the engine of growth, investment surged *after* growth reemerged and reinforced growth (De Melo et al. 1997a; Havrylyshyn and Wolf 2001).

The decline in investment was generally far greater than the decline in output, whereas the later investment expansion was all the greater in successful economies. Figure 3.7 shows the development of investment. East-Central Europe started increasing investment in fixed assets in 1994; the CIS countries reached that hurdle only in 1996. The Baltic countries took an impressive lead from 1996 to 1998. Most countries saw some decline in investment in 1999 in the aftermath of the Russian financial crash, but from 2000, investment has grown the fastest in the CIS countries and considerably more slowly in Central Europe. The superior growth in the CIS countries and the Baltics is likely to continue.

4

Liberalization: The Creation of a
Market Economy

The essence of a market economy is economic freedom – the freedom of trade, prices, and enterprise. Liberalization transformed a shortage of goods and services to a scarcity of money, which is the predicament of capitalism. The sellers' market became a buyers' market, transferring economic power from producers to consumers. The growth analysis in Chapter 3 indicates that the liberalization of prices and foreign trade were the most forceful structural reforms. Because economic freedom is the very foundation of a market economy, I discuss liberalization before macroeconomic stabilization and privatization.

Although deregulation is the most important systemic reform, for a long time, it received little scholarly attention. One reason is the paucity of relevant economic indicators, such as the degree of shortage, regional price dispersion, relative prices, product quality, and market structure. Economists had to create their own data sets, complicating empirical work.

Another reason was that economists tended to look on liberalization as something simple, done quickly, and requiring little afterthought. Initially, liberal politicians and economists harbored an excessive belief in the spontaneous formation of markets, reckoning that it was enough to eliminate central planning, destroy the administrative command system, and introduce private property (Akaev 2000, p. 39). Deregulation of the domestic economy was usually discussed as price liberalization, taking the equally important deregulation of domestic trade for granted. With few exceptions, the vital freedom of enterprise was not even on the agenda. Economists preferred sophisticated issues, such as financial markets and corporate governance, rather than bureaucratic impediments.

A third cause was that the old administration was in such disarray for a couple of years after the collapse of communism that it was no plausible threat. Moreover, the problem was not classical monopolies, which are easily handled by normal price theory, but high transaction costs, which are more difficult to analyze (Coase 1988).

In the mid-1990s, deregulation attracted new attention. There was a broad realization of how difficult deregulation actually was. Several empirical indexes on economic freedom and business environment were developed in the 1990s. As soon as deregulation could be measured, it became an object of policy action. The World Bank took the lead on business environment and governance.

The first section in this chapter outlines two contrary approaches to deregulation. Section two discusses the liberalization of foreign trade. The third section deals with labor market policy, which is remarkable because the laggards in transition became leaders in labor market liberalization. In section four, I look more closely at problems with monopoly in two major industries, natural gas and coal. This chapter concludes that a big bang was particularly important in deregulation, because most countries did not reach much farther than they did in their first jump for years.

Two Strategies of Deregulation

At the outset of transition, all countries in the former Soviet bloc undertook significant deregulation, but two diametrically opposed approaches were evident. One strategy was a radical and comprehensive deregulation to a real market economy. It was the Balcerowicz program of radical deregulation to the benefit of the population at large. The alternative model comprised gradual and partial liberalization, but it had little in common with the theoretical ideas of gradual liberalization to maximize popular support and minimize social suffering. The purpose of the actual gradual reforms was to maximize the rents to the select few in the ruling elite.

The World Bank and the European Bank for Reconstruction and Development (EBRD) composed a transition index at the outset of transition, of which deregulation was the dominant element. It is the most complete and empirical index but not very detailed. It was followed by the Heritage Foundation and the *Wall Street Journal*'s Index of Economic Freedom in 1995, which covers all the twenty-one countries discussed in this book since 1998. Unfortunately, each assessment of this index is somewhat formal (Miles et al. 2006). The Fraser Institute established its own index of economic freedom, which is more empirical but initially it covered only 1990, 1995, and 1997, and until 2002 just eleven of the twenty-one countries covered in this text (East-Central Europe, Russia, and Ukraine) (Gwartney and Lawson 2006).

Daniel Kaufmann, who was resident representative of the World Bank in
Ukraine in the early 1990s, understood that corruption was the key problem
and initiated extensive research on corruption within the Bank. The EBRD
and the World Bank carry out a major survey, Business Environment and
Enterprise Performance Surveys (BEEPS). BEEPS is based on large public opinion surveys of businesspeople in all these countries. It is detailed
and quantitative, and it covers all countries discussed herein, except for
Turkmenistan and Uzbekistan, rendering it my preferred source, although
it only exists for three years: 1999, 2002, and 2005. The World Economic
Forum has an empirical Competitiveness Index that is related to BEEPS,
but it contains only three of the twelve CIS countries. My favorite is BEEPS,
although I used the EBRD transition indicators for other years. On the
whole, all these indexes offer similar results, but the differences are often
great in areas where law digresses from reality.[1]

The EBRD Structural Reform Index measures the composite degree of
structural reform from 0 (*no market reform*) to 1 (*normal Western market
economy*). Countries below 0.50 can be defined nonmarket economies, and
countries over 0.70 are full-fledged market economies, leaving countries
in the interval of 0.50–0.70 as intermediary market economies. Central
and Eastern Europe undertook massive structural reforms in the first 3–
4 years of their transition and then little more. For the CIS reformers, reform
proceeded slowly from 1990 until 1998, when they became full-fledged market economies, whereas the CIS nonreformers (Belarus, Turkmenistan, and
Uzbekistan) have not advanced at all since 1995 (see Figure 4.1). This index
has changed minimally since 1998. Each country reached a certain degree
of deregulation in its early transition, and after that little happened. The
longer the first jump, the farther each country went.

Early, radical action was important for the course of reform. I define early,
radical reform as when a country advanced at least 0.45 on the structural

---

[1] The World Bank has undertaken another extensive study on business environment, called
Doing Business, with excellent Web design. *Doing Business* is not based on empirical surveys
but on assessments by a few prominent experts in each country. Unfortunately, several of
these assessments are rather odd. One example is that *Doing Business* alleges that it is easier
to hire and fire workers in Central Europe than in the Baltics. BEEPS and the World Economic Forum make the opposite empirical observation. Especially Poland, with its massive
unemployment, is considered more liberal in this regard than the Baltics, Bulgaria, Romania, Armenia, Azerbaijan, Georgia, Moldova, and Ukraine. This is impossible. Another
example is that *Doing Business* assesses it is much more difficult to enforce a contract in
Poland or Slovakia than in Azerbaijan, Belarus, Georgia, Russia, and Ukraine, which is
obviously untrue (World Bank and International Finance Corporation 2006). With such
evident inaccuracies about checkable data, *Doing Business* is under a cloud of relevance.

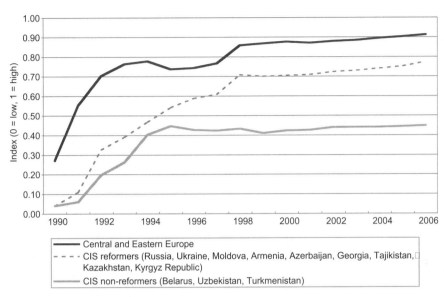

Figure 4.1. World Bank/European Bank for Reconstruction and Development (EBRD) Structural Reform Index, 1990–2006. *Note:* The formula of this index is 0.3 times EBRDs index for price liberalization and competition policy; 0.3 times EBRDs index for trade and foreign exchange liberalization, and 0.4 times EBRD's index for large-scale privatization, small-scale privatization, and banking reform. Thus this index represents liberalization to 73 percent and the rest is privatization. *Sources:* De Melo et al. (1997a); Havrylyshyn and Wolf (2001); author's calculations from EBRD (1998), (1999), and (2006).

reform index during the first two years of its transition. In Central and Southeast Europe, transition was launched in 1990 or 1991, whereas the whole former Soviet Union was thrown into transition by the Russian price liberalization through the common ruble zone in 1992. The differences in initial reform were substantial, as is evident from Figure 4.2. By this measurement, all the four Central European countries undertook very radical reforms, closely followed by Bulgaria. In addition, Estonia, Lithuania, Russia, and Kyrgyzstan passed the hurdle, a total of nine radical reformers. Moldova and Latvia barely missed the threshold.

Poland and Hungary carried out equally radical structural reforms in 1990. The only difference was that Poland concentrated its liberalization into one big bang in January 1990, whereas Hungary spread it out over a year. In January 1991, Czechoslovakia launched an even more radical and comprehensive deregulation, and Estonia and Lithuania followed in 1992–3. As Latvia advanced and kept close to Lithuania, the Balts can be discussed as a group of radical reformers, even if Latvia did not quite make it. All these

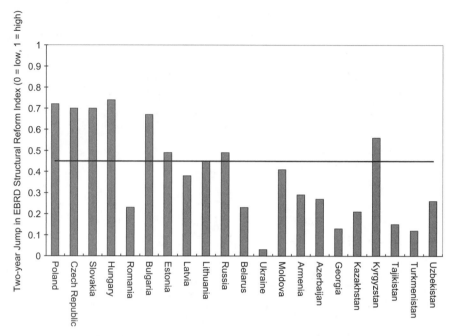

Figure 4.2. Early Reform: Radical or Gradual? *Note:* Horizontal line delineates border between radical and gradual initial reform. *Source:* De Melo et al. (1997a).

countries aspired to create real market economies with a level playing field swiftly, and by 1992 Central Europe, had already accomplished far-reaching liberalization. It has proven irreversible, and they have become full-fledged market economies.

The three other early radical reformers, Bulgaria, Kyrgyzstan, and Russia, were less fortunate. Much of Bulgaria's radical deregulation in 1991–2 was undone in 1993, when the communists came back to power. Bulgaria represents the only case of a significant reversal of a radical deregulation, which led to the horrendous financial crash of 1996, which transformed the country into a real market economy. Far out in Central Asia, President Askar Akaev launched a truly radical marketization in Kyrgyzstan in 1993, debunking the cultural myth that a country could not break with its peers and its history. Russia undertook a reasonably radical reform in 1992, but then its reforms slowed down, and only in 1996 did it cross the threshold to a full-fledged market economy.

The remaining eleven countries in the region, Romania and ten CIS countries, started with partial, slow liberalization (see Figure 4.2). Most of them undertook significant marketization. By 2000, all but three had become real market economies or came close to the hurdle after several years of partial reforms. For many, the decisive push was delivered by the financial crisis of 1998.

Three CIS countries got stuck with nonmarket economies, namely, Belarus, Turkmenistan, and Uzbekistan, and they have been unable to move out of their nonreform traps. Initially, Belarus and Uzbekistan launched some liberalization, but because their reforms were halfhearted, both countries stayed nonmarket economies, showing the danger of gradual reforms.

Price regulation was a central communist dogma. For most products, decentralized cost-plus pricing was used, and the liberalization of such prices was not controversial. The contentious prices were the heavily subsidized prices of meat and bread. Attempts at hiking them repeatedly led to popular unrest in communist Poland and the Soviet Union. Only Hungary had undertaken broad price liberalization before 1990. Radical reformers warned of the pitfalls of partial price liberalization, which could aggravate price distortions and depress output (Boycko 1991; Murphy et al. 1992). Their opponents, particularly audible in Russia, argued that price liberalization could not lead to the creation of a market economy and was even harmful, because Russia lacked the prerequisite "market infrastructure." They insisted that the far-reaching monopolization of the Soviet economy impeded market competition, so price liberalization would only lead to monopoly rents and inflation (Yavlinsky and Braguinsky 1994; Goldman 2003).

All politicians were very nervous before their great price liberalizations and feared popular riots, as had been the habit under communism. In each country, price liberalization led to a sudden price hike, ranging from 70 percent in Poland to 250 percent in Russia, but shortages disappeared and the public accepted the price liberalizations. A country did not liberalize prices much more than in its initial deregulation, as any additional freeing of prices was impeded by unending debates. Therefore, the initial price liberalization had to be as comprehensive as possible. Liberalization was both more important and difficult in the CIS countries than in Central Europe. The relative prices in the CIS countries were far more distorted, and any delay in liberalization caused enormous social costs. But a sudden freeing of prices dealt a great shock to society, as people balked at massive changes of relative prices.

One of the most confusing themes in the transition has been monopolies. As Vladimir Capelik (1994), the leading Russian specialist on antimonopoly policy, wrote: "Authors frequently see monopolistic behavior where it does not exist." Yet they did not notice real monopolies. The conviction among

Soviet economists and Sovietologists alike was that the Soviet economy was characterized by production monopolies and that numerous goods were produced by a single enterprise (Hewett 1988; Yavlinsky and Braguinsky 1994; Goldman 1996), but this was a misperception. Often a single enterprise delivered a highly specified product to the State Committee for Material and Technical Supplies (Gossnab), but there were many other producers. Annette Brown, Barry Ickes, and Randi Ryterman (1994) showed that the monopolistic industrial structure was a myth. The largest enterprises in Soviet Russia were actually comparatively small. The total number of employees in the twenty biggest Russian enterprises in 1989 was less than in the twenty largest companies in the United States, Japan, Germany, the United Kingdom, and France. In virtually every industry, Russia had too many large companies in urgent need of consolidation. The problem with the Russian enterprise structure was not that the biggest companies were too big, but that small enterprises were nearly absent. Russia's monopolies were not production but trade monopolies, maintained by state orders, monopolistic wholesale organizations, and protectionism.

These opposing perspectives on the nature of monopolies inspired two contrary approaches to liberalization of domestic trade: radical deregulation versus antitrust policy. Leszek Balcerowicz took the lead on radical liberalization in January 1990. His policy consisted of four vital measures: first, a far-reaching price liberalization; second, a truly radical external liberalization; third, the breaking up of state concerns and associations into single enterprises; fourth, and, possibly most important, a legal act allowing anybody to sell anything anytime in any place at any price to anybody. As a result, central squares in big cities were flooded with people who just started trading and soon made a living, absorbing substantial employment. Within two years, the most successful street traders had established themselves as real merchants and shopkeepers (Balcerowicz 1992; Lipton and Sachs 1990a).

In Russia, Deputy Prime Minister Yegor Gaidar took his cue from Balcerowicz and attempted a similar liberalization in January 1992. Ordinary Russians behaved exactly as in Poland, filling central squares with their wares. But the official response differed. After three months of busy street trading, the mayors of the big cities prohibited this informal trade, overruling the presidential decree. Although the police ignored skyrocketing violent crime, they imposed this prohibition rigorously. Official shops and racketeers suffered from competition with the cheap street trade, which drove down prices so that traders could no longer afford to pay racketeers their hefty charges (Åslund 1995). In collusion with city authorities, organized crime won over economic freedom. Competition remained feeble because of limited liberalization of both domestic and foreign trade, keeping Russian retail prices abnormally high.

The alternative to Balcerowicz's laissez-faire was antimonopoly policy, which came to dominate in the CIS. It was based on the lingering Soviet idea that no market was possible until its "infrastructure" had been built. The Russian Federation established a State Committee for Antimonopoly Policy and the Promotion of New Economic Structures as early as 1990 and adopted an antimonopoly law in March 1991. Rather than liberalizing trade, going after real monopolists, or breaking up enterprises, the Russian Antimonopoly Committee imposed price controls on rather small firms. By 1993, it had registered more than 5,000 "monopolists," defined as firms supplying at least 35 percent of the market for a particular good in any of Russia's 89 regions. Some local "antimonopoly" committees even demanded that an enterprise sell a certain quota locally (Capelik 1992, 1994; Slay and Capelik 1997). Russia's biggest monopolist, Gazprom, by contrast, was registered as a monopolist only in 1997. The Antimonopoly Committee did not promote competition but stifled the market, often with the intent of promoting monopolists and extorting money. The same was true of most of the CIS.

For the domestic liberalization of prices, trade, and the entry of enterprises, a big bang was necessary. Each country tended to reach as far as it jumped at its initial big deregulation. The liberalization had to be both simple and comprehensive because any complication generated rents. Sooner than anybody had expected, the bureaucracy recovered its vigor and began to thrive on extortion.

Liberalization of Foreign Trade

External liberalization also had a great positive impact on growth (see Chapter 3). The liberalization of imports was relatively easy, whereas the deregulation of exports aroused great political controversy.

With the unification of exchange rates, foreign trade tariffs started having real impact. The most reformist socialist countries – Hungary and Poland – had experimented with import tariffs, but foreign trade regulation and taxation remained discretionary until the demise of communism. Initially extremely low real exchange rates made all imports so expensive that they could not compete with domestic goods in price. Because the liberalization of imports meant an end to shortages, it enjoyed strong popular support and occurred quickly in all reformist countries. Import quotas and licenses became exceptions, and rather low import tariffs were introduced in their place. Russia had no import tariffs in the first half of 1992, and Estonia abolished them altogether.

Ironically, the early pressure to raise import tariffs to 10–15 percent came from three international organizations. The International Monetary Fund advocated low and uniform import tariffs as a suitable means of collecting state revenues. The European Union pressed the countries aspiring to accede to the Union to have at least as high tariffs as the EU, with liberal Estonia being the victim. For entry negotiations with the World Trade Organization, it was beneficial to have some import tariffs over which to negotiate. Only after several years, when real exchange rates had appreciated with financial stabilization and domestic producers recovered, did domestic protectionist pressures mount. Yet resistance against protectionism was quite strong, and average national import tariffs have stayed in the range of 3–12 percent despite much talk about the need for protection (World Bank 2005c, p. 3). The new urban middle class and entrepreneurs dependent on imports formed a bulwark against protectionism.

It was far more difficult to deregulate exports than imports because powerful exporters advocated their regulation. The domestic prices of major export commodities – energy, metals, agricultural produce, chemicals, and lumber – stayed low because of state regulation. In December 1991, the price of 1 ton of crude oil in the Soviet Union was 50 cents, while the world market price was about $100. Enterprise managers, commodity traders, bankers, and officials, who had exclusive access to export licenses, joined hands in a highly lucrative export of commodities. They bought commodities on their personal account at low domestic state-controlled prices and sold them abroad at world prices, cashing in anything from 10 to 100 times their purchasing price from 1991 to 1993. These huge rents financed strong opposition to the deregulation of exports.

At the popular level, unfounded fear reigned that the liberalization of exports would deplete the domestic market. Once, arguing with a top Ukrainian official for the liberalization of exports of grain, I encountered the conviction that "our country will be left empty." After many years of shortages, people could not imagine that the simultaneous liberalization of prices and foreign trade would balance the domestic market. They considered the domestic currency worthless and assumed that all attractive goods would be exported. Similarly, people thought most enterprises would go bankrupt if energy prices rose to world levels. Many Western economists reckoned the price discrepancy for commodities was so large that this price adjustment had to be gradual. As a means, they advocated export tariffs and the auctioning of export quotas. But in the 1990s, export tariff revenue could barely be collected. Repeated attempts at the auctioning of export quotas failed because big exporters were too powerful for the weak state. They obtained exemption from export tariffs and acquired export quotas for free.

Foreign trade went through dramatic changes. As long as high inflation prevailed, enterprises had little incentive to export because of the ease of selling at home, and exports plummeted. When macroeconomic stabilization started biting, domestic demand contracted, forcing producers to turn abroad to earn money, which they could do if exports had been liberalized. Typically, liberalizing countries experienced an early, concentrated export boost. The export potential proved great, and it was not dependent on external demand, which was always underutilized, but on domestic supply.

Few Western businesspeople saw the opening of Eastern Europe as an opportunity. Some big companies favored early establishment there, for instance, ABB, Tetra Pak, Procter and Gamble, McDonald's, and the big tobacco companies. Volkswagen undertook the biggest investment of all in the Czech Republic. Most of these companies held the view that they had to secure the market before their competitors even if they would not be able to make profits for years. But the new Eastern markets were small, risky, and immature. At the end of communism, the Soviet bloc accounted for only 2 percent of world trade and twice as much of EU trade. Nor were big Western enterprises sufficiently agile to operate in the new postcommunist economies, which required plenty of senior management time. Only after several years did foreign direct investment take off.

Many countries and regions have toyed with "free economic zones." Initially, they were promoted by reformist regions, such as Leningrad. Later on, they were favored by proponents of industrial policy as well as local interests that lobbied for tax exemptions or their right to collect central taxes. The international financial institutions resolutely resisted free economic zones, which they saw as tax loopholes, which was largely the case. Despite their staunch resistance, free economic zones were legislated in many countries. Prominent examples were the Kaliningrad exclave in Russia and the Crimea in Ukraine. They often obtained substantial tax exemptions, but they rarely thrived. Tax privileges attracted organized crime, and why liberalize one region but not another? In Ukraine, the Donetsk free economic zone became a giant tax loophole for importers, and it was abolished in 2005 after the Orange Revolution. The only flourishing free economic zone

I saw in the CIS was the Bishkek Free Economic Zone in Kyrgyzstan, which relieved enterprises from many taxes but most of all from undue government interference.

Labor Market Policy

The labor market is one of the most paradoxical areas of the transition. Widely held expectations turned out to be completely wrong. First, real wages were not driven up by strong trade unions but were depressed, and often not even paid, by ruthless managers. Second, the anticipated mass unemployment never materialized anywhere but in East Germany. Third, workers did not become a major source of unrest but proved exceedingly complacent. Fourth, labor markets in Central Europe became more regulated than in the former Soviet Union.[2]

Labor was primarily discussed as a social concern rather than as a market. Over time, three labor market paradigms have evolved. The first is the EU model, which found its most extreme expression in East Germany but was also adopted by Central Europe and Bulgaria. Old socialist regulations were maintained, and EU regulations were added to provide full social welfare. Already high payroll taxes were allowed to rise further to finance an extended social safety net, especially higher unemployment benefits because of the fear of mass unemployment and social disruption. The labor market became even more rigid than under socialism. As a result of this social democratic model, East Germany, Poland, Slovakia, Bulgaria, and Hungary saw an early and sharp rise in unemployment. In Poland and Bulgaria, unemployment peaked at 20 percent of the labor force in 2002 and 2001, respectively. Slovakia reached 19 percent in 2001 (United Nations Economic Commission for Europe 2006).

East Germany was a special case. When Germany reunified in 1990, the East German mark was set equal to the deutsche mark, and social benefits were equalized with those in West Germany. Wage setting was delegated to employers and trade unions. But because civil society and social organizations were weak in East Germany, West German trade unions and employers' associations took over. Neither had any interest in competitive wages in the East, whereas both wanted to minimize competition. Nor was the privatization agency Treuhandanstalt, which managed all state companies, concerned

---

[2] This section draws on Commander and Coricelli (1995), Allison and Ringold (1996), Commander and McHale (1996), Dmitriev and Maleva (1997), Maleva (1998), and Boeri and Terrell (2002).

about controlling wages. As a result, the amalgamated West German interests priced East Germany out of the market through excessive wage increases
(Pickel and Wiesenthal 1997). East Germany lost no less than 40 percent of
its jobs, resulting in mass unemployment, like nowhere else in the postcommunist world, of 35 percent of the labor force in 1991 (Siebert 1992,
pp. 34–9, 120–3).[3] A veritable social welfare trap had been created at a huge
cost to West German taxpayers.

In the CIS countries, a second very different model evolved. Old Soviet
labor codes stayed on the books, but managers largely disregarded them,
allowing a relatively free labor market to develop. Alas, employers did not
respect the most fundamental rule: to pay wages for work done. Wage arrears
became notorious, yet unemployment stayed surprisingly low, increasing far
less than the fall in output. The immediate cause of the small unemployment
was that real wages were extraordinarily flexible downward because they were
not indexed for inflation. All over the CIS, wage arrears became standard,
harming as much as two-thirds of the Russian workforce, not necessarily
because enterprises could not pay but because they perceived no need to do
so. Even worse, workers in Russia and Ukraine were often forced to accept
their enterprises' products as payments in kind. The saddest example I saw
was in a southern Ukrainian village in August 1996. A block of reinforced
concrete stood for sale in front of each house, representing the poor workers'
wages in kind, which they tried to hawk to passersby. As it was not necessary
to pay wages, employers had no need to lay off workers, yet at the same time
wage arrears were almost unknown in Central Europe.

At the end of communism, workers' protests had led to uncontrolled wage
rises. As transition started, reformers were greatly concerned over excessive
wage inflation and that cost-push inflation could lead to mass unemployment. Therefore, they opted for strict incomes policies. Poland launched a
tax-based incomes policy, imposing a heavy penalty tax on any wage increase
above a fraction of the inflation rate, and several countries followed Poland's
lead. Gradually, however, it emerged that no country suffered significant
wage inflation and that incomes policies were superfluous (Tait and Erbas
1995). As Jacek Rostowski (1998, p. 139) noted: "Indeed, in Poland in 1990
prices soared far ahead of wages during the first quarter of the stabilization
programme, so that wage controls are unlikely to have been important in
forming inflation expectations."

---

[3] Including open unemployment, part-time workers, employees in public works, and labor
market training.

Many analysts had presumed that, as communism was a form of socialism, workers would emerge as a strong social force when released by democracy. Socialism was not the workers' but the Nomenklatura's state, however.
Instead of the workers, the Nomenklatura rose like the Phoenix. Even where
it was understood that enterprises were controlled by their managers, their
ruthlessness surprised. For a long time, managers refused to believe in systemic change, sticking to the old system. Operating under soft budget constraints, they continued hoarding workers. Each worker was an argument in
negotiations with the authorities for more subsidies, rendering overstaffing
beneficial, and labor and tax laws provided strong incentives against dis-
missals. Enterprise managers preferred to keep workers but not pay them.
Mass layoffs were rare, and most labor mobility arose out of voluntary res-
ignations. The labor market remained tight for skilled workers (Layard and
Richter 1995; Tait and Erbas 1995; Commander and McHale 1996; Garibaldi
and Brixiova 1997; Maleva 1998).

Workers lacked effective representation, and they were fearful of unemployment. Although many countries had a formal trade union membership
of more than 80 percent, in the former Soviet Union, these "trade unions"
were sheer social security administrations. Their main task was to administer extra-budgetary funds financed out of the payroll tax for various social
benefits, such as holiday trips (Dmitriev and Maleva 1997). Many lived
by the old socialist saying: "They pretend to pay us, and we pretend to
work." Workers preferred to look for a new job while still having one. Even
if they were not being paid, they had access to enterprise's social benefits,
such as child care. Many workers started working in the informal economy,
but their old formal employment helped them escape taxation and undue
interest from the authorities. Millions of post-Soviet workers formally
retained some public employment while they roamed around as shuttle
traders or temporary laborers (Commander and Schankerman 1997). A
large part of the labor force disappeared into the lawless underground
because the economy was divided into a highly regulated official labor market with high taxes and an unregulated informal economy with few taxes or
social benefits.

Over time, a third labor market model has come to the fore, the deregulated Anglo-American model. As usual, Estonia was the pioneer. It was
followed by a rather idiosyncratic series of countries: Latvia, Kazakhstan,
Bulgaria, and Slovakia. Estonia launched its reform out of ideological commitment. Kazakhstan saw it as an element of its liberal Asian economic
model, whereas Slovakia and Bulgaria reacted to large and lasting unemployment. The reason for this convergence is that some countries wanted

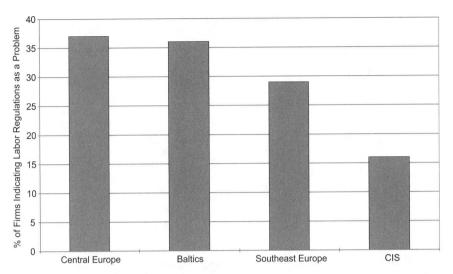

Figure 4.3. Labor Regulations as a Problem in Doing Business, 2005. *Source:* European Bank for Reconstruction and Development/ World Bank (2005).

to legalize the actual situation, whereas others wished to deregulate. The question is how fast this model will proliferate.

Labor regulations were most problematic for business in Central Europe (see Figure 4.3). They are rather cumbersome in the whole of East-Central Europe, whereas CIS labor markets are more flexible despite rigid legislation. Some undesirable rules are respected, notably two or three months of severance payment, whereas the fundamental right to be paid wages earned on time is widely disregarded. Most countries have adopted new labor codes, but only Kazakhstan has truly liberal labor legislation. Among the CIS countries, a prime purpose of labor market reform has been to legalize the existing liberal order but to make sure that workers are being paid the wages they have earned. Among the East-Central European countries, only Estonia, Slovakia, and Bulgaria have achieved such liberalization.

Most of Central and Eastern Europe, however, has established West European social democratic models, with considerable barriers to the dismissal of workers, producing even higher unemployment than in Western Europe. Although one chapter of *acquis communautaire* is devoted to labor market regulation, the EU does not impose too many rules. The European trade unions demanded regulation as exists in Western Europe, however, notably protesting against the absence of collective bargaining in Estonia and Latvia. Top politicians in Germany, Sweden, and France fretted about

How Capitalism Was Built

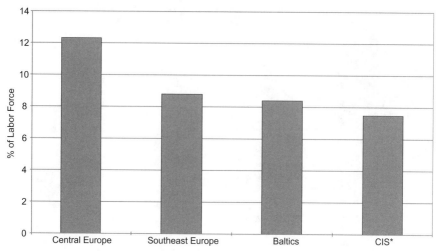

* CIS countries with plausible statistics (Armenia, Kazakhstan, Moldova, Russia, and Ukraine).

Figure 4.4. Unemployment Rate, 2005. *Source:* United Nations Economic Commission for Europe (2006).

"wage dumping" and "tax dumping," trying to bully the new EU members into taxing and pricing themselves out of the market. The EU has effectively advocated a social democratic paradigm of social welfare, even if the United Kingdom and Ireland have abandoned it. Still, the new EU members are experiencing competitive pressures to deregulate their overregulated labor markets and reduce payroll taxes, following the lead of Estonia, Slovakia, and Bulgaria, to reduce their excessive unemployment and boost their sluggish growth rates.

Unemployment reflects the severity of labor market regulations. As we would expect, Central Europe has steadily had the highest unemployment in the region with an average of no less than 12.3 percent in 2005 (see Figure 4.4). The Baltics and Southeast Europe are significantly better off with 8.4 percent unemployment. The CIS countries, for which plausible unemployment statistics exist (Russia, Ukraine, Kazakhstan, Moldova, and Armenia) have average unemployment of 7.5 percent, although they have suffered far greater economic dislocation. The harmful impact of European labor regulations is evident.

Combat of Monopoly: Gas and Coal

In each postcommunist country, the managers of a few big state monopolies resisted market adjustment at great cost to society, and they were often successful. These companies suffered from the standard shortcomings of monopolies, such as inefficiency, overstaffing, and uneconomical overinvestment. Each country went through its own drama, focusing on a few major industries – oil, gas, coal, electrical power, and railways (Slay and Capelik 1997). I focus here on Russia, the biggest and most difficult case.

The World Bank (1994b) prescribed standard principles for the regulation of natural monopolies and assisted in their implementation. An independent regulatory authority had to be established, preferably one for each industry. Prices should be raised to cover costs and allow for a moderate profit. If potential for competition existed, privatization was desirable. Some purported natural monopolies were broken by new technologies that facilitated competition, a situation most evident in the telecommunications industry. Otherwise production, transportation, and trade should be separated, because only transportation was a true natural monopoly. Production and trade could usually be subdivided into several companies. The key to achieve competition was to develop wholesale trade, and a favorite idea was wholesale auctions. Next, production companies could be privatized. Successful rent-seeking monopolists resisted any real market. Their defense of monopoly lay in the control of five levers – unified company, transportation, state ownership, prices, and trade.

To develop a market, monopolistic companies had to be broken up. In Russia, that was done in the oil and coal industry as well as in telecommunications, whereas Gazprom and the railroads have stayed unified companies. Transportation is a pillar of monopoly power. The standard international advice was to separate transportation from production, but the experiences of the Russian oil pipelines (state-owned monopolist Transneft) suggest this is not enough. The obvious solution is to allow competing private pipelines. Even when a transportation monopoly is not broken up, it often faces competition from other means of transportation. Railways compete with pipelines, shipping, and trucks. Quite a lot of privatization has occurred in telecommunications, oil, airline, and coal industries, which has generated competition. Because it is difficult to defend a private monopoly against public criticism, privatization facilitates the emergence of private competitors. Innumerable forms of price regulation have been tried, but nothing has worked in these weak states. Sensible price regulation and auctions were impossible in the face of strong monopolists. Marginal wholesale markets beside a national giant were inevitably manipulated and emasculated. Thus, the most intractable problems of natural monopolies arose out of monopolistic gas pipelines and electricity grids. Other concerns could be managed by breaking up and privatizing monopolistic companies.

Russia offers two stark examples of opposing development, its natural gas and coal industries. Gazprom, the Russian natural gas monopoly company, was the only Soviet industrial ministry to be corporatized lock, stock, and barrel. With more than 300,000 employees, it contained all the assets of the old ministry: all gas production, gas pipelines, plenty of related and unrelated enterprises (such as 200 large state farms), and even all regulatory bodies. While other enterprises were selling off social and noncore assets, Gazprom bought whatever it could in the old Soviet mode of hoarding. Gazprom's power was based both on resources and political protection. The last Soviet minister of gas industry and Gazprom's founder, Viktor Chernomyrdin, was prime minister from December 1992 to April 1998. In this role, he reinforced the company's monopoly power and undertook a large partial insider privatization to the benefit of its managers and employees, but he let the majority of the shares stay with the state. Gazprom was so powerful that its CEO was allowed to vote for the remaining state share until 2001. It had become a state within the state (Slay and Capelik 1997).

The financial dealings between Gazprom and the state were excruciatingly complex. Gazprom regulated everything itself for a long time, and it distorted prices and payments at will. Domestic gas prices were kept far below world market prices (although above costs), but the monopolist did not press for higher prices (Gray 1998). Industry subsidized households, which could be charged as little as one-sixth of the industrial price. Gazprom was prohibited from cutting off deliveries to many nonpaying users, and numerous government bodies were not given state funds to pay for necessary gas. Gazprom responded to this distorted incentive structure by accumulating barter and arrears. In 1996–7, only 7 percent of retail gas purchases were paid in cash, and arrears abounded (Slay and Capelik 1997). Rather than protesting against this state of affairs, Gazprom exploited arrears to extract substantial discounts in its taxes through offsets against their unpaid taxes, extracting implicit subsidies from the government (Commander and Mumssen 1998; Gaddy and Ickes 1998).

Gazprom's managers exploited the nontransparency to their personal benefit. Russia's gas exports to other CIS countries, especially to Ukraine, were notoriously criminal. Gazprom sold such gas to a private trading company (Itera), close to the Gazprom management, at an extremely low price. Itera charged Ukrainian purchasers high prices, but Ukrainian gas imports were heavily subsidized by the Ukrainian state through a special exchange rate until 1995. The Ukrainian government awarded a few Ukrainian gas purchasers, some state-owned and some private, regional monopolies. Because the Ukrainian state guaranteed payments for gas shipments from Russia, importers paid only for a faction. Gazprom raged against Ukraine's arrears and also accused Ukrainians of stealing gas from the pipeline, but Russia could not cut off deliveries to Ukraine, because most of its gas exports to the West went through Ukrainian pipelines. In reality, Itera and a handful of Ukrainian gas oligarchs could each year split a couple billion U.S. dollars at the expense of Gazprom and the Ukrainian state (Lovei 1998; Mercedes Balmeceda 1998; Timoshenko 1998; Åslund 2000).

The government could do little against these big state monopolies. In the spring of 1997, Russian First Deputy Prime Minister Boris Nemtsov declared a kamikaze attack on the natural monopolies, which was an apt description. Within half a year, the natural monopolies had won at the expense of Nemtsov's political career (Slay and Capelik 1997). In 2001, the resurging Russian state had grown so strong that President Vladimir Putin replaced the old Gazprom management with his own people. Rather than reforming the company, Putin continued the old monopolistic policies. Another private trading company, Eural Trans Gaz, and later RosUkr-Energo, took the place of Itera. They represented the interests of the new Gazprom management, which continued skimming off some of Gazprom's earnings.

Unlike the prosperous natural gas industry, the coal industry was perceived as hopelessly obsolete. It persisted primarily in Poland, Romania, Ukraine, Russia, and Kazakhstan. Everywhere it was terribly inefficient and unprofitable. It remained fully state-owned and was managed like one national corporation. Coal prices were regulated far below both costs and world prices, aggravating losses. In Ukraine and Russia, the coal industry became infamous for huge state subsidies, persistent wage arrears, and many strikes. The state coal managers thrived on state subsidies, which they extracted through transfer pricing and management theft, criminalizing the industry. In Russia, middlemen and mine managers typically kept one-third of the price for themselves. To add insult to injury, coal-mine managers complained that they could not pay wages to their workers, whom they urged to strike to extract more subsidies from the government. The coal miners had formed a radical, democratic force behind Boris Yeltsin in 1989, but in 1998 the miners helped to bring down the reformist Russian government under Sergei Kirienko.

After the Russian financial crash, the Russian coal industry took a sharp turn for the better. Two consecutive liberal Russian Ministers of Economy (Yevgeny Yasin and Yakov Urinson) and the World Bank had already agreed

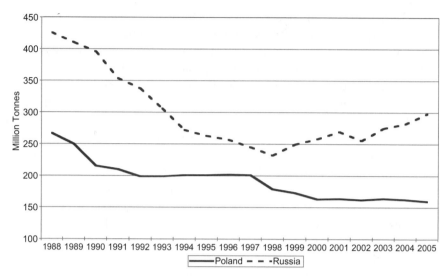

Figure 4.5. Russian and Polish Coal Production, 1988–2005. *Source:* BP (2006).

on a comprehensive reform program for the whole coal industry in 1996. The first and critical step was to break up Rosugol, the Russian coal association, which was a hybrid of ministry, industrial association, and company. The second step was the privatization of the coal mines in reasonably small portions. Soon the coal mines were consolidated in half a dozen relatively large private companies. With fragmentation and privatization, price liberalization became possible, and competition caught on. Russian coal output that had plummeted by 45 percent from 1988 to 1998 suddenly started rising, and increased by 20 from 1998 to 2005 (see Figure 4.5). Profits surged as the new private owners cut costs, fired workers, and cleaned up the finances. The World Bank prides itself of having designed a social safety net for miners and mining communities, which facilitated its popular acceptance. The Russian government could swiftly eliminate its coal subsidies, and notoriously unreliable coal supplies became predictable. This troubled industry turned healthy within a few years. Rarely have marketization and privatization proved more successful. The precondition for this success was that Russia accepted the consolidated ownership of wealthy owners, known as oligarchs (see Chapter 10). In Kazakhstan, a similar privatization of the coal industry was carried out with World Bank support, with perhaps even greater success.

The same was not true of the coal industry elsewhere. Poland had the proudest coal industry in the former Soviet bloc, and until 1997, its production decline was comparatively limited, but as late as 2006 not a single Polish coal mine had been privatized. Output continues to fall year after year, while it is rising in Russia (see Figure 4.5). The number of workers and operating mines was slashed by about one-third at great public cost. Despite high international coal prices and large state subsidies, the Polish coal industry barely managed to turn a profit, and production is set to fall further (Cienski 2006). Regardless of substantial successes in other industries, thanks to Poland's excellent big bang deregulation, Poland's coal industry failed miserably in comparison with Russia and Kazakhstan because the latter privatized, but Poland did not. Russia and Kazakhstan also allowed the consolidation of large companies in the hands of a few domestic oligarchs, which Poland resisted.

A Big Bang: Vital in Deregulation

This chapter offers rather strong empirical conclusions. Two opposing political choices were made dependent on political power. If the old elite held sway, it chose gradual deregulation, which permitted it to maintain power and extract resources with state fiat. Democratization, by contrast, led to radical deregulation, which threatened the old elite's omnipotence. Only three dictators, Lukashenko in Belarus, Niyazov in Turkmenistan, and Karimov in Uzbekistan, thought the old Soviet economy could prove viable.

Deregulation has been characterized by three important dichotomies. The first dichotomy concerns the choice of liberalization strategy. Democratic Central Europe and the Baltics opted for radical and comprehensive deregulation from the outset, whereas Romania and most of the CIS countries pursued a gradual and partial deregulation, which maximized rents for a small elite. In most countries, this hybrid system evolved into a more ordinary market economy, but three countries – Belarus, Turkmenistan, and Uzbekistan – decided to keep Soviet-style systems. The initial choice proved crucial. A country hardly reached further in domestic liberalization of prices, trade, and enterprise than it did in its first jump. The reformers had a brief window of opportunity of "extraordinary politics," as Balcerowicz (1994) emphasized. If they did not seize that chance, the rent-seeking establishment soon blocked liberalization. Their rents grew so large that the rent seekers bought political power, impeding marketization to maximize their personal rents.

Unfortunately, it is not true that "in most of the [postcommunist] states, liberalization was quickly achieved" (Lavigne 2000, p. 18). The socially oriented gradual strategy about which many Western economists and social scientists had theorized (see Chapter 2) was nowhere to be seen in real life, because gradual liberalization and a socially oriented economic policy were mutually exclusive. Even well-meaning economists who had advocated a gradual strategy became pretty radical when they joined government.[4]

A second dichotomy concerns foreign trade, where the division is strictly geographic. East-Central Europe opted for a "return to Europe" with far-reaching early liberalization of foreign trade and a reorientation toward the European Union. The CIS countries, on the contrary, had nowhere to go and tried to minimize the disruption. As a result, their trade was restructured slowly while it contracted sharply.

A third dichotomy concerns the labor market. East-Central Europe's labor market is overregulated, because it suffers from the combination of old socialist regulations and new EU regulations, which are imposed with rigor. The CIS countries have a comparatively free labor market because labor law is largely ignored, and increasingly legislation is being adjusted to reality.

In sum, early radical deregulation was of fundamental importance for a successful transition to a market economy. Any inconsistency caused problematic rents, and they were aggravated rather than resolved in the medium term, as rent-seeking interests became entrenched. Several countries were trapped at suboptimal equilibria with high rents and low output. Murphy, Shleifer, and Vishny (1993) pointed out that such suboptimal equilibria were a natural consequence of increasing returns to rent seeking. After a certain set of economic rules had been established, a powerful group of beneficiaries arose, blocking further reform. The winners did take all, both the economic system and politics (Hellman 1998). These equilibria may not be eternal, but they can last for years, especially if they are reinforced with energy rents as in Russia and Kazakhstan (Arendh 2005; Gaddy and Ickes 2005; Tompson 2005).

Fortunately for the late and slow reformers, the story did not end on this sad note. Over time, rents dissipated and dwindled. Rents between regulated prices and free prices inevitably disappeared after a few years of expanding arbitrage. Over time, most CIS countries have opened their economies. In a few cases, the CIS countries have actually chosen a more liberal approach than the Central-East European countries because of EU regulations, notably in labor market policies and agriculture. Liberal labor markets are proliferating from the East because authoritarian elites now live on profit seeking of export industries and thus benefit from freer markets. Authoritarian CIS

---

[4] The outstanding example is Grzegorz Kołodko (2000), Polish minister of finance and deputy prime minister, 1994–7.

countries, especially Kazakhstan and Armenia, have adopted the East Asian economic model with high growth based on private ownership, a small state, little regulation, but extensive corruption. As a consequence, the CIS reformers continue to make some progress on deregulation, while Central Europe and the Baltics have stopped doing so.

5

From Hyperinflation to Financial Stability

When communism collapsed, macroeconomic chaos prevailed. In late 1991, salespeople stood behind the counters of the large Moscow grocery stores, but they had absolutely nothing to sell. Even the last inedible fish and vegetable conserves had been sold out. Long lines lingered outside other shops, which had received some substandard meat. The lines could last for days, and entrepreneurial organizers distributed numbers to the queuing public, but the produce distributed could scarcely pass for meat. In the Russian language, the verbs "buy" and "sell" had been replaced by "take" and "give," showing how unequal Russians perceived the exchange between goods and money. Some *kolkhoz* (collective farm) markets that sold private produce existed, but they were few and their prices were several times higher than the official state prices. People stopped going to work because they could not use the money they earned, and they needed the time for queuing. Life was hell.

When prices were deregulated, they skyrocketed in almost all transition countries. Many major steps had to be taken to achieve reasonable price stability. First, national currencies had to be established. Second, fiscal policy had to be tightened. Third, a new tax policy was needed. Fourth, monetary policy also had to be made strict. Fifth, the exchange rate had to be unified and devalued to become competitive. Alas, these tasks were complex, and the local knowledge of macroeconomics was minimal. The very institutions of macroeconomic policy had to be built or rebuilt. The dramas of financial stabilization engaged all.

High and Persistent Inflation

All formerly socialist countries but Czechoslovakia were in severe financial crises when they entered transition. The liberalization of domestic prices in the presence of shortages and excess demand unleashed high inflation. Poland and the former Soviet republics were approaching hyperinflation, that is, more than 50 percent monthly inflation according to Phillip Cagan's (1956) classical definition. The unification and market adjustment of the exchange rate involved substantial devaluations, which further inflated domestic prices. International financial markets were largely closed, with only Hungary and Czechoslovakia being creditworthy. This was a macroeconomic nightmare. All preconditions for high inflation were at hand, and extraordinary efforts were required to vanquish it. Most CIS countries joined the International Monetary Fund (IMF) and the World Bank in the spring of 1992.

In every country, the initial price liberalization led to a greater price hike than anticipated. For Russia, the IMF had forecast a price rise of 50 percent in January 1992, but prices rose by 250 percent. In Czechoslovakia, Minister of Finance Václav Klaus (1992) argued that the height of this initial price surge could not be predicted, only its shape in case of a radical and consistent stabilization, and he proved right. The large price increases had two immediate effects. One was that the volume of money to GDP fell sharply, and the other was a strong demand for compensatory monetary expansion (Boone and Hørder 1998).

A chasm initially divided Central and Southeast Europe from the former Soviet Union, including the Baltics, where extreme inflation raged in 1992 and 1993. In 1992, Russia saw its price level surge by no less than 2,500 percent, and in 1993 inflation exceeded 10,000 percent in Armenia and Ukraine. CIS inflation peaked with ten of the twelve CIS countries experiencing hyperinflation in 1993. Even the virtuous Baltic states had approximately 1,000 percent inflation in 1992 (see Figures 5.1 and 5.2).

We can distinguish four inflationary patterns. Hungary was the single successful gradual stabilizer, with inflation never exceeding 33 percent a year. Poland, Czechoslovakia, and the three Baltic countries form a second group of successful radical stabilizers. Poland and the Baltic states started transition with high inflation, but they undertook early, rigorous, and successful stabilizations, although inflation remained in the double digits for years. The third group encompasses most CIS countries. They experienced hyperinflation in 1993 but launched serious stabilization efforts from 1994 to 1996 and brought inflation under control. Finally, five countries succeeded in reducing inflation below 40 percent a year temporarily but later faced new high inflation. These were Bulgaria in 1996–7, Romania in 1997, Russia in 1998, Belarus in 1997–9, and Tajikistan in both 1995 and 1997. Bulgaria, Romania, and Russia had all carried out late and slow stabilizations heavily dependent on strict monetary policy, but their budget deficits remained

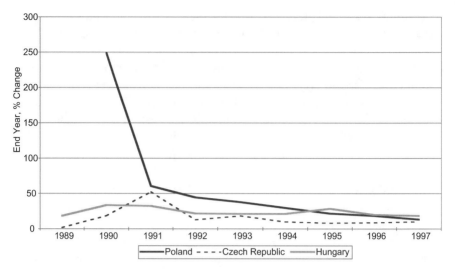

Figure 5.1. Inflation in Poland, Czech Republic, and Hungary, 1989–97. *Note:* Czech Republic numbers for 1989–90 refer to former Czechoslovakia. *Sources:* EBRD (1996) and (1999).

too large. When they could no longer raise credits to finance their excessive budget deficits, renewed inflation crises erupted, as well as debt crises, bank crashes, and large devaluations. Figure 5.3 shows the later inflationary pattern.

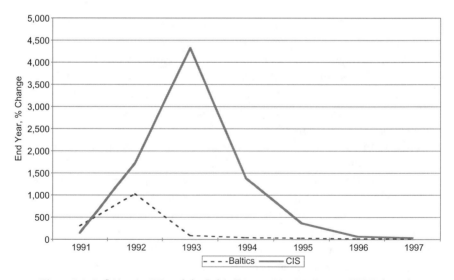

Figure 5.2. Inflation in CIS and the Baltic States, 1991–97. *Source:* EBRD (1999).

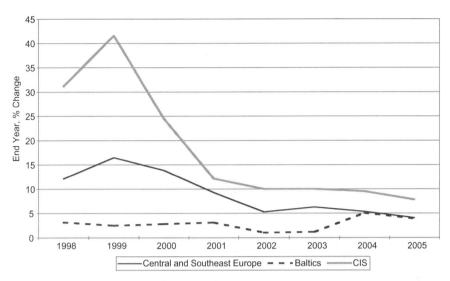

Figure 5.3. Inflation in Central and Southeast Europe, Baltics, and CIS, 1998–2005. *Sources:* EBRD (2004) and (2005).

Hyperinflation is a modern phenomenon, requiring fiat and bank money. It first emerged after World War I, and until the late 1980s, the world had recorded only 16 hyperinflations (Fischer 2005). The distinction between high inflation and hyperinflation can be illustrated with an analogy. Under high inflation, a thief steals the money and leaves the bag, but under hyper-inflation he takes the bag and leaves the money, because money is of little value. If we disregard the initial price hikes after liberalizations, the post-communist region saw no less than twelve hyperinflations during the transi-tion: Poland in 1989, ten former Soviet republics in 1993, and Bulgaria in 1997. In addition, Yugoslavia had two bouts of hyperinflation. Thus, the broader region experienced fourteen hyperinflations, almost as many as the whole world had suffered before the demise of communism.

The high and unpredictable inflation brought about not only great wealth redistribution but also a huge destruction of wealth and output, as it desta-bilized the economic environment. The bank savings of the population were inflated away, hurting particularly the well-to-do and elderly. Ironically, their anger was directed against the reformers, who liberalized prices, rather than the communists, who had issued more money than they could afford. High inflation devastated confidence in local currencies, prompting demonetiza-tion and a mass flight to dollars. As the velocity of money rose, the volume of money as a ratio of GDP plunged. Dollarization proliferated in both the consumer and enterprise sphere, and cash dollars circulated as a second currency. Capital flight caught on as the smart and wealthy transferred their money abroad to safeguard it, although such capital transfers were strictly prohibited. Relative prices vacillated sharply and unpredictably, impeding investment. The only sensible economic activity was speculative arbitrage.

Establishing National Currencies

Before any macroeconomic policy could be pursued, basic state institutions had to be built. The most important was a national currency. When the Soviet Union fell apart in December 1991, the break was not clean, because the ruble persisted as the last Soviet relict. A competitive issue of ruble credits had already started between the old Soviet State Bank and fifteen newly formed republican central banks. The more ruble credits one republic issued, the larger share of the common GDP it extracted, but the worse overall inflation became. This was a prisoner's dilemma. Everybody had a strong incentive to behave worse than others, but as a consequence, all were worse off than if they had restrained their expenditures. At the time, many CIS policy makers did not understand that credits equaled money. Only ruble currency, which was exclusively printed in Russia, was rationed. The consequence was a great shortage of cash, peaking in the summer of 1992, which led to the emission of surrogate money in the form of coupons in most CIS countries (Hardy and Lahiri 1994).

The former Soviet republics adopted three approaches to the ruble zone. The Balts wanted to leave the ruble zone as soon as possible. They regarded a national currency as their best border against Russia, and they ignored transition costs (Hansson 1993). Nationalists in Ukraine, Moldova, Georgia, and Azerbaijan favored independent national currencies in principle, but they felt poorly prepared and wanted to extract maximum benefits from cheap Russian credits and raw materials in the meantime. Therefore, they delayed their introduction of a national currency. A third group stayed close to Russia out of necessity or convenience. Neighboring Belarus and Kazakhstan considered themselves too dependent on Russia, and distant Armenia and Tajikistan sought Russia's support because they felt small and weak.

Within Russia, reformers advocated an early "nationalization of the ruble" (Gaidar 1993). They realized how costly the ruble zone was to Russia and that the competitive issuance of money would cause hyperinflation. Yet for technical reasons, such as the printing of a new currency, they thought the break could not be undertaken until the middle of 1992. Their Western economic advisors were unanimously for the instant introduction of an independent ruble (Sachs and Lipton 1993). But the old Soviet establishment prevailed. It included the Central Bank of Russia (CBR), the old Soviet ministries, and state industry, which all resisted the demise of the Soviet Union. State enterprise managers wanted to continue delivering their substandard produce to other former Soviet republics in return for Russian state credits. The sales of Russian oil and gas at very low prices to other CIS countries facilitated lucrative arbitrage for state enterprise managers, commodity traders, and bankers throughout the CIS. A rent-seeking elite benefited from the persistence of the ruble zone, as did Soviet deadbeats, whereas the broader public did not understand the issue, instinctively preferring minimal change (Åslund 1995).

The IMF was the main international agency involved. It considered the ruble zone such a politically infected issue that it preferred to be neutral. Initially, the IMF (1992) reckoned that the CIS countries needed to agree on a controlled system of emission, but this was never feasible. After the Baltic states had decided to launch their own currencies in mid-1992, the IMF assisted them. In the fall of 1992, the IMF privately urged Ukraine to leave the ruble area, but only in May 1993 did the organization publicly encourage a country (Kyrgyzstan) to depart from the zone. Because the EU was about to establish its single currency, EU spokespersons defended the ruble zone (Emerson 1992), and the EU was prominent on the executive board of the IMF. Through its neutrality, the IMF effectively supported a monetary chaos that condemned the CIS to hyperinflation (Granville 1995b, 2002).[1]

The only sensible policy was to divide the common currency zone early, as Czechoslovakia had done after the dissolution of the Habsburg Empire after World War I. All the other successor states kept the old Habsburg currency, despite the absence of a single currency authority, and plunged into hyperinflation. Czechoslovakia, by contrast, escaped the havoc by swiftly establishing its own currency and central bank. Eventually, the other successor states launched their own currencies and independent central banks and achieved financial stability with the help of international financial assistance through the League of Nations (Pasvolsky 1928). Only Czechoslovakia remained democratic throughout the interwar period. These insights were alive in the international economic debate (Sargent 1986; Dornbusch 1992). One lesson was that the best economic cure was to break up a common

---

[1] The IMF officials concerned strongly dispute that they effectively supported monetary chaos, as they urged all these countries to tighten their fiscal and monetary policies (Odling-Smee and Pastor 2002).

currency zone as soon as possible after a common monetary authority disappeared. Another was that international financial support is vital for the creation of new currencies, and a third that independent central banks help to render currencies stable. Finally, the post-Habsburg case showed the danger of dictatorship after hyperinflation, which made the population call for elementary security at any price.

Alas, all the mistakes that had been made after the dissolution of the Habsburg Empire were repeated with the ruble zone. Its breakup was protracted and agonizing. The Russian government tried to limit credit to the other former Soviet republics from July 1992, but with little success because of opposition from the CBR. As a result, ten of the twelve members of the ruble zone experienced hyperinflation in 1993. The only exceptions were Kyrgyzstan, which left the ruble zone in May 1993, and Russia, which pursued the strictest monetary policy. In Ukraine and Armenia, inflation exceeded 10,000 percent, and the hyperinflation caused economic chaos. The cost of the ruble zone to Russia in 1992 amounted to no less than 9 percent of its GDP in subsidized credits and 13 percent of GDP in implicit trade subsidy, that is, a total of 22 percent of Russia's GDP (IMF 1994a, p. 25). Although the formal gains of other CIS states were enormous, ranging from 11 percent of GDP in Belarus and Moldova in 1992 to 91 percent of GDP in Tajikistan (IMF 1994a), this flow of money did not benefit the whole nation, only individual rent seekers.

In 1993, Russia's reformist minister of finance, Boris Fedorov (1994), did his utmost to break up the ruble zone, trying to cut credits to other CIS countries and supporting Kyrgyzstan's departure. Strangely, his nemesis Viktor Gerashchenko, the old-style chairman of the CBR and the main advocate of the ruble zone, suddenly terminated the ruble zone by declaring old Soviet banknotes null and void in July 1993. Gerashchenko's intention was possibly to force other countries to accept the rule of CBR, but his action caused panic and compelled all remaining members of the ruble zone to establish their national currencies within the next few months (Granville 1995a).

Although the dysfunctional ruble zone lingered for so long, few CIS countries prepared themselves for monetary independence. They fell into complete disarray, and inflation actually surged in several CIS countries in late 1993. However, with the exception of Azerbaijan, they all had less inflation in 1994 than in 1993. The end of the ruble zone made monetary stabilization possible. Although other causes contributed, it is noteworthy that democracy failed in all the CIS countries that experienced hyperinflation in the CIS exactly as in interwar Europe.

In sharp contrast with the CIS, the Czech Republic and Slovakia repeated their post–World War I success after their peaceful split into two countries on January 1, 1993. The original intention was to divide the currency on June 1, 1993. However, an immediate run on the currency led to a separation of the Czech and Slovak korunas in mid-February 1993, and the Slovak koruna was devalued in relation to the Czech koruna. Thanks to this early division of the currencies, monetary stability was maintained in both countries (Nuti 1996).

Radical Fiscal Adjustment Was Key

Macroeconomic stabilization policy came to characterize a country's approach to postcommunist economic transformation. The two alternatives were early, radical stabilization or a gradual approach.

Poland pioneered radical financial stabilization or "shock therapy." Its main architects were Minister of Finance Leszek Balcerowicz (1992) and his advisors Jeffrey Sachs and David Lipton (Balcerowicz 1992; Sachs 1990; Lipton and Sachs 1990a; Sachs 1993; Sachs and Lipton 1990). They wanted a comprehensive radical market reform to get the fundamentals right from the outset and thought it better to play it safe than to risk failure. The budget had to be brought to balance, which could be done as price liberalization eliminated large price subsidies, and enterprise subsidies needed to be reduced. In 1991, Czechoslovakia launched a similar but even more radical program of liberalization and stabilization. Estonia escalated further. Latvia and Lithuania followed suit (Lainela and Sutela 1994; Banarjee et al. 1995). Only these six countries undertook radical stabilization programs. Even they had problems pursuing a sufficiently strict stabilization because fiscal loopholes abounded.

The apparent alternative was Hungary's halfhearted financial stabilization. The Hungarian government did as little as it could get away with. It tightened its budget deficit in 1990 but then let it lapse, borrowing as much money abroad as it could possibly service (Székely and Newberry 1993; Banarjee et al. 1995). The key difference between Hungary and Poland was the initial conditions. Poland suffered from hyperinflation, whereas Hungary only faced somewhat high inflation and a large foreign debt service. These two situations inspired different attitudes and policies, but they became two opposing models in the debate. In structural reforms, by contrast, Hungary excelled.

The real gradual alternative was little or no stabilization, which was the choice by default of most transition countries. It amounted to a very gradual policy, but without Hungary's justifications. Throughout the CIS, enormous budget deficits persisted for no good economic reason. They were financed with the hyperinflationary issue of money, as monetary policy remained very lax. Only after serious financial crisis, financial stabilization was undertaken.

The ministry of finance had to be reinforced. Because of the socialist legacy, postsocialist ministries of finance had limited control over state expenditures and revenues. Price subsidies and foreign trade subsidies were automatic. The presidential administration was beyond fiscal control, taking whatever it desired. Many state agencies established extra-budgetary funds with independent taxation and expenditures. The central bank issued subsidized credits without asking the ministry of finance. Yet under capitalism, the minister of finance must control fiscal policy and the government's purse strings. The Central European and Baltic reformers successfully centralized fiscal control to their ministries of finance, and the minister of finance became deputy prime minister in Poland, the Czech Republic, and Slovakia. In the CIS countries, Romania, and Bulgaria, this struggle lasted longer. Politically weak ministries of finance did not dare to refuse requests for expenditures, piling up far larger "planned" expenditures than they could finance.

Large budget deficits were of no benefit. Most of the region suffered from large budget deficits for a protracted period, but fiscal policies varied.[2] In the early transition, three approaches were apparent. The virtuous stabilizers (the Czech Republic, Slovakia, Estonia, and Latvia; see Figure 5.4) started their transition with more or less balanced budgets, which they maintained, suggesting that the easiest way of balancing a budget is to do so consistently. A second group (Poland, Hungary, and Lithuania) failed to reduce their budget deficits sufficiently, compelling them to undertake substantial later readjustments. They were not as successful in their budgetary restraints as the first group. The third group (all the CIS countries, Bulgaria, and Romania) had durable, large budget deficits. They all began with huge fiscal imbalances, which they found very difficult to reduce. Their revenues declined as a share of GDP, but the governments refused to face up to reality and undertake the necessary expenditure cuts.

In 1998, the picture changed completely. Approaching membership in the European Union, the Central Europeans relaxed. They allowed their budget deficits to widen to about 6 percent of GDP from 2000 to 2003, far beyond fiscal caution. The CIS countries, by contrast, were badly burned by the

---

[2] Budget statistics are amazingly poor and contradictory.

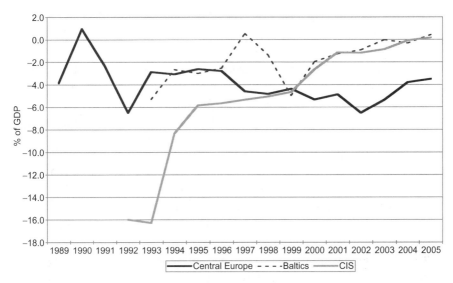

Figure 5.4. Fiscal Balance, 1989–2005. *Sources:* EBRD (1996), (2002), and (2006).

Russian financial crisis. They realized that the cost of large budget deficits was unbearable and were forced to minimize their budget deficits, because both domestic and foreign financing dried up. They now hover around 1 percent of GDP. Because little could be done to revenues in the short term, they did so by cutting their expenditures. Only the three small Baltic countries stayed virtuous throughout, with budgets close to balance.

The lesson is that the initial fiscal policy usually continues unless crisis strikes. The Baltic experience suggests that the best policy was to stick to a balanced budget. No large budget deficit has led to economic recovery, and the extensive advocacy of economic stimulation through fiscal deficit seems baseless.

State revenues contracted slowly. Socialist governments had redistributed about 50 percent of GDP through the central government, although public revenues of 15–25 percent of GDP are normal for countries at that level of economic development (Tanzi and Tsibouris 2000). Czechoslovakia topped with state revenues of no less than 61 percent of GDP in 1989, the highest level of taxation in the world in a tie with Sweden. If the purpose had been to promote economic growth, public expenditures and overtaxation should have been slashed, but an unholy alliance supported large public redistribution. West Europeans considered such a tax level normal, and many East European reformers saw Western Europe as their model. Most economists thought the state required more resources to meet the social challenges of transition. The IMF insisted on a small budget deficit but had no strong views on the level of public expenditures. A widespread fear of collapsing public revenues prompted reform governments to raise tax rates.

Surprisingly, public revenues stayed high for years. In Central Europe, total state revenues lingered at 46 percent of GDP until 1996 before moderating to 40 percent (European Bank for Reconstruction and Development [EBRD] various years). The Baltic republics, Bulgaria, and Romania soon approached an average of 35 percent of GDP. Only the CIS countries went below 30 percent of GDP by 1995. The CIS falls into two categories. One group of countries had total state revenues of 14–23 percent of GDP at the nadir in 1999, namely, the three Caucasian countries and four in Central Asia (Kazakhstan, Kyrgyzstan, Tajikistan, and Turkmenistan). The other five CIS countries (Belarus, Russia, Ukraine, Moldova, and Uzbekistan) have maintained stable state revenues averaging 35 percent of GDP.

As long as inflation stayed high, state revenues did so as well, which contradicts the standard Olivera-Tanzi effect that enterprises delay their tax payments during high inflation to reduce their real taxes. One reason was that public enterprises had no effective owners, and their managers did not mind paying taxes. Moreover, the state collected taxes through the state bank system. As a result, it extracted much of the tax in advance, reversing the Olivera-Tanzi effect to the advantage of the state treasury. When stabilization began to bite, state revenues started falling as expected because money was becoming scarce, banks no longer collected tax, and many enterprises had real owners who wanted to minimize taxes. State revenues contracted much more in countries with durable high inflation, which were also the most corrupt. The worse the macroeconomic predicament, the lower the revenues the state obtained.

Public expenditures were eventually severely cut. For years public expenditures stayed excessive. Initially, the postcommunist states tried to maintain public expenditures of around 50 percent of GDP, which they considered socially "necessary." Many countries even boosted them with new social transfers, designed to mitigate social hardship caused by the transition. Usually, public expenditures have only been curtailed because of serious crises. Exceptionally, the three Baltic states sensibly reduced their public expenditures to some 30 percent of GDP by 1995 (see Figure 5.5). Severe trouble in the early 1990s forced most CIS countries to huge cuts in public expenditures in 1994–5, although Russia stumbled on with an oversized budget deficit until its financial crisis of 1998. The Central European countries, however, never entered such a crisis and still maintain large public expenditures.

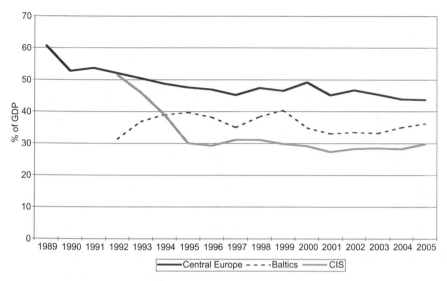

Figure 5.5. General Government Expenditures, 1989–2005. *Sources:* Tanzi and Tsibouris (2000, p. 22); EBRD (2004) and (2006).

In the CIS, public expenditures cuts have been impressive. Public expenditures plummeted from an average of 54 percent of GDP in 1992 to only 30 percent in 1996 in the midst of a large slump in output. In several countries, public expenditures were reduced by one-tenth of GDP during one year. Successful budget cuts aimed at specific items. Price subsidies were usually about one-tenth of GDP, and they disappeared with the initial price liberalization. Another early target was military expenditures. Enterprise subsidies were more difficult to reduce, although they frequently exceeded one-tenth of GDP. During the so-called shock therapy in Poland in 1990, more than 7 percent of GDP was still spent on enterprise subsidies (EBRD 1997, p. 83), and in 1998 it amounted to no less than 16 percent of GDP in Russia (Pinto et al., 1999). It normally took a severe fiscal crisis to make it politically possible to cut corporate subsidies, as in Bulgaria in 1997, Russia in 1998, or Ukraine in 2000.

Ironically, those countries that insisted on larger public expenditures than they could afford condemned themselves to high and lasting inflation, which prompted their state revenues to fall even further, eventually compelling these countries to make do with even less (Gaidar 1998). Similarly, "the stabilization process was not sustained in countries that had persistent fiscal deficits and slow structural reforms" (Fischer and Sahay 2000, p. 9). On one hand, lasting high inflation led to greater corruption. On the other, the very dysfunction of the state made it necessary to cut public expenditures more, which later would facilitate new economic growth.

Tax Policy: From Social Democratic to Liberal

Everybody agreed on the need for substantial changes in taxation.[3] The original socialist economy had no real tax system. At the end of each year, the state simply confiscated the remaining profits of state enterprises. Turnover and foreign trade taxes were nothing but the balance between arbitrarily set prices. This system of arbitrary discretion could not continue. However, tax reform was deemed too complex to be in the forefront of the transition, and all stopped at piecemeal measures. This neglect would come back to haunt policy makers and eventually cause radical innovation.

Several principles for taxation were widely embraced. First, a broad consensus supported a move from individually set taxes to universal tax rates. Second, the worry about the collapse of tax collection made governments opt for high tax rates. Even reformers accepted tax hikes, contradicting their long-term vision of low taxes. Third, a simple and transparent system was desirable. Fourth, taxes should no longer be concentrated to enterprises, but the tax base should be broadened to people. Fifth, a desire prevailed to move taxes from production to consumption. Finally, the consensus was that tax reform was so complicated that it had to be legislated and implemented over many years.

From the outset, two tax philosophies developed. One was social democratic, favoring high taxes and progressive income taxes. It originated in Hungary, which had reformed its tax system thoroughly before the end of socialism. In 1988, it had adopted the Swedish tax system with high value added tax (VAT), a progressive income tax reaching 60 percent, a payroll tax of almost 60 percent, but comparatively low profit taxes and import tariffs. This social democratic model became one standard for tax reforms in the region, adopted by Central Europe and the least reformist CIS countries – Ukraine, Belarus, and Uzbekistan.

Estonia pioneered a liberal alternative, a simple tax system with few and low taxes with minimal loopholes. Its main innovation was a flat personal income tax of 26 percent for all. Estonia also abolished all foreign trade taxes. A VAT of 18 percent was the main tax. Apart from a moderate payroll tax

---

[3] This section draws heavily on IMF, notably Tanzi (1992) and Ebrill and Havrylyshyn (1999), as well as Dąbrowski (1996), Dmitriev and Kartsev (1996), and Dmitriev (1997).

(33 percent), profit tax, and land tax, Estonia hardly had any other taxes. Even so, it collected nearly 40 percent of GDP in state revenues thanks to a highly legitimate tax system and eminent collection. Because of its high tax revenues, it was able to abolish the profit tax in 2000. As usual, Latvia and Lithuania closely followed Estonia's example (Organization for Economic Cooperation and Development [OECD] 2000b).

Under socialism, taxes had been paid by a limited number of state enterprises and automatically collected through the state bank system. Now each country needed a large new tax collection agency. From the left to the IMF, fear reigned that tax collection would collapse, but the resurgence of the communist bureaucracy was not to be underestimated. Not only East-Central Europe but also the post-Soviet states organized huge tax inspections in no time, because the old communist system mastered bureaucracy, inspection, and punishment. The CIS countries also set up tax police with full-fledged policemen, who were highly motivated because they worked on commission. These two agencies collected the same taxes from the same taxpayers in severe competition. Also the customs service and various extra-budgetary funds joined the competition for tax revenues, resulting in an overgrazing of the tax base (Shleifer and Treisman 2000).

The state monopoly of taxation had broken down and been replaced by lawless persecution of honest taxpayers. If you paid taxes to one service, you were more likely to be charged again, as the tax system was too arbitrary to offer any legal protection. Profit-making enterprises without political protection were overgrazed, often fatally so. Budding new entrepreneurs were visited by scores of new revenue and inspection agencies, which ravaged enterprises with cumbersome inspections, arrests, penalties, and fees, extorting money. A Sovietlike bureaucratic Leviathan arose in countries that needed to be liberalized from the state, and the vital legal protection of businessmen was ignored. As EBRD (1999, p. 120) put it:

Although the formal system of central planning has been abandoned, the bargaining between the state and firms has not ceased but rather changed form . . . state and enterprises engage in a web of interactions beyond the standard provision of public goods in exchange for taxes. The state gives a wide range of benefits to firms, in the form of state financing, explicit subsidies and implicit subsidies, including tax-related benefits (for example, offsets) and tolerance of arrears. Firms provide state officials with political and private benefits in the form of control rights over company decisions and bribes.

Regional and local authorities also threw themselves into the tax competition. Although a handful of taxes reaped more than three-quarters of state revenues, regional and local taxes started proliferating, because most of the major taxes were reserved for the central government, and the regional governments wanted to boost their meager revenues as well. Russia had some 200 taxes in the late 1990s, as each region invented taxes to cover its own needs. Usually, these taxes were highly cumbersome and inefficient, typically licensing fees or penalties (McKinsey Global Institute 1999). The regions had no incentive to deliver additional funds to the center. Kravchuk (1999) found that the marginal tax effect on a Ukrainian regional government exceeded 100 percent. Economically devastating extortionary raids that disrupted the work of enterprises were most lucrative to regional treasuries.

This overcentralized fiscal system seems too dysfunctional to last. Shleifer and Treisman (2000) drew the logical conclusions for Russia, arguing for a system of full-fledged fiscal federalism with separate tax bases, taxes, and tax services for the center, the regions, and the municipalities. Each level of government should be fully in charge of certain taxes, and the responsibilities for various kinds of expenditures should be clearly divided between various levels of government. Actual developments are proceeding in this direction, but very slowly.

For too long, the IMF and other Western agencies resisted tax cuts until tax administration had improved, but the tax administration could not improve much when actual taxes were confiscatory. A new tax philosophy evolved after expenditures had been slashed. One country after the other rethought its taxation, opting for fewer, lower, and flatter taxes because it made no sense to have many taxes that bred corruption and little revenues but hampered growth. This wave of tax reforms did not come from the West but from the East.

Personal income taxes were insignificant under communism. As transition started, virtually everybody wanted to raise income taxes for a mixture of social democratic ambitions, populism, and aspirations to tax people more. Hungary had a progressive income tax rising to 60 percent, but Ukraine raised its maximum personal income tax to 90 percent in 1994. As hyperinflation had boosted nominal incomes, this marginal tax rate applied to people who earned as little as $100 a month (Dąbrowski et al. 2000). Needless to say, no Ukrainian paid that tax.

Gradually, the flat tax revolution originating in Estonia in 1994 started spreading. The big breakthrough was Russia's introduction of a flat income tax of 13 percent in 2000, which led to a big boost in revenues from personal income taxes. In 2004, Ukraine followed. Slovakia introduced three flat taxes of 19 percent for personal income tax, corporate profit tax, and VAT. After a right-wing electoral victory in Romania, that country did one better in 2005, introducing a flat personal income tax, corporate profit tax, and VAT of 16 percent. President Akaev in Kyrgyzstan enacted flat tax rates of 10 percent for both corporate profits and personal income, but he was blocked by the IMF, which feared falling tax revenues. These low tax rates were introduced eventually, but only in 2006, after Akaev had been ousted in the Tulip Revolution of March 2005. The Baltics have slightly reduced their flat income tax to about 24 percent.[4] Meanwhile, corporate profit taxes in East-Central Europe have generally fallen to 15–19 percent, and tax competition is proliferating in the region. Still, in Central Europe, most taxes remain high. In Poland, the payroll tax is 48 percent, and the progressive income tax reaches 40 percent.

Despite a slow start, most of the postcommunist region has realized that it can no longer live with West European taxation. It needs fewer, simpler, lower, and flatter taxes than Western Europe. Low flat income taxes and corporate profit taxes are proliferating. Only after taxes have been reduced and simplified can tax administration be reformed.

Monetary Policy: From Loose to Strict

With transition, money became real. Reformers identified three broad tasks for monetary policy: to strengthen the central banks, to restrict the issue of money, and to move from administrative measures to market-oriented instruments. Monetary policy went through swift and complete transformation, from black to white, turning from very loose to quite strict.

Central banks faced problems similar to those of ministries of finance. In the old socialist system, the central bank was a subordinate agency for the distribution of credit and cash. Central banking was not distinct from commercial banking because the central bank issued credits directly to enterprises.

In line with the prevailing macroeconomic orthodoxy, reformers wanted to grant the central bank autonomy from both government and parliament, which had a habit of ordering the issue of money. Although the chief reformer was mostly the minister of finance, central banks reformed faster than ministries of finance. One reason was their relative independence from the state administration, which allowed their chairmen and staff comparatively safe tenure. As they were self-financing, central banks had substantial resources, permitting them to offer high salaries and attract more qualified staff, forming an elitist corps d'esprit. Western central banks offered their new colleagues effective technical assistance and good training. Many

[4] The IMF remains skeptical of flat income taxes (Keen et al. 2006).

chairmen of central banks had long tenures and became the heroes of stabilization in their countries (for instance, in the Czech Republic, Hungary, Romania, Latvia, Ukraine, and Kyrgyzstan). Russia, by contrast, illustrated the problem with an independent central bank without accountability. Thrice Chairman of the Central Bank of Russia, Viktor Gerashchenko,[5] issued more money than anybody else, causing both high inflation and currency collapse, while stalling banking reforms. His generous credits enriched so many privileged that his popularity in the elite was guaranteed.

Another priority was to stop direct commercial credits by the central bank to enterprises. In 1990, only Hungary and Poland did so, and direct enterprise credits remained substantial in most CIS countries until 1995. All CIS countries started with very low old Soviet interest rates of just a few percent, while reformers wished to raise real interest rates to a positive level and have the Central Bank interact with the commercial banks only through refinancing and open market operations (De Melo and Denizer 1999).

The money supply exploded in the early transition, and so did inflation. The high inflation led to sharp demonetization. It was used by the establishment to advocate more emission of money, although emission only increased the supply of money, not the demand. In 1989, the volume of money (M2) to GDP was 55 percent in Central Europe and the Soviet Union compared with 75–80 percent in the West. At face value, this ration looked sensible, but much of the socialist savings was involuntarily because people could find nothing to buy as a result of shortages. It was impossible to estimate how much money people would like to hold when shortages had disappeared. In addition, inflation undermined the confidence in money as a store of value and thus reduced the demand for money (Boone and Hørder 1998; De Melo and Denizer 1999). As high inflation persisted while interest rates remained low, hard currency or commodities proved better stores of values. After three to four years of high inflation, the ratio of M2 to GDP had fallen to 8–20 percent in most CIS countries (EBRD 1997, 1999, 2000).

Yet after a few years, one country after another suddenly went from soft to strict monetary policy. Temporarily, many countries opted for extremely high real interest rates – 150 percent a year in Russia and even 200 percent a year in Ukraine in 1996. They stayed high for long in many CIS countries because of sizable fiscal deficits, and treasury bonds crowded out private investment. People had learned that a loose monetary policy was socially costly, as massive cheap credits made production plummet. Another explanation of this sharp turnaround was that the benefits of cheap credits had dwindled. As demonetization proceeded, the seignorage or inflation tax

---

[5] His first term was at the UUS Gosbank.

declined because people and enterprises were no longer willing to hold much money. The beneficiaries proceeded to other forms of rent seeking, rendering high real interest rates politically possible (Åslund et al. 1996). Instead, the high yields of treasury bills became a new boondoggle (Treisman 1998).

Entrepreneurial but Problematic Banking Systems

The socialist economies had institutions called banks, but that was an undeserved compliment, because they merely carried out payments and distributed credit on government command to state enterprises (Begg 1996). State credits were seen as subsidies. Unfortunately, state banks outlived socialism. Their decisions remained politicized. They had no staff or relevant information system for credit assessment, and economic trends were enigmatic. In the absence of both skills and information, bankers gave political and personal preference to large state enterprises, which were least likely to do well. Adding corruption to this cocktail of misallocation, the bank system was dysfunctional.

Banks developed very differently in Central and Southeast Europe on one hand and in the Baltics and the CIS on the other. In Central Europe, the old state banks remained dominant, while new small private banks, usually specialized, business-oriented banks, evolved slowly. In most CIS countries and the Baltics, state banks were so bad that their role soon dwindled. Instead, hundreds of new commercial banks mushroomed in the last years of the Soviet Union. In January 1992, Russia alone had 1,360 banks registered, and their number peaked at more than 2,500 in 1994 (Johnson 2000, pp. 7, 27). These banks were subject only to the most rudimentary regulation. They had been set up under the Soviet Law on Cooperatives of May 1988 and thrived on cheap credits issued in competition by the Soviet State Bank and the Central Bank of Russia. As Grigory Yavlinsky put it: "Usually banks attract deposits from the population and give credits to enterprises, but our banks take money from the state and put it into bank accounts in Switzerland."[6] These banks were designed as rent-seeking vehicles, and many were "pocket banks" of enterprises, rich individuals, or old ministries (Johnson et al. 1993; Dmitriev et al. 1996; Johnson 2000).

Almost all countries in the region have gone through bank crises. One cause was that customers went bankrupt, another that banks miscalculated currency risks, borrowing in hard currency and giving credits at home in local currency or buying treasury bonds. Corruption and incompetence were contributing factors. New bankers made easy fortunes on high inflation

---

[6] Statement at the World Economic Forum in Davos in 1999.

in the early transition, but they suffered from stabilization. As commercial banks were collapsing, the government had to make two important choices: whether to bail out banks and whether to give priority for state banks.

Big bank crashes started in Hungary, and they led to excessive recapitalization by the state, which was soon repeated and became costly (Bonin and Schaffer 1995). When Hungary finally put its public finances into order in 1995, the government sold all the remaining state banks to foreign investors. That helped. Hungarian banks became transparent, competitive, service-oriented, and cautious, probably the best banks in the region. The large-scale admission of international banks solved the bank morass.

Once again, Estonia offered a contrast to Hungary. After its vigorous stabilization, Estonia faced a major banking crisis in late 1992. As usual, it went for a radical solution. Its commercial banks were forced to accept truly hard budget constraints. Revealing extensive fraud, the Bank of Estonia closed and bankrupted the country's three biggest commercial banks. The shareholders lost everything, and the depositors received only partial compensation because they had bet on high interest rates while facing a wide choice of interest rates differentiated by risk (Hansson and Tombak 1999). Almost all major banks in the Baltics were sold to foreigners, as in Hungary.

Surprisingly, most CIS countries followed the Balts in their severe treatment of failing banks, closing down most large post-Soviet banks. Even Ukraine closed scores of banks with little compassion for the bankers. Politically, this was possible because the banking system was not very important to the economy. With so limited monetization and credit volume, the banks lacked political leverage, and even weak governments dared to bankrupt banks. The newly rich bankers were widely disliked. The independence of central banks helped. The combination of little economic damage and limited state largess to banks rendered bank crises in the region much less costly than in other parts of the world (Hausmann and Rojas-Suarez 1996). A positive result of the fast bank expansion was that ATM machines spread like wildfire through Russia, and credit cards became widely used, developing technical sophistication in payments.

Since the completion of financial stabilization at the end of the 1990s, the postcommunist banking system has developed fast and amazingly well. Credit and deposit volumes have exploded, and the gap between lending and borrowing rates has shrunk. A new gap has opened up between Russia, which remains dominated by state banks, and most of the other countries, which have predominantly private and foreign-owned banks. The explanation is that during its financial crash in 1998, the Russian government discriminated in favor of state-owned banks. As a consequence, Russia is less monetized than Ukraine or Kazakhstan, and the Russian banking system is far less dynamic.

Capital Flight

Capital flight became a big theme in the discussion of Russia's transition. Ukraine and Kazakhstan had similar capital flight, although it was more limited in other countries. Common estimates put the capital flight from Russia at about $20 billion a year, starting in 1991. The origin of the capital flight was underinvoiced commodity exports, mainly oil and metals. This private windfall was kept in banks in offshore havens.

Capital flight went through three stages. In the initial capital flight, state managers were stealing from state enterprises through transfer pricing and evading export tariffs. Besides, they wanted to escape the unstable Soviet ruble. In 1994–5, the capital flight from Russia abated with the reduced gains on commodity arbitrage and the onset of stabilization.

A second wave of capital flight started in 1996, as the tax pressure increased and tax evasion became essential. Transfer pricing for commodities continued, because new managing owners wanted to defraud not only the state but also the other owners.

A third wave followed because of lacking confidence in local currencies and Russian banks after the bank crash of August 1998. Nobody wanted to keep more money than necessary for transactions in Russian banks. Similarly, the 1998 devaluation deterred everybody from keeping local CIS currencies for years. The so-called Bank of New York scandal that absorbed U.S. media in the fall of 1999 was a reflection of sensible Russians transferring their money holdings abroad, which the Russian state tried to prohibit in vain.

Joseph Stiglitz (1999a, 2006) has blamed capital flight on these countries' early introduction of convertibility and deregulation of capital markets, but this is incorrect. Capital flight ballooned in Soviet times in 1991, when full currency regulations were in force. Russia introduced convertibility on current account in June 1996 and Ukraine in May 1997, but currency regulation was in fact severe (EBRD 1997). Only in July 2006 did Russia introduce full convertibility. Deregulation of capital markets and convertibility were not the causes of the capital flight but vice versa. The huge capital flight necessitated the deregulation of capital flows.

Exchange Rates: Currency Board or Free Float

At the outset of transition, exchange rate policy was a major theme. Most radical reformers advocated an exchange-rate-based stabilization, using a pegged exchange rate as nominal anchor, but others preferred the money supply as nominal anchor in a money-based stabilization, allowing the exchange rate to float.

The first task was to unify the exchange rate, because all countries started with multiple exchange rates. The public saw the black market exchange rate as the "real" rate because it was set on the market. However, the black market rate was depressed by the diversion of government funds at a subsidized official rate, the domestic monetary overhang, pent-up domestic demand for imported goods, high inflationary expectations, flight from the domestic currency in crisis, and great uncertainty. Even so, when exchange rates were unified and liberalized, the initial result was huge devaluations (Halpern and Wyplosz 1996). In Russia, the average wage was merely U.S. $6 a month by the free exchange rate in December 1991, and the level was similar in other CIS countries. The higher the initial inflation and the worse the shortages, the greater the initial devaluation was. Many economists warned against these initial market exchange rates as undervalued, complicating price stabilization (Nuti 1996). Poland, the Czech Republic, Hungary, Estonia, and Russia framed the debate.

In 1989, the Polish exchange rate fluctuated wildly before the onset of hyperinflation in October. This vacillation was perceived as an unnecessary harm, leading to the thought of pegging the Polish zloty to the U.S. dollar, Poland's informal currency. The peg would serve as a nominal anchor for macroeconomic stabilization (Granville 1990; Sachs 1990, 1992). To make the peg possible, Poland needed to replenish its depleted international reserves. The country successfully raised credits of $1 billion for a stabilization fund, which was financed by Western countries (IMF 1994c). In January 1990, Poland also made its zloty convertible on current account. It presented its peg as a temporary measure, and in May 1991, it was compelled to devalue without drama. It adopted a "crawling peg," committing itself to staying within a band of moderate devaluation, which was modified from time to time. This policy of a temporary fixing of the exchange rate and an ensuing gradual devaluation was widely acclaimed. Financial stabilization was accomplished, but Poland avoided an overvalued exchange rate (Wyplosz 1999; Nuti 1996; Rosati 1996). Poland is considered a rare successful exit from a peg (Fischer and Sahay 2000).

Another big-bang country, Czechoslovakia, also pegged its exchange rate to the U.S. dollar from January 1991, with the support of a similar stabilization fund, provided by Western bilateral financing. The peg worked well as a nominal anchor, and inflation was checked. But Czechoslovakia's inflation remained higher than in the United States or Western Europe, leading to a continuous real appreciation. The increasing overvaluation of the Czech koruna hampered exports and economic growth. In May 1997, the Czech Republic was forced to abandon its peg (Begg 1998). Slovakia pursued a similar policy with the same results. For the Czech Republic and Slovakia, the temporary peg had unintentionally become permanent as a matter of national pride. The Czech example became an argument against pegs, illustrating how easily a peg could lead to an overvalued exchange rate. Several Latin America countries had similar experiences. Their successful exchange-rate-based stabilizations bred overvaluation of their currencies, which caused balance-of-payments crises (Calvo and Végh 1999). Moreover, such stabilization provided governments with little incentive to undertake fiscal reform because the low inflation was associated with the stable exchange rate rather than with a limited budget deficits (Tornell and Velasco 1995).

As usual, Hungary made a different choice from Poland and Czechoslovakia. Having attained near-convertibility by 1989, it had little reason to rush to full convertibility. With a market-adjusted exchange rate and almost constant inflation, Hungary had no need to devalue greatly or to use the exchange rate as a nominal anchor; its sophisticated monetary policy already served as a nominal anchor. Its choice was frequent but small devaluations to limit real appreciation and stay competitive. In 1995, Hungary adopted a preannounced crawling peg to limit the uncertainty and irregularity of devaluations (Halpern 1996). This pragmatic policy was successful. Through slightly different paths, Hungary and Poland arrived at the same policy of crawling pegs maintaining a reasonably valued currency. To the international community, the Hungarian example suggested that a fixed exchange rate was not necessary as a nominal anchor. This policy was cheaper because no stabilization fund, and less international funding, was required. Poland, the Czech Republic, and Hungary all adopted inflation targeting after they had exited their pegs.

In the Baltics, Estonia took the lead as usual and went for an even more radical choice than Poland.[7] As other former Soviet republics, Estonia faced near hyperinflation in early 1992, but it wanted to minimize inflation regardless of costs and integrate with the West. It was the first country to break out of the ruble zone and establish its independent currency, the kroon, in June 1992. It adopted the so-called currency board, permanently fixing the

---

[7] Estonia was lucky to have Ardo Hansson, an American of Estonian extraction with a Ph.D. in economics from Harvard University and an associate of Jeffrey Sachs, as the leading economic advisor to the Estonian government and the Bank of Estonia for years.

exchange rate of the kroon to the German mark to facilitate macroeconomic stabilization. Estonia was also the first postcommunist country to opt for full convertibility in 1994. Lithuania carried out a similar currency reform in October 1992 and opted for a currency board in April 1994 (Hansson 1997; Berengaut et al. 1998).

The lesson from Estonia was that currency boards are suitable for small, open economies with great need for macroeconomic credibility and flexible domestic markets, but a fixed misaligned exchange rate, as well as the Balassa-Samuelson effect, could lead to protracted inflation as in the Baltics, or squeeze exports as in the Czech Republic. In 1996, when Bulgaria entered a severe macroeconomic crisis, the IMF prescribed a currency board to restore its credibility. Similarly, the international community conceived of a currency board for Bosnia in 1998 (Minassian 1998). For large countries, such as Russia and Ukraine, however, it seemed inappropriate that the balance of payments would determine the money supply. Besides, it was difficult to mobilize reserves covering the whole money supply, to abstain from central bank policy, and to commit credibly to a balanced budget. The absence of a lender of last resort was also a concern (Williamson 1995; Berengaut et al. 1998).

Russia and the other CIS countries presented a very different drama. As Russia was preparing for a big bang in early 1992, Jeffrey Sachs (1995a) campaigned for a $6 billion stabilization fund for the pegging of the ruble. However, international support was not forthcoming, and the idea of further stabilization funds fell off the table as neither economically appropriate nor possible to finance. With minimal international reserves and little credibility, Russia and most CIS countries had no choice but to let their exchange rates float by default. Although the ruble's nominal exchange rate plummeted, the ruble underwent a substantial real appreciation. As stabilization was approaching in early summer 1995, even the nominal exchange rate started rising, causing worries about destabilizing exchange rate vacillation. The Russian authorities responded by introducing a broad currency band in July 1995, which contributed to the stabilization of both prices and the exchange rate. Ironically, it was too successful in attracting foreign portfolio investment because the very high domestic interest rates enticed a massive inflow of foreign funds into short-term domestic treasury bills, offering up to 100 percent a year in yield. The currency band provided a false sense of financial security, which led to too little devaluation and too soft a fiscal policy, contributing to the Russian financial crash of August 1998. The result was devaluation by 75 percent (Illarionov 1998a, 1998b). The Russian financial crash brought a lasting disrepute to currency bands and pegs, and a managed float became the favored exchange rate policy (Wyplosz 1999).

In May 2004, Central Europe and the Baltics became members of the European Union, and Bulgaria and Romania joined in January 2007. They are all supposed to join the European Monetary Union and adopt the euro in due time. To do so, they must comply with the Maastricht criteria on limited inflation, limited budget deficits (maximum 3 percent of GDP), limited debt (maximum 60 percent of GDP), and exchange rates pegged to the euro. The three Baltic states and Bulgaria have fixed exchange rates because of their currency boards, but all have too high inflation. The Central European economies have only inflation and debt ratios under control, but they have not pegged their exchange rates to the euro, and their budget deficits are excessive. They cannot adopt the euro for many years to come. The crisis of the EU after its failure to adopt the new European constitution and to impose the rules of the EU Stabilization and Growth Pact leaves the possible expansion of the euro area in a quandary.

After the Russian 1998 crash, a near consensus developed about two alternative exchange rate policies. Small open economies may opt for a currency board and eventually adopt the euro, whereas other countries are advised to let their currencies float. Yet years of stability have shaken this wisdom. The Central European countries are supposed to adopt a peg before they join euro. Moreover, does it really make sense that the small, poor CIS countries have independent national currencies with minimal financial depth?

Dramas of Financial Stabilization

A decade after the collapse of communism, inflation was under control everywhere. Inflation rates have continued to decline to the single digits. Foreign direct investment is rising steadily. Yet many countries suffered from extreme inflation for years. A myth runs thus: "All the postcommunist countries pursued similar policies aimed at curbing inflation, balancing the budget, and stabilizing the exchange rate" (Lavigne 2000, p. 18). Alas, the differences in macroeconomic policy were considerable, and the contrasting outcomes were natural consequences of these policies. Large budget deficits do nurture high inflation. A few financial stabilizations stand out: Poland 1990; Russia 1992, 1995, and 1998; Kyrgyzstan 1993; and Bulgaria 1996. Many of the facts have been discussed separately earlier in the chapter, but this section ties together the different knots.

Poland was the pioneer of transition, doing everything to control inflation. Its high inflation prompted a radical reform program. The Polish government devoted the last two months of 1989 to the double task of getting the necessary reform legislation promulgated by the parliament and of raising international financing. Both of these efforts were necessary for success, and they were accomplished thanks to the stubborn and clearheaded Minister of Finance Leszek Balcerowicz, who was rewarded by becoming the most hated man in the land. The West displayed a broad consensus on Poland from the outset, gathering in the G-24 (the then 24 members of the OECD) and pledging financing to the stabilization fund. Key elements were price liberalization, an overbalanced budget, a pegged exchange rate, an IMF standby program, substantial international funding, incomes policy, and a reasonably firm monetary policy. Still, political furor made it impossible to maintain these strict policies for long. Monetary policy eased in the summer of 1990, and the budget deficit ballooned to 7 percent of GDP in both 1991 and 1992, leading to a high inflation of 44 percent in 1992, when Poland returned to growth. Alas, in the spring of 1991 Poland failed to comply with the IMF's fiscal and monetary conditions. Consequently, the IMF suspended its disbursements for 1992 and 1993 in accordance with its rule book. Even so, or perhaps because of IMF stringency, Poland succeeded in its systemic change and stabilization, returning to economic growth first of all postcommunist countries in 1992. What was widely perceived as an excessively tough stabilization policy turned out to be wise precaution. Besides, the strong Western support for Poland was relatively cheap. The up-front cost was about $1.6 billion. Poland was a stellar example of what international support could accomplish in a postcommunist crisis (Sachs 1993).

The even more radical Estonian stabilization brought down inflation from 954 percent in 1992, to 36 percent in 1993. The currency board required a permanently balanced state budget, and it eliminated both monetary policy and public borrowing because the money supply was determined by the current account balance. The idea of a currency board arose in several quarters (Hanke et al. 1992; Hansson and Sachs 1992). Although the IMF did not initiate the currency board, it accepted the idea and provided technical assistance and insisted on adequate fiscal policies. This was a robust arrangement, creating maximum credibility both at home and abroad. Financially, the currency board was possible in Estonia because before World War II, the Estonian government had deposited its large gold reserves in Sweden, the United Kingdom, and Switzerland, and it obtained them back. The currency board and stabilization policy were introduced in a true big bang in June 1992, combined with an IMF standby program and substantial

Western financial support with great success. The currency board, together with completely free trade, minimized government interference in foreign trade, rendering Estonia the freest trader and the least corrupt postcommunist country. It attracted a large early inflow of foreign direct investment. The drawback was that inflation remained in double digits until 1998 because of the low initial exchange rate, leading to a substantial real appreciation, and the large capital inflows could not be sterilized. Again, the G-24 rose to the task and identified a financing need of $1 billion for the three Baltic States for one year, but it was more difficult to find donors this time. For such small economies, the IMF and the World Bank were constrained by their rules to pledge only $400 million. The European Union, Japan, the Scandinavian countries, and Germany saved the day with disproportionate bilateral contributions, while the United States offered no financial support (Lainela and Sutela 1994; Citrin and Lahiri 1995).[8] Although the international aid effort to the Baltics was a triumph, it revealed the West's limitations. The U.S. refusal to provide balance-of-payments support to the Baltics in 1992 marked the end of major Western aid efforts to transition countries because the Europeans were not prepared to offer financing without a U.S. share. In the future, the international financial institutions had to face the music on their own.

The abortive Russian stabilization in 1992 was heroic but partial. Its main achievement was the balancing of the budget in the first quarter, thanks to far-reaching price liberalization and cuts in military expenditures. Russia's reformer, Deputy Prime Minister Yegor Gaidar, initially slashed arms procurement by 85 percent, which eventually became 70 percent, although the military-industrial complex had been perceived as invincible (Åslund 1995). Alas, the Russian reformers failed to attract any international financing, and soon domestic political acrimony arose. The Russian reformers lacked the political muscle to undertake key reforms. First, the reformers failed to gain political control over monetary policy, and the persistence of the ruble zone warranted the competitive emission of money. Second, they lost their struggle to liberalize energy prices and exports of commodities. Third, they had no chance to abolish huge import subsidies. The outcome was near hyperinflation of 2,500 percent in 1992. Stabilization and market reform suffered a devastating blow, which reverberated throughout the whole of the CIS.

Soon after the radical reform attempt had faded in the early summer of 1992, some Western leaders woke up and realized that this attempt had been

---

[8] I was marginally involved in this fund-raising campaign on behalf of Swedish Prime Minister Carl Bildt.

genuine, but it was too late. A period of limited reforms and limited IFI financing followed from mid-1992 to October 1994. The IMF concluded several small loan agreements on soft and not very credible conditions, but Russian implementation became a persistent problem because the IFI's main Russian counterpart was no reformer but Prime Minister Viktor Chernomyrdin, an experienced Soviet industrial minister and the leader of the energy lobby. Some important structural reforms were accomplished by a few remaining reformers in the Russian government, such as the abolition of the ruble zone, import subsidies and subsidies credits, great deregulation of exports, as well as mass privatization, but no stabilization was in sight. Russians adjusted their old Soviet saying to: "We pretend to reform, and they [the IMF] pretend to finance us."

The other CIS countries watched Russia closely. They saw how spectacularly Russia failed in 1992, and they concluded that if even Russia could not attract international financial support and accomplish price stabilization, they had no chance, so why challenge their own establishments (Akaev 2000)? Their only short-term hope was Russian price subsidies and subsidized credits supplied through the ruble zone. Thus, the West's refusal to support the Russian reformers brought disaster on the rest of the CIS. Their financial stabilization was delayed by a few years, and reforms were not only delayed but distorted, breeding extraordinary corruption.

The first CIS country to opt out of the ruble zone and undertake a successful financial stabilization was faraway Kyrgyzstan. It did so with an IMF program and substantial international financing in May 1993. Despite considerable expenditure cuts, it maintained a large deficit, mainly financed with international loans. As a compensation for soft fiscal policy, it pursued a very strict monetary policy with high positive real interest rates. Because of scarce reserves, its exchange rate was left floating. Kyrgyzstan's inflation declined from 1,363 percent in 1993 to 32 percent in 1995. Moldova undertook a similar stabilization later in 1993, and Armenia, Georgia, Azerbaijan, Kazakhstan, and Uzbekistan followed in 1994, Russia in 1995, and Ukraine in 1996. A problem with these stabilizations was that they relied too much on monetary policy, resulting in very high interest rates, whereas the budget deficits of most CIS countries remained excessive. Their fiscal laxity was to come back to haunt them.

Russian stabilization was renewed in 1995. In October 1994, a currency crisis woke the Russian establishment up. After the budget deficit and monetary emission had expanded excessively, the ruble exchange rate plummeted by 27 percent in a single day, and inflation shot up. Money had assumed economic significance, and this currency crisis suddenly made macroeconomic stabilization a political priority. Russia's successful privatizer, Anatoly Chubais, became first deputy prime minister for macroeconomic policy. The Russian government sharply reduced the budget deficit and concluded its first full-fledged standby agreement with the IMF in April 1995. With the authority of real financial support, Chubais won the intragovernmental struggle over the reduction of subsidies and the elimination of tax exemptions for privileged lobbies. By the summer of 1996, financial stabilization had been attained, and inflation dropped to 22 percent (Åslund 1999).

Many factors made the Russian stabilization of 1995 possible. First, the initial transition rents from high inflation had shrunk because subsidized credits and import subsidies were gone, and export rents were small. Second, the currency crisis of October 1994 created a political momentum for reform. Third, the emission of treasury bills denominated in rubles had created a strong constituency for a more stable exchange rate (Treisman 1998). Fourth, the reformers in the government fought better than ever, hitting all important interest groups rather than offering them trade-offs, delivering a shock to rent seekers. Although the government was dominated by industrial lobbies, enterprise subsidies and regional transfers were cut by two-thirds. The paradigm switched from rent seeking toward profit seeking. Fifth, finally the Russian government and the Central Bank were pursuing a coordinated economic policy, aiming at macroeconomic stabilization, which enhanced credibility.[9] Sixth, for the first time, the IMF offered substantial credits. Its standby loan amounted to 2 percent of Russia's GDP in one year, giving the IMF substantial political weight. Finally, Gaidar's reformist party, Russia's Choice, was the largest parliamentary faction, providing the reformers with a strong base in the State Duma. All these factors taken together generated credibility.

Bulgaria's ex-communist government had undertaken a halfhearted stabilization, but in 1996, it bumbled into a serious fiscal crisis. As the budget deficit exceeded 10 percent of GDP, it could no longer service its external debt. The dominant state banks had been doling out subsidies to government cronies, which were replenished by the state budget. Eventually, however, the state had to let plenty of banks go bankrupt. Because of external default, the exchange rate went into tailspin, and hyperinflation was a fact in February 1997. The GDP collapsed by 10 percent in 1996, and Bulgarians protested in the streets and democratically ousted the irresponsible ex-communist

---

[9] President Yeltsin sacked Viktor Gerashchenko as chairman of the Central Bank of Russia after the October 1994 currency crisis.

government through the ballot boxes. In 1997, Bulgaria adopted a currency board and economic polices similar to those of Estonia five years earlier, and they worked.

The Arrears Crisis

One of the most perplexing macroeconomic anomalies of postcommunist transformation has been the proliferation of arrears, barter, offsets, and other forms of nonmonetary payments. Reformers did not anticipate them, and their critics invoked the rise of arrears and barter as evidence that ordinary market economic laws did not apply to postcommunist reality.

Any attempt at macroeconomic stabilization rendered money scarce. As a consequence, enterprises tried to avoid paying anybody, piling up debts to banks and other enterprises, tax debts to the state, and wage arrears to their workers (Rostowski 1993, 1994). Their inclination not to pay showed that their incentives had changed. In the old socialist system, state banks had regularly netted out arrears by issuing credit. People were unaware that unpaid bills and their collection are normal under capitalism and that trade credits of a few months' duration were standard. They thought something was seriously wrong (Schaffer 1998).

However, there were several real problems. One was that creditors had no effective tools to extract their claims. For years, bankruptcy laws were missing. Courts were ineffective, and debt collection notoriously poor. Even so, enterprises could make sure that they were paid, mostly by insisting on prepayment (Begg 1996). Another problem was that the payment systems were rudimentary. Payments were manual and slow because ordinary mail was used. Banks lacked the capacity to service the rising number of enterprises and payments under capitalism. In Poland, this problem was resolved easily by allowing everybody to pay in cash. In the CIS countries, however, bank transfers remained compulsory to avoid tax evasion, which allowed inept and power-hungry central banks to clog the payments system for years. Commercial bankers further delayed payments to utilize their customers' money for themselves in the meantime.

A more fundamental problem was the credibility of stabilization programs. If enterprise managers assumed that no stabilization would take hold, they would be fools to pay because their debts would be inflated away. Enterprise managers collectively demanded the traditional netting out of mutual debts, as happened all over in hesitant stabilizers – Romania, Azerbaijan, Belarus, Kazakhstan, Russia, Turkmenistan, Ukraine, and Uzbekistan. They all benefited from new cheap state credits, each netting out operation-bred demands for new bailouts, while the monetary expansion boosted high inflation (Citrin and Lahiri 1995). A serious moral hazard had arisen.

A simple mechanism in the Soviet payments system facilitated collective action among enterprise managers: all bills were paid in chronological order of filing by the banks. If more credit was issued, everybody would be paid, and nobody could jump the queue, extracting a payment before the others. Therefore, all enterprises pressured government and central banks to issue more credit. Hungary and Poland had liberalized their payment systems under socialism, but it lingered for years in the CIS (Sachs and Lipton 1993). Only after the old payments system had been abolished did stabilization take hold.

The Russian Financial Crash of 1998

The greatest stabilization drama was the Russian financial crash in August 1998. At the time, it was widely perceived as the end of the market economic experiment in Russia (Lloyd 1998; Stiglitz 1999a). The idea of trying to build capitalism in Russia was condemned as absurd (Reddaway and Glinski 2001). Joseph Stiglitz (2000) blamed the IMF and the U.S. Treasury for flawed interventions. Both he and Andrei Illarionov (1998a, 1998b) saw the overvaluation of the ruble caused by the currency band as the main shortfall. Clifford Gaddy and Barry Ickes (1998) pointed to the underlying problem of extensive and rising barter, which facilitated tax avoidance and diverted tax revenues from the federal government to regional governments. Others emphasized the unsustainable fiscal deficit and all the unmanageable debt burden (Åslund 1998; Kharas et al. 2001). A proper analysis of the Russian crisis of 1998 is vital for our understanding of postcommunist transformation.

Russia's financial crisis was reminiscent of Bulgaria's. After the initial stabilization of 1995, the Russian government had irresponsibly allowed the budget deficit to rise to some 9 percent of GDP in 1996 and 1997 (see Figure 5.6). This deficit was financed with international credits and short-term domestic bonds, many of which were bought by private Western portfolio investors. Their purchases resulted in a massive inflow of portfolio investment of $46 billion, or 10 percent of GDP, into Russia in 1997 (Russian European Centre for Economic Policy 1999). This inflow boosted the exchange rate within its currency band. The Russian stock market was booming and quadrupled in value in 1996 and 1997, but investor sentiment to emerging markets suddenly reversed in the wake of the Asian financial crisis in late 1997. Contagion effects from the East Asian crisis hit Russia hard.

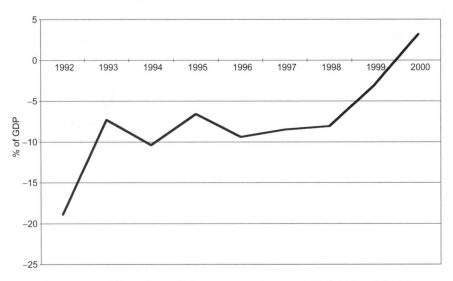

Figure 5.6. Russia's Budget Deficit, 1992–2000. *Source:* EBRD (1999) and (2004).

In March 1998, President Yeltsin unexpectedly sacked his long-time Prime Minister Viktor Chernomyrdin and replaced him with a young liberal Sergei Kirienko. It made sense to blame Chernomyrdin for having been too complacent facing the burgeoning crisis, but it took a month for Kirienko to be approved by the parliament, and another month to form a government. Furthermore, the new government seemed insouciant and unaware of the severity of Russia's financial crisis.

By May 1998, investors lost confidence in Russia's macroeconomic policies, but most of Russia's public debt was very short term, and it required persistent refinancing. As a result, yields were driven ever higher, making the Russian treasury bills appear a Ponzi game. Meanwhile, the currency inflow had turned into an outflow, which accelerated quickly. In July 1998, the IMF and the World Bank organized a substantial financial package with the prodding of the U.S. Treasury. The IMF disbursed $4.8 billion, but the Russian State Duma rejected the key fiscal measures proposed by the government as part of the IMF conditions for this loan. Russia had failed to shore up its fiscal policy, which was no longer tenable (Owen and Robinson 2003; Odling-Smee 2004).

Until August 1998, Russia managed to defend the exchange rate with its declining international reserves. Inflation was kept low, while output started decreasing because of the extremely high interest rates and the high valuation of the ruble. On top of everything, the world price for Russia's oil exports plummeted to a low of $10 per barrel. Realizing that Russia's policy improvements fell far short of what was necessary, the IMF decided not to offer any additional financial support. The U.S. Treasury concurred. By letting Russia default, the IMF reinforced its credibility. On one hand, the IMF had done its utmost to get Russian fiscal policy on a sustainable track, and it had provided substantial financing. On the other hand, when Russia evidently ignored agreed conditions, the IMF stood by its standards.

On August 17, 1998, the Russian government let the exchange rate float downward, defaulted on its domestic bonds, and declared a moratorium on foreign debt payments for 90 days. The reformist, but powerless, government of Sergei Kirienko fell within a week. The result was devaluation from 6 to 24 rubles per dollar and an inflation of 85 percent that year (Illarionov 1998a, 1998b). Yet a little-noticed fact was that Russia's current account never turned to a deficit. Russia seemed set to follow Bulgaria toward hyperinflation. The economy came to a standstill, as the banking system closed down for several days. Now the queues were outside the banks instead of the grocery stores. Russians lost their ruble and bank savings once again.

But soon events took a different turn. In the absence of both domestic and international financing, the government was forced to eliminate its budget deficit, sharply reducing expenditures as well as arrears. The profligate regional governments suddenly faced a hard budget constraint, forcing them to cut enterprise subsidies. The default on the domestic debt reduced total public debt substantially, and the devaluation led to a competitive undervaluation of the ruble. Because the government had chosen to devalue when international reserves remained substantial (about $10 billion), no large foreign loans were needed to replenish reserves. The worst half of the banks closed down, and the payment system improved. At long last, the Russian economy faced the shock therapy that its reformers had failed to deliver because of insufficient political credibility. Russia took a decisive step to defeat rent seeking and cement a profit-seeking market economy with a reasonably level playing field. Russia's opening to short-term international financial flows exposed the country to the vagaries of world financial markets, which ultimately forced Russia to accept their discipline. With its open economy, Russia had little choice but to adjust to world market standards.

Russia's fundamental macroeconomic problem was its large budget deficit. The federal tax revenues were small because most of the revenues stayed with the regional governments. In July 1998, the Russian government tried to transfer more regional revenues to the federal budget, but a triumvirate of forces defeated the government in the State Duma. The regional governors refused. Many politically influential oligarchs ignored to pay taxes, and the communist-dominated majority in the State Duma regularly voted for more public expenditures, neglecting revenues. Although the reform-oriented Kirienko government was formally responsible, these three groups dominated the Duma. Because they were the obvious villains, they lost most of their political power to the federal government in the next few years (Citrin and Lahiri 1995; Åslund 1999; Komulainen and Korhonen 2000).

The diversion of federal tax revenues to regional governments and businesspeople was facilitated by the rise of barter. Contrary to expectations, barter had steadily expanded from a nadir in May 1992, when barter accounted for only 4 percent of industrial sales, to peak at 54 percent in August 1998 (*The Russian Economic Barometer* 2000). Barter was most prominent in industry and construction, whereas little barter was used in the consumer or service sectors. Stabilization was not a cure, but nor had the abundant emission of money been helpful, so monetary policy was not the issue. One idea was that barter had been inherited from the old system, but it had risen during the transition. It could be seen as another transitional distortion. The masters of barter trade were big companies selling natural gas, electricity, metals, and construction materials, which could all be sold on the market (Aukutsionek 1998).

The main answer to the enigma of rising barter was delivered by Gaddy and Ickes (1998). They showed that different companies and the state had an interest in the development of a virtual economy. Enterprises that failed to sell their produce for real money resorted to barter, but enterprises selling valuable goods also did so because they could extract tax discounts from the state through barter. Barter prices were inflated by 40–50 percent, facilitating manipulations. An offset usually implied that a government agency accepted payment in kind instead of money. By not paying taxes, enterprises extracted public contracts at favorable prices, often for unplanned construction projects. A variety of absurd legal rules, such as restrictions on sales below prime cost, were avoided. Regional governments could formally fulfill their tax collection targets and increase their share of total tax revenues through offsets. Both loss-making companies and the profitable energy companies colluded through barter and other nonmonetary transactions against the state to extract additional subsidies at the expense of the federal government and the rest of society, making clear that the cause of barter amounted to tax avoidance. Barter and offsets were just the latest fashion in rent seeking (Commander and Mumssen 1998; Gaddy and Ickes 1998; OECD 2000a).

The implicit subsidy of the participants in barter and nonpayments was great, justifying a transaction cost of 20–30 percent of the gross price (Broadman 1999). A study by Pinto et al. (1999) estimated the implicit Russian budget subsidies through barter and nonpayments at 7.6 percent of GDP in 1996, rising to 10.4 percent of GDP in 1998. Total subsidies to the Russian enterprise sector amounted to no less than 16.3 percent of GDP in 1998. Barter of this type was localized to Russia, Ukraine, and Moldova (Hellman et al. 2000).

In August 1998, barter seemed a permanent ailment of the Russian economy, but after the financial crash, barter plummeted in both Russia and Ukraine. The dominant reason was that the governments cleaned up their finances, reducing subsidies as well as government arrears. In particular, they insisted on all taxes being paid in cash and they prohibited offsets. Meanwhile, bankruptcies soared. The crash itself lent credibility to the hard budget constraints that reformers had failed to deliver because of their political weakness. It brought about a flight to quality payments, that is, money. Cash became king in the aftermath of the crisis. A change of payments meant also a switch from the rent-seeking transitional economy to a more normal market economy (Braguinsky and Yavlinsky 2000). Paradoxically, the crash convinced entrepreneurs that the market economy had come for good.

Naturally, it was wrong to depend on the sales of huge volumes of treasury bills at outrageous yields. The size of the federal debt service was unsustainable and precipitated a default (Kharas et al. 2001). It would have been preferable to devalue the ruble earlier, but until the summer of 1998 huge foreign portfolio investments were flowing into the Russian economy. The prospect of yields in the order of 100 percent a year was just too attractive. This was particularly true of the Russian banks, which had borrowed in hard currency abroad to buy Russian ruble-denominated treasury bills. Half of them would have been bankrupted by devaluation already in the late spring because of imbalance between foreign currency credits and ruble assets. The most prominent victims in the Russian bank crash of 1998 were the banks whose high quality the World Bank and the EBRD had certified and supported with international financing (Johnson 2000, p. 211). These two organizations thought postcommunist enterprises suffered from a dearth of financing, but their primary problem was, on the contrary, soft budget constraints.

In hindsight, Russia's financial crash seems an economic catharsis. Suddenly, the Russian government undertook all those measures it should have carried out in 1992. In Moscow, somebody put up posters with the text: "Nobody will help us but ourselves." What had been politically impossible for years was quickly done. The budget deficit was eliminated, and since 2000 the Russian budget has shown a significant surplus, as enterprise subsidies were cut and barter and offsets were eliminated. Social transfers were indexed at less than the rate of inflation. A larger share of the tax revenues went from the regional governments to the federal government. The fiscal cleansing paved the way for a comprehensive liberal tax reform, which reduced the number of taxes and lowered their rates, and other market reforms were carried out. Russia has let its currency float, but it has kept the exchange rate low by accumulating huge reserves, reaching $315 billion by the end of 2006. In 1999, Russia started a period of high economic growth averaging nearly 7 percent a year. The recovery was facilitated by rising oil and commodity prices. The one serious mistake in economic policy was that the bank crash was utilized for a substantial renationalization of the bank system (Owen and Robinson 2003).

The rest of the former Soviet Union looked on the Russian drama with awe. They were all hit. The Russian demand for their exports declined, as did their total exports. International financing also dried up for them. The CIS countries got frightened, and, exactly like Russia, they reduced their budget deficits and undertook long-delayed structural reforms. Since 2001, their average economic growth has been as high as 9 percent a year.

Major Lessons from Postcommunist Stabilization

The macroeconomic policies pursued by transition countries have been remarkably different, but the outcomes have also varied greatly, and they suggest several general conclusions.

First, macroeconomic stabilization was very difficult, requiring great attention and political will. The political resistance to stabilization was enormous. It came primarily from a small elite that made fortunes on inflation. The chief issue was whether the rent seekers could be brought under political control.

Second, a radical, early, and comprehensive stabilization proved the best cure, because it minimized the rent seeking connected with high inflation. The early stabilizers also excelled in institutional reforms, showing that these reforms were complementary. All the strictures of excessive focus on financial stabilization and "monetarism" were unfounded.

Third, contrary to all gradualist arguments, a prolonged period of high inflation incurred far greater costs than the process of stabilization, because high inflation precluded economic growth, whereas rent seeking transferred incomes to the wealthiest. The early stabilizers became the first growth countries. No risk of overshooting is in evidence, because no country overdid stabilization and proceeded too early to low inflation.[10] Even in relentlessly radical Estonia, inflation was as high as 29 percent in 1995, three years after its ambitious stabilization, and examples of insufficient stabilization policies abound. Inflationary inertia has been considerable (see Figure 5.3).

Fourth, large fiscal deficits had to be eliminated. Otherwise, these time bombs exploded and devastated the economy. An early shift to a strict budgetary policy was vital for successful financial stabilization. The key to fiscal balance was the realization that expenditures had to be slashed rather than revenues increased. An excessive fiscal deficit usually led to a financial crisis, which necessitated more severe budget cuts at a higher social cost. Successful expenditure cuts were targeted. Enterprise subsidies were the critical stumbling blocks. In most countries, they could be cut only after a severe financial crisis. Social transfers are much more difficult to cut in democratic states, and excessive social transfers have become a lasting handicap of Central Europe. Since 2000, the whole postcommunist world, apart from Central Europe, has impressed with nearly balanced state budgets (see Figure 5.4)

Fifth, public expenditures have remained too large in most transition countries (see Figure 5.5). Not a single country has small public expenditures by international standards. One of the greatest shortfalls in fiscal policy has been lacking emphasis on expenditure cuts. Only the Baltic governments intentionally slashed them from the outset. Other countries have done so after protracted stagnation or severe crises. Today, Central Europe is stalemated by excessive public expenditures. Cuts of public expenditures have generated not only macroeconomic balance but also economic growth, and they have limited the damage caused by corruption.

Sixth, the breakup of the ruble zone was a necessary precondition for any stabilization in the former Soviet Union. This common currency zone generated monetary irresponsibility because of the competitive emission of money. Its perseverance for more than one and a half years after the collapse of the Soviet Union was probably the greatest single mistake in transition. Belonging to the ruble zone in 1993 is a dividing line between success and failure in the early transition.

Seventh, ordinary macroeconomics applied perfectly well to the transition countries. More vigor and rigor were needed for stabilization in postcommunist countries than elsewhere, because of the weakness of institutions. Moreover, rent seeking was outlandish, and the powerful old elite utilized all possible means to perpetuate it. Both factors complicated macroeconomic

---

[10] Azerbaijan and Armenia recorded deflation in 1998, but that was long after their stabilization.

stabilization, especially in weak states. After a few years, however, most rents had dissipated, and businesspeople could be persuaded to switch from rent seeking to profit seeking.

Finally, the IMF has played a crucial role in macroeconomic stabilization in transition countries. No country has stabilized and undertaken market reforms without the assistance of the IMF, both with financing and technical advice.

If no serious fiscal adjustment is undertaken, financial crises erupt. They involve large social costs, but they are highly pedagogic both to the elite and the population. If people cannot learn from the bitter experiences of others, they have to go through purgatory themselves. Crises lead to the political activation of people as in Poland in 1989, and in Bulgaria and Romania in 1996. They render hard budget constraints credible for governments and enterprises. Crises force governments to make sound fiscal adjustments and render necessary expenditure cuts politically possible.

Initially, the transition countries had limited current account deficits because so little international funding was forthcoming. With financial stabilization and the opening of their economies, substantial international financing has been forthcoming, and many countries have sustained large current account deficits for many years. The Baltic star performers have average current account deficits around 10 percent of GDP, and Central and Southeast Europe had 7 percent of GDP in 2005 (see Figure 5.7). As long as these deficits are financed with foreign direct investment and other forms of long-term equity investment, even large deficits are sustainable. The CIS countries have had small current account deficits since 2000, partly because they could not obtain large foreign credits any longer and most attract limited foreign direct investment.

Amazingly, public debt has declined to such an extent that it is no longer a concern in all but the poorest CIS countries and Hungary. For total foreign debt, including the private sector, trends are diverse. The Baltic countries that have no net public debt have attracted all kinds of international finance, especially loans to foreign-owned subsidiary banks by their parent company, swelling their external debt. The CIS governments are still shocked by the 1998 crisis and are steadily reducing their external public debt, which also reduces their total foreign debt. In addition, their debt to GDP ratio has declined because their GDPs in dollar terms have risen with substantial real appreciations. As private inflows increase, their external debt will rise. Central and Southeast Europe offer a middle path with a rather constant external debt (see Figure 5.8).

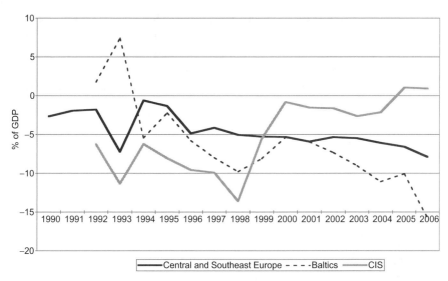

Figure 5.7. Current Account Balance, 1990–2006. *Source:* International Monetary Fund (2007).

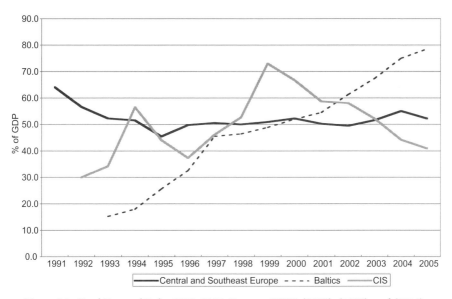

Figure 5.8. Total External Debt, 1991–2005. *Sources:* EBRD (1999), (2000), and (2006).

A general observation in the economic growth literature is that financial depth is beneficial for economic growth (e.g. Levine and Renelt 1992). In the early transition, by contrast, the correlation between financial depth and economic growth was negative. The explanation is that growth is spurred by hard budget constraints that activate supply, and hard budget constraints arise when money becomes scarce. Remonetization is still under way. When it is complete, the usual positive correlation between financial depth and economic growth might emerge.

6

Privatization: The Establishment of Private Property Rights

The postcommunist privatization was unprecedented. In one incredible decade, more than 150,000 large and medium-size enterprises, hundreds of thousands of small firms, and millions of apartments and houses have been privatized (Djankov and Murrell 2002).[1] The private sector went from being nearly nonexistent to producing almost two-thirds of GDP. This was the most fundamental change brought about by the transition.

Strange as it may sound today, the privatization of public enterprises was a novelty that was introduced by British Prime Minister Margaret Thatcher after her election in 1979, and President Augusto Pinochet in Chile at about the same time. The United States did not start advocating privatization abroad until 1985 (Williamson 1990), and the now abundant privatization literature started in 1987.[2]

Nothing aroused more passion than privatization. It involved everything – politics, law, justice, morals, and economics. It was the fundamental dividing line between a socialist and a capitalist society. No obvious precedent existed for such a profound transformation. Thatcher had leisurely privatized less than a dozen enterprises a year. Such a pace would have condemned the postcommunist countries to socialism for many years to come. This need for novel approaches contradicted one of the radical reformers' battle cries, "no more experiments." Privatization also provoked emotions because it was so concrete and visible. All people wanted their own piece of property for living or work ("I want to own my house!"). This concreteness confused people about the value of enterprises. As state factories were badly

---

[1] Useful review articles that are general sources for this chapter are European Bank for Reconstruction and Development (1999), Havrylyshyn and McGettigan (2000), Megginson and Netter (2001), and Djankov and Murrell (2002).

[2] However, the concept of reprivatization was coined in Nazi Germany in 1934, and it became topical after the collapse of the Nazi system (Bel 2006).

managed, obsolete, and overstaffed; many were worthless smokestacks, but few understood that.

The nationalization of the means of production was one of the most sacred Marxist-Leninist dogmas. Nobody in the communist world dared to discuss large-scale privatization seriously until 1988.[3] Then, however, a consensus quickly formed that privatization was both necessary and urgent in that "public enterprises are inefficient because they address the objectives of politicians rather than maximize efficiency" (Boycko et al. 1995, p. 109). In the East, popular disillusion with public enterprises was extraordinary. In contemporary Russian, *kolkhoz* (collective farm) is a synonym for chaos. Suddenly, the question was not whether to privatize but how.

"Private" might appear an obvious concept, but it is not. Most postcommunist countries require 70 percent private ownership to classify an enterprise as private because the state possessed additional levers as owner. Even so, in numerous companies, the state has retained a "golden" share, granting it a veto, undermining the rights of other owners. Privatization was often encumbered with government restrictions, forbidding a new proprietor to change the profile of a shop, lay off workers, choose suppliers, change its interior design, and so on, blurring the dividing line between deregulation and privatization.

An intense discussion erupted on privatization, and disagreements have not abated to this day as reported in section one. Privatization was discussed in three categories: small enterprises, large and medium-size enterprises, and land and real estate. Section two considers small enterprises, which were most easily privatized. The privatization of large and medium-size enterprises was the most complex assignment, attracting the fiercest disputes, discussed in section three. Section four is devoted to land reform and the privatization of real estate. These implied the largest transfer of wealth, but they aroused less national interest because they were often handled as local issues and constrained by traditional claims. Section five observes the importance of new enterprises, which was not much noticed early on. Section six discusses the relative success of various forms of privatization. Finally, overall conclusions are pondered.

Differing Aims of Privatization

It made perfect sense that the privatization debate was so intense, because no other measure had as great an impact on the formation of the new

---

[3] Astoundingly, the first substantial discussion of privatization even in Poland was Dąbrowski et al. (1989).

society. The most fundamental goal of privatization was political – to divide enterprises from the state, which was the very foundation of democracy and pluralism. The second goal was to build the foundation of a market economy. This required independent enterprises, and they could be nothing but private. A third major issue was justice. Finally, initial claims to ownership and actual control over property constrained privatization. On the basis of all these considerations, national privatization strategies were formed.

The Political Goal: Depoliticization of Enterprises

The dominant political aim of the reformers was to break up hegemonic state power and make private ownership the foundation of freedom and democracy, inspired by Friedrich Hayek's *The Road to Serfdom* (1944/1986, p. 78), "the system of private property is the most important guarantee of freedom, not only for those who own property, but scarcely less for those who do not."

Maxim Boycko, Andrei Shleifer, and Robert Vishny (1995), the main thinkers behind the Russian privatization, published a brief but forceful book, *Privatizing Russia*, which served as a lucid handbook for privatization. Their view was that "at least in Russia, political influence over economic life was the fundamental cause of economic inefficiency, and that the principal objective of reform was, therefore, to depoliticize economic life. Price liberalization fosters depoliticization because it deprives politicians of the opportunity to allocate goods. Privatization fosters depoliticization because it robs politicians of control over firms" (pp. 10–11). Under communism, managers had been selected and promoted by political criteria. The only cure was to separate politicians from property: "In our view, controlling managers is not nearly as important as controlling politicians, since managers' interests are generally much closer to economic efficiency than those of politicians. Once depoliticization is accomplished, the secondary goal of establishing effective corporate governance can be addressed" (p. 65).

The state could not be separated from enterprises once and for all, because the state easily reemerged in many shapes. Reformers saw a threat in industrial ministries, but they were defeated with surprising ease in Hungary, Poland, and the former Soviet Union by an alliance of reformers and state enterprise managers. Even so, numerous proposals for new holding companies, reminiscent of the old ministries, recurred for years. The networks between regional officials and state enterprise managers were strong and tenacious. The worst opponents of reform were the natural monopoly ministries, which stayed largely unified.

Another important liberal political objective was to build a new middle class of educated and property-owning people. For this reason, Václav Klaus (1994) and Yegor Gaidar (2000) favored voucher privatization as well as new startups.

In the end, "privatization is a political process, reflecting the art of the possible" (Kaufmann and Siegelbaum 1996, p. 439). Politically, one scheme of privatization could not be rammed through, and little legal privatization occurred until a broad coalition had been formed, built on a compromise between the strong claims of many stakeholders, such as managers, employees, ministerial officials, and regional officials. The key to successful reforms was to establish consent among these interests (Boycko et al. 1995). The strength of these demands varied with country, prior legislation, and the distribution of power, and privatization schemes had to adjust accordingly. In most cases, only stakeholder privatization could be undertaken, but it contradicted the aspirations of effective corporate governance, because the leading stakeholders were incumbent managers and employees, who were widely considered the least suitable owners of large companies. This circumstance complicated postcommunist privatization. A cure to any initially problematic distribution of property rights was to make shares freely tradable.

The Key Economic Goal: Building the Foundation of a Market Economy

Privatization had at least seven major economic objectives.

A well-functioning market economy. The foremost aim of privatization was to build the foundation of a well-functioning market economy and breed new private enterprises. Czech Minister of Privatization Tomáš Ježek (1997, p. 480) put it succinctly: "the primary purpose of privatization in Czechoslovakia was not to increase the efficiency of particular companies, but to create market structures to encourage private businesses. Fundamentally, this meant that privatization sought to bring about an essential transformation of the role of the government in the economy." Ludwig von Mises's (1920/1972, p. 81) profound truth came home to roost: "Socialism is the abolition of rational economy. . . . Exchange relations between production-goods can only be established on the basis of private ownership of the means of production." No clear line delimits a socialist economy from a capitalist economy, but no Western economy has a public sector that produces more than one-third of GDP. Increasing empirical evidence shows that on average private and privatized enterprises outperform public enterprises all over the world (Megginson et al. 1994; Megginson and Netter 2001). Although this was true even in Western countries with well-run public corporations, the situation was obviously far worse in the former socialist countries where the mismanagement of public enterprises was notorious and obvious to the naked eye.

Enterprises needed real owners. A leading theme in the socialist reform debate was that state enterprises had no real owners. Under Gorbachev a prominent slogan was that enterprises must be given real "masters" (*khozyayeva*). The conclusion was that only privatization could establish real owners.

Companies had to be made independent. State enterprises were linked to one another through multiple networks imposed by the state. Privatization was needed to break enterprises free from such noneconomic considerations and make them truly independent of one another. As Kyrgyzstan's President Askar Akaev (2000, p. 47) stated: "Efficiency is primarily determined by the market structure and the development of competition. The main goals of privatization are, therefore, to change property relations, to form the market structure and to reinforce competition." Foes of privatization tried to argue that competition and demonopolization were more important than privatization (Bogomolov 1996; Stiglitz 1999a), but no such contradiction existed. No competition agency succeeded in breaking up state enterprises, but this occurred on a mass scale in the privatization process (Slay 1996).

Privatization helped impose hard budget constraints on enterprises. Although governments may also give subsidies to private firms, state enterprises receive more subsidies (European Bank for Reconstruction and Development [EBRD] 1999). Politically, it is much easier to defend subsidies to public corporations. Socialist countries were littered with rundown and malfunctioning factories, which often crowded out new enterprises and polluted city centers. Even today, a huge old power station fumes opposite the Kremlin. A key goal was to facilitate the exit of such obsolete enterprises, and the entry of new firms to accomplish Schumpeter's (1943/1976) creative destruction. A hard budget constraint was a precondition and bankruptcy the ultimate verdict. For years, few companies went bankrupt, but many were compelled to sell underutilized assets, creating an asset market and breeding new enterprises.

Enterprise restructuring and corporate governance. Although the effects of privatization on the economic system are most important, analysts of privatization have been preoccupied with the narrow topic of enterprise restructuring and corporate governance. Enterprise restructuring is typically categorized as the improvement of allocative efficiency (the reallocation of resources from old to new activities) and X-efficiency (restructuring within surviving firms) (Blanchard 1997). Only strong owners (principals) could control and motivate managers (agents). Obviously, one single powerful owner was ideal from this perspective, whereas highly dispersed ownership to the public was considered dangerously ineffective. The dominant view was that outside owners were economically preferable, but inside ownership dominated and employees with their many disparate interests were unlikely to focus on profitability. Another risk was that their property rights could be usurped by their manager. Western experts have persistently emphasized the qualitative superiority of foreign direct investment, involving management skills, capital, and technical know-how (Havrylyshyn and McGettigan 2000).

The creation of a real capital market. Large-scale privatization was a precondition for the creation of a real capital market, leading to a more rational allocation of capital. Most privatization schemes were not likely to engender an efficient initial structure of ownership. Therefore, it was vital that small owners who had received their shares because of their employment could sell them to facilitate the accumulation of shares by strong new owners. Stock markets had to be developed early on, and they needed to be sufficiently transparent to provide meaningful corporate governance (Frydman and Rapaczynski 1994).

Investment. Although investment, especially foreign investment, was widely considered a major objective of the privatization process, confusion reigned. Many argued for sales of enterprises rather than free distribution because they wanted more investment, not realizing that such payments for enterprises were supposed to be state revenues and did not involve any real investment. Logically, reformers opposed sales because they diverted private savings to the state treasury (Ježek 1997). Furthermore, the initial hopes for foreign investment were exaggerated by the lasting communist belief that international capital was dying to enter the former communist countries.

State revenues. In the West, state revenues are usually a major reason for privatization, but this was a subordinate issue in most transition countries, where systemic change and justice dominated the debate. Considering that public corporations were usually extremely badly managed and the enterprise environment was hazardous, their market value was small. The exception was Hungary, where enterprises were reasonably valuable because of prior reforms, and its patent budget deficit required financing. With few exceptions, a postcommunist government was financially better off giving its enterprises away than trying to run them itself, because only strong private owners could undertake the necessary restructuring, and annual tax revenues from successful privatized enterprises soon dwarfed the highest possible sales prices of an enterprise.

What Justice?

Privatization was a matter of justice, but four moral imperatives guiding it contradicted one another: restitution to old owners, equitable free distribution to the people, free distribution to the employees, and market sales to the benefit of the state.

Restitution. The return of property to the original owner or legal inheritors was what was meant by restitution. This principle was strongly embraced in the Baltic republics for national reasons and in East Germany because of German legal principles and West German political interests. Liberal economists, in particular Václav Klaus, objected to restitution. Many people had suffered in different ways from communism. Why compensate for the loss of property but not for deaths, incarceration, and so on? There were technical complications too. Communists, World War II, and fires had sometimes destroyed documented titles of land. Nor was the legal system prepared to handle all claims. In East Germany, which instantly imported both legislation and courts from West Germany, some 2 million claims were presented, clogging the courts for years and stopping thousands of construction projects because of uncertain legal claims. Some restitution occurred in most Central European countries, particularly of farmland and real estate, whereas the restitution of medium-size and large enterprises was avoided. In the CIS, restitution was hardly an issue, because communism there had lasted for more than seventy years (Frydman and Rapaczynski 1994; Klaus 1994; World Bank 1996a).

Property distribution through privatization. The moral upshot from the conclusion that the suffering under communism could not be assessed was to distribute all property evenly to the whole population through mass privatization. All citizens could be given vouchers with claims to state property, and the state could auction property for vouchers. Milton Friedman is credited as the originator of voucher privatization, whereas in Russia this idea was broached by the neoliberal Moscow economist Vitaly Naishul, who wrote a book on voucher privatization in 1987 (Chubais 1999). Václav Klaus became its main protagonist in the postcommunist world. Opponents argued that this radical solution was communism in reverse and accused the adherents of "market bolshevism" (Glinski and Reddaway 1999).

Share distribution to workers. A more socialistic idea was the free distribution of shares to the workers of each enterprise. This view was much stronger in the Soviet Union than in East-Central Europe, and it was most popular in small enterprises, which had often been cooperatives under communism. Managers often exploited this argument to their own benefit.

Property sold at market price. A contrary, right-wing stand was that no property should be given away, but sold at a market price, because what was given for free would not be respected. Such a position was widely held in Hungary, Estonia, and Poland, where a domestic bourgeoisie had evolved before the end of communism, and the state functioned. Yet moral objections were strong because only four controversial groups possessed enough money to buy enterprises in the early transition: communist officials, organized criminals, dubious new businessmen, and foreigners. With a large supply of property but little demand, property would inevitably be sold cheaply, which would benefit those lucky to be endowed with cash. In addition, sales would require more time than mass privatization. A plausible argument was to utilize the large monetary overhang for privatization, but in practice it proved impossible to organize privatization before price liberalization had been unleashed.

In the former Soviet Union, bank savings were inflated away by massive monetary emissions under socialism and ensuing price liberalization. Those hurt demanded compensation, possibly through privatization. This option was investigated in Russia, but the state Savings Bank (Sberbank) insisted that it could not open privatization accounts for lost savings faster than after three years, which dissuaded the reformers (Chubais 1999). In Ukraine, the liberal Deputy Prime Minister Viktor Pynzenyk revisited this idea after stabilization in 1996. A law established state liability for lost savings, and valued them at 160 percent of GDP. "Compensation certificates" for lost savings were issued to be used as privatization vouchers. However, this liability would only be paid when budget means were available and this state debt was not indexed. Actual repayments have been limited to only some 0.1–0.2 percent of GDP each year, and this scheme aroused no appreciation (Yekhanurov 2000).[4]

The Specter of Spontaneous Privatization

When communism collapsed, control over enterprises varied by country. In the Soviet Union, the Law on State Enterprises of 1987 had made incumbent state enterprise managers quasi-owners by rendering them independent of the industrial ministries, which could no longer sack them. The managers controlled the enterprises but were not entitled to their cash flows (Åslund 1991). In Poland, workers' councils had assumed power, arousing parallels with Yugoslav workers' self-management, which had boosted workers' wages and state investment per worker, at the expense of high inflation

---

[4] Additional information from the International Monetary Fund.

and unemployment (Lipton and Sachs 1990b). In Hungary, workers' councils existed, but their strength was in doubt. The state and its industrial ministries remained the real owners of state enterprises in Czechoslovakia, Romania, and Bulgaria. The politics of privatization differed accordingly, but the relative strength of political groups was poorly understood in advance. The power of workers, trade unions, and industrial ministries was exaggerated, whereas the power of state enterprise managers was underestimated.

Ownership rights to an asset are usually divided into control rights and cash flow rights. Control rights encompass the rights to decide on the usage of an asset, including its sale or lease, whereas cash flow rights are the rights to the yields. The standard problem in the former communist countries was that these rights had been separated. The state formally maintained cash flow rights and part of the control rights, namely, the eventual sale; state managers had most of the control rights over state enterprises. These property rights had to be united to allow for efficient enterprise management. Otherwise, the managers' incentives were to divert the cash flow to themselves with little consideration of the cost to the enterprise (Boycko et al. 1995; Kaufmann and Siegelbaum 1996).

Incumbent state managers had already started a large-scale spontaneous privatization in Poland, Hungary, and the Soviet Union. Often a manager "leased" the state enterprise he managed, gaining control also over its cash flow. Usually, leasing gave the manager, or nominally the workforce, the right of a gradual management–employee buyout at a very low price. Managers also tapped money from "their" firms through transfer pricing. A manager sold the output of "his" state enterprise, or a part of it, to his private firm at a low price, reselling the product at a much higher price, thus seizing the whole profit from the state. Even in the Czech Republic, where the government possessed the greatest power over state enterprises, Minister of Privatization Tomáš Ježek (1997, p. 480) observed: "Managers of state-owned enterprises typically established private companies under their ownership and siphoned state-owned assets into these companies through various dubious techniques." So-called tunneling or management theft through transfer-pricing has remained notorious in most postcommunist countries. Managers often indulged in asset-stripping and stole "their" enterprises bare (Grosfeld and Hare 1991; Johnson and Kroll 1991). An early focus of privatization was to stop spontaneous privatization, which was seen as inequitable, slow, and inefficient, benefiting the incumbent managers. Reformers feared it would arouse a popular political backlash against reform, as indeed happened all over the region (Kaufmann and Siegelbaum 1996).

The urgency of privatization varied with the degree of economic and legal crisis. The Soviet Union was in a rampant economic crisis, with output in free fall and widespread lawlessness. The saying went "what is not privatized will be stolen," underlining the need for speedy privatization. In the absence of any effective state authority, a common conclusion was: "The only way of remedying the crippling inefficiency of post-socialist state enterprises is to move as fast as possible toward a genuine property regime" (Frydman and Rapaczynski 1994, p. 13).

Neither rules nor institutions for the selling of property or enterprises were in place. The only capital markets socialist countries had permitted were marginal markets for summer houses and small machinery. Hungary had a formal stock market, but it was a bogus institution at which state banks traded marginal stocks in state banks for no economic purpose. Without markets, no asset prices existed, and book prices or historical costs reflected the old distorted prices. When property markets started emerging, they were illiquid and thus haphazard, with low and arbitrary market prices (Frydman and Rapaczynski 1994). Commercial law was rudimentary, although more developed in Poland and Hungary because of their substantial legal private sectors, enabling them to opt for more complex schemes of privatization than other countries.

Naturally, no state administration for privatization existed, and the old industrial ministries were unsuitable for managing privatization, which they either opposed or wanted to exploit. Each country built up a relatively decentralized, large privatization administration, leaving most real estate and enterprises to be privatized by regional and local administrations. The privatization authorities persistently fought the old industrial ministries over control of state enterprises. Legal, commercial, or administrative expertise for privatization was lacking, and Western consultants and investment bankers did not have the right know-how. In the early 1990s, an American investment banker told me that his firm was only interested in advising on the privatization of enterprises worth $100 million or more given their fee level, but only a score of enterprises in the region were of such value.

Hungarians argued in a normal Western fashion that privatization had to be proper, creating strong owners with good corporate governance, and that the state should receive due revenues: "State property must not be squandered by distributing it to one and all merely out of kindness.... The point now is not to hand out the property, but rather to place it into the hands of a really better owner" (Kornai 1990, pp. 81–2). The precondition for such a view was that the state was in such good shape, that it was capable of managing public enterprises. Only Hungarians, Poles, and soon Estonians could share Kornai's positive view of the state: "But the state is alive and well. Its apparatus is obliged to handle the wealth it was entrusted with carefully until a new owner appears who can guarantee a safer and more efficient guardianship" (1990, p. 82). Then, speed was less significant.

In the post-Soviet chaos, however, state enterprises were subject to extraordinary theft, not least through the ongoing spontaneous privatization by incumbent managers. Privatizers also hoped to thrive on chaos, launching privatization before the old establishment had recovered and reinforced its claims on public property. Because the transaction cost and time of illicit deals were high, reformers were offered a window of opportunity, which was a strong argument for mass privatization. Their aim was to create a critical mass of private enterprise to secure the survival of a market economy. The vast unregulated public property would inevitably entice many top officials into corruption. High pace required the mass mobilization of people, which would render privatization more equitable as well. Hence, privatizers saw mass privatization as a way to regularize and speed up privatization, and all postcommunist countries but Hungary, East Germany, and Azerbaijan opted for some mass privatization (Åslund 1992; Boycko et al. 1995; Kaufmann and Siegelbaum 1996; Chubais 1999).

Choices of Privatization
Initially, the eventual scope of privatization was barely discussed. Reformers privatized in accordance with the law of the least resistance, as public property abounded. Still, a tacit understanding was that Western Europe had a public sector of "normal" size.

Some industries caused special problems. In the Czech Republic, an early debate raged over the "family silver," enterprises of emotional national value, which would not be privatized. In Russia, the kernel of the defense industry was excluded from privatization. In Ukraine, the communists specified thousands of enterprises to be excepted. Natural resources and monopolies were controversial everywhere because people feared they would be sold off too cheaply. Domestic ownership of agricultural land was treasured by peasants, who feared speculative purchases by absentee landlords. Few opposed the privatization of multiple small and medium-size enterprises and most big manufacturing enterprises. A standard compromise was to establish a list of industries or enterprises that would not be privatized for the time being.

This discussion led to a fair degree of consensus on some broad principles:

1. Privatization had to lead to real, clearly defined, private property rights.
2. The new owners must effectively control management.
3. Economic efficiency should be promoted both within the privatized enterprises and in the economy as a whole.
4. Privatization had to be socially acceptable.

On other points a choice had to be made between contradictory positions:

- Some emphasized speed, others the quality of privatization.
- Some favored insiders, and others preferred outside investors.
- Principles of justice and political convenience weighed against economic efficiency.
- Some desired swift adjustment, whereas others aspired to minimal change.

The choice of privatization method varied with the nature of the property, political situation, bureaucratic capacity, and prior claims. The five main alternatives were as follows:

1. open sales,
2. management or employee buyout,
3. mass privatization,
4. restitution, or
5. bankruptcy and liquidation.

In contrast to the strife over liberalization and macroeconomic stabilization, both reformers and rent seekers aspired to privatization. The rent seekers wanted to benefit, whereas reformers adopted all conceivable positions. The process of privatization has involved many surprises for everybody, and the inability to predict outcomes probably facilitated privatization. The drawback is that many participants now regret the outcome of privatization because they miscalculated their personal benefit – or as most of them would argue – were cheated.

Small-Scale Privatization: If Started, Swiftly Done

The most reformist countries had pioneered limited small-scale privatization of retail shops before the end of communism, and in every country small shops and kiosks were easily privatized, but it was vital to get it done.[5] Normally, small-scale privatization took off grandly, but it was not automatic. Even reformist Kyrgyzstan did its small-scale privatization as late as 1994–6, and Ukraine pursued it in 1995–6.

Several preconditions had to be in place. First of all, the government had to authorize local authorities to privatize small public enterprises because the central government lacked the necessary administrative capacity. Second, local governments needed to establish a privatization administration. Third, local governments had to decide to sell rather than lease, often persuaded by a financial squeeze. Usually, small-scale privatization was delayed until these decisions were made, but once the process started it was swiftly completed within two years because everybody realized they had to act fast to seize their share.

Before small-scale privatization, a heated discussion raged about whether shops should be sold at auctions, which liberal economists favored, or cheaply to the employees, preferred by them. Some auctions took place in many countries, but the bulk of small enterprises was sold cheaply to insiders. Auctions led to faster structural changes, not least because of fewer liens and residual regulations.

After privatization, most problems were caused by local regulations, such as short leases on premises, licenses that must be renewed each year, limited rights to change the profile of a shop, restrictions on the laying off of workers, and dependence on state wholesale trade. Although these problems arose from the lack of freedom of trade, they were often reinforced by conditional privatization. For years, no difference could be noticed between state shops and privatized shops in Moscow, whereas new private shops looked splendid. Frequently, even the staff did not know whether their shop had been privatized or not. Yet after small-scale privatization, market forces started biting. In the region as a whole, hundreds of thousands of small enterprises have been privatized, and the success of small-scale privatization is underscored by the absence of discussion about it.

Large-Scale Privatization: The Biggest Headache

Large-scale privatization was the greatest drama of transition, and it remains controversial. Here all the political, economic, and technical problems of

---

[5] Earle et al. (1994) offer an exhaustive account of this process in the Czech Republic, Hungary, and Poland, and the World Bank (1996a) accounts for the whole region.

Table 6.1. *Methods of privatization of medium-sized and large enterprises*

	Sale to outside owners	Voucher privatization (equal access)	Voucher privatization (significant concessions to insiders)	Management-employee buyouts	Other[a]
Central Europe					
Poland	Tertiary	Secondary	–	Primary	–
Czech Republic	Secondary	Primary	–	–	–
Slovakia	–	Secondary	–	Primary	–
Hungary	Primary	–	–	–	Secondary
Southeast Europe					
Romania	Secondary	–	–	Primary	–
Bulgaria	Primary	Secondary	–	–	–
Baltics					
Estonia	Primary	–	–	Secondary	–
Latvia	Secondary	Primary	–	–	–
Lithuania	–	Primary	–	Secondary	–
CIS					
Russia	Secondary	–	Primary	Tertiary	–
Belarus	–	–	–	–	–
Ukraine	–	Secondary	–	Primary	–
Moldova	Secondary	–	Primary	Tertiary	–
Armenia	–	Primary	Secondary	–	–
Azerbaijan	–	–	–	–	–
Georgia	Secondary	–	Primary	Secondary	–
Kazakhstan	Secondary	Primary	–	–	–
Kyrgyzstan	–	Primary	–	–	–
Tajikistan	–	–	–	Primary	–
Turkmenistan	–	–	–	–	–
Uzbekistan	–	–	–	Primary	Secondary

[a] Includes asset sales through insolvency proceedings and a mass privatization program based on preferential credits.
Source: European Bank for Reconstruction and Development (1997, p. 90).

privatization coalesced. The debate was lengthy and acrimonious, resulting in extensive and complex legislation.[6]

The questions were as many as they were daunting. Governments had to decide what to privatize and who should do it. A vast volume of legal acts had to be drafted and adopted by parliaments. Some enterprises were broken up first. The property of each enterprise had to be specified. Then, enterprises were corporatized, and sales were organized by special privatization committees. Often, privatization vouchers or coupons were distributed. Demand and supply had to be matched. Frequently, the legal and technical problems became so cumbersome that mass privatization was stalled for years in countries as different as Poland and Ukraine.

The design of large-scale privatization varied significantly between countries that otherwise pursued similar reforms. Typically, one country opted for one primary method of large-scale privatization but pursued other options in parallel, and failure could abort the initial choice. Most strikingly, the Polish government opted for mass privatization but could not agree on its details for years, and liquidation became a major form of privatization by default. This accidental pluralism ascertained progress in privatization.

Statistics on privatization are amazingly poor. In Table 6.1, the EBRD gives us an approximate picture of the dominant methods. Sales to outsider owners dominated only in East Germany, Hungary, Bulgaria, and Estonia. The main alternative, mass privatization with vouchers, prevailed in the Czech Republic, Russia, Latvia, Lithuania, Moldova, Armenia, Georgia, Kazakhstan, and Kyrgyzstan. Unexpectedly, management-employee buyouts were most prominent in Poland, Slovakia, Romania, and Ukraine. In Belarus and Turkmenistan, no large-scale privatization took place.

The choice of privatization strategy went through two phases. Initially, privatization was an intellectual and idealistic exercise, which gave birth to the many voucher schemes and untold harebrain schemes. Next, powerful economic and political interests were mobilized, and privatization became the art of the possible. As a consequence, the strategies that were the most equitable and the least corrupt emerged first, but over time they were downgraded to the benefit of strategies that accommodated vested interests. Out of the five major privatization strategies for large and medium-size enterprises, voucher privatization and international public offerings are, in

---

[6] The literature on large-scale privatization is enormous. The privatization programs and principles of most countries have been publicized in several anthologies. When not indicated otherwise, I have drawn the facts on the various national privatization programs from Earle et al. (1993), Frydman et al. (1993a, 1993b), Borish and Noël (1996), and Lieberman et al. (1997).

principle, transparent and involve little administrative discretion. They should generate the least corruption. Reformers fought primarily over these two options, but neither has become all that significant. Instead, the dominant privatization strategies have been management and employee privatization, spontaneous privatization, and direct sales, which offer no transparency but allow great administrative discretion. The cleanest form of privatization, liquidation, has played only a minor role, because few understood its charm. Equity has played some role, promoting voucher privatization and employee privatization as the most equitable forms of privatization.

Initial public offerings. In the West, initial public offerings (IPOs), that is, sales of stocks on the stock exchange, have been the standard form of privatization of large companies. In the 1980s, this practice was finessed in the United Kingdom, and its practitioners looked for new markets. Immediately after Poland had announced that it would privatize, half a dozen of London-based investment banks sent their missionaries to Warsaw to preach the virtues of IPOs, largely at the expense of the UK Know-How Fund.

Many sound arguments favored IPOs. First, it was the most public and transparent form of privatization, with extensive disclosure of information. Second, the privatization would be open both to the public and foreign investors. Third, outside investors would enter with the right incentives and fully entitled to restructure the company. Fourth, the pricing would be done by the market, guaranteeing the maximum revenue for the government. Fifth, corporate governance would be ideal, and IPOs would form the basis for a sound stock exchange. Yet there were serious objections. First, the required information would not be available for years, delaying privatization. Second, the cost of an IPO was so large that few enterprises could come into question. Third, IPOs could alienate the population because foreign investors were likely to dominate, and they would acquire their stocks cheaply because of the dearth of domestic capital. Fourth, existing stakeholders had no incentive to accept IPOs. Hence, IPOs could not be a major avenue of privatization (Lewandowski and Szomburg 1989; Lipton and Sachs 1990b).

In the first decade, Poland, Hungary, and Estonia undertook a score of IPOs each, but hardly anybody else did. IPOs provided an excellent foundation for the Warsaw Stock Exchange, but they became insignificant for privatization during the first decade of transition. The critics proved right: IPOs were never a feasible option for substantial privatization.

Direct sales or investment tenders. The advantages of direct sales or investment tenders were that one or a few outside owners would acquire dominant ownership and be motivated to restructure enterprises, and they could attract foreign investors. Through investment tenders, the state could demand substantial investment, and reap considerable state revenues. For certain big enterprises in need of a specialized Western owner, this was the only plausible option for survival.

The disadvantages, however, were palpable. Direct sales were not transparent, and investment tenders even less so. The many conditions that were negotiated with government officials bred maximum administrative discretion and corruption. They were the least equitable privatizations, and they offered no incentives for stakeholders who resisted them. This was the worst form of formal privatization. All countries have undertaken some direct sales and investment tenders, but they became the primary form of privatization only in East Germany, Hungary, Estonia, and Bulgaria, and they were perceived as successful merely in Hungary, Estonia, and the Czech Republic, the countries with the best public administration. Only in these countries did privatization become a substantial source of state revenues, and these countries became major recipients of foreign direct investment (FDI) per capita.

The East German privatization was presented as an extraordinary success at the time, which must be one of the greatest achievements of government propaganda on record, because the outcome is anything but impressive. The German government's Treuhand privatization agency sold 13,000 state-owned enterprises in East Germany from 1990 to 1994, surprisingly fast but at an extraordinary cost. "Prices charged for firms being sold were low, and the Treuhand often paid new owners to take over state-owned enterprises and to guarantee their future. Thus, in the course of its existence, the Treuhand took in $50 billion but spent $243 billion on privatization" (Brada 1996, p. 71). This was by far the most costly and wasteful privatization. The sales were heavily concentrated to West German companies, signifying a very closed shop. Treuhand was the world's most generous corporate welfare agent, which was apparent to outside observers early on (Akerlof et al. 1991; Brada 1996; Kaser 1996). Among other postcommunist countries, only Estonia followed the East German example, and the unpopular privatization strategy is considered to have contributed to the loss by the Estonian reform government in the 1995 elections (Åslund et al. 1996).

Looking to the east and south, the results of direct sales and investment tenders have been uninspiring. The state revenues have been insignificant, because these "sales" were akin to corrupt giveaways to the rich and powerful. Investment commitments were hardly ever substantiated. In Bulgaria, direct sales to the elite lay the ground for business empires, such as Multigroup, which contributed to the financial collapse of 1996–7. When Pavlo

Lazarenko was the prime minister of Ukraine in 1996–7, he considered the privatization of large enterprises so sensitive that he took them over himself and privatized many to his own benefit.[7] In Kazakhstan, major metallurgical assets were sold off to dubious businesspeople in discrete deals. In Russia, the infamous "loans-for-shares" sales of stocks in a dozen major companies took place in late 1995 after voucher privatization had ended and all other forms of privatization had been blocked. In particular in Russia, Ukraine, and Kazakhstan, such privatizations coincided with the evolution of large "financial-industrial groups." Still direct sales were preferable to leaving enterprises with the state. In the longer term, the economic results of the oligarchic groups improved spectacularly (see Chapter 10). The economic recovery of Russia, Kazakhstan, and Ukraine was driven by large financial-industrial groups in energy and metals. But the political reaction against the oligarchs rendered their property rights insecure.

Voucher privatization. Voucher privatization was the pet idea of liberal economists and the chief invention of postcommunism. It became the dominant form of privatization in the Czech Republic, Russia, Latvia, Lithuania, Moldova, Armenia, Georgia, Kazakhstan, Kyrgyzstan, and initially in Slovakia, but almost all countries issued some vouchers. Mass privatization through vouchers, distributed to virtually the whole population, was theoretically attractive. It was fast, and it would create a market and an equitable wealth distribution. The distribution of vouchers alleviated the shortage of domestic demand for property purchases. Because the whole population would benefit, it had great popular potential. Its administration was much less costly and complex than IPOs, since voucher auctions simplified evaluation problems. However, voucher privatizations were riddled with many practical, administrative, and political problems. Their main economic disadvantage was that they led to dispersed ownership with ineffective corporate governance.

A major dispute between reformers and managers was which enterprises, and how much of each, should be privatized through voucher auctions. In Russia, Minister of Privatization Anatoly Chubais was committed to a maximum of voucher privatization, but only 20 percent of the stocks in the 16,462 enterprises that went through voucher auctions until June 1994 were sold for vouchers, and 51 percent of the shares were usually given cheaply

---

[7] Information from the State Property Fund of Ukraine and the Ukrainian Cabinet of Ministers at the time. Lazarenko was later sentenced in the United States for having laundered some $130 million.

to managers and workers (Blasi et al. 1997, p. 192), showing how managers defeated the state. Moreover, the most attractive enterprises were usually withheld from voucher auctions (Marcinèin and van Wijnbergen 1997). As a result, people were disappointed, obtaining less than their anticipated share of national property, especially as their expectations had been exaggerated by the reformers' propaganda about the potential benefits of privatization.

Privatization involved many sensitive technicalities. Initially, the new voucher funds in the Czech Republic appeared genial, facilitating investment by ordinary people, but popular enthusiasm evaporated when the head of the biggest voucher fund eloped to the Bahamas with a considerable fortune. These investment funds were a late improvisation, and time did not suffice for their regulation. After they had emerged as major owners, they opposed regulation (Ježek 1997). Furthermore, they became closely linked to state-owned banks, reducing the impact of the privatization. In Russia and Ukraine, voucher funds emerged but just faded away, offering no benefit to their many tiny investors (Pistor and Spicer 1996). As no country managed to solve the problem of corporate governance of investment funds, it was probably insolvable.

Even so, voucher privatization made a huge contribution to privatization. Thanks to voucher privatization, two-thirds of many CIS economies were actually privatized. The alternatives were no privatization or much more corrupt privatization. In Kyrgyzstan, President Akaev (2000, p. 48) noticed with satisfaction: "The fast mass privatization allowed us to sharply restrict the informal privatization, which had been named 'Nomenklatura *prikhvatizatsiya* (grabbing).'" Initially, the Czech Republic excelled with eminent enterprise restructuring thanks to dominant outsider ownership (Frydman et al. 1997). In the long run, however, the murky nature of the Czech voucher funds might have hampered the country's economic development. Voucher privatization suffered from exaggerated popular expectations, but those expectations facilitated privatization. It has become commonplace to blame voucher privatization for any unrelated problem, including insider privatization and management theft (see Stiglitz 1999a). After 1999, however, mass privatization appears to have been the distinguishing feature of the countries with the highest economic growth (Bennett et al. 2005). A positive revision of voucher privatization appears justified. It facilitated the fastest, biggest, and least corrupt privatization at minimal administrative costs. It was also comparatively equitable, and after some delay, it has facilitated substantial industrial restructuring. Most important, the resulting property rights are widely accepted as legitimate.

Manager or employee privatization. In many countries, managers and employees had such strong claims to state enterprises that nothing but insider privatization was feasible.[8] The real choice was between giving ownership to insiders and leaving enterprises in nebulous collective ownership while subject to extensive management theft. This was true of Poland and most CIS countries. Management or employee privatization dominated in a motley group of Poland, Slovakia, Romania, Ukraine, Tajikistan, and Uzbekistan. Only the Polish privatization was geared toward employees, whereas elsewhere managers took charge. In Russia, managers typically owned about 20 percent of the stocks and employees about 40 percent after so-called voucher privatizations. In Ukraine, managers owned about 30 percent, and Georgian managers were usually majority owners (Blasi et al. 1997; Djankov 1999). The term "buyout" is a misnomer, because insiders paid next to nothing.

Insider privatization had three great advantages. It was fast. It created legitimate property rights. Administratively, it was the easiest form of privatization. Otherwise, insiders would block privatization whenever they could (Lipton and Sachs 1990a; Boycko et al. 1995). Some argued that management-employee buyouts could enhance efficiency because the incentives for managers and employees would improve (Earle and Estrin 1996; Shleifer and Vasiliev 1996). A drawback was that incumbent managers, who needed to be replaced by outsiders, were entrenched. The insiders had poor incentives to act fast, which was likely to slow down restructuring. The privatization of highly valuable companies to its managers transferred huge wealth to a privileged few. Some of the wealthiest companies in the region underwent insider privatization benefiting their managers. Outstanding examples are Gazprom and the two respected Russian oil companies, Lukoil and Surgut. These managers were allowed to get away with their booty, because they were not only strong but also considered competent, and they wisely accepted privatization. Lukoil and Surgut were initially slow to restructure, but they have accelerated.

Curiously, insider privatizations are probably the least criticized major privatizations, and a positive revision of insider privatization is also due on the same lines as the voucher privatization. The resulting property rights are widely respected, although insider privatizations are not at all equitable.

Bankruptcy and liquidation. Bankruptcy is one of the best forms of privatization, but little studied and poorly understood. First, the very threat of bankruptcy imposes a hard budget constraint on enterprises. Second,

---

[8] A general survey on employee ownership is Uvalic and Vaughan-Whitehead (1997).

it ousts failing managers. Third, it is the most effective and comprehensive means of restructuring of enterprise assets, because all old debts are wiped out. Executors may split up a misconceived company and sell off its assets piecemeal. Fourth, a bankrupt enterprise is sold through executive auction, the preferred method of privatization. Fifth, bankruptcy improves the competitive environment and levels the playing field because government subsidies to loss-making enterprises are terminated. It opens markets captured by subsidized producers and frees up underutilized productive resources. Finally, bankruptcy is a complete sale, leaving no residual state equity (Mizsei 1993; Kaufmann and Siegelbaum 1996; Balcerowicz et al. 1997; Gray and Holle 1997).

Bankruptcy took time to catch on. Bankruptcies gained early significance in Central Europe and the Baltics. In Poland, liquidation with ensuing sales of the enterprise became a major means of privatization of medium-size firms. Atypically, Hungary introduced a draconian bankruptcy law with an automatic trigger in 1992, which resulted in an explosion of more than 14,000 bankruptcies that year (Balcerowicz et al. 1997). Only Estonia embraced liquidation intentionally as a privatization strategy, and the results have been excellent (Nellis 1994; Kaufmann and Siegelbaum 1996). Many other countries introduced bankruptcy laws, but it took long time before they became effective. In Russia, bankruptcy became significant only with a new Bankruptcy Law in March 1998, the edge of which was reinforced by the financial crash of August 1998. Bankruptcy dealt a devastating blow to the old system (Åslund 1995; Novoprudsky 2000).

For bankruptcy to become effective, several related laws had to be in place, a commercial code, a civil code, and some laws regulating debts. Bankruptcy proceedings were personnel intensive, and they were delayed by understaffed courts. In addition, few had any incentive to initiate a bankruptcy, because creditors doubted legal recourse would give them any money. The state was reluctant to challenge powerful enterprise managers or provoke unemployment, and tax revenues were no top priority. Bankruptcy fell between all stools. To economists, hard budget constraints, creative destruction, and the reallocation of scarce assets were laudable, but bankruptcy was left for lawyers, who cared little about these phenomena. In the CIS, American lawyers provided most legal advice, and they saw bankruptcy as the rehabilitation of enterprises in line with Chapter 11 in the U.S. bankruptcy law, which concurred with the vested interests of lame-duck Soviet enterprises. In a populist vein, the opponents of bankruptcy frightened people that all companies would go bankrupt, leading to mass unemployment and depression. Such fears postponed the introduction of bankruptcy.

Eventually, bankruptcy produced a credible threat of exit for those who did not pay.

Bankruptcy also had drawbacks. One was that it required the usage of courts, which stood out for their malfunctioning and corruption. As a result, bankruptcy has become a favorite means of corporate raiders in CIS countries, and they may undermine the security of property rights. Overall, however, bankruptcy was highly useful, and for years it was one of the greatest sins of omission in the postcommunist transformation.

Privatization of Land, Real Estate, and Housing

The ownership of land, real estate, and housing differed greatly in various socialist countries for arcane historical reasons. In the German Democratic Republic, residential real estate was predominantly private, as in the Russian countryside, whereas Czech and Slovak houses were thoroughly socialized (Åslund 1985). Nor was their privatization particularly related to other reform policies. Because these privatizations were so peculiar, I discuss them only briefly.

Real estate falls into three major categories: agricultural land, commercial real estate, and housing. The efficacy of their privatization depended on the existence of a legitimate form of privatization, and only two forms were perceived as legitimate: restitution to former owners and privatization to tenants. Restitution was exercised widely in the whole of East-Central Europe, especially for housing and collective farmland, accounting for about three-quarters of all farmland in East Germany, Czechoslovakia, Hungary, Bulgaria, Romania, and the Baltics (Swinnen 1999). Usually, old land titles had remained on the books and could be restored, and a lot of land and housing soon found legitimate owners. In Czechoslovakia, agricultural land held by collective farms had never been formally socialized, facilitating its restitution. In 1990, Romania undertook a swift spontaneous land reform by allowing peasants to retake their old land. The other form of legitimate privatization was the transfer of ownership to occupants of agricultural land or housing, which became standard in the CIS, where residents possessed such strong quasi-property rights to their apartments that they claimed them for free.

Little has been as difficult to privatize as commercial real estate. Because communism had not recognized private property, new commercial real estate had been neither properly delineated nor registered. The various property rights – formal ownership, beneficiary of sale, beneficiary of rent, right of utilization, and approval of disposal – were often distributed among several state organizations in an unwieldy fashion. This fragmentation of property rights meant that a simple lease of a commercial unit could require permission by as many as seven agencies. Before anything could be privatized, the property rights had to be unified in one hand, which often took many years (World Bank 1996a; Harding 1995).

The privatization of land and real estate was even more political than other forms of privatization. In the end, it was not important how privatization was undertaken, but it was crucial that it took place and resulted in property rights that were respected and could be freely transferred through sales. When this was not the case, for example, in Russian and Ukrainian agriculture, local magnates with good contacts with the regional governors accumulated hundreds of thousands of hectares. As usual, restrictions benefited the wealthy and well-connected rather than the original landholders, who received a lower price because of liens. In many countries, it took about a decade to sort out the property rights of commercial real estate and only then a long-delayed construction boom could take off to respond to the pent-up demand for new offices. Even in 2006, a quarter of Warsaw, especially its center, was stagnant and dilapidated because its property rights remained in dispute. Poland is the only East-Central European country that has never promulgated a law on restitution.

The conclusion is that all economic arguments about how to undertake real estate privatization were at best irrelevant but probably harmful because political perceptions were all-important. Restitution was most effective both in processing privatization and generating legitimate property rights, whereas auctions were rare and unpopular. After privatization, normal land and real estate markets have evolved where governments allowed them. The second best solution was to just let people possess their housing and agricultural land.

New Enterprise Development: The Ultimate Success

Lenin cherished the idea of the whole country as one big company, and gigantomania was the hallmark of communism, especially in the Soviet Union and Romania. This idea was popular. Many Soviet citizens could not imagine that small enterprises could be productive or relevant for economic growth, seeing no point in facilitating their entry even after the end of communism.

A few countries differed. The main exception was Poland, where communists failed to collectivize agriculture, which had remained private. From 1956, Poland and Hungary accepted a revival of small, urban enterprises.

By the early 1980s, these two countries already had a class of self-made, wealthy, private businesspeople, making Poles and Hungarians realize the economic significance of small entrepreneurs and a good business environment (Åslund 1985). So did the Balts, who cherished a petty bourgeois ideal of peasants, craftsmen, and shopkeepers that represented the normality of the interwar period, when they had enjoyed independence. They lived for E. F. Schumacher's slogan "small is beautiful," and they wanted to revive their old beautiful world of smallness.

Over time, the understanding of the need for small enterprises grew, but two very different perspectives on how to promote small entrepreneurship took hold. The radical reformers, led by Leszek Balcerowicz, emphasized economic freedom: he imposed this policy in Poland, and the small enterprise sector flourished in no time. His policy consisted of two major elements. The first was to grant small entrepreneurs nearly complete freedom to do virtually anything without government permission. The second element he had inherited. Most communist countries had lump-sum taxes for individual entrepreneurs. In Poland, they had laid the foundation for the large private sector before the end of communism (Åslund 1985). At their best, lump-sum taxes guaranteed low, stable, and predictable taxation, as well as liberation from government inspectors. Given the dearth of small enterprises under communism, the formation of new enterprises was essential. The first transition countries followed Balcerowicz's liberal line, and hundreds of thousands of new small enterprises emerged in every country (Johnson 1994).

The other view, which dominated in the CIS countries, was permeated with statist, paternalist thinking: small enterprises could not manage without support from the state through subsidies, subsidized credits, and tax exemptions. Everything was wrong with this approach. State officials wanted to "help" small entrepreneurs in exchange for personal "commissions," whereas the entrepreneurs wanted freedom. State committees and funds for the support of small business were set up in several countries, but they allocated small financial resources to friends not necessarily possessing small enterprises, becoming nothing but breeding grounds for corruption. The same was true of discretionary tax exemptions, which also had to be paid for. Rather than stimulating private enterprise with economic freedom and a level playing field, these governments suffocated them with regulation and extortion. Even so, the transitional chaos offered sufficient freedom for legally registered private enterprises to mushroom in Russia during the first two years of transition, but then the bureaucrats came back with a vengeance, and they had not retreated much. In the CIS, small enterprises remained sparse, because enterprise entry was increasingly restricted by a ubiquitous bureaucracy that made extortion its bailiwick. The opportunity to liberalize entry was missed (Åslund 1997b; Hellman et al. 2000; World Bank 2002).

For a long time, the door to the liberalization of small enterprises seemed closed for good. But then Kyrgyzstan adopted low fixed land taxes in connection with its land reform in 1996, which boosted agricultural production by some 8 percent a year for years. Surprisingly, in 1998 both Ukraine and Kyrgyzstan undertook far-reaching deregulation of small enterprises. Their secret was a single, fixed lump-sum tax from small entrepreneurs. In no time, Kyrgyzstan had 650,000 and Ukraine more than 6 million small entrepreneurs mainly in trade and various services. Single businesspeople were left alone because they were too small to pose a threat to big business and they were not attractive targets for extortion (Åslund and Johnson 2004).

In early inquiries, entrepreneurs assured that most important for their development was a decent tax system, freedom from bureaucratic interference, free foreign and domestic trade, and access to a market for premises (Johnson 1994). One of the most comprehensive surveys of new firms was undertaken by Simon Johnson, John McMillan, and Christopher Woodruff (2000) in Poland, Slovakia, Romania, Russia, and Ukraine in 1997. They found Poland and Romania far advanced, with Slovakia slightly behind, whereas Russia and Ukraine were backward. The profits of an entrepreneur depended primarily on the efficiency of the resolution of commercial disputes and secondly on the unofficial and official taxes actually paid. Contrary to the perception of lawlessness, courts were widely used by businesspeople in all these countries, and they worked, although much less efficiently in Russia and Ukraine. Total official taxes paid were substantial, amounting to 16–17 percent of sales in Central Europe but 24 percent in Russia and Ukraine. Coincidentally, the Russian and Ukrainian entrepreneurs also had to pay about 50 percent more in unofficial payments to government officials than the 4 percent of their sales paid in Poland and Slovakia. The higher the taxes, the higher bribes tax inspectors could extort.

Notwithstanding many problems, entrepreneurs proved a tremendous force. People throughout the region built up good and mighty companies from nothing in a very short time. As early as 1995, Simon Johnson, Daniel Kaufmann, and Andrei Shleifer (1997b) estimated that 33 percent of GDP in the region arose in startups. This share ranged from half of GDP in Poland, Estonia, and Latvia to 10 percent of GDP in Belarus (see Figure 6.1). Naturally, the size of the legal private sector as well as the small enterprise

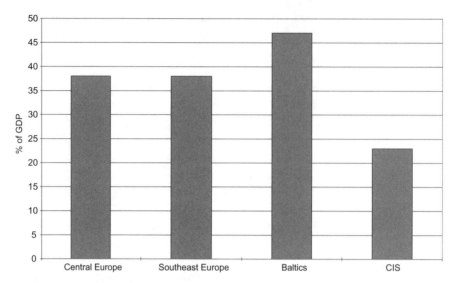

Figure 6.1. De Novo Share of GDP, 1995. *Source:* Havrylyshyn and McGettigan (2000).

sector was inversely related to the underground economy, which was caused by excessive regulation and taxation (Johnson et al. 1997b).

Virtually every enterprise survey verified that startups were most efficient in every regard. The best early explanation was provided by Simon Johnson and Gary Loveman (1995). Because everything socialist enterprises had done was wrong from a market economic standpoint (see Chapter 1), it was so difficult to transform them that it was better to start anew if they did not possess extensive physical capital. Firms needed to produce better products; develop marketing that had been rudimentary and reach out to new markets; establish proper accounting, with cost controls and adjustment to a different cost structure; cease hoarding excessive supplies of input and labor; and change suppliers of inputs and often equipment. At the same time, they needed to stop the piecemeal theft that was institutionalized at state enterprises and introduce a mentality of honesty and service-mindedness. Most companies needed total change, but then new firms were likely to do a better job, which explains the success of the startups. As much of the socialist production was value detracting, much of the socialist organizational capital was negative (Dąbrowski et al. 2000).

Great Achievements of Privatization

Too often, privatization is judged by the degree of restructuring in privatized enterprises, but that was only one of the aims of privatization. It was

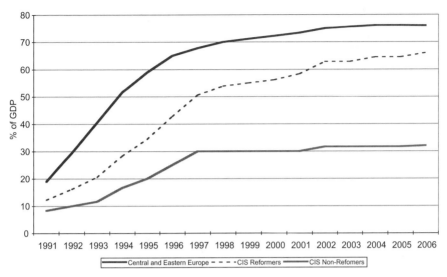

Figure 6.2. Private Sector as Share of GDP, 1991–2006. *Sources:* EBRD (2000) and (2006).

supposed to change the whole economy and society. It must be judged by democracy, structural reforms, and market structure as well.

Extraordinary expansion of the private sector. The world has never seen anything like this expansion. In the first decade of postcommunist transition, more than 150,000 large and medium-size enterprises, hundreds of thousands of small firms, and millions of apartments and houses were privatized (Djankov and Murrell 2002; Nellis 2001). Figure 6.2 depicts the overall picture of the share of GDP originating in the private sector with three groups of countries, East-Central Europe, nine CIS reformers, and the three CIS nonreformers. At this aggregate level, the picture is clear. The three curves have stayed separate and stabilized at different levels. East-Central Europe privatized most radically and reached 76 percent by 2006, close to the standards of the Western Europe. The CIS reformers advanced the most gradually to around 66 percent. Belarus, Turkmenistan, and Uzbekistan reached 30 percent in 1997 and stopped.

Democracy. The foremost political aim of privatization was to break up the socialist state hegemony and facilitate democracy. The correlation between democracy and privatization is strong (see Figure 6.3). The logic is evident. All countries with a private sector of more than 60 percent of GDP in 2005 were considered free or partially free by Freedom House (2006). The leaders in privatization (as well as in structural reform) in Central Europe and the Baltics are fully democratic, whereas semiprivatized countries tend to be semidemocratic. The three countries with minimal privatization are true

Figure 6.3. Democracy and Privatization, 2005.

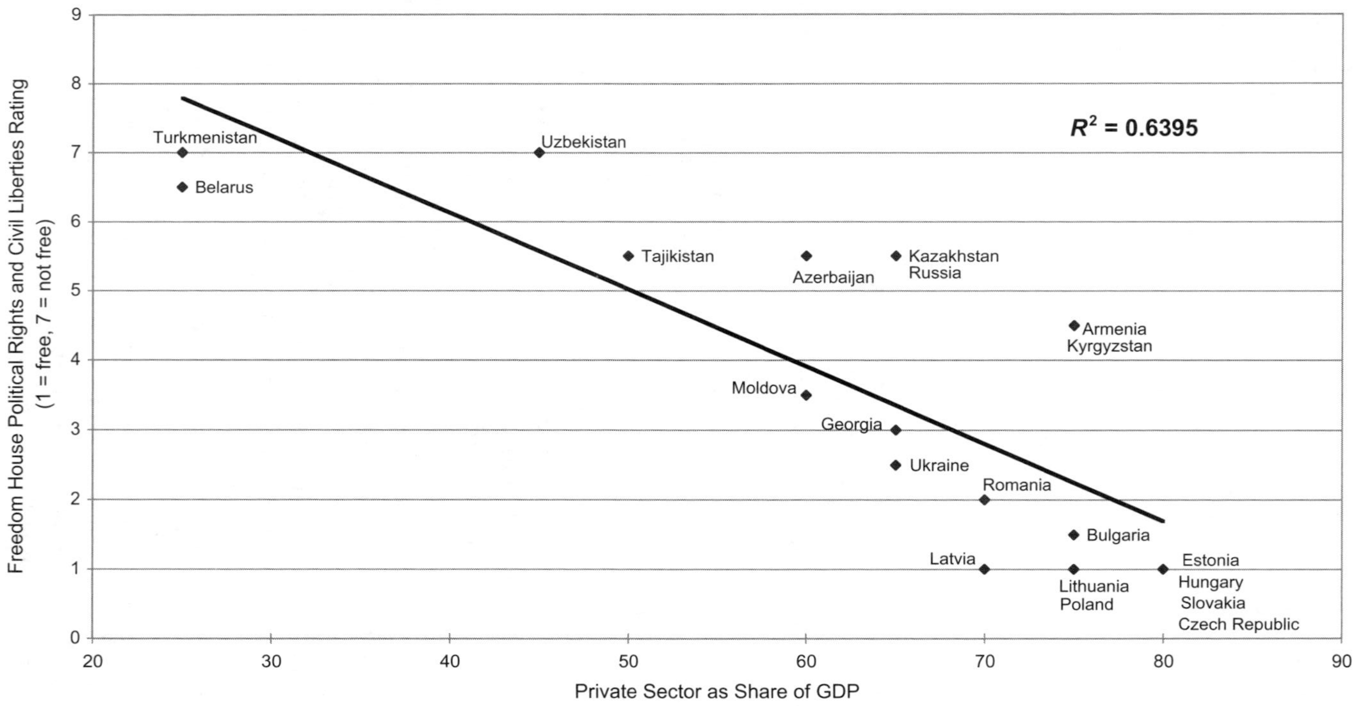

Freedom House Political Rights and Civil Liberties Rating
(1 = free, 7 = not free)
Private Sector as Share of GDP
R^2 = 0.6395
9
8
7
6
5
4
3
2
1
0
20
30
40
50
60
70
80
90
Turkmenistan
Belarus
Uzbekistan
Tajikistan
Azerbaijan
Kazakhstan
Russia
Armenia
Kyrgyzstan
Moldova
Georgia
Ukraine
Romania
Bulgaria
Latvia
Lithuania
Poland
Estonia
Hungary
Slovakia
Czech Republic

Sources: EBRD (2005) and Freedom House (2006).

tyrannies. A state that is hegemonic through ownership, such as Belarus and Turkmenistan, leaves little room for democracy.

Formation of a market economy. The countries that have privatized most have also undertaken most other structural reforms, and the correlation between liberalization and privatization is extremely close (Åslund et al. 1996). This was the intention of the privatizers: "It is precisely because of privatization, and the creation of groups with a vested interest in protecting their own property, that the Russian government began to take steps to create market-supporting institutions" (Shleifer and Vishny 1998, p. 10).

Hardening of budget constraints. Enterprises have been depoliticized and made independent from the state. A prime objective of privatization was to terminate enterprise subsidies. Opponents of fast privatization have argued that "soft budget constraints and rent-seeking are not unique to [state-owned enterprises]. Private firms also lobby to get subsidies and to seek rents" (Roland 2000, p. 7). Although this is true, subsidies are highly concentrated to state-owned enterprises throughout the region. In 1999, state enterprises received 26 percent of all financing for fixed investment from the state, compared with only 3 percent in privatized enterprises, whereas startups received virtually no subsidies (EBRD 1999, p. 137). Even in Central Europe and the Baltics, state enterprises obtained one-fifth of their investment financing from the state, showing that good structural reforms were not enough to terminate these subsidies without privatization. Privatization has made a major contribution to the hardening of budget constraints.

Competition. Critics of privatization argue that competition is more important than privatization, but this is a false dichotomy because privatization breeds more competition. With privatization, the number of enterprises increases, and thus competition likewise increases. The countries with the largest private sectors also have most startups. Finally, there is much less competition among state firms. Nearly 30 percent of the state-owned enterprises in the region face no competitor, but this is true of only 5 percent of the new entrants and 9 percent of the privatized enterprises (EBRD 1999, pp. 135–6).

Enterprise restructuring has been extensively studied. At a first stage of enterprise restructuring, managers can be replaced. A second stage involves defensive restructuring, essentially cost cutting. A third stage comprises offensive restructuring, with the expansion of sales, profits, exports, and employment as well as the introduction of new products and new investments. A fourth stage arises when substantial equity capital is raised through the stock market. At each stage, various factors influence enterprise performance, and ownership is only one of them. By 2000, a broad agreement about the overall outcome of privatization for enterprise management had surfaced (Havrylyshyn and McGettigan 2000; Megginson and Netter 2001; Djankov and Murrell 2002):

1. Private firms perform better than state enterprises.
2. Startups perform the best.
3. Privatization to outsiders leads to higher efficiency than privatization to insiders.
4. Foreign ownership is mostly beneficial.
5. Firms privatized to insiders, especially employees, perform about as badly as state-owned firms.
6. Partially privatized companies do much better than completely state-owned firms.
7. New outside managers perform better than the original managers.
8. Investment funds have played an ambiguous role. They facilitated privatization but left the new private sector in an ownership limbo.
9. The positive results from privatization were immediate in East-Central Europe but took years to emerge in the CIS countries.

Since 1999, the massive economic growth in the CIS countries, which mostly carried out mass privatization, has changed this picture. Using data from 23 transition countries from 1990 to 2003, one ambitious study found that mass privatization is associated with a positive structural break in the growth process unlike other privatization methods (Bennett et al. 2005). One explanation is that the incumbent manager usually stayed on for some time after privatization, but little happened until an outsider bought the privatized company and changed managers. Moreover, because of lagging structural reforms, the CIS enterprise environment was too inhospitable until 1999.[9]

Replacement of enterprise manager. From 1988, it was all but impossible to oust a Soviet enterprise manager. The first goal of privatization was to facilitate managerial turnover. The managers never had it so good, enjoying more freedom, power, and money than ever before or later. They held quasi-property rights over "their" enterprises without accountability. Privatization proved a potent threat to managers. Wherever privatization took place,

---

[9] Another extensive study of enterprise productivity in manufacturing in Hungary, Romania, Ukraine, and Russia until 2002 showed strongly positive results of privatization in Hungary and Romania but negative results in Russia (Brown et al. 2005). Presumably, the explanation for Russia's poor result lies in the choice of industry. Manufacturing has not spearheaded Russia's economic recovery, and Russia's old manufacturing plants might simply have been so poor that greenfield investment made more sense.

a normal turnover of managers started, even when insider privatization dominated. Blasi et al. (1997, p. 203) recorded that the manager changed in 33 percent of the privatized Russian enterprises they surveyed from 1992 to 1996. The threat of hostile takeovers had appeared, and in Russia they became common. By 1999, managerial turnover reached about 10 percent a year in both state-owned and privatized enterprises in the whole region (EBRD 1999, p. 139; Mau 1999).

Defensive restructuring imposed by hard budget constraints. The second transition task at firm-level was defensive restructuring to enhance efficiency by cutting the large unjustified costs of labor, inputs, investment, and unrelated activities. Liberalization gave managers a freedom of choice, and their incentives changed when money became scarce. Even if state enterprises enjoyed more subsidies than private firms, their budget constraints grew harder as well. Surprisingly, all kinds of enterprises, including state enterprises, undertook substantial restructuring (Pinto et al. 1993). Grosfeld and Roland (1995) found that 600 large state enterprises in Poland, the Czech Republic, and Hungary shed some 30 percent of their workforce in the first two years of transition. The explanation is that macroeconomic stabilization was the main tool imposing hard budget constraints and thus prompting cost cutting (Commander and Mumssen 1998).

Privatization needed for offensive restructuring. The third step, offensive restructuring, was a much more complex undertaking. It required the development of an expansionary business strategy with new products, innovations, expanded sales and exports, new investment, and more staff, leading to greater profitability. In the West, a new manager is usually desired for such efforts. Now greater differences between various kinds of enterprises emerged, and ownership was critical. In sales, startups did far better than both state enterprises and privatized firms, followed by privatized companies (EBRD 1999, p. 133). New entrants and privatized enterprises changed suppliers approximately as often in the whole region, whereas state enterprises were more conservative (EBRD 1999, p. 134; Earle and Estrin 1997). The expansion of employment was one of the best indicators. As expected, startups were most expansive, followed by privatized firms, with state enterprises coming last (EBRD 1999, p. 134; Frydman et al. 1997). The essence of successful performance is higher profitability, but here statistical problems are palpable. Several early studies, which controlled for the selection bias of privatized enterprises, come to the overall conclusion that they outperformed state-owned enterprises (Claessens and Djankov 1997; Grosfeld and Nivet 1997; Frydman et al. 1998). One would expect private enterprises to be more innovative than state enterprises, but the state enterprises in Russia and

Ukraine are actually doing as well as privatized enterprises in Central Europe and the Baltics (EBRD 1999, p. 134). The explanation is presumably that the high-tech military-industrial complex in Russia and Ukraine remained state owned, and underemployed researchers continued to invent new products. One study of Central Europe concluded: "Privatization is effective in enhancing revenue and productivity performance of firms that come to be controlled by outsider-owners, but produces no significant effect in firms controlled by insiders" (Frydman et al. 1998). Over time, however, insider-owned enterprises did better than state-owned enterprises, although worse than those subject to outsider privatization, including mass privatization (EBRD 1999).

The evolution of stock markets. As one would expect in an economy characterized by market failures, retained earnings are the dominant source of financing for new and growing enterprises because of high risks, poor information systems, moral hazard, and insufficient regulation and supervision (Pleskovic 1994). By 1999, retained earnings provided half of the funding for fixed investment in Central Europe and the Baltics and about two-thirds in the rest of the region (EBRD 1999, p. 137).

The importance of the initial distribution of stocks depends on the ease with which they can be redistributed. The Coase theorem states that under perfect competition, private and social costs will be equal (Coase 1988, p. 14). To Coase, this was only a theoretical construct; he argued that transaction costs determined the design of economic institutions. The privatizers hardly harbored this illusion, but the idea that the original distribution of titles was of limited importance enjoyed great currency. The redistribution of property depended on the efficiency of secondary markets, which was bound to be inadequate for years (Sutela 1998). Both Western and local stock market specialists focused on superficial technical features, such as electronic trading systems. Early on, Kiev received as technical assistance a modern stock exchange equipped as in Lyons, but for years only three or four stocks were traded, and the Kiev stock market remained rudimentary in 2006. Key problems were instead legal regulation (the registration of titles, custody, externally audited accounts, corporate governance, and the supervision of stock exchanges) and the supply of stocks.

In the 1990s, stock markets took off in only four countries: Hungary, Poland, Estonia, and Russia. The first three went through a similar evolution, based on privatization through IPOs. Their quality was fine, but market capitalization stayed low because of limited supply of stocks. Major companies, such as energy and telecommunications, were not privatized. Slovakia, Latvia, and Lithuania followed in the footsteps of the pioneers, but their markets were smaller and less reputable. The supply of stocks remains small, because foreign direct investors buy whole companies and take them off the local stock exchange, and IPOs are few. The Baltic stock exchanges have merged with the Scandinavian stock markets, and Vienna is gathering the Central European stock markets. The Czech stock market never thrived because after the voucher privatization, it was flooded with a couple of thousands of listed stocks, most of which were not actively traded, and regulation was poor. In all countries with real stock markets, brokerages and investment banks swiftly developed, and the stock markets have contributed to international financial integration.

The Russian development has been a world apart, being big, wild, and spontaneous (Frye 2000). A couple of hundred exchanges had arisen before the end of communism as wildcat entrepreneurship, and thanks to the large-scale privatization, the country was awash in stocks from 1993. If an enterprise was of value, a market for its stocks developed easily, and ownership was consolidated by new core owners who bought up its stocks in Moscow. Local stockbrokers visited such enterprises and purchased stocks from the workers, delivering large packages of stocks to Moscow. Particularly valuable companies, such as telecommunications, utilities, and oil, surged in a first stock market boom in 1994, which was followed by a minor bust. In 1996 and 1997, the Russian stock market quadrupled, becoming the best-performing market in the world in both years with a market capitalization peaking at $100 billion, one-fifth of GDP at the time or ten times more than the Polish market capitalization. However, Russia's market capitalization plummeted by 84 percent between October 1997 and August 1998. Apart from the Russian financial collapse, pervasive dilution of minority shareholders deterred foreign equity investors. Russia had promulgated amazingly good legal standards after its mass privatization, but the Federal Security Commission had little power and failed to implement most rules. The Russian stock market revived spectacularly. By 2005, valuations reached such a level that a flood of IPOs reached the market, and equity had become important for raising capital. The Russian stock market, however, has largely emigrated to London, which has become the stock market of the whole of Eastern Europe. Primarily, this is a result of the globalization of financial markets, but it has been spurred on by Russia's failure to develop a credible rule of law. By the end of 2006, Russia's stock market capitalization reached $1 trillion equaling the GDP. This dynamic but speculative stock market is more reminiscent of New York or London before World War I or Hong Kong in recent years. Even if the Russian stock trade mainly occurs abroad, its stock market has become a strong force, facilitating both financing and enterprise restructuring.

Justice? Looking at postcommunist privatization from today's perspective, the overwhelming impression is that much has been accomplished, and little economic recovery occurred until a critical mass of private enterprise had been assembled. Private enterprise has driven the long-lasting economic boom. It is difficult to understand the vitriol that has been characteristic of so much of the Western literature about privatization, especially just after the Russian financial crash (e.g., Stiglitz 1999a, 2002; Reddaway and Glinski 2001; Ellerman 2003; Goldman 2003), which reflects a similar tone in the Russian literature. A general complaint is that privatization was not fair and that the oligarchs accumulated huge fortunes, which I discuss in depth in Chapter 10. Another concern was that the privatization became lawless, but law and order broke down before the collapse of communism. Naturally, regulation lagged behind as hundreds of new laws had to be adopted and calibrated through repeated amendments. Finally, some complained about the new businesspeople having paid too little to the state, but that was no major goal in any of these countries with the exception of Hungary. In short, people got upset when others benefited more than they. The complaint that privatization did not lead to economic recovery in the CIS countries has been disproved by the high economic growth after 1999.

The ultimate accusation against privatization was that it bred corruption. However, the sale of an enterprise to the private sector limited state officials' opportunities to extort bribes for that property, and a once-for-all price could hardly discount all their future rents. A slow start of privatization led to the entrenchment of an establishment that thrived on state ownership in corrupt ways, exactly as Kaufmann and Siegelbaum (1996) had predicted. Even in reformist Latvia, an observer reported in 1996:

Many members of Latvia's new political elite serve on the boards of directors of large state enterprises, where their salaries in most cases are several times higher than those for governmental or parliamentary posts. Officials in such positions have diverted funds through state enterprises by having the enterprises guarantee loans to private firms in which the officials themselves had interests. Those loans were seldom repaid. (Paeglis 1996, p. 37)

Similarly, Polish politics has suffered from the corrupting influences of many large enterprises remaining state owned, which are considered vital for campaign financing. This is another example of dangerous path dependence leading to a suboptimal equilibrium. With minimal or limited initial privatization, the danger was great that strong vested interests would thrive on state ownership and impede further privatization. The correlation between corruption and privatization is strong and negative, showing that privatization does not boost corruption (see Figure 6.4).

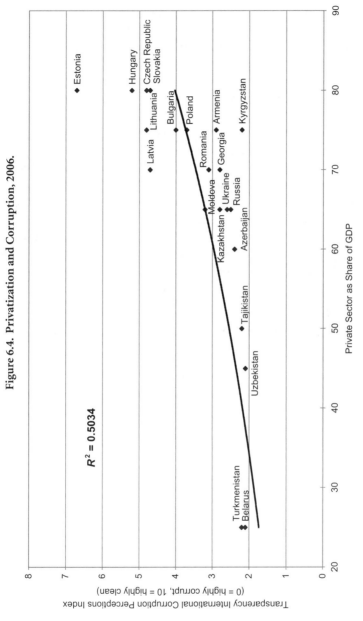

Figure 6.4. Privatization and Corruption, 2006.

Sources: EBRD (2006) and Transparency International (2006).

The performance of enterprises with various types of ownership has repeatedly upset the conventional wisdom. The first surprise was that small startups outperformed all other enterprises. A second revelation was that even the dinosaurs, the large old state enterprises, could undertake defensive restructuring because cost cutting depended primarily on hard budget constraints and not on ownership. Third, initially voucher privatization disappointed because of ineffective corporate governance, but after having been sold to new entrepreneurs many of these enterprises have shone. Fourth, few expected so many strong new entrepreneurs to emerge so fast. At the end, however, the pattern is approximately as expected. Private ownership has proved to be the key to economic revival. Startups and foreign-owned enterprises are the star performers. Privatized enterprises comprise a second group, and state-owned enterprises perform the worst. The old organizational capital of state enterprises was largely harmful and was best liquidated, but the physical capital was better than many had thought, and the human capital was excellent but underutilized (McKinsey Global Institute 1999; Dąbrowski et al. 2000).

Vital: Speed and Legitimacy of Property Rights

Mass privatization was the greatest innovation of postcommunist transition, and it touched everybody. Little surprise that it has been so controversial and so differently assessed. Two major questions remain. One is the relationship between timing and quality of privatization, and the other is the durable respect for resulting property rights.

A standard assumption both in the theoretical political economy literature and the public debate has been that privatization could be undertaken either soon or later, but this is a dubious premise. Privatization has not been a continuous process, and strong path dependency is apparent. Each country adopted a path of privatization that was not easily altered. State enterprises remained dominant until a government undertook a concerted effort at large-scale privatization, leading to a major boost in the private sector in one or two years. In countries with little privatization, notably Belarus and Turkmenistan, no such jump occurred, because minimal large-scale privatization took place. As the dictatorial state recovered its economic and political control, privatization stopped altogether. Ukraine and Moldova launched their privatization late, and they moved ahead but only after Herculean efforts. Thus, the real choice was between fast privatization and little privatization.

Another popular view has been that the timing and pace of privatization do not matter, but that the quality of privatization is important and that policy makers had a choice between fast privatization or slower privatization of higher quality (Murrell 1992b; Murrell and Wang 1993; Roland 1994, 2000). This idea presupposed the absence of positive complementarity between the volume of privatization and other structural reforms, which contradicts the evidence. It also presumes a strong state, which is equally unrealistic. It is based on a comparison between Poland, which failed to undertake its intended mass privatization, and Russia that succeeded in little but its mass privatization. As a result, Russia caught up with Poland in privatization, and from 1997 to 1999, 70 percent of the Russian GDP was considered by the EBRD to come from the private sector, but only 65 percent in Poland. For most other years, Poland's private sector was larger than Russia's. A substantial literature has developed on the basis of this odd incidence, ignoring that Poland had carried out many more reforms than Russia, that all the other Central European countries had privatized more than Russia, and that the measurement is in doubt. This is monocausal reasoning at its worst. It makes more sense to compare Russia with its East Slavic neighbor, Belarus, which had very similar preconditions. Russia, with its mass privatization, proceeded with structural reforms, whereas Belarus, with a minimum of privatization, regressed into a state-regulated economy. In the CIS and Southeast Europe, the choice was not between a late privatization of high quality and an early dirty privatization but between early privatization and no privatization. Countries that started their major privatization efforts late, such as Ukraine and Moldova, suffered qualitatively worse privatizations than in Russia because more stocks went to insiders, corporate governance and minority shareholders' rights were more limited, stock markets faltered, and fewer market reforms occurred (Djankov 1999; Yekhanurov 2000).

A third common technocratic view is that each polity has a free choice in its country's privatization, but the options of privatization have been severely constrained by initial claims on property, political power, legal and administrative capacity, prior privatization, and other reform policies. The harsher the prior dictatorship, the more dominant state ownership, and the worse both state and corporate governance have become. What works in one country might be detrimental or impossible in another, and the feasible methods have been fewer than usually understood. Only three countries have successfully undertaken the qualitatively most advanced form of privatization – initial public offerings – on a significant scale, namely, Poland, Estonia, and Hungary, countries also renowned for being the least corrupt. Outside these three countries (and the Czech Republic), direct sales have been exceedingly corrupt, and they incurred incredible losses on the state in East Germany. As widely anticipated, initially voucher privatization led to poor corporate governance, but more was privatized than otherwise possible in several difficult countries. For nationalist reasons, Ukraine did not want to follow the Russian example of voucher and insider privatization, but the prolonged debate over privatization aroused such acrimony that little privatization was executed until Ukraine implemented an essentially Russian scheme in 1996 (Yekhanurov 2000). The real choice CIS countries faced was minimal and very corrupt privatization or combined voucher and insider privatization.

This leads to conclusions at variance with the conventional wisdom about privatization. A first conclusion is that there is a strong positive correlation between the degree of privatization and output (see Chapter 3).

Second, a major concentrated privatization effort was necessary in all countries but Poland to ascertain the dominance of the private sector.

Third, the earlier this major privatization was undertaken, the higher the quality of privatization was likely to be, because privatization was a vital lever against corruption and the period of revolutionary disruption was propitious.

Fourth, the breakthrough in privatization was always a large-scale privatization effort, regardless of how it was undertaken. The purported choice between large-scale privatization and new enterprise development was another myth. The real choice was whether to undertake large-scale privatization and promote new enterprise development or do neither.

A fifth conclusion is that it is less important how large-scale privatization was undertaken than that it was carried out. The choice of privatization was primarily a matter of what was politically possible.

Finally, privatization was a prerequisite for the sustenance of democracy. All postcommunist countries with less than 60 percent of its GDP arising in the private sector are classified as unfree by Freedom House (2006).

Liberalization, stabilization, and privatization are all positively correlated both logically and empirically. Their relative impact has varied over time. Liberalization was necessary to create freedom of choice, but enterprise restructuring only started when enterprises faced hard budget constraints, which required that stabilization had taken hold. A competitive environment encourages further restructuring, but private ownership and good corporate governance are required for strategic expansion.

The concerns about the respect for resulting property rights have risen over time. Virtually all countries have serious privatization scandals that involve multiple top politicians and businesspeople. The obvious, oft-proposed solution would be to issue a statute of limitation for violations of privatization legislation. In some countries that has happened, but they are unpopular. Voters want to punish the rich, whereas other wealthy business-people aspire to pick up the spoils. The cure is uncertain. In democracies as well as authoritarian states, politicians appeal to populist sentiments against the wealthy. After Ukraine's Orange Revolution, reprivatization from certain oligarchs became the craze, and at the time of this writing, President Putin pursues a renationalization campaign, with Russian state-dominated companies buying well-run private companies to the apparent benefit of the personal enrichment of Russian top officials.

Future respect for property rights is one of the weakest links in post-communist states. Over time, it appears to matter less economically how privatization is carried out, but the respect for the resulting property rights, or the political legitimacy of privatization, is crucial. Therefore, mass privatization and insider privatizations by the old management and workers have become more attractive in hindsight, and sales of big enterprises to outsiders remain controversial. Ownership arising from secondary sales is respected, however low the prices were. Similarly restitution and privatization to occupants and tenants appear effective because they bred respected property rights as well. These observations cast doubt on the relevance of a large literature measuring the economic effects soon after privatization. The time perspective was too short, and the key to good long-term economic performance is the sanctity of property rights, on which medium-term economic performance offers little or no guidance.

7

An Inefficient Social System

The main aim of economic policy is to enhance economic welfare. When transition to capitalism began, however, everybody anticipated social suffering, and in its early stages, postcommunist economic transformation was often presented as a social catastrophe. There was certainly trauma, and results have varied greatly among transition countries, but the initial perception of social disaster was exaggerated.[1]

Chapter 3 concluded that the decline in registered output was highly exaggerated. Although we know even less about real incomes, they must have fallen less than output. Initially, real incomes plummeted, but they have surged with economic recovery. Income differentials have increased everywhere, but much more in the east and the south than in the west. Countries pursuing more radical initial reform, which generated less rent seeking, saw a smaller increase in inequality. Poverty ballooned in the poorer CIS countries, but much poverty was shallow and has shrunk with economic recovery, as I discuss in the first section.

The most disturbing social development, considered in section two, was declining life expectancy among Eastern Slavic and Baltic men, who found it difficult to adjust to the change of system. Infant mortality, by contrast, has fallen sharply in most of the region, except in six of the least reformist CIS countries. This suggests that health care has improved in most countries, but it is still in poor shape because of lagging systemic reform.

The education system is the theme of section three. It has seen a dynamic but erratic development. Public financing has held up well, and substantial

---

[1] This chapter draws heavily on work carried out by the World Bank (2000b, 2005b), particularly Branko Milanovic (1998). The Carnegie Moscow Center undertook a social policy project in the second half of the 1990s, largely by my former Carnegie colleagues Mikhail Dmitriev and Tatyana Maleva, which is another major source (Åslund and Dmitriev 1996; Maleva 1998).

private funding has been added. An extraordinary expansion of higher education has taken place, although quality might have deteriorated. Primary and secondary education has been neglected throughout the CIS, and in the poorest countries, universal literacy might be on the wane.

Because of the expected social suffering, politicians agreed to increase social expenditures both as a share of GDP and in absolute terms in most postcommunist countries, as discussed in section four. The most developed transition countries have become encumbered by untenably large social expenditures, whereas they have contracted in the poorest countries. Unfortunately, social transfers have not been very social because they often were not targeted at those in the greatest need but rather at privileged groups. Reforms are needed to target social benefits at neglected groups.

As a consequence of disparate social policies, the countries in the region are developing three social models. Central Europe has adopted a West European social welfare system, and some CIS reformers are moving toward an East Asian model with much smaller social expenditures. Southeast Europe and the Baltics occupy intermediary positions. The three CIS nonreformers are maintaining an expensive but inefficient Soviet model.

Incomes: Differentiation and Poverty

From the outset, the common assumption was that postcommunist transformation would involve great social trauma because incomes would plunge with output. Another assumption was that income differentials would widen, because rapid economic restructuring would alter the relative values of professions and income differentials had been artificially compressed under socialism. A third assumption was that poverty would be aggravated because of the contraction of average incomes and a widening of income differentials. However, nobody had a clear sense of the dignity or speed of these changes.

In Chapter 3, I discussed the strong downward bias in official output statistics in the transition. Whatever is true of output statistics is even more applicable to personal income statistics. All show that "real" incomes fell more than output, which is impossible. The most important reason for this statistical distortion is that in their death throes, the communists gave people more money instead of goods or services, and this mounting monetary overhang bolstered statistical "real" incomes just before price liberalization. A huge chunk of these monetary incomes was illusory, reflecting increased shortages and queuing. Personal incomes were less recorded and thus more underestimated than virtually anything else, because auxiliary private incomes, tax avoidance, tax evasion, and social transfers ballooned in the new market economy, whereas wages from their main state employer had dominated people's incomes in socialist times. Unlike the old declining heavy industry, much of the new and unofficial economy benefited consumers. In addition, as investment and defense expenditures decreased as shares of GDP, the private consumption share expanded. Hence, average incomes must have contracted much less than GDP.

Curiously, household surveys give us an even stranger picture of personal incomes than official statistics (Milanovic 1998). Without going into details, the unfortunate conclusion is that we have little idea of what happened to incomes in the early transition. In all likelihood, a substantial decline in personal incomes occurred in the initial transition, but how large it was we dare not say, and it was followed by a substantial and long-lasting rise.

Consumption statistics are partial and unreliable, although slightly better than income statistics. According to official statistics, Poland stood out as an unchallenged star, with an increase in total consumption of 36 percent from 1989 to 1999. The Czech Republic and Romania also exceeded their communist level of consumption by 1999, but the others fared considerably worse (United Nations Economic Commission for Europe 2000, p. 161). The actual standard of living is difficult to assess because of the radical alteration of relative prices and consumption baskets, as well as access to new goods and improved quality. Those who want to show how arduous the transition was use consumption of meat as a yardstick, showing radical declines, but meat was the most subsidized product under communism. Those who want to play down the costs of transition, on the contrary, emphasize the rapid increase in the volume of fruits, vegetables, cars, household appliances, and consumer electronics, whose relative prices dropped. People queued for a new car for up to ten years under communism (Berg and Sachs 1992). Like incomes, living conditions deteriorated everywhere during the end of communism and the early transition, but we dare not say by how much, and this decline was followed by a substantial rise. "Mirroring the growth in output, there has been a sharp upswing in average wages in all economies in the Region. For example, in the low income CIS group, real wages have almost doubled since 1997 . . . this upswing has been shared alike by unskilled and skilled, poor and nonpoor" (World Bank 2005b, p. 16).

Income differentials are still more difficult to measure, but their development is easily understood. On the whole, income differentiation increased approximately as expected. In Central Europe, income differentials were the most compressed in the world, and no market economy could maintain such extreme egalitarianism. The average Gini coefficient of disposable income in

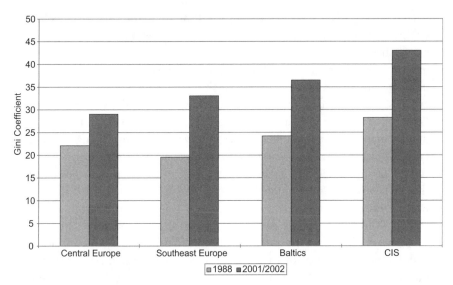

Figure 7.1. Inequality: Change in Gini Coefficients, 1988–2002. *Source:* UNU-WIDER (2006).

Central Europe rose from a Scandinavian level of 22 in 1988–9 to a low West European level of 29 in 2001–2 (see Figure 7.1). The rise in differentiation was concentrated to the first few years of transition and leveled off around 1995. In the Baltics and Southeast Europe, differentiation went a bit further to a level slightly higher than in Western Europe.

Inequality grew much more in the CIS countries. Initially their degrees of inequality diverged, with reformist Georgia and Kyrgyzstan reaching extreme levels of income differentiation, and little happening in the nonreformers. Over time, however, their levels of inequality converged. The most extreme measurements of inequality proved inaccurate, whereas late reformers and nonreformers saw their inequality surge.[2] The Gini coefficients of the CIS countries have risen from a West European level of 28 to the U.S. level of 43, but this is still significantly below the Latin American level. Oddly, the course of reforms did not have much impact. The high new growth in the CIS countries led to a decrease in inequality in those countries between 1998 and 2003, whereas no trend was apparent in Central and Eastern Europe (World Bank 2005b, p. 13).

---

[2] Gross wage statistics show the greatest income disparity, which decreases in steps when taxation, additional monetary earnings, additional nonmonetary earnings (from the widespread private plots), state transfers, and, finally, private transfers are added (Keane and Prasad 2000).

Here, too, statistical challenges are daunting. In a fine analysis of Polish statistics, Michael Keane and Eswar Prasad (2000) debunked the prevailing view that Polish inequality had increased substantially and showed that the inequality in incomes and consumption was virtually the same in 1997 as in 1989 and even fell in the early transition. Although wage differentials expanded, larger social transfers fully compensated for them. Presumably, Poland was an outlier because of its successful early reforms and its broad development of new small enterprises, but we are left wondering whether Poland excels because of better policies or more accurate statistics.

The income differentiation reflected the prior distribution of power. In the Soviet Union, the Nomenklatura was much more dominant than in Eastern Europe. It collectively imposed a partial reform strategy, which allowed it to usurp a share of the wealth that corresponded to its power. This observation is an argument for both radical comprehensive reform and democratization prior to a change of economic system. A more prosaic explanation is that more initial economic distortions caused more rent seeking, breeding greater income differentials.

Any newspaper reader would presume that the increased inequality reflects the predominance of a few tycoons, but they fall outside any statistics. Instead, the main cause of widening income differentials is to be found in wages (Milanovic 1998). In the mid-1990s in Russia, wages accounted for no less than three-quarters of the increased inequality, indicating the emergence of a large new middle class, which flourished in the new private sector. Increased wage differentials also explain most of the gulf between the former Soviet Union and Central Europe. Next, our newspaper reader would assume that the reduction of social transfers, such as pensions, has aggravated inequality. In fact, social transfers grew as a share of GDP, but they did not help the poor much. Particularly in the former Soviet Union, they actually aggravated inequality because a disproportionate share of pensions went to the privileged (Misikhina 1999). Surprisingly, entrepreneurial incomes hardly contributed to recorded inequality, but these statistics are probably especially unreliable.

Because GDP has developed very unevenly in the region, regional disparities in personal incomes have increased. Previously, Kazakhstan and Kyrgyzstan were similar in economic development, but today the average dollar wages in Kazakhstan are five times higher than in its southern neighbor Kyrgyzstan, which still has twice as high a dollar wage as its southern neighbor Tajikistan, which has become the poorest postcommunist state.

If income disparities rise dramatically in relatively poor countries with falling output, poverty is bound to rise. Recorded poverty soared shockingly in the early transition. The World Bank (2005b) chose $2.15 per person per day in 2000 prices in purchasing power parties as a standardized poverty line. By this standard, in 2003, poverty was minimal in East-Central Europe, below 5 percent in all countries but Romania (12%). Not very plausibly, the World Bank claims that poverty was minimal in Belarus, Ukraine, and Azerbaijan. Only Russia and Kazakhstan form a middle ground with 9 and 21 percent poverty, respectively. The low-income CIS countries, by contrast, suffered from extensive poverty ranging from 43 percent of the population in Moldova to 74 percent in Tajikistan. Seven poor CIS countries, Tajikistan, Kyrgyzstan, Georgia, Armenia, Uzbekistan, Turkmenistan, and Moldova, have become trapped in deep and widespread poverty. No comparison with the Soviet situation is possible because the Soviets denied the possibility of poverty, but poverty has undoubtedly increased substantially in most CIS countries. About two-thirds of all the poor are working adults and children, with unemployed and elderly accounting for the rest. The four characteristics that indicate a high-poverty risk are youth, rural living, unemployment, and low level of education (World Bank 2005b).

The saving grace about poverty in the region is that most of it is relatively shallow, with many people living just below the poverty line. An anomaly in comparison with the rest of the world is that the poor are literate and comparatively well educated. Under propitious political and economic conditions, this should lead to a fast decline in poverty (Milanovic 1998), and that has indeed happened. The number of poor has plummeted during the long economic boom that started in 1999 in the CIS. The overall poverty rate for the region fell from 20 percent in 1998 to 12 percent in 2003, as more than 40 million people in the region moved out of poverty. Much of this poverty reduction occurred in the populous middle-income countries Kazakhstan, Russia, and Ukraine, but poverty dropped almost everywhere. Alas, in recent years poverty in the low-income CIS countries has deepened, whereas it remains fairly shallow in the richer CIS countries and in Southeast Europe (World Bank 2005b).

Life and Health

One of communism's proudest claims was well-developed, free public health care. However, the system was neither efficient nor effective because it focused on the consumption of certain inputs, especially hospital beds, rather than health outcomes. Actual health standards were poor in comparison with countries at a similar level of economic development.[3] This inconsistency between public claims and reality became obvious toward the end

---

[3] Communist Cuba and China, by contrast, have quite impressive life expectancy.

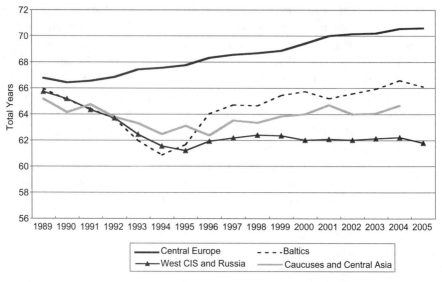

Figure 7.2. Male Life Expectancy, 1989–2005. *Source:* World Bank (2006).

of communism. Yet transition has been accompanied by such disturbing tendencies as declines in life expectancy, population, and nativity, prompting the question of what has happened to life and health.

Declining Male Life Expectancy

The early fall in life expectancy in many transition countries was the most shocking development. The average life expectancy at birth for all the transition countries decreased insignificant from 70.3 years in 1989 to 70.0 years in 1995 (United Nations Development Program [UNDP] 1998, p. 213). The shock was sharply declining male life expectancy in nine post-Soviet countries – the three Baltic states, Belarus, Ukraine, Moldova, Russia, Kazakhstan, and Kyrgyzstan. Russia experienced the greatest decline – seven years – from 1989 to 1994, when male life expectancy at birth reached the deplorable nadir of 57.6 years, 14 years less than for Russian women, the greatest gender disparity in the world. Disturbingly, it has stayed very low, around 59 years (World Bank 2006).

In Central Europe, male life expectancy rose by 3.6 years from 1989 to 2004, and in Southeast Europe by one year. Strangely, the war-ridden countries in the Caucasus did not suffer, nor did the destitute Central Asian states, Tajikistan, Turkmenistan, and Uzbekistan, although their poor statistics may not tell us the whole truth (see Figure 7.2). The countries concerned do not form any clear economic pattern.

The low male life expectancy in Russia has been thoroughly analyzed. Most of the additional deaths are due to cardiovascular diseases and accidents. One obvious explanation is that alcohol sales increased with the falling relative price of alcohol, following Mikhail Gorbachev's severe antialcohol campaign (Brainerd 1998). A fine regression analysis by Vladimir Shkolnikov et al. (2000) examined all possible health-related causes and socioeconomic factors and found no other explanation among them. The health problems of Russian males seem psychological. Judith Shapiro (1995) suggested that the problem might be men's inability to handle stress caused by uncertainty in the transition, and Shkolnikov et al. (2000) concurred. The problem was not starvation or abject poverty. Nor was it deteriorating health care. Instead, the dilemma was that East Slavic and Baltic men were typical company men with little ability to handle change. Their cultural response to transition was to start drinking even more heavily than usual, which reduced their life expectancy. In recent years, "[d]eclines in male life expectancy ... have generally been arrested. However, many of the proximate causes of high male mortality, notably the high incidence of cardiovascular and circulatory disease and death from accidents and acts of violence, remain" (World Bank 2005b, p. 25).

Falling Infant Mortality

Infant mortality is a more relevant indicator of the quality of health care. It was always much higher in the communist countries than in the West. Most postcommunist countries have experienced a considerable reduction in infant mortality since 1989, and this decline is positively related to reform. Central Europe has recorded a stunning fall in infant mortality by no less than 65 percent from 1989 to 2005, and the Czech Republic has one of the lowest infant mortalities in the world – reflecting truly remarkable progress (see Figure 7.3). The Baltic countries have done almost as well with a decline by half from 1992 to 2005. Within the CIS, two opposing patterns are evident. The six most reformist CIS countries (Russia, Ukraine, Armenia, Georgia, Kazakhstan, and Kyrgyzstan) experienced a respectable 40 percent reduction in their infant mortality from 1989 to 2005. By contrast, the six least reformist CIS countries (Belarus, Moldova, Azerbaijan, Tajikistan, Turkmenistan, and Uzbekistan) faced a substantial rise in their infant mortality of almost 30 percent from 1990 to 2005. Remarkably, relatively wealthy and purportedly socially oriented Belarus made no advances in infant mortality, whereas poor Armenia, Georgia, and Kyrgyzstan did. The conclusion is that radical economic reform helped reduce infant mortality. A complementary argument is that more democratic polities are more responsive to their people and offer better health care than dictatorships.

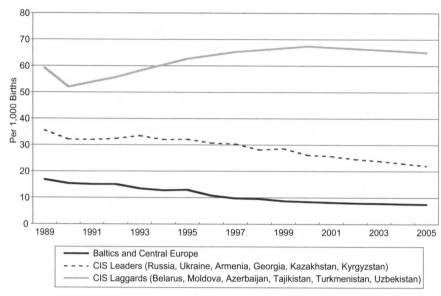

Figure 7.3. Infant Mortality, 1989–2005. *Source:* U.S. Census Bureau (2006).

Contrary to popular perception, health expenditures did not collapse after communism but have been reasonably stable in real terms rising as a share of GDP. For instance, Russia's real public health spending exceeded the 1990 level as early as 1994 (Davis 2001). Hungary (8.4%) and the Czech Republic (7.5%) spend a higher percentage of their GDP on public health care than some of the richest countries. Seven countries, Georgia, Azerbaijan, Kazakhstan, Kyrgyzstan, Moldova, Tajikistan, and Uzbekistan, spend less than 3 percent of GDP on public health care, which appears to be too little (World Bank 2005b, p. 184). The most relevant measure, however, is the region's total health expenditures as a share of GDP. They increased by no less than half from 4 percent of GDP in 1990–1 to 6 percent of GDP in 2003 (World Bank 2006, UNDP 1998, p. 215). Even so, 1990–1 was a time of radical increase in health budgets because of populist pressures throughout the region. This is almost a West European level of health care spending, and it is highly respectable for countries at this level of development, suggesting that people care about their health and can influence such spending. A major explanation behind this counterintuitive development is that private expenditure on health has risen sharply.

The contrast with public health care in the Soviet Union is stark. A Soviet economist reported in 1988: "The USSR has 4,000 district hospitals, but more than 1,000 of them have no sewage system, 2,500 no hot running water,

600 have neither hot nor cold water" (Bolotin 1988). In 1985, Soviet public health care funding had fallen to a dismal 2.2 percent of GDP, although it rose to 2.9 percent of GDP in 1990 (Goskomstat 1991, pp. 9, 16). Health indicators improved greatly under Gorbachev, but only temporarily because of his brief and unsustainable campaign against alcohol. After this last Soviet campaign faded away, the long-term decline in most health indicators recurred in most former Soviet republics.

Although the level of health expenditures is respectable, most public health care systems are deplorably inefficient. At the beginning of the 1990s, East European countries had over 50 percent more hospital beds for their population than EU countries, and hospitals accounted for over 70 percent of the health care budget compared with less than 50 percent in most EU countries (*Eurohealth*, Autumn 2001, p. 1). Most countries had too many hospital beds and too many specialists but not enough general practitioners, nurses, medicines, and modern medical equipment. Under communism, health care was free in theory, but bribes and tips were commonplace. A large gray sector has persisted, as medical staff use the capital of the public health care system for informal private work instead of setting up expensive private clinics. In transition, health care systems have remained highly centralized, stifling local initiatives. The performance of the health care system probably deteriorated for a few years despite large budget allocations. Unlike other parts of the postcommunist economy, it has hardly benefited from any privatization.

Health care has attracted a lot of policy attention. The first political ambition was to raise health care expenditures, but reforms have been late. They have aimed at the separation of the funding of care, the purchasing of medical services and medicines, and the provision of care as in most Organization for Economic Cooperation and Development (OECD) countries. The Hungarian, Czech, and Polish governments have launched far-reaching medical insurance schemes financed with a payroll tax, and so has Kyrgyzstan. Many other countries have introduced some medical insurance, but most of these schemes have been partial (Nicholls 1999; World Bank 2005b).

Health care reforms have perked up efficiency somewhat, but initial results have been humble. Funding levels have stabilized or increased, but quality has barely improved. The health care system has too much real estate and staff, and resources for basic public health activities are insufficient. One outcome has been repeated failures to stem communicable diseases (World Bank 2005b). The restructuring of health care has accelerated since the mid-1990s in most countries. Often, reforms have taken on a decentralized life of their own, when hospitals and other local bodies have gained some

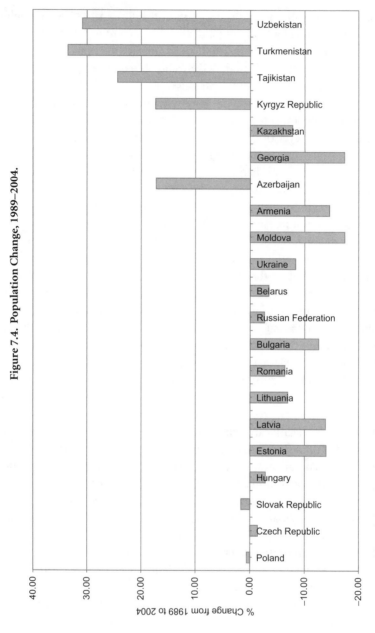

Figure 7.4. Population Change, 1989–2004.

Source: World Bank (2006) and United Nations Economic Commission for Europe (2006).

independence. A good measure of rationalization is the reduction of the previously abundant hospital beds. All postcommunist countries but Poland reduced the number of hospital beds from 1989 to 2003, but in 2003 Belarus and Russia had the largest number of hospital beds per population, revealing that they had undertaken the least health care reform (World Bank 2006).

Few reforms are as complex as health care reforms. No good model exists, although elementary West European public health care system serves as a model. The medical systems involve large numbers of staff, who have often resisted reforms. This is particularly true of senior administrators, the main beneficiaries of the gray economy in health care. Little competition between service providers has developed, and the corruption of public health care breeds inefficiency and dissatisfaction (Chernichovsky et al. 1996; Nicholls 1999). One of the greatest improvements lies outside of the public health care system because with the introduction of a market economy, all kinds of medicines have become available.

Confusing Demographic Developments

Demographic changes have been dramatic. Four major demographic trends are apparent. In the whole European part of the region, fertility has been far below the human net reproduction rate of 2.1 children per woman, and death rates have been high. As a result, all European postcommunist countries, apart from catholic Poland and Slovakia, have recorded a natural decline in their population. Azerbaijan and the Central Asian countries, except Kazakhstan, by contrast, have had a substantial natural population growth because of high birth rates. A second trend has been that Russians, and people ethnically close to them, have emigrated from the Baltic states and Central Asia, partially to Russia. Third, the ethnic core population too has emigrated on a large scale from the poorest and war-ridden countries – Armenia, Moldova, and Georgia – but also from all the poor Central Asian countries. Finally, many citizens of the poorest EU accession countries, as well as Moldova and Ukraine, have sought work in the EU countries.

The overall population picture is diverse. The region can be divided into three groups with regard to population developments. A first group of ten countries have experienced a considerable decline in their populations. According to official statistics, five countries lost about 15 percent of their population since 1989: Georgia, Armenia, Estonia, Latvia, and Bulgaria (see Figure 7.4). In reality, Moldova and Ukraine should be added to this group, and Armenia, Georgia, and Moldova actually lost as much as one-fifth to one-quarter of their populations. Other countries with substantial decreases of their populations are Lithuania, Romania, and Kazakhstan.

A second group of five countries, Azerbaijan, Kyrgyzstan, Tajikistan, Turkmenistan, and Uzbekistan, has experienced a strong population growth of 17 to 33 percent from 1989 to 2004, according to the official statistics. These numbers are somewhat exaggerated because of significant unregistered emigration, mainly to Russia and Kazakhstan.

A third group comprises six countries: the four Central European countries, Russia, and Belarus. They are the only countries with more or less stable populations. Considering all the talk about Russia's demographic crisis, it may come as a surprise that its population is among the most stable among transition countries, but this is the average between a substantial natural decline and large immigration from other former Soviet republics.

New threats are rising. The whole region has one of the most rapidly growing infection rates of HIV/AIDS in the world, particularly in Russia, Ukraine, and Estonia, because of the increased use of injected drugs, high migration rates, and limited government response (World Bank 2005b), but the impact has been limited as yet.

Education Adjusting to Demand

The situation in education resembles health care, but it is much better because of more private initiatives. Comprehensive education was the pride of communism, and unlike socialist health care the education system could boast of considerable achievements. The whole region enjoyed 99 percent literacy. Secondary education was standard, and university education was as common as in Western Europe. In particular, the communist countries were strong in mathematics and engineering.

Education was a real priority of communism. In 1990–1, the transition countries spent on average 5.9 percent of their GDP on education, even more than the 5.4 percent of GDP in the OECD countries (UNDP 1998, p. 217). By 2002, average public spending on education remained high at 5.0 percent of GDP in the postcommunist countries, compared with 5.3 percent of GDP in the rich OECD countries. Yet a few countries (Armenia, Georgia, and Tajikistan) had such low public education expenditures that basic education for all was endangered (World Bank 2006). Private expenditures on education have surged, but they are not well surveyed. Real total expenditure on education has probably risen after communism.

Unfortunately, the public education system is poorly managed. Teachers have suffered from low wages and long-lasting wage arrears, and shortages of textbooks have prevailed. The most worrisome tendency is that primary school enrollment is no longer comprehensive in several former Soviet countries. A poor underclass might be dropping out of education, although since 1998, enrollment in the compulsory education has improved.[4]

University education offers the real surprise. Definitions vary, but the number of university students has risen greatly, approximately doubling from 1989 to 1999. The new EU members have as high a share of their youth enrolled in higher education as the old EU members (World Bank 2005c, p. 83). This surge is particularly marked in Poland, Bulgaria, Hungary, Armenia, Russia, and the whole of Central Asia (UNDP 1998, pp. 74, 217). The expansion of university education seems a response to increasing demand, with the greatest rise in enrollment in business administration (Pleskovic et al. 2000). At the beginning of the transition, many in the region reckoned that higher education was no longer of significance for their earnings because only the ability to trade counted, but that view lasted only a couple of years. Soon people realized that investment in their human capital was worthwhile. Youngsters decided to learn economics, business administration, law, and languages. These subjects were no specialties of the old universities and institutes, so numerous new institutions developed. During a trip to St. Petersburg in 1992, I learned that the city harbored no fewer than 200 institutions that proudly, although somewhat pretentiously, called themselves business schools. Many barely existed and most closed down, but the degree of entrepreneurship in higher education, particularly business training, has been extraordinary. As reflected in the rising income differentials, the return on human capital soared with transition.

In a study of economic education in twenty postcommunist countries, we found a proliferation of new, usually private, universities. This development was most prominent in relatively liberal CIS countries, notably Russia, Ukraine, the Caucasus, Kazakhstan, and Kyrgyzstan. Small Georgia took the prize with no fewer than 279 officially registered institutions of higher education. People are evidently drawing the sensible conclusion that the old public universities in the Caucasus and Central Asia are no good, establishing new institutions, but the new pluralistic and competitive climate has reinvigorated the old universities as well. In the Baltics, Central Europe, and Southeast Europe, the old universities have remained dominant, and much fewer new schools, primarily business schools, have been added. Although education is politically sensitive, most postcommunist countries have evidenced considerable openness to private initiative and outside funding, except the

---

[4] Alas, the two main sources of data, the World Bank and United Nations Educational, Scientific and Cultural Organization, present numbers that are completely contradictory (World Bank 2005b; TransMONEE database 2006).

hard dictatorships of Belarus, Turkmenistan, and Uzbekistan (Pleskovic et al. 2000).

Another positive aspect of postcommunist higher education is the vast volume of private financing that has become available. In the CIS, about half of the students pay tuition fees. Because bribes for admittance were common in Soviet days, and still are, people easily accept formal tuition fees. In recent years, local businesspeople have started giving substantial donations for education. Unfortunately, state financing is extremely centralized, and the private financing that often accounts for half the funding of state universities is gray, inciting university administrators to illicit actions. Reformers demand that universities become independent foundations, accountable to a board of trustees. The increased reliance on private financing has led to a new dominance over the education system by the middle class, reflected in the greater emphasis on university training at the expense of primary and secondary education reminiscent of Latin America.

Both the old state institutions and the new private universities suffer from severe problems with quality. Bribery has became pervasive both in private and public institutions of higher learning, especially in the Caucasus and Central Asia. In many CIS countries, professors demand bribes for exams, which reduces the students' incentives to study. Falling standards of higher education have become a serious concern, particularly in the Caucasus and Central Asia. As a reaction, reformers demand standardized national tests and entrance exams, without subjective interviews, but university presidents, who benefit from corruption, put up severe resistance. A major bottleneck is the training of university teachers and researchers. Few good graduate programs in social sciences exist in the region, rendering the education of a new corps of teachers in the West necessary, as well as the building of new institutions in the region. For natural sciences, the problem is low funding and salaries, which have convinced tens of thousands of Soviet scientists to emigrate to the West or to the local private sector (Pleskovic et al. 2000).

Unlike the Chinese government, these postcommunist governments have shown little interest in organizing major scholarship programs to send students abroad. The main exception is Kazakhstan, which in 2006 increased the number of scholarships for study abroad to 3,000 a year. The best institutions of higher education in the former Soviet Union have been set up in cooperation with foreign institutions and donors, but in many cases, the foreign partners have lost interest or financing after several years, and many projects have collapsed. Among the best new universities are a series of American Universities in Bulgaria, Armenia, and Kyrgyzstan. There are also excellent graduate schools, the main one being George Soros's Central European University in Budapest. Virtually all of the best education establishments in the region have been cofinanced by George Soros (Pleskovic et al. 2000).

The situation is better with textbooks. Many Western textbooks have been translated from English into local languages or written anew, again through George Soros's generous financing, and the free book market swiftly spread modern textbooks throughout the region, providing a strong base for better education in social sciences. Similarly, the curricula of good Western university courses have swiftly proliferated, especially at new universities. Unfortunately, mediocre professors with old training insist on using their own textbooks, denying their students the benefits of better textbooks.

In sum, education has seen far more entrepreneurship and experimentation than the health sector, as postcommunist people seem more prepared to invest in their brains than in their health. Part of the explanation might be that the young want education, whereas the old demand health care. Moreover, teaching requires less starting capital. Yet young customers are not necessary well informed and many students are trapped in expensive education of poor quality. Like the public health care system, the public education system calls for profound reforms. Fewer resources should be wasted on real estate, and qualified teachers need higher salaries. Universities and school districts require financial independence from the central governments, although they should be accountable to local boards. The state should administer standardized national tests and exams to combat the deleterious effect of pervasive bribery, and it must not stifle initiative through bureaucratic interference. Poor quality and high cost are the main concerns in education (World Bank 2005b).

Social Transfers and Pension Reform

Social support is one of the most misperceived elements in the transition.[5] The main problems have not been collapsing social support systems, but the expansion of social transfers beyond a sustainable level and their misdirection to the relatively wealthy. In the first years of transition, social transfers increased sharply as a share of GDP in Central Europe, the Baltics, and the Slavic states of the former Soviet Union (UNDP 1998 p. 94). Only in the Caucasus and Central Asia did they shrink, but they still exceeded East

---

[5] This section draws on Åslund and Dmitriev (1996), Dmitriev (1996), Goleniowska (1997), Holzmann (1997a, 1997b), Kramer (1997), UNDP (1998), and World Bank (2005b).

Asia's level. The exceptions were Georgia and Tajikistan, states that were on the verge of disintegration. In addition to direct social support, substantial subsidies to enterprises, housing, and utilities have been maintained in some countries. Social transfers were outsized and unaffordable for middle-income countries, without providing effective social protection. A transition to a more efficient and targeted system has started, but developments are diverse.

Over the 1990s, social transfers were scaled down. By 2000, their share had declined to 6.5 percent of GDP in the poor CIS countries (Armenia, Azerbaijan, Georgia, Kyrgyzstan, and Moldova), whereas they were 13.8 percent in the new EU members. Pensions constituted 70 percent of the social transfers in the new EU members and 50 percent in the poorest CIS countries (World Bank 2005b, p. 118). Compared with other countries at the same economic level, social transfers are still high.

The Dilemmas of a Social Safety Net

The old social benefits were not very social, because a relatively limited share went to the poorest. A sharp line falls between Russia and Ukraine on one hand and Central Europe together with the Baltics on the other. In the former, about 10 percent of all social transfers has gone to the poorest 20 percent (Milanovic 1998, p. 113). A couple of hundred "categorical" benefits remained on the books in Russia and Ukraine in 1999, and they were targeted at the old Nomenklatura, which received such benefits instead of higher salaries. In 1998, the Russian Ministry of Labor and Social Affairs found that 70 percent of all social transfers went to the wealthiest 30 percent households (Dmitriev 1999; Misikhina 1999). Central Europe and the Baltics, on the contrary, had relatively efficient social assistance, which helps to explain their more even income distribution (Milanovic 1998).

Family and maternal allowances are very small, in the range of 1–2 percent of GDP, although families with children belong to the poorest. Little wonder that these countries suffer from extremely low nativity. In recent years, many countries have raised child support to stimulate nativity. This has occurred as a matter of national policy – for instance, in Ukraine and Russia – because young parents with small children do not constitute a pressure group.

Under communism, the government provided large price subsidies, but workers paid for these with their artificially low wages. Some countries tried to maintain subsidies for essential foods, but the outcome was shortages. In 1992, the government of Kyrgyzstan fixed low milk prices, which led to the mass slaughtering of cows to the long-term detriment of milk and meat production (Chu and Gupta 1993, p. 25). Politically most difficult were housing and utilities subsidies, which were defended tooth and nail by the upper middle class in the big cities, the main beneficiaries. Transportation subsidies were also politically sensitive, but they were small.

The old Soviet-type social support system was corporatist, although pensions comprised a centralized state system. Health care and education were centralized state systems, but ministries and enterprises had their own facilities. Because many social benefits were provided by enterprises, no comprehensive social welfare system existed (OECD 1996). After communism, the countries in the region developed rather different social support systems, which can schematically be divided into three distinct models.

Hungary and Poland opted for West European social democratic welfare systems in the late 1980s and maintained them after communism. The advantage of this model was that the social welfare system became universal, independent of enterprises, but the costs of social protection in Hungary and Poland rose to 30–35 percent of GDP, which was not sustainable. The Czech Republic and Slovakia emulated these developments, although they checked the costs and chose a slightly less rigid model. These high expenditures are forcing the Central Europeans to undertake significant social welfare reforms. In 2004, Slovakia parted company with the other three more social democratic countries, but these reforms contributed to the loss by the reformist center-right government in the 2006 elections to left-wing populists.

The Baltic states were more liberal and radical, not least because they had less money. They chose a mixture of a liberal and a social democratic social welfare model, developing the most modern and efficient social welfare system in the region. Their model was both less costly and more flexible. Among the Caucasian countries, Kazakhstan, and Kyrgyzstan, public revenues dropped below 20 percent of GDP, forcing them to prioritize among their public expenditures. The result has been some radical social welfare reforms. Kazakhstan and Kyrgyzstan have sought inspiration from East Asia and international liberal ideas. Together with the Baltic states, these five states have undertaken the most far-reaching and sensible social welfare reforms.

The most conservative countries are Russia, Ukraine, Belarus, Moldova, and Uzbekistan, which largely maintain the old Soviet model of social welfare. Russia and Ukraine are suffocated by bloated bureaucratic systems because of their sheer size, whereas the rulers of Belarus and Uzbekistan have been hostile to most reforms.[6] Until the end of the 1990s, they maintained

---

[6] Turkmenistan has let its social sector decline because its priority is to build palaces for the omnipotent President Niyazov.

substantial enterprise subsidies – 8 to 10 percent of GDP in Russia and Ukraine – and big housing and utilities subsides – steadily around 4 percent of GDP in Russia. Their social support was extremely inefficient. The old elite maintained such power that it was able to concentrate social benefits to themselves. The Russian financial crash in 1998 forced Russia, Ukraine, and Moldova to undertake significant social reforms, but they are still lagging behind Kazakhstan and Kyrgyzstan.

Curiously, a motley group of the Baltics, Kazakhstan, Kyrgyzstan, and recently Slovakia feature the most modern social support models. Poland, Hungary, and the Czech Republic labor on with an old-fashioned and expensive model, but the awareness of the need for reform is insufficient. Belarus and Uzbekistan stand out as unreformed old Soviet corporatist systems.

After the first bout of populism at the end of communism and in the early transition, domestic support for social safety nets has been limited. It is difficult to reach the truly poor with targeted support in the former Soviet Union, considering the lack of reliable data on personal incomes and the corrupt public administration. Too much of the purported social benefits go to middlemen rather than the poor. Branko Milanovic (1998) wisely concluded that an OECD-like minimum income guarantee would hardly work in the CIS because of the great income underreporting. Instead, support to specific groups – pensioners, children, and the unemployed – will have to suffice. In the CIS, it makes sense to raise the minimum wage as a social protection for poor workers, considering that they have so little clout, as Russia and Ukraine have done in recent years. A decent unemployment benefit for half a year is one way to reach a truly poor group. Because families with children form an exposed group, family allowances – whether universal or means tested – can help. Altogether, this does not amount to much. Means-tested local social welfare is still needed for the truly poor because there is no plausible solution with such a poor information basis and corrupt delivery system.

Private transfers are also important. In low income CIS countries, remittances and other private transfers by far exceeded public transfers. In Moldova, remittances account for more than 10 percent of GDP and boost consumption levels, including among the poor, helping to reduce poverty (World Bank 2005b).

On the whole, little has been done to create an effective social safety net targeted at the truly poor. One explanation is that the young and middle-aged poor have been disorganized, lacking political representation. The communists have shown little interest in this conundrum, but have fought tooth and nail for Nomenklatura privileges and pensions. Moreover, no delivery system can easily reach the poor, whereas the centralized pension systems were in comparatively good shape. The government has little real knowledge of personal incomes, and its apparatus is quite corrupt. The social administrations, which are large and conservative, have resisted reform. Finally, the socialist principle that "those who do not work should not eat" was popular in the CIS, breeding opposition to public payments to the poor.

An Expensive but Inadequate Pension System

The pension system provides the most important social transfers. All the socialist countries had comprehensive public pensions, although millions of Soviet citizens were excluded from old-age pensions until 1985. However, the old pension systems suffered from many shortcomings. They were rather expensive, with costs ranging from 4.4 percent of GDP to 9.1 percent in the European part of the Soviet bloc in 1989. Even so, the postcommunist regimes raised pensions substantially, and by 1994, the costs of pensions had surged to 6.5–15.8 percent of GDP. By comparison, the OECD average was about 7 percent of GDP, ranging from 2 percent in Iceland and Australia to 13 percent in Italy in 1995 (Impavido 1997, p. 107). Poland took the lead, doubling the real costs of its pensions to almost 16 percent of GDP, the highest share in the world. The first Polish reform government decided to index pensions fully, maintaining real pensions even when real incomes fell, to mitigate the resentment of the elderly (Goleniowska 1997). The old were angry in any case and voted disproportionately for the communists, and the young had to pay their high pension costs.

The large costs were not caused by a high level of benefits but by excessive coverage. The retirement age in the Soviet Union was the lowest in the world – 55 for women and 60 for men, whereas 60 for women and 65 for men were standard in Central Europe. Many professional groups, ranging from coal miners and ballerinas to colonels, were entitled to early pensions. In exaggerated fear of mass unemployment, the Central European reformers encouraged workers to take early pensions. Altogether, about one-quarter of the population was entitled to pensions.

The pensions were financed with exorbitant payroll taxes. Hungary had the highest total payroll tax, peaking at 62 percent in 1993. The old Soviet payroll tax of 38 percent was actually the lowest, but most former Soviet republics had raised them to 40–50 percent, compared with 15 percent in the United States (Holzmann 1997a). These payroll taxes were not tenable. They led to massive tax evasion and the flight of a large share of the labor force into the underground economy.

The pension system was unjust as well. Contributions and resulting pensions were barely related. The Nomenklatura enjoyed special high state pensions paid directly from the state budget. Working pensioners received full pensions and paid little or no tax because their pensions were not subject to taxation. Politicians meddled with pensions, rendering them unpredictable. In the CIS, pension arrears became as notorious as wage arrears. In Ukraine, pensioners had to wait six months for their pensions in the mid-1990s. As state finances worsened in the CIS countries, the state could no longer afford reasonable pensions, driving average pensions down and below subsistence minimum in the poorer countries. Notwithstanding a very expensive pension system, CIS pensioners could not entrust their survival to ordinary pensions. With the financial crash in Russia in 1998, the average Russian pensioner fell below the official poverty line. Unlike other social benefits, pensions were actually paid out to everybody entitled, even if delays occurred. A fundamental pension reform was needed.

Discussion on pension reforms started in the early 1990s, when the excessive costs and insufficient social protection became evident. This debate has developed in three waves, which have affected different regions under the influence of international experiences. Initially, the International Labor Organization (ILO), the OECD, and the EU took the lead. They proposed a West European pension system, maintaining the basic state system but with higher retirement age, taxation of working pensioners, closer connection between contributions and pensions, and the elimination of various privileges. They wanted to fix the pay-as-you-go system rather than replace it (Holzmann 1997a). Only Estonia succeeded in undertaking such a reform, but a radical increase in the retirement age was not popular with anybody and it contributed to the demise of its young, reformist government in the elections in 1995.

A more radical reform was necessary. In 1994, the World Bank (1994a) published its report *Averting the Old Age Crisis*, which propagated new thinking about pension reform. As a consequence, the organization became the leading international agency on pension reforms. Its approach was inspired by the Chilean pension reform and ensuing reforms in Latin America, but it did not go as far, favoring a three-pillar pension system. The first pillar would be a minimum pay-as-you-go state pension for all. The second pillar was to be a funded system based on compulsory saving in individual accounts, and the third would be voluntary private pension savings. Apart from securing pensions and lowering the payroll tax, such a reform would stimulate savings, the development of the capital market, and ultimately economic growth. From 1998 to 2004, this system was legislated by all countries in Central Europe and the Baltics (World Bank 2004). This more radical reform had political advantages. The connection between contribution and benefit became credible, transforming pensions from an entitlement to savings and insurance, which generated middle-class support. Retirement age became a matter of personal choice rather than a political battle.

In the CIS, citizens distrusted the state and its competence much more than in Central Europe and the Baltics, where the old pension system still functioned. Reformers in Kazakhstan opted for a pure Chilean pension reform, with private, funded pensions, maintaining minimal state pensions for those in the old system and the poor. By doing so, they joined a liberal international ambition to privatize social security. Kazakhstan adopted such a system in 1998, with a contribution rate of 10 percent of incomes, but old pensions were not touched (Holzmann 1997a). Three major problems arose. The first was the paucity of sensible investment objects in Kazakhstan, because the stock market was underdeveloped, and the treasury bill market hardly offered positive returns. Another problem was that funding was diverted from the old pension system, but its expenditures burdened the budget (Cangiano et al. 1998). The third problem was that the private pension savings were insufficient. As a result, the government of Kazakhstan reintroduced a minimum state pension for all in 2006, and it is considering reintroducing a payroll tax on enterprises to raise pension benefits.

A bizarre incident occurred in Ukraine in 2004. Although the country had partially legislated a three-pillar system in 2003, it was thrown back to the populism of 1990 in the presidential election in 2004. The incumbent government doubled pensions, and Ukraine's pension costs shot up to nearly 16 percent of GDP, the highest in the world. The government formed after the Orange Revolution did nothing to scale back these excessive pensions because it was considered too politically sensitive. Ukraine thus repeated Poland's mistake in the early transition and may have formed a social welfare trap.

Pension systems in the region remain comprehensive and expensive. The pendulum has swung back to the middle-of-the-road World Bank's three-pillar system, whereas both the pure Chilean model as well as the old West European pay-as-you-go model are out of fashion.

Three Alternative Social Models

Today the wilder claims about a universal collapse in living standards and social expenditures can be left aside as misperceptions. A more relevant observation is that three alternative social models have arisen that correspond to three models of taxation.

Belarus and Uzbekistan have retained the old Soviet social model. Their social expenditures are still large as a share of GDP, but their efficacy and efficiency are deplorable, as is evident from their rising infant mortality. They maintain the Soviet social welfare system that primarily benefits the old Nomenklatura.

The second model is the social democratic social welfare system that Hungary and Poland introduced toward the end of socialism, and the Czech Republic has a similar system. The characteristic of this system is large social transfers, which require high taxes. These two features go together with an overregulated labor market (see Chapter 4). This model is a social welfare trap. Still all these countries have greatly improved the functioning of their public health care and education sectors, and they have undertaken pension reforms. Their states function well enough to convince many citizens to favor the public sector.

The third model is liberal, represented by the three Baltic states, Kyrgyzstan, and Kazakhstan. They all have a much smaller state, lower social transfers, and consequently lower taxes. They offer a larger role for the private sector and the market. Kazakhstan has gone the furthest in liberal pension reform and labor market reform. Arguably, Armenia, Georgia, Bulgaria, and Romania are moving in this direction along with most of the late CIS reformers.

Many social developments appear unrelated to these three models. One of the most important dividing lines is democracy. Amartya Sen established that famines had disappeared with democracy in India (Drèze and Sen 1989). In the same way, the efficacy of social support systems is positively correlated with democracy. The fully democratic countries in Central Europe and the Baltics have comparatively well-functioning and equitable social support systems. In the not very democratic CIS countries, the prime problem with the social welfare system has been that it mainly benefits the upper middle class, and social transfers remain regressive. Especially in Russia and Ukraine, it has been politically controversial to reduce the old Nomenklatura benefits, and it has been equally difficult to raise unemployment benefits.

A similar explanation can be hypothesized for the increased income disparities. Income inequality appears to rise with authoritarian rule. In democratic East-Central Europe income differentiation has widened to a West European level, whereas in the not very democratic CIS, income inequality has reached a U.S. level regardless of economic system. Similarly, the public education system throughout the CIS has become exceedingly focused on the interests of the middle class, whereas the supply of education appears more balanced in East-Central Europe.

The reason for the fall in male life expectancy in Russia, the Western CIS, and the Baltics is completely different. The simple but sad reason seems to be that East Slavic and Baltic men are company men who found it exceedingly hard to adapt to the transition and instead fell for the temptation of heavy drinking, causing many to die young. Because the initial fall in life expectancy was equally scary in radically reformist Estonia as in nonreforming Belarus, the cause cannot be sought in the nature of their reforms. After several years, however, the Baltic states saw their male life expectancy rise almost as in the Central European countries, so in the longer term, the economic system mattered.

Large public systems supplying social services, notably health care and education, have been among the slowest to reform and restructure, which explains why people complain so much about them. They suffered from being state-owned and centralized, allowing neither private nor local initiative. It is illuminating that unreformed Belarus has about the worst development of mortality and vitality indicators, although it boasts little initial output decline and high economic growth.

The demographic situation is the most complex. Several countries have already lost one-fifth to one-quarter of their populations. One group is the war-ridden and poor countries, such as Moldova, Armenia, and Georgia, but other countries, such as Estonia, Latvia, and Bulgaria, suffered a large decline in their population because of a combination of low nativity and large emigration. The Muslim countries in Central Asia and Azerbaijan, by contrast, are seeing a substantial increase in population.

Finally, resources matter. The poorest countries in the region have suffered the most, as is evident especially from their high poverty rate. High infant mortality and poor education are other indicators of poverty.

Although social reforms arrived late, they gained momentum in the late 1990s. They were driven by rising costs, declining public revenues, and increasing public dissatisfaction. The first concern was to secure sufficient financing for basic needs, such as health, pensions, and basic education, which has largely been accomplished. The next issue was to check costs and improve efficiency through systemic reforms. Two focal points have been health care, which has been strikingly inefficient, and pensions, which have been expensive yet left everybody dissatisfied. Much remains to be done; complex social reforms take a lot of time, and large public institutions are the most difficult to reform. Substantial social reforms are discussed in many countries and do occur, but resistance is entrenched and remains severe.

8

Democracy versus Authoritarianism

An important reason for the breakdown of the communist dictatorship was a split in the old elite, the Nomenklatura. Liberals in the old establishment thought they would be better off economically and also freer under a more liberal regime. Many "members of the old elite were now discovering that they could maintain their privileged positions in society even without the ideology...the party was no longer a monolith. And once it ceased to be a monolith, it was no longer viable" (Dobbs 1997, pp. 373–4). The party reformers were opposed by dogmatic hardliners who wanted to maintain the old order, and the escalating struggle between these two factions made it possible for outside reformers, often true democrats, to start playing a political role (McFaul 2001).

When communist power collapsed, the political situation changed in a revolutionary fashion. Usually, two dominant political forces emerged. One was a broad popular movement embracing democracy and freedom, and its opponent was the reformist part of the old elite; the hardliners simply disappeared. The dilemma for the rising democrats was whether to opt for a full defeat of the old system or for a compromise with its more progressive members, with whom they had cooperated until the end of communism. The new political leaders made different choices depending on preconditions, popular opinion, and their own preferences. All Central European countries started off with roundtable negotiations, whereas the abortive hard-line 1991 coup in Moscow forced abrupt transitions on all the Soviet republics. The same was true of the violent uprising in Romania. Ironically, the more sudden the collapse of the old system was, the greater role the old establishment assumed, as liberal opposition had little time to evolve. Democracy never had a chance in Turkmenistan, Uzbekistan, and Kazakhstan, where the old rulers stayed in power, just abandoning their communist cloaks.

Democratizing new regimes had to choose between fast and slow democratization in the same fashion as they had to choose economic reform strategy. The fundamental problem with the communist state was that it worked for the Nomenklatura rather than for the people. Democratization meant making the state work for the population instead. At this time, however, able members of the old elite exploited the weakness of the political and economic institutions to enrich themselves at the expense of society through extraordinary rent seeking. Defeating rent seeking and democratization were two sides of the same coin. They both required an early and radical break with the old system. Otherwise the Nomenklatura could amass sufficient fortunes to purchase political power for the foreseeable future.

In the same way as market forces check monopolies and rent seeking, democracy restricts the political power of the elite. Democracy was crucial for a successful market economic transition: the higher the quality of democracy, the more far-reaching market economic reform was. To render democratic pressures effective, the structure of the constitution and political representation was essential. Real political parties had to be allowed, and they were best promoted through proportional representation, with a threshold for representation in parliament. An early election after the collapse of communism facilitated the consolidation of parties and impeded their proliferation.

In this chapter, I consider political issues of significance for the economic reform process. Section one explains why democratic breakthrough was critical for a successful early economic transformation. Section two notes that democratization is not a sufficient political precondition for successful market reform. The rule of the old elite must also be broken. Otherwise society might be captured in an underreform trap. Colored revolutions have transformed semidemocratic societies, as discussed in section three. Section four considers how electoral rules and constitutions matter. A true challenge is how to tame the Leviathan that was the communist state apparatus, outlined in section five. Section six is devoted to public opinion and the role of ideology. The final section ponders over the future of democracy in the region and the ineffectiveness of democracy aid.

Democratic Breakthrough: Critical for Successful Transformation

The basic purpose of a state is to provide external and internal security. If the borders of a state are not secure or if anarchy rules within the country, people are naturally too preoccupied with these questions to think about anything else. We should not expect countries that in the early transition were ridden by civil wars (Tajikistan and Georgia), war (Armenia and Azerbaijan) or attempts by territories at violent secession (Georgia and Moldova) to be democratic. This fundamental line of thinking goes back to Thomas Hobbes (1651/1968) and was elegantly specified by Dankwart Rustow (1970, pp. 350–1): "National unity must precede all other phases of democratization" (cf. McFaul 2001).

For countries in peace, the next question is: For whom is the state working? Two opposing views stand out. One sees the state as good, but the people are unable to understand their real interests, which easily becomes a justification for more or less enlightened despotism. The other camp worries that the elite exploit the state for its own purposes. Instead, such classical liberals want the elite to be held accountable, seeing democracy as the cure. An intermediary position is that the state is good and that you have to make peace with the old elite to build a stable democracy.

The first position, that the state was good and the people foolhardy, was shared by traditional social democrats as well as some conservatives of the modernization school. An outstanding social democratic example was Nobel Prize laureate Gunnar Myrdal, who advocated dictatorship in Third World countries to speed up their economic and social development. His argument ran: "The experience of the countries in central, eastern, and southern Europe after the First World War suggests that when a democratic form of government is imposed on an economically and politically imma-ture nation it rapidly succumbs to authoritarian pressures and does so for internal reasons" (Myrdal 1968, p. 774). As an enlightened social engineer, Myrdal put his ideals of modernization over democracy: "Yet it may be doubted whether this ideal of political democracy – with political power based on free elections and with freedom of assembly, press, and other civil liberties – should be given weight in formulating the modernization ideals" (p. 65). "An authoritarian regime may be better equipped to enforce a social discipline, though its existence is no guarantee of this accomplishment" (p. 67).

The idea that democracy was the preserve of the West and countries of high economic development was deeply embedded in modernization theory, whose leading representative is Samuel Huntington. As late as 1992, he argued that "authoritarian governments are better positioned than democratic governments to promote economic liberalization" (Huntington 1992–3, p. 12). When transition started, many argued that the precondi-tions for democracy had to be built first. A premature move to democracy could hinder growth by increasing the influence of special interest groups and fostering political instability (Isham et al. 1997). This idea of benign authoritarianism is paternalistic, and it is shared both by social democrats and some conservatives.

The most extreme advocates of authoritarian modernization may be labeled the "Pinochet school." They argued that a temporary dictatorship was needed to introduce a market economy. Not surprisingly, the Pinochet argument has been more popular among old communists (for instance, Brucan 1992) and Russian industrialists than among supporters of a liberal market economy. It has been a key argument for the Chinese model. Yet some Russian economic liberals have called for a Russian Pinochet (e.g., Aven 2000).

The opposing view is that the state is evil, a Leviathan, and that it has to be minimized and controlled. The original authors of that view were the classical liberals, such as Jeremy Bentham and John Stuart Mill (1859/1975). They considered the state a means of oppression of political and economic freedom by the rulers. The best people could hope for was that the state would leave them alone, a line of thought leading to laissez-faire. In the nineteenth century, the state developed the instruments for the rule of law. Its expenditures expanded during time of war, whereas the social welfare state is a product of the last century (Tanzi and Schuknecht 2000). Many political scientists have long reckoned that democracy and a market economy belong together, but this positive correlation has been tenuous (Lindblom 1977).

A second school drew the corollary to this view, that early democratization was essential to defeat the old Nomenklatura, which was the main obstacle to market reform. Strangely, this was a minority view, but it found a home in the influential *Journal of Democracy*. Prominent advocates of combined early democratization and radical economic reform were Larry Diamond (1995), Valerie Bunce (1999a, 1999b), Michael McFaul (2001). Larry Diamond (1995, p. 108) argued:

There are powerful logical, theoretical, historical, and empirical reasons to expect a close association between capitalism and democracy, with a logical relationship flowing almost inescapably from the very definitions of these terms. Capitalism is an economic system based on private ownership of the means of production and the determination of prices and rewards through competition between private producers.... Democracy is a political system based on the autonomy and freedom of individual citizens, and the determination of public power and policies through competition between groups of citizens, based in parties and interest groups. Economic freedom and political freedom thus would appear, at a minimum, to be natural companions, even if one does not strictly require the other.

In one large cross-country regression for the whole world, Robert Barro (1996) established a universal positive correlation between democracy and growth. However, he argued that when the effects of the rule of law, free markets, small government consumption, and high human capital were set aside as well as the initial level of GDP, the overall effect of democracy on growth was weakly negative, but those effects are typical consequences of democracy. No free markets and no rule of law exist in postcommunist tyrannies.

The reputation of democracy was greatly enhanced in the late 1980s after the economic reforms in Latin America, which were usually preceded by democratization (Maravall 1994). "Only in Asia does authoritarianism appear conducive to economic liberalization" (Geddes 1994a, p. 107), which could be explained by the very limited role of the state in East Asia, the traditional macroeconomic discipline, and so on. Most dictators reveal limited compassion for their people, caring more for the fortunes of their families and friends. After all, the many dictatorships in Africa have not been known for socially inclined policies. Barbara Geddes (1994a, p. 113) summed up the new democratic insights thus: "In many countries the biggest, and certainly the most articulate and politically influential, losers from the transition to a more market-oriented economy are government officials, ruling-party cadres, cronies of rulers, and the close allies of all three. These are groups whose ability to make effective demands does not decline as regimes become less democratic, which explains why many authoritarian governments have had difficulty liberalizing their economies."

Larry Diamond (1995, p. 131) pursued the democratic case for postcommunist countries, arguing for the early adoption of a new constitution and the consecutive holding of parliamentary elections: "the state in these last decades of communist rule had ceased to represent *any* common national interest, and its collapse left nothing but powerful congeries of rent seekers, utterly contemptuous of law, with the skills and ruthlessness to accumulate enormous wealth, rapidly and illegitimately. Permitting them to do so risks discrediting the entire new order."

Valerie Bunce (1999b) argued that the uncommonly inert socialist institutions could not stand the challenges of domestic as well as international change in the 1980s. The self-destructive nature of the socialist institutions also explained the course of change. A natural consequence of this argument was that the socialist institutions were no asset but a hindrance to market reform, which led Bunce to argue for rapid institutional cleansing and for democratization as a support for market economic transformation.

In later empirical work, the slow political and economic reforms are targeted as causes of failure of both economic reform and democratization. For instance, Steven Fish (2005, p. 247) found that Russia's failure to democratize was explained by "too much oil, too little economic liberalization, and too weak a national legislature."

A third school was called "transitology." It was dominant in comparative politics, and it was based on studies of the democratizations in South Europe and Latin America in the 1970s and 1980s, which Samuel Huntington (1991) named the "third wave" of democratization. Most transitologists were social democratic. Their key idea was that a regime change should be "pacted," that is, agreed in a negotiation between the old and the new regime. Terry Lynn Karl and Phillipe Schmitter (1991), major authors of transitology, argued that negotiated, pacted transitions produced more successful democratic outcomes than nonnegotiated transitions, but they were likely to produce restricted democracy. Rather than calling for a defeat of the old elite, the transitologists wanted to avoid intimidating it. Therefore, they warned against overloading the transition. They argued that economic and political transition should not be undertaken simultaneously (O'Donnell and Schmitter 1986).[1]

Adam Przeworski (1991) specified the transitologist arguments for the postcommunist world. Like Myrdal and Huntington, Przeworski saw a choice between democracy and radical economic transformation, seeing radical reform as a threat to democracy. As discussed in Chapter 2, all his main arguments have been disproved. First, radical reform did not cause a greater but a smaller fall in output than gradual reform. Second, people did not rise against reform or endangered democracy because of steep falls in recorded output, as long as their governments appeared serious about reform. Third, the threat to democracy did not come from the people but from the elite. Furthermore, that people would be so preoccupied with short-term economic results that they would let them jeopardize democracy runs against any consideration of expectations.

Similarly, Jon Elster, Claus Offe, and Ulrich Preuss (1998, p. 272) summarized two kinds of vicious circles that they had anticipated. Either "the unrestrained use of democratic freedoms would undermine any national

---

[1] Meanwhile, Latin American growth has stalled because of insufficient structural reforms, caused by the perseverance of old vested interests, which raises the question whether the delay in economic reforms might have been harmful for Latin America, but that query goes beyond this study.

Figure 8.1. Democracy and Market Reform, 2005.

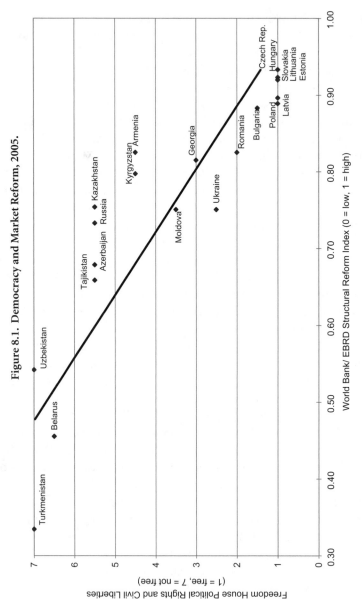

Freedom House Political Rights and Civil Liberties
(1 = free, 7 = not free)

World Bank/ EBRD Structural Reform Index (0 = low, 1 = high)

Source: EBRD (2005) and Freedom House (2006).

program of economic recovery because the citizens would use their newly acquired voting power to remove out of office every government that dared to impose on them economic and social hardships." Or "the unrestrained use of state power to impose economic reform of the 'shock therapy' kind on society irrespective of the social costs would necessarily provoke active or passive resistance of society against the reform and at the same time cause a considerable number of people to live in poverty and even misery." They concluded, however, that "fortunately neither of these hypotheses has come true in their extremely pessimistic versions."

As a result of the limited explanatory power of transitology for the post-communist world, this scholarship has not evolved much empirically, but it was the dominant mind-set in comparative politics supported by a large number of academic luminaries at the outset of transition. Its significance for shaping the Western thinking about postcommunist transformation at the early stage must not be belittled.

This book concurs with the second school advocating early democratization to be undertaken simultaneously with a radical market reform. The strife over radical market reform versus gradual reform was a matter of whether the interests of the people or a small rent-seeking elite dominated over society. The same was true of politics. A democratic breakthrough could best ensure the dominance of the popular interest over the state. Therefore, we would expect the correlation between democracy and successful market economic reform to be particularly strong in postcommunist transition. First, the communist state was far more dominant over economy and society than anywhere else in the world. Second, its elite was tightly knit, forming an isolated cast. Third, the few checks and balances of communism faded with its demise, leaving the powerful without constraints. Fourth, the opportunities for rent seeking were extraordinary.

Not surprisingly, in one of the first substantial regression analyses De Melo et al. (1997a) found such a strong correlation between political freedom and economic liberalization and it has persisted. If we plot the Freedom House index for political and civil rights against the EBRD structural transformation index for 2005, all the nine East-Central European countries are both the most reformed and the most democratic countries, whereas the nonreformers Belarus, Turkmenistan, and Uzbekistan are the most authoritarian (see Figure 8.1). Initially, most democracies in the region opted for radical reform, and the others for at least gradual reform, and the dictatorships chose little or no market reform (cf. Bunce 1999a; Havrylyshyn 2006).

From Figure 8.1, we can specify combinations of political regime and reform strategy that have reinforced one another either in a vicious or a virtuous circle. Focusing on the state of democracy and market economic transformation in 2005, we obtain four groups of countries:

1. *Full democracies with normal market economies: East-Central Europe.* These nine countries are full democracies, and they have established normal market economies. Most of them started off with radical reform strategies, although Bulgaria and Romania were greatly helped onto the right track by their severe financial crises in 1996–7. All these countries are members of the European Union, which has proved a strong anchor both for democracy and market transformation.

2. *Full-fledged authoritarian systems with Soviet-type economies: Belarus, Turkmenistan, and Uzbekistan.* Uzbekistan is still ruled by its last first communist party secretary; but without ideology. In Belarus, Alexander Lukashenko was elected with overwhelming majority in 1994 as a populist raging against the corruption of the Communist Party, but he has consolidated a dictatorship. None of these countries undertook much reform, and their economies are completely dominated by the state, serving the interests of their dictators.

The remaining states are usually labeled "captured" or oligarchic. Most of them started off as semidemocratic and undertook gradual reforms, which generated extraordinary rent seeking, leading to great inequality. The ruling elite achieved substantial economies of scale in its rent seeking, which reinforced the economic distortions. To maximize its rents, the ruling elite strengthened its political control, rendering the state more authoritarian. In that way, rent seeking contributed to authoritarianism. Although these countries are often discussed as "captured," they are actually changing the most dynamic with regard to both democracy and market economic transformation. In 2006, they can be described accordingly:

3. *Mildly authoritarian states with rent seeking dominated by the rulers: Azerbaijan, Kazakhstan, Russia, and Tajikistan.* In these countries, the president and the people closest to him maintain a firm grip on both the economy and politics, but market economies prevail. State power has been consolidated in the hands of the president. Although private ownership dominates, property rights are conditional on the political approval of the ruler. Hardly by chance, the first three countries in this group are major energy exporters, and they seem to have fallen victim to the "oil curse." The question arises whether the current rulers can sustain their dictatorial powers if the world oil prices fall substantially.

In these countries, transitional rent seeking has been reinforced by natural rents (Arendh 2005; Gaddy and Ickes 2005).

4. *Semidemocratic oligarchic states with market economies: Armenia, Kyrgyzstan, Moldova, Ukraine, and Georgia.* This group is the most diverse and unstable. All these countries are electoral democracies, but their degree of democracy varies considerably. They are market economies with significant distortions, and they are pervasively corrupt. They may either evolve toward full democracies with normal market economies, or some president may consolidate power in an authoritarian regime.

These regimes vary not only by political nature but also in stability. The full democracies are most stable, followed by the full-fledged dictatorships, whereas the semidemocratic oligarchic states and the mildly authoritarian states are rather unstable. Kyrgyzstan, Georgia, and Ukraine were all mildly authoritarian states before their colored revolutions.

A major cause as well as purpose of authoritarian rule is high-level corruption. Not surprisingly, the Freedom House index for civil and political rights is closely correlated with the corruption perception index of Transparency International, as is evident from Figure 8.2. The competitive political system has acted as a check on corruption, and the opposite of corruption has been radical reform (cf. Rose-Ackerman 1999).

An Underreform Trap

A democratic breakthrough was a necessary but insufficient condition for successful early market economic reforms.[2] Outside democrats had to oust the old ruling elite, because political discontinuity was a prerequisite for successful early reforms. The political logic of radical market programs was that people in the midst of drastic decline in output and high inflation would vote for economic stability and long-term economic growth. This idea runs counter to the perception that communist parties soon made a great electoral comeback.

In reality, however, neither was true. The outstanding Bulgarian political scientist Ivan Krastev (2000) has pointed out that the postcommunist region can be divided into two parts. In the not very democratic CIS countries that were still electoral democracies, the governments (almost) always win

---

[2] This section draws on Åslund et al. (2001).

Figure 8.2. Democracy and Corruption, 2005.

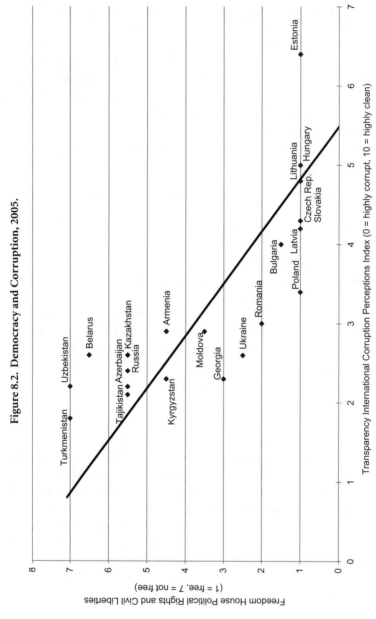

Transparency International Corruption Perceptions Index (0 = highly corrupt, 10 = highly clean)

Freedom House Political Rights and Civil Liberties
(1 = free, 7 = not free)

Source: Transparency International (2005) and Freedom House (2006).

elections, whereas in democratic East-Central Europe governments (almost) always lose elections. The explanation is that voters focus on corruption, and the incumbent government is naturally deemed responsible. Remarkably few incumbent parties have won reelection in postcommunist democracies. The swings are often huge from one election to the next. We must be careful not to draw far-reaching conclusions from single elections because ideological preferences are more submerged by such protest votes.

To test these contradictory perceptions on the electoral record, we examine all parliamentary elections in democracies in the area from 1989 until 2000.[3] Fifteen countries in our postcommunist region enjoyed a reasonable degree of political freedom, being classified as free or partly free by Freedom House, whereas seven countries were not even partly free and are excluded (Azerbaijan, Belarus, Kazakhstan, Kyrgyzstan, Tajikistan, Turkmenistan, and Uzbekistan; Freedom House 1999). Electoral outcomes are most easily classified by the size of the national Communist Party. Even if renamed, one party is usually its evident successor. Communist parties have become social democratic in Poland, Hungary, Slovakia, and Lithuania, although throughout the 1990s, they remained hard-line in their opposition to market economy in the Czech Republic, Bulgaria, Romania, and throughout the former Soviet Union – all countries that saw little democratization before the end of communism.

The results from all these parliamentary elections contrast sharply with conventional wisdom. Communist parties fared poorly regardless of country and policy (see Table 8.1). By 1998, no Communist Party in the region had attained one-third of the votes cast in the most recent democratic election. The communist parties in Italy, France, and Finland were actually larger during the Cold War. Their main strength was relative unity and solid organization. A few governments contained the odd communist minister at times (Slovakia, Russia, and Ukraine), but the Communist Party was not the senior partner in any government. Apparently, the popular nostalgia for communism was very limited. A cross-country regression for postcommunist countries shows that governments pursuing radical reform fared better in democratic elections than gradualist governments. Most governments lost their second election in the transition, but all nonsocialist governments that had opted for gradual reform lost, and some of those that had chosen radical reform won (Åslund et al. 1996).

---

[3] Presidential elections tend to be dominated by personal factors, whereas local elections are not very relevant for national policy, and participation is limited. The countries considered democratic have varied minimally, and I picked 1998 as a neutral standard.

Table 8.1. *Ex-communist vote share in parliamentary elections in postcommunist countries, 1989–2000 (percent of total votes cast)*

	First Election	Vote Share	Second Election	Vote Share	Third Election	Vote Share	Fourth Election	Vote Share
Armenia	1990	Minority	July 1995	12.1	May 1999	12.0		
Bulgaria	June 1990	47.2	Oct. 1991	33.1	Dec. 1994	43.5	April 1997	22.1
Czech Republic	June 1990	13.6	June 1992	14.2	May 1996	10.3	June 1998	11.0
Estonia	March 1990	Minority	Sept. 1992	13.6	March 1995	5.9	March 1999	6.1
Georgia	Oct.–Nov. 1990	Tiny minority	Oct. 1992	2.7	Nov. 1995	3.8	Oct. 1999	Tiny
Hungary	March–April 1990	10.9	May 1994	33.0	May 1998	32.9		
Latvia	March–April 1990	Minority	June 1993	12.0	Sept.–Oct. 1995	12.9	Oct. 1998	14.7
Lithuania	Feb.–March 1990	Minority	Oct.–Nov. 1992	42.6	Oct.–Nov. 1996	9.5	Oct. 2000	31.1
Moldova	Feb. 1990	Majority	Feb. 1994	22.0	March 1998	30.1		
Poland	June 1989	Minority	Oct. 1991	12.0	Sept. 1993	20.4	Sept. 1997	27.1
Romania	May 1990	66.3	Sept. 1992	37.9	Nov. 1996	21.5	Nov. 2000	37.0
Russia	March 1990	Majority	Dec. 1993	12.4	Dec. 1995	22.7	Dec. 1999	24.3
Slovakia	June 1990	13.6	June 1992	15.2	Sept.–Oct. 1994	13.1	Sept. 1998	14.7
Ukraine	March 1990	Majority	March 1994	Minority	March 1998	24.7		

Countries that were classified by Freedom House (Karatnycky et al. 1999) as not free have been excluded. They were Azerbaijan, Belarus, Kazakhstan, Tajikistan, Turkmenistan, Uzbekistan, and Yugoslavia. Kyrgyzstan has not had any party elections.

Notes:

1. The June 1990 election result for the Czech Republic was for all of Czechoslovakia.
2. Political parties were not allowed during the 1990 elections in any of the former Soviet Union or in the 1994 elections in Ukraine.
3. In September 1992 in Estonia, the parties Safe Home, Our Home Estonia, and the United People's Party qualify as Communist Parties, although they were primarily Russian national parties.
4. For the October 1992 result in Georgia, the number shown is share of seats not votes.
5. Latvia has had a series of Russian nationalist parties (Harmony for Latvia – Rebirth of the Economic Union and the National Harmony Party), but they have been true Communist parties, led by the old hard-line communist leaders.
6. The June 1989 election in Poland was only partly free.

Source: Inter-Parliamentary Union (www.ipu.org).

Table 8.2. *Communist Party electoral performance and market economic transformation, 1998*

	Communist parties doing well		Communist parties doing badly	
Radical Transformation	Hungary	(0.93)	Czech Republic	(0.90)
	Poland	(0.86)	Estonia	(0.90)
			Latvia	(0.86)
			Lithuania	(0.82)
			Slovakia	(0.90)
Incomplete Transformation	Bulgaria	(0.79)	Armenia	(0.76)
	Moldova	(0.76)	Georgia	(0.79)
	Romania	(0.76)		
	Russia	(0.64)		
	Ukraine	(0.65)		

Note: The borderline between "radical transformation" and "incomplete transformation" has been put at a high 0.80 on the structural reform index for 1998 (in the brackets), and as borderline between "communist parties doing badly" 20 percent of the votes in the last election before 2000 has been chosen (see Table 8.1).

Source: Table 8.1 and author's calculations from European Bank for Reconstruction and Development (1999).

Still, the strength of the Communist Party mattered. By its performance, these countries can be divided into two groups – those where the communist parties received more than 20 percent of the votes cast in the latest parliamentary election before 2000 (seven countries), and those where they obtained less than 20 percent (seven countries). This is a natural threshold with no country in the interval of 16 to 21 percent. Our summary classification is displayed in Table 8.2, matching this political division by their degree of market reform in 1998, splitting the democratic transition countries into four quadrangles.

We can distinguish three typical electoral paths. First, the top left box in Table 8.2 contains two countries that undertook radical transformation, but even so their communist parties did well. In Poland and Hungary, the former communist parties were initially almost routed, but they staged strong comebacks to about 30 percent of the vote, as they were thoroughly reformed early on. They could be described as right-wing social democratic parties by West European standards.[4] The success of these countries' market economic transformation convinced even communist leaders to reform,

---

[4] If we had chosen a different time, the similarly reformed Lithuanian postcommunist party could have joined them.

securing their political survival. Their conversion verified the formation of a market economic consensus.

In seven countries the communist parties were devastated, receiving only 10 to 16 percent in the most recent elections before 2000. All went through substantial market economic transformation and achieved considerable and lasting growth and are in the right upper box in Table 8.2 (or just below). These communist parties undertook far-reaching reform, but they did not reform fast enough. A broad consensus in favor of market reform was achieved without them.

The bottom left box in Table 8.2 contains five countries where communist parties have been relatively successful, although the market economic transformation was incomplete. These five countries are Bulgaria, Romania, Moldova, Ukraine, and Russia. All these countries were in an underreform trap during most of the 1990s.

Russia, Moldova, and Ukraine endured the most long-lasting rent seeking. Their old communist parties remained strong, gathering 20 to 30 percent of the votes cast. Although not formally in power in Ukraine or Russia, the communists were highly influential in parliament because the electoral system made them overrepresented, allowing them to block reform legislation. That suited powerful "oligarchic" business groups, which thrived on an all-intrusive state, demanding high taxes from all but them, whom the state offered ample subsidies instead. Thus both communists and oligarchs favored similar economic policies, forging a consensus around a rent-seeking state. The concentrated economic power around the state circumscribed democracy, and politics became polarized between oligarchs and communists.

The liberal right was weak, because the performance of the partial market economy was mediocre, and few strong independent entrepreneurs had emerged. Liberals faced the unenviable choice between compromising with oligarchs (Anatoly Chubais in 1996) or staying in the political desert, rendering themselves politically irrelevant (Grigori Yavlinsky). Electorally, the communists remained strong because of dissatisfaction with the poorly functioning semireformed system, whereas most noncommunist voters supported oligarchs as the strongest opponents of the communists. As a consequence, communists stayed both strong and unreformed when market-oriented economic transformation was slow.

The best examples of communists and oligarchs helping each other to dominate politics were the Russian presidential elections in 1996 and the very similar Ukrainian presidential elections in 1999. In both cases, a communist systemic threat convinced all anticommunists to unite behind the victorious incumbent president, with the oligarchs as the main beneficiaries. The natural outcome was an oligarchic economic and political power structure. Interestingly, the European Bank for Reconstruction and Development ([EBRD] 1999) found that state capture, that is, the influencing of government policymaking by a narrow set of interest groups, was the greatest in these semireformed countries.

Southeast Europe, Russia, Ukraine, and Moldova represented a political underreform trap. The combination of political polarization between communists and oligarchs and their common economic program of rent seeking was difficult to break. But this underreform trap burst. In Bulgaria, the horrendous financial crisis of 1996–7 discredited the ruling ex-communists as well as undermined them financially. As a result, the Bulgarian people elected a nonsocialist parliamentary majority, and a liberal government launched radical market reform. In Romania, the financial crisis of 1996–7 was sufficiently severe to lead to the democratic ouster of the ex-communist government, although the new government pursued somewhat less radical reforms than Bulgaria. In both cases, the underreform trap broke under the combined pressure of financial emergency and democracy (cf. Drazen and Grilli 1993). Similarly, the Russian financial crash undermined the most corrupt oligarchs, regional governors, and the communists, who appeared most responsible, but the crash led to state consolidation and authoritarianism rather than liberalism and democracy. In Ukraine, the shock of the Russian financial crash was sufficient to discipline the oligarchs to allow radical reforms. Exceptionally, the Communist Party has consolidated its hold on power through elections in Moldova, which is the country that has suffered the most economically after communism.

Renewed Democratization: Colored Revolutions

By the time of the Russian financial crash of August 1998, the perception had taken hold that some countries had been lastingly captured by rent-seeking elites. Many thought little could be done in these countries, in which predatory mismanagement bred stagnation. But then something happened, both economically and politically.

Two contrary politically developments occurred. In some oligarchic countries, notably Russia, Kazakhstan, and Azerbaijan, the central state power was reinforced and the oligarchs were weakened. In another group of countries, Georgia, Ukraine, and Kyrgyzstan, botched elections led to so-called colored or color revolutions, because of the locally adopted names. In November 2003, the Rose Revolution overthrew President Eduard Shevardnadze in

Georgia. It was followed by the Orange Revolution in Ukraine in November–December 2004, and finally by the Tulip Revolution, which toppled President Askar Akaev in the Kyrgyz Republic in March 2005.[5]

These three political transformations have a lot in common, as they do with the revolution in Serbia in September 2000. All the prior regimes were semidemocratic and allowed elections, but their democracy was constrained. The spark for each regime change was a fraudulent national election. The dominant revolutionary claim was that the old regime was highly corrupt, and the revolutionaries called for freedom and democracy. In Ukraine, a major slogan was "Bandits to prison!" Both the incumbent regime and the opposition honored certain constitutional rules, such as when elections were to be scheduled and how they were to be undertaken. The opposition could hold the regime to its own standards. A general sense prevailed that the old president and his regime had outlived themselves and did not know what to do next. People wanted change, but they doubted that the forthcoming election would allow it. All these revolutionary situations ended without the massive use of violence by either the state or the opposition, although the opposition groups used extra-constitutional tactics. In Serbia, Georgia, and Ukraine, but not in the Kyrgyz Republic, the new regime appears to have become more democratic (McFaul 2006).

The three post-Soviet colored revolutions – in Georgia, Ukraine, and the Kyrgyz Republic – had seven common conditions for democratic breakthrough. The fundamental condition that made these regime changes possible was that the incumbent regimes were neither strong nor united. They were no centralized dictatorships but semidemocratic or mildly authoritarian polities, which a skillful old president managed by playing various oligarchic groups against one another. In Ukraine, only one oligarchic clan fully supported the presidential candidate of the old regime (Viktor Yanukovych), whereas the others were lukewarm (Åslund 2006).

A second related fissure went through law enforcement. Its various branches were rivals, pursuing competing oligarchic interests. Because the troops were not very reliable, the old regime did not know whether it could deploy them against demonstrators. In Georgia, the security forces were called out but refused to shoot in defense of Shevardnadze.

A third condition was that the old regime had an unpopular leader. In Georgia and the Kyrgyz Republic, Shevardnadze and Akaev seemed inclined to stay on, whereas in Ukraine, President Kuchma tried to appoint a

---

[5] This section draws heavily on Åslund and McFaul (2006), especially McFaul (2006). See also Wilson (2006).

successor. All of them had originally been popular, but corruption or nepotism had eroded this.

Fourth, a strong and well-organized opposition existed. The opposition was reasonably structured in a limited number of major parties that acted together. It had a popular leader, who had substantial executive experience and parliamentary representation. In the Orange Revolution, the billionaires supported the regime, but the multimillionaires opposed it, generously funding the Orange Revolution (Åslund 2004b).

Fifth, the opposition had access to independent media. The Orange Revolution marked the breakthrough of the Internet era, as an Internet newspaper, *Ukrainskaya pravda*, became the foremost news medium. Mobile phones, which could also take photos, transmitted revolutionary news. Strangely, both the Georgian and Ukrainian old regimes permitted the opposition access to a minor TV channel, which proved very important. These countries were sufficiently free so that foreign broadcasting could not keep up with events and meant little to the locals (Prytula 2006).

A sixth condition was timely and credible independent election monitoring undertaken on a national scale, and the instant spreading of the actual election results. This required strong domestic nongovernmental organizations as well as international election monitors. Exit polls as well as alternative vote counts were carried out, and finally the actual fraud was revealed, verifying the vote rigging.

A final critical condition was the ability of the opposition to mobilize the population, which required strong nongovernmental organizations. A model student organization, *Otpor*, developed in Serbia, and a similar organization, *Kmara*, emerged in Georgia. Next, the Belarusian *Zubr* evolved, but no revolution took place in Belarus, and in 2004, the youth organization *Pora* was formed in Ukraine. These organizations started street demonstrations, but they would have mattered little if the population had not followed them. The number of people in the streets was vital for the success of the protest. The mobilization was facilitated by the public sense that it was now or never because the election had evidently been stolen.

In all these regime changes, foreign actors were conspicuous. Western nongovernmental organizations happily assisted with the training of activists, election monitors, and independent journalists. The Orange Revolution was top TV news throughout the world for one month, and prominent international politicians went to Kiev to participate in a roundtable with the Ukrainian leaders on how to conclude the revolution peacefully. The Kremlin and other incumbent dictators labeled the colored revolutions Western conspiracies. That was an exaggeration, but the opposition enjoyed strong Western sympathy. The colored revolutions showed that these "captured" regimes were not all that entrenched but harbored seeds of democracy. According to more stringent definitions of "revolution," the colored revolutions do not quite qualify. They were peaceful, and constitutions were obeyed. No major redistribution of property occurred. It might be more appropriate to call them democratic breakthroughs (McFaul 2006).

The colored revolutions bred a counterrevolution in the remaining, more authoritarian, oligarchic regimes. In April 2005, an armed uprising in the Uzbek city of Andijan was quashed in bloodshed costing hundreds of lives. In Russia, the Kremlin drew the conclusion that it needed to become more autocratic to stay in power. It tightened authoritarian controls over all factors that may have contributed to the colored revolutions. Effective one-party rule was imposed. All media of significance were brought under Kremlin control. A new restrictive law on nongovernmental organizations gave the Kremlin arbitrary control over their registration and funding. Independent election monitoring was prohibited by law, as was criticism of public officials. Judicial reform was halted to the benefit of arbitrary secret police action. Still the question remains whether the remaining oligarchic regimes will evolve into democracies or strict dictatorships in the longer term.

Parties, Electoral Rules, and Constitutions

The essence of democracy is institutions that effectively represent the public interest, and elections are the main vehicle in their construction. The timely execution of political institution building was vital, and timely meant early. A few seemingly technical aspects of the first elections have been essential for the political development of each country.

First, political parties had to be built to represent a broader public interest. Their formation depended greatly on whether parties were permitted in a founding election (McFaul 1997). Central and Southeast Europe launched ordinary party elections from the outset, but all the elections in the Soviet Union in 1989 and 1990 precluded any formal role for political parties, which rendered them merely semidemocratic. As a consequence, the post-Soviet electorates and the ensuing parliamentary factions were neither structured nor disciplined, and the deputies were accidental figures accountable to nobody. The only exceptions were the Baltic states, Georgia, and Armenia, where the national popular fronts had grown so strong that they became real political parties despite the electoral system. In Ukraine, parties were proscribed even in the second parliamentary elections in 1994. The result was the freewheeling corruption of individual deputies in an unruly parliament. About one-third of the Ukrainian deputies elected in both 1994 and 1998 were active businesspeople. Their purpose was not to facilitate deregulation but to extract their share of rents through legislation benefiting their enterprises or by selling their votes to other businesspeople.

Another important election rule was the choice between proportional representation and majority election in single-mandate constituencies. The East-Central Europeans and Balts chose proportional elections, whereas the CIS countries opted for mixed systems. Some had proportional representation (Armenia and Georgia); some single-mandate constituencies (Belarus, previously Ukraine and Kyrgyzstan); and some had a combination of both (Russia, Ukraine, and Kyrgyzstan). In the countries with proportional representation, the party system gained strength, and those are the strongest democracies in the region (Kitschelt et al. 1999), and there is a trend toward proportional elections. As elsewhere in the world, proportional representation facilitated the formation of strong parties and thus reform efforts (Geddes 1994b). The challenge from the Communist Party often forced the other political groups to get organized and improve the efficacy of their democracy.

A third election rule with great impact was whether any threshold for proportional representation existed, usually 4 or 5 percent of the votes cast. Some countries introduced such a hurdle from the beginning, and they obtained neatly structured parliaments with up to six parties. This was true of East Germany, Hungary, the Czech Republic, Slovakia, Bulgaria, Romania, Estonia, and Lithuania. The main exception was Poland. In its first freely elected *Sejm* in 1991, Poland had no less than 28 parties. Initially, hurdles left a large share of the votes cast without representation because of the large number of small parties. Georgia took the prize in its October 1992 parliamentary elections; more than two-thirds of the votes were cast for small parties that were not represented. Soon people learned and increasingly selected parties that gained representation (McFaul 2000).

A fourth important factor for the future party structure was the timing of the first founding parliamentary elections (McFaul 1999). The population was most enthusiastic for economic reforms just after their launch, when they focused on vision rather than costs. The later the first elections after democratization were held, the worse the result was for reformers. Countries that had mobilized to overthrow communist rule tended to unite around one popular movement. If elections were held within less than a year, these movements could be transformed into large democratic parties; any further delay caused divisions. Successful early elections took place in East Germany, Hungary, and the Czech Republic. Poland, Russia, and Latvia, on the contrary, held their first parliamentary elections very late, almost two years after they had attempted radical economic reform programs. These late elections resulted in a complete fragmentation of the popular movement for democratization and serious backlashes against reform. In Poland, Solidarity was broken up into a score of parties, and in Russia the once impressive popular movement Democratic Russia dwindled into insignificance. Latvia saw its popular front fractured and demolished.

National peculiarities do matter. None of the postcommunist countries has a party structure that resembles that of any other postcommunist country, showing more originality than West Europeans (Kitschelt et al. 1999). The degree of stabilization of the party structure varies, but big parties still come and go even in Central Europe. Yet the party elections, proportional representation, hurdles for representation, and timing of a founding election have had the predicted great impact (McFaul 1997).

The impact of the choice of constitution was even more profound. The fundamental alternatives were parliamentary or presidential rule. The former communist countries were left with a contradictory constitutional inheritance. On one hand, they had written constitutions that had been promulgated. On the other, these constitutions had never been applied. These bogus communist constitutions assumed real life only after communism. To a surprising extent, constitutions and politics were seen as national prerogatives, and most countries tried to draw on precommunist national history, however miserable it had been, and international experience was ignored. The impact of Western models was much more limited than in the economic sphere. Fortunately, in the western part of the region, one of the dominant slogans was "return to Europe," and the European Union had definite ideas about political systems, offering its advice to East-Central Europe. As a result, East-Central Europe has by and large adopted the democratic rules of Western Europe.

The most dramatic constitutional conflict concerned the division of power between the president and the parliament. They were worst in CIS countries with some democracy – Belarus, Ukraine, Moldova, Russia, Kazakhstan, Kyrgyzstan, Georgia, and Armenia. This strife escalated because the principle of the division of power, which had prevailed in the rest of the world since the late eighteenth century thanks to Montesquieu (1748/1977), had never been accepted by the communists, since it circumscribed the power of the Communist Party. The public understanding of the benefit of the division of power was absent.

The Soviet parliament was a rubberstamp institution that convened twice a year to adopt one or two laws each time. Its members were often token representatives of various social strata, such as picturesque milkmaids, rather than powerful individuals. According to the Soviet Constitution of 1977 and its republican varieties, however, the parliament was powerful and sovereign. On this basis, post-Soviet parliamentarians demanded substantial executive powers, notably in fiscal and monetary matters as well as privatization, just trying to grab what they could. These constitutional problems were aggravated by the lack of party structure and the not fully democratic parliamentary elections in early 1990.

Initially, the presidency was given strong powers in most countries to offer firm leadership. Only Hungary chose a pure parliamentary system from the beginning. The Czech Republic, Slovakia, Bulgaria, and the Baltic republics had ambiguous constitutions, but inspired by Western Europe, the powers of their presidents have been increasingly circumscribed. Legislation became the concern of parliament, and the government was responsible to parliament, and the president focused on constitutional and international issues.

In the former Soviet Union, presidential powers have persistently been much stronger than in East-Central Europe, but parliaments have challenged them, leading to virulent conflicts. Presidents reacted to irresponsible parliaments by demanding more power, but the parliaments usually refused, pointing to the corruption of the government. The most dramatic strife occurred in Russia in September–October 1993, ending with bloodshed after the president had dissolved the predemocratic and unrepresentative parliament, which launched an armed uprising. Similar conflicts occurred in Armenia, Belarus, Moldova, Ukraine, Kazakhstan, and Kyrgyzstan, but they were resolved without bloodshed. Over time, some clarity has been established. The less democratic a country is, the stronger its presidential powers. Moldova, Ukraine, Armenia, and Kyrgyzstan have moved in the direction of stronger parliamentary system, whereas all the other CIS countries have reinforced presidential powers, which has coincided with the strengthening of authoritarian rule.

Throughout the postcommunist world, establishments have claimed that political stability, consensus, and strong leadership are necessary for successful market economic reform. These views are so common that many Western political scientists do not even query the benefit of political stability, seeing it as a goal in itself (Elster et al. 1998, pp. 292–3). Yet, a good rule of thumb is whatever the old communist elite wanted must be wrong, however sensible it sounded. Empirically, government instability has actually been an advantage. The five countries with the most frequent changes of governments are Poland, the three Baltic states, and Bulgaria, some of the most successful reform countries. Their governments have lasted only one year on average. A plausible explanation is that frequent changes in the executive mean that vested interests cannot control the government, which becomes more transparent, more accountable, and less corrupt, better corresponding to the public interest. Initially, Bulgaria illustrated the danger of inconsistent policies and erratic policy reversals, but in the end its economic reforms have succeeded. So far, vested interests have been a far greater threat to sound economic policies in transition than disorder. After all, the Central Asian dictatorships – Turkmenistan and Uzbekistan – have had the most stable governments. The main problem has not been to maintain government stability but to accomplish sufficient change and to secure the public interest through the establishment of checks and balances.

Instinctively, many people think that a one-party majority government is preferable. However, in transition the most successful reform governments have been broad-based, multiparty coalitions. Illustrative examples are multiple Polish, Estonian, Latvian, Lithuanian, and Czech governments. This is logical if the main threat is that the old establishment will corrupt the new government, because a coalition government involves political competition, transparency, and accountability. With several parties in government, no single group can capture the state. Transparency is enhanced because each coalition partner sees what is going on. Each party fends for its own long-term reputation, which makes any coalition partner object to another partner ripping off the country. Naturally, corrupt deals may be struck, but the risk is less than in a majority government. Government instability and coalition governments indicate a competitive political system, and countries with the most competitive political systems have achieved most economic reform. Democratic systems can constrain the capacity of narrow elite groups that exercise undue influence on government (EBRD 1999).

Several key principles need to govern the constitutional order. First, there must be a clear division of executive and legislative powers, which the democracies in the region have accomplished. Second, law should rule society. Concretely, the parliament must possess substantial legislative powers, whereas the rights of the government and the president to rule by decree should be restricted. Third, the government must be transparent and accountable, which is a strong argument for parliamentarianism, because a parliament can supervise a government relatively closely, while presidents and their administrations are patently nontransparent and unaccountable. Under the existing conditions, parliamentary rule is preferable to presidential rule in the whole region. The purported need for a strong president is a variety of the myth of the need for a dictator. A strong state is a legal, transparent, and accountable state.

Persson and Tabellini (2000, 2003, 2004) have spearheaded an extensive theoretical and empirical literature on the impact of constitutions and electoral rules on economic policy in recent years in up to 80 democracies, primarily Western and Latin American countries. Although some of their lessons apply to the postcommunist countries, others do not. The main commonality is that "a parliamentary form of government is associated with better performance and better growth-promoting policies, measured by indexes for broad protection of property rights and of open borders" (Persson and Tabellini 2004, p. 95).

Strangely, Persson et al. (2000) presumed that a presidential democracy would have stronger accountability because of a straighter chain of command and a clearer separation of powers and thus stronger checks and balances, although they noted that this result does not hold true for weak democracies. Kunicova and Rose-Ackerman (2001) received the more plausible empirical result that presidential systems are associated with more widespread corruption. As a postcommunist presidential system represents a continuation of the arbitrary rule by the Party apparatus, it is naturally subject to few checks and balances and more inclined to corruption, and therefore it is also likely to be less democratic.

Persson et al. (2003) argued that voting over individuals correlates with lower corruption, but the opposite is true in the postcommunist states. The less corrupt East-Central European countries have proportional elections, whereas the more corrupt CIS countries predominantly pursue personal elections. It has been easier to purchase individually elected seats than party-list seats in the mixed Russian and Ukrainian systems. The resulting coalition governments in East-Central Europe have been much better at controlling corruption than the CIS governments, contrary to Persson and Tabellini's argument. Some of their more specific points on economic policies, however, appear valid, namely, that proportional elections lead to higher public spending, higher taxation, and larger budget deficits.

The limited applicability of this political economy of constitutions to the postcommunist countries raises the question what is wrong with it. One possibility is that East-Central Europe and the CIS countries are different. Another possible explanation, suggested by Daron Acemoglu (2005), is great covariance with unobserved variables. The peculiarities of the parliamentary systems that predominate in Europe might pertain to the European social welfare ideology, the EU rules, or recent policy fads, especially given that the period of these studies is very short. The degree of democracy is important, and it must not be seen as exogenous but endogenous because authoritarian and semiauthoritarian regimes prefer presidential rule. Finally, policy in the transition period should differ from stable conditions. Its purpose is to construct a new system rather than to manage an old one, and its rent seeking was most peculiar. The declining relative economic performance of the Central European countries could be explained with their transition having been completed, rendering further reforms almost as difficult as in reform-shy Western Europe.

How to Tame the Leviathan: Reform of the Communist State

The new postcommunist governments had to seize control over the state apparatus and rebuild it. In the communist states, the formal government and its state apparatus were only appendices to the real state, the Communist Party. The Party stood above the law, intervening however it found convenient without accountability. Unfortunately, the communist institutions did not just go away. After communism, the Central Committee of the Communist Party was transformed into a presidential administration, and the regional party committees into gubernatorial administrations. By communist tradition, these administrations could interfere at will. The presidential administrations were quite large – in the late 1990s, 6,000 people in Russia and 1,000 people in Ukraine.[6] These bureaucracies became centers of rampant corruption because of their large assets, freedom of intervention, and absence of accountability.

People who never dealt with communist states are usually unaware of how problematic they were. The communist state did too much and the wrong things, while vital state functions were ignored. Communist states did not regulate but managed enterprises. To get bureaucrats out of enterprises, the government had to be separated from business, which was the basic reason for privatization (Boycko et al. 1995). Numerous state bodies designed for the management of industries and enterprises had to be abolished, ranging from the State Planning Committee, its subordinate State Material Supply Committee, and the State Price Committee, to scores of industrial branch ministries. Poland and Hungary had completed these changes before the end of communism, but abolished branch ministries reemerged in most post-Soviet countries because their functions had not been eliminated. Intrusive

---

[6] Personal information from work with these governments.

state intervention persists in enterprise decisions throughout the region (EBRD and World Bank 2005).

For communism, secrecy was even more sacrosanct than openness is for democracy. A first step toward transparency was to publish all legal acts, which authoritarian post-Soviet countries are still reluctant to do. Eventually, their publication on the Internet is likely to solve this problem in democracies and semidemocratic countries. Another novelty was public audits of the government. Under communism, Poland exceptionally had a strong Auditing Chamber, but now most countries have established an independent auditing agency.

The reform of the communist bureaucracy has caused extraordinary headache. Under communism, senior officials were members of the Communist Party, muddling the distinction between politicians and civil servants. Communist bureaucrats had the wrong qualifications, being largely engineers rather than economists and lawyers. Many had been preoccupied with intricacies of a command economy, without relevant knowledge of a market economy. In the gerontocratic Brezhnev era, officials were promoted by seniority rather than merit. These officials represented a negative human capital, and their layoff was urgently needed. Depoliticization, rejuvenation, and professionalization were crucial.

The reform of the government was a daunting challenge, and only one country was really successful in this undertaking: Estonia. Under the truly radical Prime Minister Mart Laar (2002), the young Estonian government concluded that a maximum of disruption was desirable to stop communist telephone rule and corruption. It drew up a completely new government structure with clear borderlines between political and civil service positions. It laid off all civil servants, allowing everybody to apply for the new government jobs, and their applications were judged on merit. Amazingly, Estonia succeeded in this radical reform, and it can boast of the least corruption of all postcommunist countries. However, one important reason for its success was probably that Estonia was the smallest of all the transition countries. In Russia, President Yeltsin and his advisors were painfully aware of how the abolition of the tsarist foreign service by the liberal Russian government in early 1917 had led to chaos and they concluded that it was necessary to work with the old administration (Pipes 1990; Åslund 1995; Havrylyshyn 2006).

The greater the initial turnover of political elites was, the higher the probability of successful market reforms. Communist governments that retained power have been reluctant to reform. Progress in liberalization has been "twice as high in countries where the political executive has been replaced as in those where the incumbent from the communist era remained in office" (EBRD 1999, p. 106). Indeed, in several countries liberalization and stabilization were delayed until the incumbent postcommunist government was finally removed through elections, notably in Bulgaria, Romania, Moldova, and Ukraine. This is a strong empirical argument for lustration, that is, the exclusion from senior government service of secret policemen and party officials. It was undertaken systematically only in East Germany and the Czech Republic, although several other countries made some efforts, notably the Baltic states, Poland, and Bulgaria. The counterargument is that old officials can make amends, and if allowed to make a comeback, they can contribute to advantageous competition. The exclusion of a large group of people has serious implications for civil rights and the legitimacy of democracy as well. In the successful reform countries, especially Poland, Hungary, and Estonia, civil service reforms were impressive, clearly improving the quality of public administration.

Contrary to the general perception, the communist administration was not all that large, and most transition countries saw their bureaucracies swell or even double. One reason was that the government assumed a number of new functions, notably tax collection. Another cause was the absence of hard budget constraints, which led to a wasteful expansion of the bureaucracy. A third explanation is that many additional bureaucrats, who were largely inspectors, made their own living in the name of the state, by extorting money for "paid services."

Not surprisingly, it has been extremely difficult to reform government. The EU has made the greatest contribution. Although numerous necessary changes are obvious, many of those working in the government apparatus have little reason to welcome such changes, because of their perverse incentives. Quite a few officials are more interested in enriching themselves through extortion and theft (Hay and Shleifer 1998; Shleifer and Vishny 1998). How to defeat these enemies from within has been one of the most difficult tasks of the transition. Andrei Shleifer and Robert Vishny (1998, p. 12) concluded that "deregulation and liberalization are far more important for fighting corruption than the improvement of incentives and personnel selection inside the bureaucracy."

Public Opinion and Ideology

Do people support reform? A large number of opinion polls have been conducted in former communist countries. For our purposes, the European Union's *Eurobarometer* is most useful, because it posed the same questions to the population of up to fifteen countries in our region annually from 1990.

A first question was whether people thought their country was going in the right or wrong direction (European Commission, various years). In countries that had launched a serious economic reform, people tended to be positive about the direction of their country just before and at the beginning of the reform, whereas sentiments often turned sour later on (Poland, the Czech Republic, Slovakia, Bulgaria, and the Baltic states). The only two countries where the population was persistently optimistic were the most radical early reformers, the Czech Republic and Estonia. When the Czech reforms ran out of steam in 1997, the mood plummeted. Most countries did not undertake very radical reforms, and their populations were highly dissatisfied. All this suggests that people favor quite radical reforms.

The second question is even more telling, namely, whether people reckoned the reform in their country had been too fast or too slow. This query was only meaningful at an early stage of reform, and European Commission's *Central and Eastern European Eurobarometer* shows that in 1994, an overwhelming majority in fifteen postcommunist countries thought reform in their country was too slow. The radically reforming Czech Republic was the only exception where only a slight majority advocated faster reform. Apparently, the problem was not the people but the ability of the political process to translate their will into radical market reform.

But why do people in opinion polls indicate that the material situation has deteriorated? Even in East Germany, where people admit to massive material improvements on all specific questions, they claim a general deterioration. The causes are multiple. They involve real effects, changed income distribution, psychological reaction to change, altered social status, and increased uncertainty and risk. Some people adjusted fast and benefited. Others were unable to handle change and risk and started drinking. Income differentials increased, rendering the winners fewer than the losers. Social status changed rapidly in favor of entrepreneurs, but they were few. In the CIS, wage and pension arrears became notorious. Hyperinflation ate up bank savings. People were not used to negative publicity about their own society, because it had been prohibited under communism, and they presumed that bad news reflected real deterioration. Law and order declined, and all kinds of risks increased. People do not think of total welfare or even their own welfare but of their relative position. Considering the multitude of momentous changes, it would be strange if not many people were upset by one aspect or another, which does not necessarily say anything about their real standard of living.

Postcommunist transformation was an intensely ideological process, albeit this was concealed by antipolitical slogans, such as "no more experiments," which repudiated the complete politicization of communism. Virtually all the leading economic reformers – Leszek Balcerowicz, Václav Klaus, Mart Laar, Einars Repše, Yegor Gaidar, and Anatoly Chubais – were committed neoliberals, with favorite books such as Friedrich Hayek's *The Road to Serfdom* (1944/1986) and *The Constitution of Liberty* (1960). They were no sheer technocrats but professed an alternative vision of a more humane society. Transformation was not only about economic efficiency and welfare but also about freedom and human dignity most clearly formulated by Václav Klaus (1992, 1994). One of his favorite expressions was: "The third way leads to the Third World." The prime purpose of the reformers was less to win elections than the public debate, reestablishing the norms of Western civilization in these morally degenerate communist states (Dąbrowski et al. 2001). The ideological commitment of these reformers provided their societies with a sense of direction. The importance of ideology is best illustrated by a society with no sense of ideology, such as Belarus. When society has no evident purpose, all that is left is interests in a society dominated by a small elite, rendering dictatorship and the prevalence of rent seeking the natural outcomes in line with Ivan Karamazov's thesis in Fyodor Dostoyevsky's *The Brothers Karamazov*: "If there is no God, everything is permitted."

Successful reformers have also nurtured a strong national commitment, often seeing the rebirth of their nation as their goal. This was particularly apparent in the Baltics but also in Central Europe and Armenia. The nonreformers, on the contrary, harbored little national purpose, as is evident in Belarus and Central Asia. Ukraine and Moldova cherished national consciousness, but their people were not very confident. The nationalists in these two countries joined hands with the old communist elite because their own strength was insufficient, whereas the old elite realized that they could no longer rely on Moscow. As a result, these countries were captured by the old elites, which indulged in massive rent seeking, while the nationalists lacked economic program.

When Leszek Balcerowicz (1992) launched radical economic reforms in Poland, one of his greatest concerns was strikes and other forms of social unrest. Two years later in Russia, Yegor Gaidar (2000) was of a similar opinion, and worries were rampant in many other countries, such as Hungary, Bulgaria, Romania, and Ukraine, which had experienced serious strike movements that had undermined the power of the old communist dictatorships. However, labor relations changed instantly with transition. Fears of strikes and labor unrest proved exaggerated, and the problem has not been too many but too few strikes. When more than half the workforce is not paid its salaries in time and in full, as was the case in Russia and Ukraine, workers *should* go on strike. The most active trade unions were those that could extract the largest public subsidy per person. The frequent misperceptions of how labor would react were based on a lack of understanding of the perversity of the old official communist trade unions. Previously, labor unrest, especially coal miners' strikes in Poland, Russia, and Ukraine, had been expressions of democratic pressures rather than of trade unionism. Much of the early political activities took the form of trade unions or environmental movements. When the Polish trade union Solidarity was formed in 1980, it was an actual national front. Similarly, the environmentalism that thrived in Estonia and Lithuania from 1987 was primarily an expression of national and democratic opposition. When real national fronts were formed in 1988, the previously strong environmentalism faded.

Each government that liberalized consumer prices was afraid that people would take to the streets in protest. After all, Poland had experienced bloody riots because of price increases, primarily on meat, in 1956, 1970, 1976, and 1980, and even the Soviet Union had seen a massacre in Novorossiisk in 1962, unleashed by a meat price hike. In many other countries, notably in North Africa, bread price rises had unleashed serious riots. To great positive surprise, no single postcommunist price liberalization aroused social unrest. I was in Moscow around the time of the price liberalization. The atmosphere was tense. Before the deregulation, a public fear prevailed, as if a Damocles sword was hanging in the sky, and people who were expecting the sky to fall upon them suddenly became very kind to one another. When the prices were liberalized, they rose instantly by 250 percent, but there was no sign of protest. People took it calmly and serenely as in all the other postcommunist countries. Why was there no public reaction? A price increase for a limited number of commodities is politically less acceptable, because people can measure how much they lose personally and figure out that the privileged escape. A price rise is directed against certain groups. With general price liberalization, on the contrary, the whole economic paradigm changed, and nobody could assess the effect on specific groups, rendering collective action difficult.

People were not completely passive. When a country pursued an ostentatiously hopeless and damaging economic policy, people took to the streets. The best examples are Bulgaria and Romania in 1996, when huge mass protests broke out, although the economic mismanagement had gone very far before people reacted.

On the whole, society reacted as a student of Mancur Olson's (1971) *Logic of Collective Action* would have assumed. Civil society and all kinds of organizations were weak. Hence, only small and tightly knit interest groups with a great deal to benefit were able to collude, and they represented primarily the rent-seeking elite.

Democracy and Democracy Aid

The future development of democracy in the postcommunist countries is by no means obvious. There are many reasons to presume that democracy will be sustained in most of the current democracies and erupt in some authoritarian states, but there are also contrarian tendencies.

A fundamental precondition for democracy is peace and secure borders. Wars have been significant in postcommunist transition. Even excluding Yugoslavia, five countries have endured wars: Tajikistan, Georgia, Armenia, Azerbaijan, and Moldova, in approximate order of damage, not to mention Russia's war in Chechnya. The initial effect of war was unambiguous. Output fell sharply, notwithstanding that much of the official decline reflected an expansion of the underground economy. Georgia and Armenia now belong to the most corrupt countries in the world. Yet after considerable suffering, both countries have undertaken significant reform, and especially Armenia has attained impressive economic growth. Georgia and Armenia experience the least state intervention in enterprise decisions (EBRD 1999). They might represent an example of Mancur Olson's (1982) thesis that the destruction of obsolete state structures through war may facilitate the establishment of more adequate state structures than a gradual reform within the old institutional structure could have done. Olson used the examples of West Germany and Japan after World War II. Both countries were well endowed with human capital, which was a precondition for Olson's thesis because it is an asset for which allocation can be improved. Yet the Georgian and Armenian governments deliver few public goods, not even elementary law and order. The so-called frozen conflicts persist: Transnistria in Moldova, Abkhazia and South Ossetia in Georgia, and Nagorny Karabakh in Azerbaijan. In Chechnya, warfare continues. So far, Dominic Lieven's (2000) judgment holds that no empire has collapsed as peacefully and with as little bloodshed as the Soviet empire. Although national strife can emerge, it is most remarkable how submerged it has been outside of the Balkans.

Most of the classical preconditions for democracy exist in the former Soviet bloc (Lipset 1959). The level of education is remarkably high. The same is true of urbanization and industrialization. With some exceptions, the postcommunist countries are economically upper-income countries. Most such countries in the world are democracies. In addition, they are enjoying high and sustained economic growth.

The main threat to democracy in the region may lie in corruption, which can delegitimize the political system. Ivan Krastev's judgment holds. Corruption is the main theme in almost all elections, and nearly all governing parties lose elections, because they are blamed for corruption. Seymour Martin Lipset (1959, p. 86) taught us: "Legitimacy involves the capacity of a political system to engender and maintain the belief that existing political institutions are the most appropriate or proper ones for the society." Many Russians think that their state is unique and has to be authoritarian and corrupt. The post-Soviet states have serious problems with the efficacy and therefore legitimacy of the state.

Many of the worst threats to democracy reside in history, both distant and recent. Authoritarian ideology remains strong in the former Soviet Union. In an excellent recent book on Russian conservatism, the grand old man of Russian history Richard Pipes (2005, p. 1) concluded: "The dominant strain in Russian political thought throughout history has been a conservatism that insisted on strong, centralized authority, unrestrained either by law or parliament." The current Russian regime draws parallels with Count Sergei Uvarov's famous triad "Orthodoxy, Autocracy, Nationality," which became the ideological foundation for the reign of Tsar Nicholas I (Pipes 2005, p. 100). Characteristically, the Russian governments have accepted the economic laws of the market as universal and applicable to Russia, but they have perceived their politics as uniquely Russian. They have by and large ignored the insights of foreign political scientists. The absence of democratic traditions and inherited democratic institutions is a problem. A particular threat is old antidemocratic elites, notably the old security services, which currently rule Russia. For the former Soviet people, continuity as a source of democratic legitimacy is not available.

In more recent history, the multiple collapses in the Soviet Union in 1991 make many Russians hanker for security regardless of cost. None of the countries emanating from the Habsburg Empire that experienced hyperinflation stayed democratic until World War II. The same can now be said about the former Soviet Union. Of these fifteen states, only the three Baltic states, which escaped the ruble zone in mid-1992 and thus hyperinflation, have stayed persistently democratic.[7] The cost of the fateful attempt to preserve the ruble zone after 1991 does not diminish in hindsight but big political

---

[7] At the moment of writing, Freedom House (2006) assesses Ukraine as free.

damage is added to its economic dread. A similar argument could be made about the breakdown of law and order and the collapse of other essential state functions, such as the payments of pensions and wages.

The radical reform program has been criticized for the clear and specific answers it provided, but this book suggests that this broad body of the mainstream Western economic advice was amazingly appropriate, both theoretically and practically. Out of the twenty-one countries we discuss in this book, eighteen are market economies. Democracy building, by contrast, has been as relative failure. Only nine of these twenty-one countries have become sustainable democracies. Looking upon how democracy building was been attempted, this failure is no surprise.

As discussed at the beginning of this chapter, unlike economists, political scientists had not reached any broad agreement on how democracy building ought to proceed. The authoritarian modernization school and the dominant transitology turned out to be outright wrong on just about everything, and the protagonists of the successful combination of early democratization and radical economic reform were a small minority.[8]

Consequently, political scientists could not agree on any consistent body of policy advice such as the radical reform program. When advice was offered it was surprisingly vague. Literature about democracy aid typically suggests which questions should be discussed as well as methodology but refrains from concrete policy advice on key issues (e.g., Carothers 2000). The sound answers that actually existed were not understood, compiled, or spread. The best summary of the main lessons from the building of democracy was oddly published by the EBRD (1999) in its *Transition Report 1999*, from which many of the conclusions in this chapter are drawn.[9] The dominant orthodoxy, transitology, has proved inadequate. No widely appreciated body of concrete policy recommendations existed.

The Western world did not provide relevant advice on most of the big political questions posed in the postcommunist world. Should early parliamentary elections be held after the democratic breakthrough, or should a nation stick to old constitutions and roundtable agreements? Russia, Poland, and Latvia suffered badly by holding parliamentary elections about two years after their democratic breakthrough, missing their chance of having their democracy consolidated in an early election. Western political scientists are divided about the merits of presidential versus parliamentary system,

[8] Michael McFaul (1997, 2001), Larry Diamond (1995, 1999), and Valerie Bunce (1999a, 1999b) took positions close to those expressed here.
[9] The main author of the political chapter was Joel Hellman.

whereas postcommunist practice shows that presidential systems recreated the Communist Party apparatus. Nor do most of them have any principled position on the choice between proportional and majoritarian elections in one-person constituencies, whereas practice has shown that proportional elections with a reasonable hurdle for representation of a party work best for effective democracy. When it comes to more difficult questions, such as how to organize a government effectively, the West has little advice to offer but imitation of its own institutions.

Most political scientists even braced themselves against giving policy advice, as if that would degrade their academic professionalism. Unlike the classical political philosophers, few contemporary political scientists dare to be normative in sharp contrast to many economists who went to the countries in question and made very concrete policy suggestions. Political scientists stopped at more or less academic seminars, for which leading policy makers have little time.

Nor does any international organization have the mandate to build democracy, as the IMF takes responsibility for global macroeconomic stability and the World Bank for privatization. The nearest substitutes are USAID and the EU, but neither organization professes any explicit ideal of democracy beyond the most obvious elements, such as free and fair elections.

The complaint is often made that Western democracy aid has been too small, but given the lack of substance, this is hardly the main problem.[10] It is true that most policy makers showed little interest in international advice on democracy building, but considering the paucity of relevant content in what was presented to them it is not very surprising that highly occupied politicians decided that they could spend their scarce time with something more useful.

The main exception to this failure of international support for democracy building has been the organization of democratic elections and their monitoring, which has become an important and successful part of Western democracy assistance. Two international organizations, the Organization for Security and Cooperation in Europe and the Council of Europe, have developed a healthy competition in election monitoring. Several international nongovernmental organizations, notably George Soros's Open Society Institute, Freedom House, the International Republican Institute, and the National Democratic Institute have also committed themselves to the promotion of democratic elections and election monitoring. What to do

---

[10] The spectacular U.S. failure to build democracy in Iraq with virtually unlimited resources verifies how little knowledge about democracy building the U.S. government has absorbed.

after a democratic election, however, remains as confused as a decade earlier, leaving the nations of the colored revolutions floundering. In hindsight, it is all too clear that the newly elected president Yushchenko should have been advised to dissolve the old parliament and hold fresh, fully democratic elections.

The only successful method of building democracy in the postcommunist world has been the wholesale emulation of EU institutions through the twinning of various state agencies in one postcommunist country with one EU country. This worked because the EU countries are much better at applied bureaucracy than at the formulation of ideas. Arguably, the EU's greatest contribution to postcommunist institution-building has been its proliferation of democracy. The EU has imposed the idea that no decent state can be anything but a democracy, and the East-Central European countries have accepted and internalized that standard. The CIS countries had no such peer states.

9

From Crime toward Law

One of the key Soviet tenets was that the Communist Party must not be constrained by anything. Consequently, the Party refuted the rule of law. With the bureaucratization of communist power, some law or rules became necessary, but the socialist legal system served the Party. Its function was to enforce the commands of the government that was subordinate to the Communist Party. Formally, crimes against the state were judged more severely than crimes against individuals, although that idea never took root in public sentiment.

The socialist states had many rules that were alien to a market economy. Most private enterprise or entrepreneurship was criminalized as "speculation." Unemployment was not pitied but prohibited as "parasitism" and was punished with labor camp. Because only a minimum of personal property was allowed, little legislation existed for the defense of private property rights. Nor did the state have any need for financial legislation, although Central European countries maintained some prewar legislation on their books.

A legal system with prosecutors and judges had existed under socialism, but, peculiarly, the public prosecutors were superior to the judges. Defense councils were not common and had little authority. Soviet judges were not particularly corrupt, but they were obeying political orders and the prosecutors. They were few and poorly trained for commercial disputes. Debt collection services barely existed.

Even so, communism was a system of kleptocracy, working for the enrichment of the Nomenklatura. The extremely centralized socialist economic system was so inconsistent that the only way of making it work was to allow state managers to trade on the side to make sure that they could acquire the necessary inputs to fulfill the state production plans. Law was so subordinate that few bothered about its consistency. The Nomenklatura was

241

supreme and did what it wanted within certain informal boundaries. The absence of a clear borderline between right and wrong led to the need for a huge law enforcement apparatus of police and secret police as well as many and severe punishments. The Soviet Union had the largest number of prison inmates as a share of the population in the world.

The communist legal system was inefficient at the height of totalitarianism, and it was at complete loss in the transition. Meanwhile, the Nomenklatura persisted and enriched itself through rent seeking, and its members honored only loyalty to other members of the Nomenklatura. The daunting task of reformers was to transform this kleptocratic monster into a law-abiding state, serving the interests of the people. Old Nomenklatura networks had to be broken, or the negative organizational capital of the communist dictatorship had to be disbanded (Shleifer and Vishny 1998, p. 233). A maximum disruption was desirable, but at the same time public order had to be maintained.

The collapse of the old order was particularly troublesome in law enforcement, which allowed ordinary crime to rear its ugly head, which is discussed in the first section. Institutions that protect property rights are crucial for economic growth and particularly for investment (North 1981) because they diminish transaction costs, but the question was how to create them. A new legal system had to be built, but that was possibly the most complicated task of postcommunsim, which is reviewed in section two. In the void of an effective legal order, corruption evolved, which is discussed in section three.

An Explosion of Crime

Crime exploded during the collapse of communism and the initial transition, which was a natural consequence of the breaking down of the old order. The explosion of crime shook society. Crime statistics are not standardized, but most transition countries probably saw an approximate doubling of their crime rates. The rise in crime seemed related to how the old regime eased up. A more radical reform brought about an earlier peak in crime followed by stabilization, whereas the gradual reformers saw a longer but steady increase. Poland and Hungary experienced the sharpest surge in their crime rates in 1990, their first year of reform, after which they stabilized (Åslund 1997a). The reformers, Russia and Kyrgyzstan, faced a doubling of crime from 1988 to 1992, whereas the crime rate grew more gradually in the most conservative countries, Turkmenistan and Uzbekistan (Mikhailovskaya 1994).

The disorganized individual crime became unbearable. New business-people complained that they were visited by different racketeers, and they did not know whom to pay, but they had to pay protection fees to save their lives. Numerous entrepreneurs were murdered, and many more saw their premises burn. The former Soviet Union had a great supply of potential protectors – war veterans from Afghanistan, former police and military officers, sportsmen and traditional Soviet criminals. Law and order effectively broke down as the old police stayed passive, generating great demand for protection. This was a truly Hobbesian world. Diego Gambetta's (1993) economic analysis of the evolution of the Sicilian mafia appears perfectly applicable, and a young Russian social scientist, Vadim Volkov (2002) has written an excellent analysis of the Russian evolution of crime.

Crime evolved in response to market forces and organized itself spontaneously. Through great violence, organized crime imposed its own order with racketeering fees and divided the business world into well-defined mafia districts. Businessmen actually appreciated the organization of crime that occurred in 1993–4. First of all, they knew whom to pay, so the risk of double-paying disappeared. Second, their risk of being shot declined. Russia's very high murder rate peaked in 1993. Third, racketeering fees declined as the security business became standardized. The drawback, of course, was that most Russian businesses were compelled to pay racketeering fees. The main exceptions were enterprises under solid state protection, such as enterprises belonging to the military-industrial complex and the Ministry of Interior. As Volkov (2002, p. 19) put it: "Since the actions of the state bureaucracy and of law enforcement remain arbitrary and the services provided by the state tend to have higher costs, private enforcers (read: the mafia) outcompete the state and firmly establish themselves in its stead." The state played a very small role in the early 1990s.

Curiously, this seemingly impenetrable system of organized crime did not last for long. Three forces brought it down. First, the awestruck Russian reformers made a masterstroke: they legalized private security companies in 1992. Swiftly, organized crime legalized itself as private security companies, which the state could increasingly supervise and regulate. Step by step, the private security companies became more orderly and legal in their activities.

Second, new big businesspeople, oligarchs, thought the fees of the protection rackets were too high – originally 20 percent of turnover, falling toward 10 percent of turnover over the years. Instead the oligarchs set up their own security forces. By the mid-1990s, 8 percent of the employees in a typical oligarchic corporation were occupied with security, both guards and counterintelligence, finding out what their enemies were doing. The top oligarchs hired a deputy minister of interior to run their security and a deputy chairman of the KGB to manage their counterintelligence. As early as 1995, the oligarchs had squeezed out organized crime.

Third, both the dangers and temptations of organized crime were excessive. Within a few years, almost all the famous mafia kingpins had disappeared. Many had been killed by one another or the police. Others had been sentenced to long prison terms, while successful criminals had the choice of selling out and retiring in the West or gentrifying (Brady 1999). Very few organized criminals were able to legalize themselves at home. Among the current 60 known billionaires in Russia and Ukraine, only a few might have started as racketeers, although most were black marketeers.

Despite the many books written about the exciting post-Soviet organized crime, it lasted for only a brief period, approximately 1992–5, although it persists in many places. As late as 2006, the Russian city Novgorod was run by seven organized crime gangs, and the Russian state does not interfere.

Also the oligarchic period of legal private security prevailed for only a brief period, from 1995 until 1998. By 1998, the state had come back. Gone were the complaints from the early transition that the criminals had stronger cars, better arms, bulletproof vests, and computers, unlike the police; but the new, well-equipped police were not necessarily a legal force.

In 2000, I sat down with a driver in Bishkek in Kyrgyzstan and asked him how many racketeers had stopped him when he had driven his newly bought, secondhand Mercedes from Germany to Kyrgyzstan. He had counted – 120 times. On my question how many of the racketeers where private and how many were policemen, he answered: "They were all policemen. There is hardly any private racket left in the CIS." They took over much of the organized crime and racketeering, especially in the CIS. The official law enforcement bodies had the advantage of being legally armed and entitled to make raids and arrest people. Little wonder that it came back and took over within seven years.

Courts are often seen as the key defenders of property rights, but they can do little without an effective police. In a survey of shopkeepers in Warsaw and Moscow, Timothy Frye (2001) found that shopkeepers considered the performance of the police more important for the security of their property rights than the courts, and the Polish police were more inclined to abide by the law than their Russian colleagues (cf. European Bank for Reconstruction and Development [EBRD] 1997, 1998). Violence has been consolidated anew in the hands of the state through its police. The big remaining problem is to make the police obey the law and work for the public good. Essentially, that is an issue of democracy.

Attempts at Building a Legal System

Today it is obvious that the construction of an effective legal system should be one of the foremost tasks of postcommunist transition.[1] In the early transition, however, that was not so evident. A legal system existed, and nonlawyers assumed that it somehow functioned, not quite realizing how abnormal it was. It was bound to deteriorate, because capitalism required more active courts, and as the judges became more independent and powerful, they also became more corrupt.

The corps of socialist lawyers was a major impediment to legal reform. Most of them were conservative civil servants who desired no change. They served the state at its pleasure rather than the law. Prosecutors fought tooth and nail for the preservation of the old Stalinist system that granted them a maximum of power. Independent lawyers were few, and most of them were also dependent on the state. The best of them flourished on commercial work and stayed out of politically controversial reforms. The few reform-minded lawyers were intent on writing their country's constitution, following in the footsteps of Thomas Jefferson. A larger group of lawyers engaged in drafting commercial legislation, yet the vital reform of the whole legal system was left aside for years.[2]

A nonlawyer would assume that the academic discipline of comparative law would have a clear theory of how legal systems evolve, that a sensible set of policy advice would exist and that experienced international legal advisors would be forthcoming to advise governments how to reform their legal systems, but little emerged. A book on law during the first decade of transition makes the stunning statement "that applied analysis of the effects of legal and institutional reform is still in its infancy" (Murrell 2001, p. 8). The lawyers were so detached that "[i]ronically, economists rather than lawyers have been the promoters of the new relevance theory of law for corporate governance" (Pistor et al. 2000, p. 326). Alas, economists started with odd side issues closest to their hearts, such as privatization and corporate governance, while mainstream legal issues, such as criminal law and legal procedural codes, were long left untouched.

---

[1] An overall source to this section is Anderson et al. (2005).
[2] I owe some of these observations to Judge Bohdan Futey, judge U.S. Court of Federal Claims, Washington D.C.

Nor did any international organization specialize in the promotion of legal reform. An exception was the American Bar Association's Central European and Eurasian Law Initiative, which started working in Central and Eastern Europe in 1990 and in the CIS in 1992, but it was only a national nongovernmental organization.

All the postcommunist countries had a legal tradition. They were part of the European civil law tradition, based on centralized legislation, as opposed to the Anglo-American common law tradition, which draws extensively on precedence. A substantial literature has evolved around the importance of legal origin (La Porta et al. 1998), but these countries had no real choice because they were already so deeply entrenched in the civil law tradition. And that was no tragedy. Many developing countries with French civil law, such as Chile, Morocco, the Philippines, and Turkey, rank high in terms of property rights (Levine 2005). After all, before World War I, France had a larger stock market capitalization in relation to GDP than the United States (Rajan and Zingales 2003).

The leading reformers, most of whom were economists, started with what they understood – legislation. At a rapid pace, hundreds of laws were drafted, notably civil codes and privatization legislation. Both the European Union and United States Agency for International Development (USAID) were keen on financing the drafting of legislation, which was effective and influential. This was the area of the greatest competition between the EU and the US; both sides wanted to have their legal standards spread. The initial quality of draft laws was often poor, but as soon as one law had been adopted, proposals for its amendment developed, and legislation quickly improved. The spurt of legislation during the first decade of transition was impressive almost everywhere, but the progress in legislative activity varied greatly depending on the dynamism of a few reformers in each country. Some reformist countries, such as Georgia and Ukraine, still display a disconcerting lacuna of legislation, whereas Azerbaijan and the Kyrgyz Republic have promulgated an impressive array of laws (Anderson et al. 2005, p. 24).

The adoption of thousands of new laws in the region has brought about some stunning improvements: "In fact, many of the countries of the former Soviet Union which received legal technical assistance primarily from the United States can today boast higher levels of investor rights protection on the books than some of the most developed market economies, such as France or Germany" (Pistor et al. 2000, p. 357). A new irony is that Russia's Gazprom in 2006 had a market capitalization that was three times larger than that of the biggest German company, Siemens or Eon, not least because Russia has more shareholder-friendly corporate legislation than Germany.

The popular demand for knowledge of the new legislation was impressive. In the early transition, collections of laws and legal handbooks could be found at every street stand, together with management books and dictionaries of foreign languages. Enterprise surveys in Russia showed that both large and medium-size enterprises paid for legal services and kept themselves well informed about new legislation (Hendley et al. 1997). The Internet provided new opportunities to publicize laws, decrees, and court judgments. Despite much bureaucratic resistance, the transparency of law has greatly improved.

Unfortunately, "the quality of the law on the books has little or no explanatory power for the effectiveness of legal institutions" (Pistor et al. 2000, p. 345). Some early judicial reforms were undertaken. Most countries added a constitutional court to their judiciary system to hold the government accountable. Judges were given independence from the state and were depoliticized, securing safer tenure for them and rendering the judiciary more self-governing. Over time, the salaries of judges have risen, and court budgets have improved. The problem is that the judges obtained freedom without accountability.

What businesspeople demand from courts is fairness, honesty, strength of enforcement, speed, and affordability. In fact, demand for judicial services appears to be driving judicial reform. Central Europe and the Baltics stand out with both the greatest demand for judicial services and the best capacity to deliver them. The demand for judicial services, in turn, depends on the progress of market reforms (Anderson et al. 2005, p. xvi).

The European Union and its accession process have greatly influenced legislation and judicial reform. Every EU accession country had to adopt the common EU legislation, *acquis communautaire*, which consists of some 170,000 pages. The EU has also set standards and regularly assessed the progress of candidate countries in their legal development.

Still a World Bank survey of judicial systems concluded that "less overall progress has been made in judicial reform and strengthening than in almost any other area of policy or institutional reform in transition countries since 1990" (Anderson et al. 2005, p. xiv). There is no sign of the new EU members catching up with the old members in terms of court performance. Comparing judicial reforms and the effectiveness of judicial systems in various countries, the idiosyncratic variations from country to country are most striking, suggesting that a few legal reformers did wonders where they existed. The disconnect between legislation and efficacy of laws is equally astounding (Anderson et al. 2005, p. 28). Courts are persistently rated among the most corrupt bodies.

Considering the weakness of the legal system and the poor compliance with law, one would assume businesspeople ignore courts, but enterprises are suing both each other and the government more each year (Hendley et al. 1997). The logical conclusion is that over time, new laws change businesspeople's behavior.

For commercial disputes, an alternative to the corrupt public courts has been private arbitration courts, usually attached to Chambers of Commerce at home or abroad. Foreign companies have typically insisted on arbitration in an international court, usually in Stockholm, Vienna, Zurich, or London. Their judgments have been recognized by national courts though with certain resistance.

In practice, businesspeople have different possibilities of defending their rights. In an article distinguishing the enforcement of property rights and contract, Daron Acemoglu and Simon Johnson (2005) found that "property rights institutions have a major influence on long-run economic growth, investment and financial development, while contracting institutions appear to affect the form of financial intermediation but have a more limited impact on growth, investment, and the total amount of credit in the economy." Indeed, contractual payments can be secured by many means. The standard solution is to request advance payments. Leasing has proliferated because the creditor can easily seize the leased property without going to court. A supplier can also ask for collateral. Finally, international arbitration courts can be used. By contrast, little can be done to secure real estate by alternative means, which is inevitably under local jurisdiction.

Considering the minimal policy attention devoted to legal developments, the results are not all that disappointing. Just a few years ago, some scholars argued that it was impossible to implant one country's legal system into another country. Soon it emerged that the world was dominated by four legal systems, the Anglo-American common law and three variants of European civil law, and that the postcommunist countries already had a centralized civil law system. A large volume of legislation of rising quality has been promulgated in most countries. The knowledge about this legislation is quickly spreading. The demand for judicial services is steadily increasing, and the judicial systems have been reformed, even if the appreciation of the improvements is scant. Ever more lawyers are being trained, and the resources of the court systems are increasing. The major shortfall has been that the corruption of courts has increased with their importance, and the judges are painfully unaccountable. Yet in the last few years, the measurement of court performance has developed, and whatever is measured tends to improve. A precondition of improvement, however, is that the government does not oppose it. The last step in judicial reform is to make the collection effective. Especially East-Central Europe has taken a giant step from communist kleptocracy and lawlessness toward the rule of law.

Corruption: The Bane of Transition

Corruption is defined as "the misuse of public power for private gain" (Rose-Ackerman 1999, p. 91). It means the malfunctioning of the state, with politicians and civil servants selling public goods for private gain rather than working for the goals of society as a whole.

At the collapse of communism, the preconditions for corruption were particularly propitious. The Soviet Union had a strong tradition of corruption, particularly in the three Caucasian countries and Central Asia. Empirically it takes a long time to amend corruption (Treisman 2000). In transition, the formal powers of the state remained nearly complete, and the discretion of state employees was greater than ever because they no longer had to obey their superiors. The old apparatus of repression had ceased to function, but no new rule of law existed. Most countries did not even have laws against corruption, rendering it nearly unpunishable.

There was no clear understanding of what corruption was. The idea spread that civil servants should be allowed to work on commission. When the old system collapsed, its administration attracted little attention because of its near complete chaos. Its employees were demoralized, keeping a low public profile. Few could imagine that these small gray men would soon come back and make big money on corruption, but that was what happened. Their demoralization was all the greater because most of them regretted the demise of the communist system, and their real salaries became ridiculously small with hyperinflation. For several years, the best civil servants departed for the private sector, where senior staff could instantly catch up to 100 times higher incomes. The remaining staff was often poorly qualified and appointed because of personal fiat. A popular belief evolved that transition has boosted corruption, widely seen as the greatest bane of the transition.

Quantitative measurement of corruption did not start until the mid-1990s, but since then a number of alternative measurements have evolved.[3] Five overall tendencies in the region are evident from the end of the 1990s. First, the total volume of bribes has increased. Second, the average "bribe tax," that is, the percentage of annual revenue a firm pays in bribe, declined

---

[3] The most relevant and extensive is the EBRD-World Bank business survey, BEEPS, which is based on queries among businesspeople, although its validity in severe dictatorships is doubtful. Unfortunately, it has only been undertaken in 1999, 2002, and 2005.

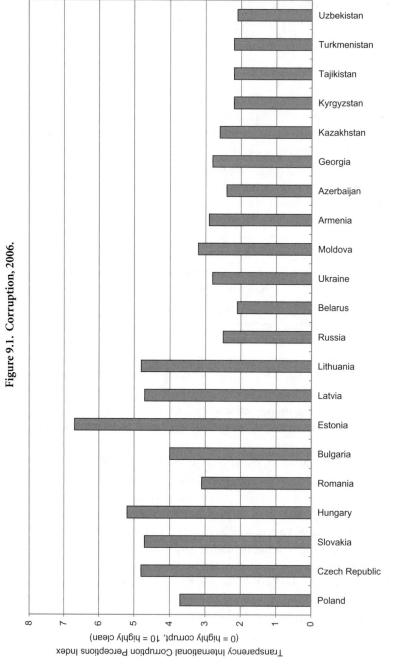

Figure 9.1. Corruption, 2006.

Transparency International Corruption Perceptions Index
(0 = highly corrupt, 10 = highly clean)

Source: Transparency International (2006).

from 1.6 percent in 2002 to 1.1 percent in 2005 for the whole region, according to Business Environment and Enterprise Performance Survey (BEEPS). Third, corruption has been rationalized. The frequency of bribery has declined, prices have been standardized, and people better understand what they pay for. Fourth, nuisance extortion in taxation, customs, business licensing, and all kinds of inspections has declined, but corruption has increased in courts and government procurement. Fifth, businesspeople see corruption as a big but steadily declining problem (Anderson and Gray 2006). Overall, corruption seems to have become more pervasive but also standardized and more rational. Therefore, it has become more tolerable.

Corruption has maintained a strong hold with a clear geographic pattern. According to Transparency International, it is worst in Central Asia and the Caucasus, and almost as bad in Russia, Belarus, Ukraine, and Moldova, whereas Southeast Europe has less corruption, and Central Europe and the Baltics are the least corrupt (see Figure 9.1). Estonia has persistently been far ahead of the others, followed by Hungary. Good governance is closely correlated with the degree of market reform.

Initially, graft in Russia appeared especially harmful, damaging economic development more than elsewhere. One particular complaint by people who paid bribes was that they did not receive the services that they paid for (Shleifer and Vishny 1993). Another grievance was that the extortion by officials was unnecessarily cumbersome. In 1996, Daniel Kaufmann (1997) found that Ukrainian enterprise managers spent more than one-third of their time with government officials, but by 1999, this time had fallen by half (to 17 percent) – an impressive improvement in an economy that was perceived as totally stalemated by bureaucracy (Hellman et al. 2000). Apparently, businesspeople and officials rationalized their relations, lowering the transaction costs caused by inspectors stopping production and wasting management time through bargaining.

The degree of bribery varies with type of enterprise. Private firms pay more bribes, and they view corruption as a bigger problem than do state-owned firms. Small private firms pay more bribes as a share of their revenues than big firms because they are more vulnerable. Manufacturing firms pay the most bribes because they are sitting ducks for predatory government inspectors. Firms in urban areas pay more bribes than firms in small towns or rural areas because more inspectors are present there. The longer a firm has been in business, the less subject to extortion it becomes. Foreign firms pay fewer bribes. This pattern makes clear that most of the corruption is extortion, forcing the most vulnerable firms to pay more (Anderson and Gray 2006, p. 24).

Few phenomena clarify the need for both radical and comprehensive reform better than the rise of corruption. The array of possible and effective measures is extensive, and it touches on all kinds of policies. The fundamental cause of corruption is that "corrupt incentives exist because state officials have the power to allocate scarce benefits and impose onerous costs" (Rose-Ackerman 1999, p. 39). Democracy was vital to break the power of the elite and to discipline politicians and bureaucrats, introducing transparency, free media, and checks and balances. Unfortunately, transparency has made surprisingly little headway. Only Estonia has adopted a full-fledged public information act as exists in the Scandinavian countries. In most post-Soviet countries, the Stalinist practice of secret but legally binding decrees persists. The repetitive corruption scandals that oust politicians and governments in East-Central Europe show that voters do care about corruption and that democracy is an effective check.

The "opportunities to engage in corruption need to be scaled down by reducing the government role in the economy" (Tanzi and Schuknecht 2000, p. 169). The first BEEPS showed a strong positive correlation between state intervention and corruption (EBRD 1999). The power of the state apparatus had to be reduced through deregulation, which would diminish the power of officials to extract bribes, by legalizing previously prohibited activities, such as private enterprise, by abolishing licenses and permissions, and by freeing prices and trade. State monopolies were notorious dens of corruption, maintaining as many distortional regulations as possible. Naturally, officials opposed truly radical liberalization, because a simple and draconian deregulation was most likely to beat them.

"Privatization can reduce corruption by removing certain assets from state control and converting discretionary official actions into private, market-driven choices" (Rose-Ackerman 1999, p. 35; cf. Kaufmann and Siegelbaum 1996). Even if privatization itself inevitably is discretionary and therefore often fraught with corruption, it can be completed once and for all. The alternative to full privatization is leasing from the public sector, which seems highly corrupt all over the world.

The next step is to deprive the state apparatus of material resources by cutting public expenditures. Reductions of public expenditures have proved vital for the return to economic growth in the CIS countries (Åslund and Jenish 2006). These cuts do not need to be antisocial. In corrupt states, public investment and subsidies typically crowd out investment in human capital through education and health care (Tanzi and Davoodi 1997; Mauro 1995, 1998; Knack and Keefer 1995).

A large number of fiscal changes are important for the reduction of corruption, as discussed in Chapter 5. The self-financing of state inspection agencies through penalties must be prohibited. Taxation in some countries degenerated into tax farming, in which tax rates were at most nominal and taxation was a matter of negotiation rather than law. The assessment and payment of both taxes and customs fees should be separated and formalized to avoid corruption-generating negotiations.

On the expenditure side, corruption-prone items such as subsidies and public investment need to be kept short. A strange communist feature was that the state invested directly in enterprises, and these practices have continued even after enterprises have been privatized. Unfinanced mandates should be abolished, because otherwise the agencies in question try to extract financing in corrupt ways. Program budgeting is needed so that the state budget covers all costs necessary to carry out government programs. Similarly, sequestration should be avoided, because when an adopted budget is tampered with, the wrong programs are cut to the benefit of administration and public investment, as was persistently the case in Ukraine in the 1990s (Åslund and de Ménil 2000).

One peculiar feature of postcommunism was a multitude of inspection agencies. Some were new, such as the huge tax inspection, the ferocious tax police, and the antimonopoly committees, but most had existed before. Suddenly, dozens of agencies were out inspecting enterprises. Inspectors made money for both their employers and themselves by penalizing businesspeople. Many of these agencies should simply be abolished or at least merged. Their huge labor forces must be cut, and they should be prohibited from visiting enterprises. In 1997, I visited a small factory in Ukraine and learned that seven or eight tax inspectors visited the company every day. I checked how that could be the case and received the explanation that Ukraine had 70,000 tax inspectors but only some 10,000 real taxpaying firms, and one single tax inspection was allowed a year, so the tax inspectors distributed themselves on different enterprises that had to take care of them and feed them the whole year. Naturally, the inspectors fought tooth and nail for their rights to onsite inspection. In Kyrgyzstan, I actually encountered "extra-budgetary" police, that is, police in uniform who were not paid by the state, which sounds like the definition of legalized racketeering. The Internet offers wonderful opportunities for hands-off contacts between state and citizens, such as income declarations on the net and e-procurement. To combat corruption the state needs to minimize contacts that can lead to extortion, minimize discretion, and standardize the remaining contacts.

During years of high inflation, salaries in government service fell sharply, with pay scales becoming compressed, often making it impossible for even a minister to live on his or her salary. It has been extraordinarily difficult to raise salaries for senior officials, offering no incentives for hard and honest work. For many civil servants, additional incomes became a necessity. They were often extracted as bribes, but entrepreneurial activity was also common. Substantial fringe benefits in kind, such as free apartments, dachas, cars with drivers, and holiday trips, are still distributed to senior officials in the CIS countries in a more or less discretionary fashion. Commission remuneration has proliferated on a grand scale. Especially CIS tax police and customs officials have become used to receiving certain shares of the state revenues they extract. Rather than satisfying their needs, these commissions whetted their appetite. Characteristically, CIS tax police have focused on easy and fat prey, such as foreign investors, aggravating an already unjust tax burden. As an effect, the public service was partially privatized, and the dividing line between public and private was blurred further.

The whole civil service is steeped in conspicuous conflicts of interests. In the late Soviet period, ministers boasted about being so progressive that they set up private enterprises, not realizing that it was an obvious conflict of interest. Communist officials had learned Pierre-Joseph Proudhon's thesis that property was theft, and they thought they might as well start their career as capitalists by stealing state property. Only gradually have multiple employments and "commissions" extracted by public servants been prohibited. Clear lines must be drawn between business and the state, prohibiting all combinations of the two. Explicit codes of ethics defining bribery are needed. The widespread practice of appointing government ministers to supervisory boards of enterprises, through which they can earn much more than their official salary, is another unacceptable practice. The many fringe benefits should be minimized and replaced with money because they inevitably breed crime. One of the most effective checks on corruption would be to allow public access to the income declarations of all citizens, as in the Scandinavian countries.

Ultimately, the civil service needs to be reformed to become competent, meritocratic, and regulated. Standardized civil service exams and depoliticization are also needed. Estonia undertook a profound homemade reform of the state apparatus, and the EU has assisted other accession countries. To reduce and improve the quality of the public service has proved very difficult and to discipline it even more so. Naturally, violations of discipline should be punished, but punishments must be proportional to the crime to be taken seriously.

In the end, the legally armed law enforcement agencies are likely to win out in corruption and crime, as is apparent from the police taking over racketeering almost all over the CIS, and the current rule of KGB officers in Russia. The advantage of this concentration of power is that the monopoly of violence is being restored. The problem is that democracy has not taken root in most of the CIS countries so that the population does not control the state, which does not serve the people.

Estonia has been the champion in virtually all measures that can reduce corruption, and the result is impressive. Although Estonia belonged to the Soviet Union for forty-six years, it is now the twenty-fourth least corrupt country in the world according to Transparency International (2006). One may object that Estonia is a special case with only 1.4 million inhabitants, but Hungary, which has done significantly less still, comes forty-first in the world. Clearly, corruption can be controlled if a government makes it a priority, but it requires rigorous and comprehensive reforms that challenge the elite.

The approach to the development of crime, corruption, and law stands in stark contrast to the economics of transition. Although economists both in the region and abroad fought over postcommunist transition, few lawyers seemed to care. Nobody presented a relevant theory for the transformation of the legal system, and few were working on it. Consequently, no appropriate set of policy advice could be available. Some local lawyers were admirable reformers, but they were few. The absence of international organizations focusing on the legal transition was striking. Interpol is a minimal organization for exchange of police information. There is no international supreme court. Lawyers' associations are usually very national, apart from those dealing with international commercial law. In recent years, the EU, USAID, and the World Bank have engaged in legal issues, but none with the single-mindedness of the IMF in its pursuit of macroeconomic stability. Considering all these shortfalls, it is no surprise that the development of the legal system and legality has been the weakest part of the transition.

10

The Role of Oligarchs

Suddenly, the Russian steel industry has become a hot topic in the international business community. A few years ago, this would have seemed a crazy notion. During the Soviet era the Russian steel industry was ridiculed for its obsession with planning targets and was a byword for inefficiency. But since the break-up of the Soviet Union, a series of large and powerful steel companies has been created from the privatization of previously government-owned steel operations in Russia.

Financial Times, June 14, 2006

Nothing is as controversial as "oligarchs." The opening quote marvels over how Russian oligarchs have transformed the Russian steel industry, but as if to avoid praising them, the word "oligarch" is avoided (Marsh 2006). "Oligarch" is an ancient concept, and an "oligarchy" is defined as "government in the hands of a few" by the *Oxford University Press Dictionary*. In that sense of the word, the semidemocratic countries in the former Soviet Union may be described as oligarchic.

In Russia and Ukraine, "oligarch" became a popular label for the wealthiest tycoons around 1994, as the first truly rich people emerged. The meaning of oligarch in the two countries is similar.[1] An "oligarch" is a very wealthy and politically well-connected businessperson, a dollar billionaire, or nearly so, who is the main owner of a conglomerate of enterprises and has close ties to the president. Oligarchs or robber barons are few and tremendously wealthy. Bradford DeLong (2002, p. 179) has suggested that a present-day billionaire would be a good proxy for a robber baron. It might be more appropriate to call them plutocrats, because their aim is to make money

---

[1] There are four excellent journalistic books on the Russian oligarchs, showing how they evolved and how they operated, Brady (1999), Freeland (2000), Klebnikov (2000), and Hoffman (2002). Less has been written on the Ukrainian oligarchs; see Puglisi (2003), Åslund (2006), and Grygorenko et al. (2006).

rather than to rule the state. Joel Hellman (1998) has coined the phrase "state capture" to characterize the relationship between big businesspeople and the state in a country such as Ukraine, because these businesspeople influenced the state by multiple means.

Many mix up old-style state enterprise managers with these newly rich upstarts. Others confuse oligarchs with the godfathers of organized crime. Much of the literature on privatization argues that no privatization is better than privatization to well-connected businesspeople at prices below the market level (Black et al. 2000; Goldman 2003). Opinion polls show that oligarchs are the most hated people in Russia. As a consequence, the public condoned the Kremlin's lawless confiscation through taxation of Russia's biggest and best oil company, Yukos, and the Ukrainian government discussed widespread reprivatization in 2005 after the Orange Revolution.

The many questions about oligarchs deserve a separate chapter. In section one, I consider who the "oligarchs" were. Section two discusses the economics of oligarchy, and section three its political aspects. Section four argues that the standard complaints about oligarchs are a matter of ideology. Section five concludes that the key policy issue is to reinforce property rights. The final section considers Russian President Vladimir Putin's attempt to resolve the issue of oligarchs.

Who are the Oligarchs?

Oligarchs are by no means unique to Russia and Ukraine. Much of the discussion about economics in Latin America has circled around the entrenched power of oligarchs (Dornbusch and Edwards 1991). Rafael La Porta, Florencio Lopez-de-Silanes, and Andrei Shleifer (1999a) studied the ownership of the twenty biggest listed companies in 27 predominantly Western countries. They found that even very large corporations have controlling shareholders in most countries, and they are usually extremely wealthy families. The diffuse corporate ownership characteristic of the United States and the United Kingdom is highly exceptional. Having surveyed recent literature on ownership around the world, Randall Morck, Daniel Wolfenzon, and Bernard Yeung (2005, p. 693) concluded: "Control pyramids effectively entrust the corporate governance of the greater parts of the corporate governance of the greater parts of the corporate sectors of many countries to handfuls of elite, established families, who can quite reasonably be described as *oligarchs.*" Rather than considering oligarchs an exception, as most of the Anglo-American literature about Russia does, we must accept them as the international standard.

The most remarkable observation might be that oligarchs are not very common in most former Soviet bloc countries. Out of our twenty-one countries, people are preoccupied with oligarchs in only three: Russia, Ukraine, and Kazakhstan. In East-Central Europe, few billionaires have been allowed to develop, and the richest man in Central Europe, the Pole Jan Kulczyk, was forced to escape abroad in 2004. In the small, poor countries Kyrgyzstan, Moldova, and Tajikistan, no billionaire is to be found, and that is also true of the lingering socialist economies, Turkmenistan, Belarus, and Uzbekistan. In East-Central Europe, billionaires are barely allowed to develop, and in most CIS countries the ruling family possesses most wealth. The formation of an oligarchy indicates more openness.

The historically most prominent oligarchs are the so-called robber barons in the United States. The *New York Times* referred to the new big businessmen in America as robber barons in the 1850s, alluding to the knights who lived in castles along the Rhine and extorted fees for passage. That label stuck. The robber barons were the men who built great industrial and transportation empires in the late 19th century in the United States (Steele Gordon, 2004, pp. 211–12).

I focus here on the most prominent postcommunist oligarchs, those in Russia and Ukraine. They have displayed greater similarities with the American robber barons than is usually understood because time has beautified U.S. history, and we can better understand the Russian and Ukrainian oligarchs by comparing them with their American colleagues. In all three countries, big businessmen responded rationally to the existing economic, legal, and political conditions. The oligarchs stood out as the true *homos oeconomicus* in a world of bewilderment.

By 2005, the social features of the oligarchs are easy to establish. Most of them are around 40 years of age. They were about to graduate from university when the Soviet Law on Cooperatives was adopted in 1988, which usually formed the legal basis of their first enterprise. Almost all of them are engineers, and several are doctors of engineering, from the best schools in the Soviet Union, primarily in Moscow. Their social origins are mostly humble, and many of them come from the provinces, but the Soviet education system gave them the opportunity thanks to their outstanding mathematical skills. Initially, the dominance of Jews was striking, but the ethnicity of the oligarchs has become more varied. Nearly all the oligarchs manage huge companies. All but one of the Russian billionaires are men.[2] By all criteria,

---

[2] The single woman is the wife of Moscow Mayor Yuri Luzhkov, who has proved highly skillful in Moscow real estate.

the current oligarchs are outstanding self-made entrepreneurs, although most made their fortunes on the reanimation of existing Soviet mastodons rather than developing new enterprises.

The Russian oligarchs are typically preoccupied with oil and metals. Of 26 Russian billionaires identified by *Forbes* in 2005, twelve had made most of their money on metals, nine on oil, and two on coal (Kroll and Goldman 2005).[3] Ukraine had no less than ten billionaires in 2006, and six of the biggest Ukrainian oligarchic groups concentrate on steel.[4] An oddity is the dearth of bankers among the current Russian oligarchs, which is explained by the state dominance over the Russian banking system after the financial crash of 1998, which was used as a means of renationalization.

Curiously, many oligarchic groups in Russia are run by tight groups of friends, typically school friends, suggesting a surprising degree of trust outside the family in that country. A consequence of this great trust among Russian business partners is that several of the big enterprise groups generated multiple billionaires: Yukos seven, Alfa three, Interros two, Mechel two, and so on (Kroll and Goldman 2005). The uncommonly large number of billionaires in Russia is partially explained by the country's strong partnerships. Also in Ukraine, two of the four biggest oligarchic groups have three billionaire owners each (Privat Group and Industrial Union of Donbass).[5]

The Economics of Oligarchy

Let us look more closely at the economic and legal conditions that generated oligarchs in the United States as well as in the former Soviet Union.

One fundamental cause of this generation and concentration of wealth in America after the Civil War was the sudden achievement of great economies of scale in certain industries, especially metals, oil, and railways. Such economies of scale cannot be attained in a small country. The super-rich mainly emerge in countries with large markets, which may partially explain why they are only prominent in the three largest post-Soviet economies (Russia, Ukraine, and Kazakhstan).

A second feature common to the U.S. industrialization and postcommunism was rapid structural change, which facilitated great accumulation of wealth among those few who knew how to take advantage of the trends of

---

[3] In oil: Yukos, Lukoil, Surgut, TNK, Sibneft; in metals Rusal, SUAL, Norilsk Nickel, Severstal, Evrazholding, NLMK, MMK, Mechel, and UMMK.

[4] System Capital Management, Interpipe, Privat Group, Industrial Union of Donbass, Zaporizhstal, and MMK imeni Ilicha (Korrespondent 2006).

[5] Interviews with owners of both groups in March 2003 and December 2004, respectively.

the day. In the United States, the period of reconstruction after the Civil War was characterized by radical changes, and in the former Soviet Union, the state and the economic system collapsed.

A third economic characteristic was the presence of rent, which is often difficult to distinguish from economies of scale. The U.S. antitrust case against Microsoft attempted to determine whether Microsoft's profits depended on rent or economies of scale and failed to make this distinction to anyone's satisfaction. Most of the original U.S. robber barons made their money on railways, which generated large monopoly rents until competing lines had been built. Other robber barons focused on the natural rents of resource industries, John D. Rockefeller on oil and Andrew Carnegie on steel (DeLong 2002). The Russian and Ukrainian oligarchs focus on oil and metals, industries with ample natural rents.

Fourth, the U.S. robber barons benefited from the free distribution of state assets, notably land around the railways, and cheap state credits because multiple early railway investments ended up in bankruptcy because of insufficient state support to attain the desired economies of scale (DeLong 2002). In the postcommunist world, privatization took place through cheap sales of old assets either through direct privatization, as the loans-for-shares privatization in Russia, or the accumulation of vouchers or stocks on the secondary market. Given that the state enterprises were mismanaged and thus lost international competitiveness until they were privatized, early privatization was vital.

Fifth, the absence of strong legal institutions also determined the rise of oligarchs. Well-functioning legal systems are a recent invention, and even within the West legal systems are subject to many flaws. Many Western countries adopted insider legislation only in the last two decades. As multiple corporate accounting scandals, from Enron to WorldCom, illustrate, corporate governance remains poor in the West even today. John Steele Gordon (2004, pp. 207–8) has eloquently captured the state of law in the United States in the 1860s, which saw the rise of the robber barons:

Nowhere was ... corruption more pervasive than in New York, and especially on Wall Street. ... In 1868 the New York State Legislature actually passed a law the effect of which was to legalize bribery ... the popular English *Fraser's Magazine* wrote that "in New York there is a custom among litigants as peculiar to that city, it is to be hoped, as it is supreme within it, of retaining a judge as well as a lawyer."

By comparison, the current legal practices in Russia and Ukraine appear nothing but normal for this stage of capitalist development. Poor judicial systems breed poor corporate governance, impeding the evolution of financial markets. Without strong corporate legislation and a potent judicial system, partners find it difficult to agree or resolve conflicts. Nor can principals (owners) control their agents (executives), so they are compelled to manage their companies themselves. As a consequence, businesspeople with concentrated ownership tend to be more successful than those who have to deal with many minority shareholders. "When institutions are weak, doing business with strangers is dangerous and unreliable" (Morck et al. 2005, p. 672). Therefore, businesspeople want to escape the hazards of concluding too many contracts that they cannot secure in court. They rationally opt for vertical integration to avoid the hazards of arbitrary court judgments about contracts; that is, they prefer corporate hierarchies to horizontal markets (Williamson 1975). Tarun Khanna and Jan Rivkin (2001) investigated business groups in fourteen emerging economies that are not postcommunist. They conceived of business groups as responses to market failures and high transaction costs and found that group affiliation had a profound, positive effect on profitability.

The combination of all these five factors – large economies of scale, vast economies, fast structural change, the prevalence of rents, and poor legal systems – led to the concentration of fortunes in oil, metals, and railways in the United States in the nineteenth century, as well as in the same industries in Russia and Ukraine today. It is difficult to see how a market economy could be introduced under these conditions without generating super-rich businesspeople, and the emergence of oligarchs seems nothing but a natural consequence of the development of capitalism under the prevailing conditions.

Economically, the oligarchic systems have proved highly adaptive. It is inaccurate to equate oligarchic enterprises with state-owned enterprises as Anne Krueger (2002 p. 3) has done, arguing, with reference to politically connected big businesspeople in East Asia, that state-owned enterprises "are almost exactly the same in their effects as cronyism." The difference between oligarchic companies and state companies is immense. Big state enterprises tend to be monopolies or quasi-monopolies, whereas the oligarchic corporations typically indulge in vicious competition rather than price fixing. Characteristically, the domestic Russian prices of oil and coal have been liberalized for many years, but the prices of state transportation, natural gas, and electricity are still regulated. Large state enterprises enjoy ample access to subsidies, and their investments are often decided by the government, whereas oligarchic enterprises have had to make do without subsidies since 1998. Russian state enterprises are notorious for acquiring assets and wasting resources, presumably to the benefit of management, rather than undertaking productive investment. Russian state-dominated enterprises, such as Gazprom and Rosneft, patently fail to boost production organically, in which private Russian oil, coal and metallurgical companies have excelled. Gazprom has succeeded in maintaining a negative cash flow regardless of how high gas prices have surged, whereas the private oil and coal companies are flooded with profits despite much more severe taxation. After the financial crash of 1998, the Russian oligarchs swiftly streamlined their business structures, and mergers and acquisitions caught on. State-dominated companies such as Gazprom, by contrast, not only resisted selling noncore assets but bought more. The oligarchic corporations excelled in buying international services of all kinds, whereas the state companies resisted doing so until it had become standard. In short, the oligarchic companies have proved highly innovative in management, whereas the state enterprises are the last acceptors of any novelty (Dynkin and Sokolov 2002; Shleifer 2005).

Standard advice to foreign investors in the former Soviet Union is not to touch old, unrestructured Soviet enterprises with more than 1,500 employees, because their operation is too complex. Many such enterprises are viable, but only locals appear to possess the relevant skills to turn them around. Just think of all the skills that are required! For truly big enterprises, strong and good relations with both the central and regional governments are necessary. In the absence of a functioning legal system, the owner/manager must be able to secure property rights and contracts in the most effective and affordable extra-legal fashion. One of the prime tasks on a Soviet plant is to outroot rampant theft by the employees. Post-Soviet countries have plenty of social regulations, but only some of these are actually honored. Soviet enterprises were chronically overstaffed, but only local businesspeople tend to have the guts and ability to cut the labor force down to an economical size. Soviet factories were typically overloaded with equipment. Most of it must be scrapped, but foreign businesspeople tend to gut the factories, using little but the premises, whereas local businesspeople with less capital are anxious to utilize valuable physical capital and technology. Soviet management had its peculiarities, and in factories with tens of thousands of workers, knowledge of the old management is necessary for its successful renewal; financial skills and management consultants can easily be brought in from outside. Therefore, there are many reasons to expect that local businesspeople can do better than foreign investors in basic industries, such as metallurgy and other resource industries, especially at the early stages of restructuring, if they get the chance to own them despite limited capital.

Yegor Grygorenko, Yuriy Gorodnichenko, and Dmytro Ostanin (2006) studied a sample of almost 2,000 Ukrainian companies. They found that oligarchs picked underperforming firms with large capital stock and sales, and they established that firms owned by oligarchs had much higher productivity growth than others. This tallies with a relatively early empirical study of Russian financial-industrial groups in the mid-1990s, which found that these hierarchical groups were more efficient in their real investment than independent owners (Perotti and Gelfer 2001).

The only plausible alternative owners of large factories are foreign investors and the state. In Central Europe, the public insistence on "fair" privatization at full prices was so great that most large enterprises remained state-owned for far too long. They deteriorated for years and stayed unprofitable. Some big enterprises were finally sold to foreign investors, who usually proved themselves both clueless and hapless. As a result, most large industrial enterprises in Central Europe have closed down, and the myth has evolved that such enterprises could not be restructured. In Russia and Ukraine, by contrast, the old large metallurgical and chemical industries are booming as never before because skillful oligarchs are allowed to own them. The other alternative was not to privatize. Belarus is an eminent example. Its economic restructuring has been tardy, and neither market economy nor political pluralism has evolved.

Two major conclusions can be drawn. First, only a few businesspeople with concentrated private ownership and supreme knowledge of the informal rules could manage large Soviet enterprises in the early transition. The real alternatives were to keep them state owned and unreformed until they collapsed or to sell them off to foreign investors, who usually closed down most of the original enterprise because they did not know how to manage it. The question was whether the state would allow local big businesspeople to emerge or not, and only a few countries did so. They have successfully restructured large Soviet mining and metallurgical industries.

The second conclusion is that the oligarchs were not guilty of the conditions that arose, but they responded rationally to the existing conditions. Whenever state regulation created wedges between fixed state prices and market prices, they arbitraged between these prices to their personal benefit. When privatization was launched, they transferred state property to themselves in the cheapest way. During the mass privatization, they bought vouchers and stocks. Given that so many enterprises were privatized simultaneously, they had no time to develop a business strategy but bought opportunistically what they could get cheaply until mass privatization had been completed. Meanwhile, they did little to their newly won enterprises because they obtained the greatest marginal value by acquiring more assets rather than investing in their enterprises. After the mass privatization was completed, the oligarchs elaborated business strategies; streamlined their assets, specializing in a few industries; and invested heavily (Brady 1999; Dynkin and Sokolov 2002; Shleifer and Treisman 2004).

The Politics of Oligarchy

The key legal and political issue in emerging capitalism is property rights. Hernando de Soto (2000) has pointed out how the absence of property rights harms the poor in middle-income countries and the developing world today, but the rich face the same hazard. Nothing could be done by law when laws were in disarray, the courts unreformed, and the law enforcement ineffective (Gaidar 2003). The question was how to handle state failure.

In the early postcommunist period the business world was Hobbesian. "In the state of nature, property rights exist only as long as they can be protected by the claimant" as Vadim Volkov (2002 p. xi) formulated it. Before the oligarchs, organized crime prevailed. The oligarchs broke through in this world of organized crime. Initially, they bought security from organized crime as everybody else, but soon they established their own security services, which were cheaper and more reliable than criminal gangs.

Later on, the oligarchs increasingly purchased state services, or politics, to reinsure their shaky property rights. They used the agency that appeared most effective at the time in a typical succession: reliance on organized crime, their own security forces, government agencies, and politics (cf. Klebnikov 2000).

Oligarchs could act in two contrary fashions depending on their sense of security and access to political power. If they were strong, they acted in line with "the concept of *economic entrenchment* as a feedback loop, whereby weak institutions place sweeping corporate governance powers in the hands of a tiny elite group, who then lobby for weak institutions to preserve their concentrated control over the countries' large corporations – oligarchic capitalism" (Morck et al. 2005, p. 711; cf. Shleifer 1997). Or as Konstantin Sonin (2003) wrote: "In unequal societies, the rich may benefit from shaping economic institutions in their favor." Boris Berezovsky's behavior and his and Vladimir Gusinsky's attack on the Russian government because of their decent privatization of the state telecommunications holding Svyazinvest in the summer of 1997 may be described in that way (Freeland 2000; Klebnikov 2000). Common tricks by powerful oligarchs were to send tax police, prosecutors, and other law enforcement agencies on competitors with poorer political connections.

If the oligarchs felt weak by contrast, they would act in the opposite manner: "But sometimes, highly concentrated corporate control does not induce economic entrenchment. Strong institutions develop and diffuse capitalism takes hold" (Morck et al. 2005 p. 711). The conclusion is that the more competition oligarchs are exposed to, the better they behave. Because oligarchs stand out as the ultimate *homos oeconomicus*, we would expect their behavior to vary with the situation. The ultimate success is when an oligarch tries to gentrify after a few years of dubious enrichment, as Mikhail Khodorkovsky, the main owner of Yukos oil company, did.

Politics offer a number of attractive goods. Starting from the top, business-people can buy presidential decisions, usually not directly from the president but from his family or closest aides. The difference between the administration of U.S. President Ulysses Grant (1869–77) and that of Boris Yeltsin or Leonid Kuchma is less than Americans want to recognize. Although the U.S. robber barons arose in the 1850s (Commodore Cornelius Vanderbilt is considered the first one), it was not until the early 1900s that President Theodore Roosevelt opposed them. The Russian situation has changed profoundly since 2000, when President Putin came to power. Now, oligarchs are extorted by the Kremlin rather than being entitled to buy its services. The problem with Russia is rather that the oligarchs have proved too weak to resist the large-scale renationalization undertaken since 2003 in Russia by President Vladimir Putin. Unlike in the United States, the Russian oligarchs are hardly strong enough to safeguard their property rights when the ruler turns against them.

The second kind of political good on sale is legislation from the national parliament. The United States has not prohibited the purchasing of legislation, or lobbying, but legalized and regulated this process, rendering it transparent. President Putin complained that Yukos blocked minor tax legislation directed against oil companies in Russia in June 2003. He used this as an argument for his demolition of the company and the jailing of its owner. But the United States can tax energy much less because of its strong energy lobby. The corporate lobbies in the legislatures of the United States, Russia, and Ukraine were long strengthened because parliamentary elections were dominated by one-man constituencies, but the introduction of full proportional elections, in Ukraine in 2006 and in Russia in 2007, is likely to weaken their power. Individual candidates needed to mobilize their own campaign financing, which is much easier if the candidates themselves are rich or have a few large contributions. The U.S. Senate was called a Club of Millionaires in the Gilded Age of the 1880s, as is the Ukrainian parliament today. After the March 2002 elections, Ukraine had its most oligarchic parliament. It was commonly said that 300 of the 450 deputies in its Supreme Rada were dollar millionaires, and until the Orange Revolution, half the Supreme Rada was dominated by nine oligarchic factions, each representing the interests of one major business group (Åslund 2006).

A third group of political goods is government decisions. Several of the ministers of President Ulysses Grant's administration were direct beneficiaries of corrupt payments from railway companies (Steele Gordon 2004, p. 219), and the corruption of cabinet ministers has been a patent problem in the United States. With the U.S. revolving doors between government and the private sector, conflicts of interest slightly detached in time have become almost impossible to prosecute. By contrast, in the 1990s the Ukrainian and Russian oligarchs devoted amazingly little attention to government posts. Ministers tended to be civil servants. In Russia, the half-year appointments of the oligarchs Vladimir Potanin and Boris Berezovsky to senior government posts were exceptions. Russian businesspeople preferred to buy services from officials or purchase public jobs for their helpers. Again, Ukraine has been far more oligarchic than Russia. Two prime ministers in the 1990s, Yukhum Zviahilsky (1993–4) and Pavlo Lazarenko (1996–7), were major businessmen themselves (Åslund 2000). Even so, the Ukrainian government remained dominated by civil servants until November 2002, when the country's first coalition government was formed under Prime Minister Viktor Yanukovych, and big businesspeople moved from Parliament to top government jobs. President Viktor Yushchenko promised to draw a sharp line between business and government, but his first administration contained three substantial businessmen.[6] In August 2006, Yanukovych became prime minister, and a group of big businesspeople joined his cabinet.

A fourth political good of great value is court decisions. The earlier quote about New York courts in the 1860s says it all about American courts at that time. In Russia and Ukraine, the use of courts has risen steadily as law has evolved. Alas, as courts have become more important and independent, they have also become more corrupt, and the prices of court decisions have likewise risen.

Media is a fifth, mostly private, political good. In the United States, media owners have enjoyed a free hand for a long time. Publicity has long been traded freely in Russia and Ukraine, which is legal. In Boris Yeltsin's Russia, the oligarchs Boris Berezovsky and Vladimir Gusinsky dominated the media. President Vladimir Putin has gradually expanded government control and

---

[6] Petro Poroshenko, Yevhen Chervonenko, and David Zhvania.

ownership over media, but the trade in "news" publicity for commercial purposes is continuing as before, and public relations agencies in Moscow provide price lists, specifying how much it costs to buy news reporting by various prominent TV personalities. In Ukraine, oligarchs (primarily Viktor Medvedchuk and Victor Pinchuk) purchased a lot of media, especially TV, before the presidential elections in October 1999, inspired by the Russian presidential elections of June 1996. "Oligarch" even acquired the additional meaning of "media owner."[7] The main media have so far stayed in the hands of a few oligarchs.

Thus, considering the economic, legal, and political conditions of oligarchy, the Russian and Ukrainian oligarchs are by no means atypical. They are responding rationally to the prevailing conditions to maximize profit and security. How well or badly they behave depends on how much competition they are exposed to. A major concern caused by the current Russian renationalization and the recent Ukrainian discussion about reprivatization is that the oligarchs are too weak politically to achieve a balance of power with the state that could secure property rights for the future.

Complaints: A Matter of Ideology

Oligarchs are controversial, and so were the American robber barons (Veblen 1899/1994). The primary political complaint about Russian and Ukrainian oligarchs is their excessive wealth. The number of billionaires is large in Russia. By its number of billionaires, Russia ranks as the third country in the world after the United States and Germany (Kroll and Fass 2006).

A related argument is the considerable inequality in Russia and Ukraine, but it is similar to that of the United States, and far below the average of Latin America (see Chapter 7). Inequality is substantial but hardly inordinate and more or less constant.

Criticism of the oligarchs has focused on the purportedly flawed privatization, perceived as the key to their wealth. This is the popular view in Russia and Ukraine as well as in the West. That a view is widespread does not mean it is well founded. Volumes have been written about the Russian loans-for-shares privatizations in late 1995, which marked the rise of the Russian oligarchs, but the relationship between privatization and oligarchs was more tenuous.[8] The oligarchs in question were all known as such before these privatizations. The loans-for-shares privatizations did not make them

---

[7] I owe this observation to Olena Prytula, editor-in-chief of *Ukrainskaya Pravda*, Kyiv.
[8] The best are Freeland (2000) and Hoffman (2002). See also, Blasi et al. (1997).

oligarchs, and most of them did not participate in the loans-for-shares privatizations.[9] Moreover, unlike many other privatizations, substantial money
was paid in the loans-for-shares deals, even if the amounts were paltry in
comparison with the potential values of the enterprises. Several of the dozen
enterprises involved in loans-for-shares did extremely well, especially Yukos
and Sibneft, which led the revival of the Russian oil industry. Soon they
paid as much in taxes in one year as anybody could possibly have asked
in return for these enterprises in 1995 (Shleifer 2005). A majority stake in
Yukos was privatized for $310 million, but at the time nobody suggested
that a maximum price of more than $4–5 billion was feasible. As early as
2000, Yukos paid no less than $6 billion in taxes that year. Thanks to the eco-
nomic success after its privatization Yukos's market capitalization peaked at
$45 billion in 2003 before Putin destroyed the company.

Economically the Russian loans-for-shares privatizations were an unmit-
igated success. The state would have lost greatly if it had retained these
companies and privatized them later, regardless of the eventual sale price.
That was the fate of Central Europe's now moribund steel industry and
coal mines. People detest privatizations more than straightforward theft of
money because they can see privatized factories with their naked eye. They
do not react when billions of dollars are spirited out of the state treasury
because they do not see them. Privatization is too transparent, making the
wealth of the few apparent to ordinary people (Shleifer and Treisman 2000;
Åslund 2002). The conspicuous success of others is rarely appreciated.

In Ukraine, privatization was later and messier than in Russia (Yekhanurov 2000), which bolstered the power of the oligarchs. Until 2000,
Ukraine's oligarchs focused on gas trade and little else. One leading oligarch, Ihor Bakai, stated famously: "All really rich people in Ukraine have
made their money on gas" (Timoshenko 1998). The oligarchs' rent-seeking
excesses delayed economic recovery for longer in Ukraine than in Russia.
Finally, in 2000, substantial economic policy changes occurred against the
will of the Ukrainian oligarchs, which contributed to high economic growth
(Åslund 2001). The big controversial privatizations in Ukraine took place in
2002–4, when its oligarchy was at its peak. Although the oligarchs increased
their wealth more than ever, competition from emerging big businesspeople challenged the oligarchy. After the Orange Revolution, Prime Minister

---

[9] Of the seven famous oligarchs in Russia in 1996 and 1997 (Petr Aven, Boris Berezovsky,
Mikhail Fridman, Vladimir Gusinsky, Mikhail Khodorkovsky, Vladimir Potanin, and Alek-
sandr Smolensky), only three participated (Boris Berezovsky, Mikhail Khodorkovsky, and
Vladimir Potanin).

Yuliya Tymoshenko directed the popular anger against two leading oligarchs, Victor Pinchuk and Rinat Akhmetov. They had made the transition from commodity trading to production and developed large steel corporations, with transparent and efficient corporate structures. The shadier oligarchs, by contrast, escaped the brunt of the critique. Admittedly, Pinchuk and Akhmetov were the beneficiaries of the most disputed privatization in Ukraine,[10] but the point is rather that the most successful, transparent, and productive businesspeople were the focus of the public fury.

A common complaint about oligarchs was that they bribed, stole, and committed all conceivable crimes. The profound problem with postcommunist society, however, was that it was lawless in the exact meaning of the word. Multiple ordinary human rules were not codified in law. Worse, many such rules were criminalized. Under these circumstances, it was difficult to establish the requirement for legal behavior. Contracts had to be enforced somehow and payments collected, but courts would not do so.

Oligarchs were also accused of being parasites, of not producing anything. As discussed earlier, however, the less rent seeking and the more productive oligarchs became, the more unpopular they were. At the time of the Orange Revolution in 2004, Ukraine's GDP was growing at a staggering pace of 12 percent a year. Much of its steel was produced in the oligarchs' mills, and many other branches of industry were taking off in the oligarchs' hands. The oligarchs became subject to much greater public criticism when they no longer stole but produced. Similarly, the popular reaction against the Russian oligarchs caught on around 2000 after several of the major oligarchs had decided to become fully legal and legitimate, pay taxes, declare their ownership and spend substantial amounts on charitable donations. This voluntary transparency might have been the greatest mistake the Russian oligarchs ever made. People find the transparency of wealth hard to tolerate.

Marshall Goldman (2003) argued that American robber barons were better than the oligarchs because they invested and built new enterprises, but that distinction hardly holds. After the Russian and Ukrainian oligarchs acquired their enterprises, they invested heavily by any standard (Shleifer 2005). Moreover, why should big old enterprises be wasted? Only oligarchs have proved able to save them.

Alas, economic utility and popular acclaim seem negatively correlated. Insider privatization, which dominated in the early transition, has been

---

[10] In the summer of 2004, just before the presidential elections, they acquired the huge Kryvorizhstal steelworks for $800 million without real competition. The Yushchenko government reversed the privatization and sold Kryvorizhstal to Mittal Steel for $4.8 billion.

found economically less effective, but politically it has been more easily accepted. If the first beneficiary squandered his funds, he was easily forgiven, or at least forgotten. Also, if somebody buys a mismanaged privatized enterprise on the secondary market for a penny, nobody complains. Nor do people react much if somebody takes over a well-managed company at a low price after ordering law enforcement agencies to engage in lawless persecution.

The *sense morale* is not pretty. The shadier the machinations through which oligarchs made their money, the safer they are from public condemnation. The more productive and transparent they become, the more criticized they are, and the more taxes they pay, the more exposed they become, as Yukos so well illustrates. Admittedly, time heals all wounds, and so does failure. Today few are concerned about the retired organized criminals who emigrated (even if they were serial killers) or state enterprise managers who lost their fortunes after having run their ill-gotten enterprises aground.

So what is the problem with oligarchs? People dislike successful capitalists for purely ideological reasons. The U.S. government did not react against the robber barons in the 1860s and 1870s when their excesses were worst, but it did so only in the early 1900s, when populism grew strong under the influence of Thorstein Veblen, Louis Brandeis, and Theodore Roosevelt. It helped little that Andrew Carnegie was giving away his wealth at an unprecedented pace (Morris 2005).

In the end, the acceptance of large fortunes and certain inequality is a matter of ideology. People do not accept others' affluence, unless they believe that great riches are permissible. This is the secret of the economic success of the Western world, and it is not limited to the Anglo-Saxon world. Forbes reckons that Germany is the country in the world with the second largest number of billionaires, and the whole of continental Europe has dominant family groups owning their biggest companies (La Porta et al. 1999a). Postcommunist nations find it difficult to accept the amassment of huge personal fortunes because socialist ideas opposing the very rich persist. The situation has become more dramatic by economic and legal conditions skewered in favor of the formation of oligarchs. Property rights remain feeble and are easily questioned. The very speed of change suggests that it may be reversed. Contrary to popular convictions, the peculiarity of postcommunism is not that oligarchs have arisen but that they have only been permitted to evolve in three countries. The economic problem of postcommunism is not oligarchy but society's ideological inability to accept large fortunes and ultimately private property rights. If the property rights of the richest are not secure, no property rights are. The best formulation of such an ideology for the acceptance of the formation of wealth and its inheritance is probably Friedrich Hayek's (1960) book *The Constitution of Liberty*.

Ironically, postcommunist reforms were not sufficiently ideological, as Hillary Appel (2004) has shown in her comparison between privatization in the Czech Republic and Russia. She concluded that in the Czech Republic Václav Klaus wisely used classical liberal ideology to facilitate privatization. Although the Russian privatizers were equally radical liberals, they chose to justify privatization with concrete material benefits, advocating the participation of various stakeholders (Boycko et al. 1995; Chubais 1999). The Russian public felt cheated when their anticipated material benefits did not materialize, whereas the Czechs happily reelected Klaus because he promised nothing but ideology. Neither large-scale fraud by the investment funds nor low growth upset the clear-sighted Czechs. The riches of the Russian and Ukrainian oligarchs can hardly be accepted by the public if these people do not embrace capitalist ideology.

The main enemy of liberalism is no longer socialism, even if many socialist sentiments linger, but populism. Populism is no longer directed against the laws of macroeconomics, as was the case in Latin American in the 1970s and 1980s. Today the value of macroeconomic stability is widely understood throughout the world. Instead, the new postcommunist economic populism pokes into a less well understood area of economics, namely, property rights. It agitates for redistribution of property. As usual, populism is driven by a combination of forces. Some suffer from the lack of justice, and others want to make fortunes by undermining the property rights of others. No sound capitalism can develop without respect for property rights, however. The origins of Western property rights are not pretty. Indeed they made Pierre-Joseph Proudhon exclaim "Property is theft" in 1840, but capitalism succeeds in the West because property rights are accepted even so.

After the Orange Revolution in Ukraine, the new government spoke of the possible reprivatization of up to 3,000 enterprises. The redistribution of property is often considered a characteristic of a revolution (Mau and Starodubrovskaya 2001), but the complications of a large-scale re-privatization would be immense. Only very recent privatizations could be effectively reversed, because many enterprises had changed hands. How would partial sales and investments be valued? Obviously, the oligarchs would resist their expropriation, and their willingness to spend money on politics and courts in a corrupt state made it likely that they would win. Nor would new case-by-case privatizations be successful, because they rarely are in weak post-communist states (Havrylyshyn and McGettigan 2000). In a revolutionary situation, many businesspeople, especially respectable foreigners, are prone to stay out of competitive privatizations, although the Ukrainian oligarchs could be replaced by Russian oligarchs. The old owners would undoubtedly sue the state. Primarily as a consequence of this harmful debate, Ukraine's growth rate plummeted from 12.1 percent in 2004 to 2.6 percent in 2005 as the oligarchs slowed down their economic activities. The Ukrainian economy speeded up again after the parliamentary elections in March 2006 put an end to the danger of reprivatization.

After the Rose Revolution in November 2003, the new Georgian regime under President Mikheil Saakashvili also questioned the existing property rights. It arrested dozens of businesspeople whom it considered criminals and let them out for a fee, arbitrarily set at an amount from $300,000 to $1 million. In tiny Georgia, the positive effect on the treasury was palpable. The public complained, however, that friends of the new regime were not asked to pay up, regardless of how they had earned their money. The amounts were perceived as arbitrary extortion, and the guarantees of property rights have not been proved.[11] Complaints have arisen that the government has continued on its initial arbitrary track of extortion.

The obvious alternative policy option would be to guarantee the oligarchs full property rights without asking them for compensation, which is, of course, the preferred choice of the oligarchs. The Russian and Ukrainian oligarchs are trying to develop this option with huge charitable donations primarily to the social sector, taking their cue from Andrew Carnegie and John D. Rockefeller.

A Question of Property Rights

In the mid-1990s, young locals took on the challenge to transform seemingly moribund Soviet smokestacks. They succeeded beyond any expectation, revitalizing old factories and spawning economic recovery. Soon, some new owners became conspicuously rich, because economies of scale were great, rents ample, and only enterprises with concentrated ownership could make it because of the weakness of the legal system. Because their property rights were weak, the new entrepreneurs, commonly called oligarchs, reinsured their property rights by buying politicians, judges, and other officials, which is called corruption or state capture. Ironically, the present problem is to safeguard the civil rights of the generators of this unprecedented boom.

[11] Personal information from Theresa Freese, a journalist living in Georgia, on May 12, 2005.

Recently, both Russian and Ukrainian politics have been driven by a popular urge to defeat corruption, identified with oligarchs. In the Gilded Age, the United States faced the same dilemma: how to quell the excesses of the new big businesspeople. Russia under Putin has instigated confiscatory taxation of the biggest oligarch and extorted the rest with periodic payments. Ukraine considered a large reprivatization scheme, which destabilized both politics and economics, not to mention law.

The problem with these schemes is that they are driven by the wrong ideology – a populist dislike of the rich plus a desire by rising businesspeople to grab the assets of the old oligarchs, and disrespect for both law and property rights. Neither should be encouraged. The emergence of oligarchs must be understood as a natural consequence of the prevailing economic, legal, and political conditions in the aftermath of communism and needs to be accepted by the public. This requires that the public understands and embraces the fundamental principles of capitalism.

In a theoretical paper, Daron Acemoglu (2003) took a dispassionate view of the problems of property rights in an oligarchic versus a democratic society. He defined an "oligarchic society" as a "society where political power is in the hands of the economic elite," and he compared the trade-off between the distortions of such a society with those of a democracy, where political power is more equally distributed.

The big problem he saw with a democracy is high taxes, which redistribute income from entrepreneurs to workers, discouraging entrepreneurial investment. This is exactly what is described in Chapters 3 and 6. Democratic East-Central Europe has higher taxes, greater public redistribution (notably social transfers), and lower investment growth than the oligarchic CIS countries. In addition, the democratic countries have much more regulated labor markets and thus higher unemployment (see Chapter 4). The problem with an oligarchic society, in Acemoglu's view, is that it offers a less level playing field. It restricts the entry of new enterprises, distorting the allocation of resources and redistributing income toward the entrepreneurs by reducing labor demand and wages.

The growth rate in the respective case depends on which distortion has the greatest economic impact. Acemoglu (2003) argued that the typical pattern is that an oligarchy first becomes richer but later falls behind a democratic society. As in so many other respects, the early postcommunist transition is peculiar. As discussed in Chapter 3, democracy was strongly positively correlated with all kinds of market reforms and economic growth until 1998. The explanation is that democracy was the most effective lever against the extraordinary rent seeking. From 1999, by contrast, the negative effects of high taxation, high social transfers, and overregulated labor markets have kept growth in Central Europe low. In addition, its inability to accept the rise of oligarchs left the productive capital of old industrial giants underutilized.

The CIS oligarchies have performed in the opposite fashion. Until 1998, their economic elites behaved utterly irresponsibly. They attempted to maximize their rents, ignoring that their rent seeking caused economic decay to their countries. The Russian crash of 1998 radically realigned the incentives of the economic elites of the CIS oligarchies. The inflationary rents were gone, and their main revenues arose from the production of commodities for export. Suddenly the oligarchs became interested in high economic growth and low taxes because the resurging state power forced even them to pay taxes. The oligarchs favor a free labor market because it benefits their economic interests. They care little about corruption, which they can handle; it limits entry of new competitors, generating rents for the happy incumbents. For now, the handicaps of the East-Central European democracies appear more damaging to economic growth than the high corruption of the CIS oligarchies (Åslund and Jenish 2006).

Yet the liberal argument for the leveling of the playing field, the reduction of corruption, and the facilitation of entry of new entrepreneurs remains strong and sound. At some stage, this may give the East-Central European countries the upper hand again in economic growth. Ideally, the CIS oligarchies would become democracies after they have exploited the benefits of their current incentive structure fully. Arguably, that is what happens when successfully developing semiauthoritarian countries become democracies. Another possibility is that the East-Central European countries succumb to tax competition, as is currently happening, and slash taxes as well as social transfers to boost their economic growth. The outcome of this competition is not obvious, but it is positive in itself.

Today it might sound implausible, but oligarchs can also be combated through a social democratic approach, with high progressive taxation. Bradford DeLong (2002) pointed out that the United States hardly generated any billionaires from 1930 to 1980, because even there social democracy was victorious for half a century. The outstanding feature of this period was high progressive taxation, which exceeded 90 percent for the truly rich after World War II until 1962 (Steel Gordon 2004). Even under the otherwise liberal U.S. conditions, the high progressive taxes on the very rich stemmed the emergence of new billionaires. Would the new U.S. multibillionaires, who gave birth to the new wave of enterprises in high-tech, finance, and trade, such a Microsoft, Intel, and Wal-Mart, have developed, if the United States had maintained a marginal income tax of more than 90 percent? I doubt it. Fortunately, such high progressive taxes run counter to the mood of our time, which cherishes flat taxes. Nor are such high taxes likely to harm the oligarchs, who are likely to avoid them either by buying themselves sufficient legislative clout or through emigration. Wealthy aristocrats as well as the inheritors of the entrepreneurs a century ago persist in many European countries despite high progressive income taxes, whereas new entrepreneurs tend to sell out to the old families (Morck et al 2005). But countries with few entrepreneurs need to cherish them.

Naturally, law must be imposed on the oligarchs. If the state is able to guarantee property rights to big businesspeople, their need to capture the state with large political payments will plummet. Then a normal legal system, which can discipline the oligarchs, can evolve. In the end, no political solution is likely to hold if it is not supported by a strong and broad ideological commitment to the sanctity of private property. If people are not convinced that they need capitalism for their own good, they are not likely to accept the perseverance of the super-rich.

Oligarchs have proved highly useful economically after the rampant rent seeking ended. They have evolved as a natural product of large economies of scale and weak legal security, and very large enterprises can hardly function without their firm management. A major problem is that oligarchs spend inordinate amounts to ensure their property rights, which could be cured by guaranteeing the private property rights of all people, including oligarchs. If not even the property of the richest is safe, how can anybody trust his or her property rights? Such a guarantee of property rights marks the crossing of the threshold to mature capitalism. Oligarchs may become more palatable politically if they are charged additional taxes or induced to undertake large-scale charitable donations. Ultimately, the acceptance of oligarchs is a matter of ideology. Do we accept the very rich or not? Mature capitalism does, but lesser systems do not.

A final observation on oligarchy is that it does not appear very stable. East-Central Europe has established stable democratic systems, and Belarus, Turkmenistan, and Uzbekistan have reinforced strict dictatorships. The other nine CIS countries may be called more or less oligarchic political regimes, which are intermediary between democracy and dictatorship. They can develop in either direction, and they have changed considerably in recent years. Under Putin, Russia has been transformed from a semidemocratic oligarchy to a centralized police state. With the Orange Revolution in November–December 2004, Ukraine took a big step in the opposite direction toward full-fledged democracy with a more parliamentary system. The main question in the region is how these oligarchic regimes will evolve.

Putin's Alternative: Centralized Dictatorship

In early 1998, the Russian oligarchy had reached its zenith. A common view was that the country's transformation had been completed and that the oligarchy was to last for the foreseeable future. The oligarchs appeared to deal with the state as a self-service boutique, but their demise came faster than anybody expected. All of a sudden, the state was back with an unquestioned monopoly of power. Renationalization replaced privatization, and secret police took over both power and wealth from the oligarchs. The man embodying this defeat of the oligarchs was Russia's President Vladimir Putin. The oligarchs, who had seemed omnipotent, suddenly surprised with their weakness.

The financial crash of August 17, 1998, brought a sudden end to the paradise of the oligarchs. They had been big purchasers of domestic treasury bills, and they had financed their purchases with large loans in Western currencies. When the Russian government defaulted, they lost big. Most of the large oligarchic banks went bankrupt. Only Alfa Bank was left standing. Incredibly, Viktor Gerashchenko, who had caused so much damage to Russia's economy and had been sacked because of the currency crisis in October 1994, was reappointed chairman of the Central Bank of Russia. He secured the state banks' dominance, which remains to this day, marginalizing the oligarchs in the financial sector.

The financial crash forced President Yeltsin to appoint an old-style government with prominent communist ministers and the former foreign intelligence chief Yevgeny Primakov as prime minister, curtailing the role of oligarchs in Russian politics. Although a couple of oligarchs assisted in the nomination of the former KGB lieutenant-colonel Vladimir Putin as prime minister and president from 2000, his presidency became the defeat of the oligarchs.

Also the regional governors, who had been major culprits behind the Russian financial crash, lost political power. They had refused to allocate more tax revenues to the federal treasury and they had defrauded the center through barter schemes and offsets.

The third group to lose out politically was the communists, who had opposed all the fiscal measures that had been needed to salvage the Russian economy as well as market economic legislation. Although the communists seemed to gain the upper hand through their appointments to Primakov's government, they lost badly in the parliamentary elections in December 1999 to Vladimir Putin's new centrist party of power, United Russia.

As discussed in Chapter 5, the Russian financial crash led to a remarkable sanitation of Russia's public finances. The government swiftly balanced the state budget, primarily by slashing enterprise subsidies but also by reducing real pensions and by centralizing tax revenues. Remarkably, Russia has maintained very strict macroeconomic policies, leading to ever-larger budget surpluses from 2000. As oil revenues rose with higher world market prices, they were amassed in a special stabilization fund, and international currency reserves exceeded $300 billion by the end of 2006 (Owen and Robinson 2003). Russian society had been so shell-shocked by the crash of 1998 that these strict policies reflected a broad consensus.

Putin's first term as president, 2000–3, was characterized by substantial market economic reform, such as the adoption of a liberal new tax code with fewer and lower taxes, the development of the Civil Code and the promulgation of a new Customs Code. Considerable deregulation occurred, and Russia undertook most steps necessary to join the World Trade Organization. Privatization proceeded, and corruption declined. Russia seemed to be completing its market economic transformation (Åslund 2004a).

An ominous parallel development, however, was a gradual but far-reaching centralization of political power. Initially, elementary state power was restored. The regional governors were forced to succumb to federal law. In the 1990s, regional governors and businesspeople had corrupted courts. Now, they were brought under the control of the presidential administration. Initially, Putin intimidated the oligarchs to stay out of politics, but in October 2003, he had the wealthiest oligarch, Mikhail Khodorkovsky, arrested and eventually sentenced to eight years in labor camp. By bankrupting Khodorkovsky's oil company, Yukos, through lawless and confiscatory taxation, Putin made a joke of both his tax reform and of judicial reform.

In Putin's second term, nearly all the institutional developments were regressive. Gradually, he let the state or loyal businesspeople take over all media of significance. Through a multitude of dirty tricks, elections at all levels were manipulated. Candidates and parties were declared unfit for the flimsiest formal reasons. After the free but unfair parliamentary elections of December 2003, the Russian parliament was without consequence, and even partial democracy was over. The political parties were sapped of independence and content. The members of upper chamber, the Federation Council, became appointed and thus without significance. By naming a feeble prime minister in early 2004, Putin rendered the government equally irrelevant. Nongovernmental organizations were suffocated with red tape.

In September 2004, Putin decided that also regional governors would be appointed rather than elected, losing independence. In this fashion, Putin systematically deprived all political institutions but the presidency of power and significance (Fish 2005).

Putin accomplished an amazing de-institutionalization, leaving the presidency as the only institution of relevance, supported by secret police and media monopoly. Its main source of legitimacy was the president's personal popularity, whereas the Russian Orthodox Church, Russian nationalism, and naked repression did not evoke a wide appeal. The president was left standing alone in front of the people without any mediating institutions, much like Russian tsars.

The high economic growth and the accompanying rising standard of living were mitigating factors, but increasingly the economic growth depended on the high international prices of Russia's energy exports and the momentum of prior market reforms. By 2005 and 2006, the industrial growth, which may be seen as the underlying growth, had faded to a mere 4 percent a year. The hallmark of Putin's second terms was renationalization, as big, sluggish state corporations purchased successful private enterprises. Sometimes the prices were too high, arousing suspicions about substantial kickbacks. In other cases, the prices were too low, making evident that the sales were not voluntary. Leading state officials, mostly hailing from the KGB, assumed control over large state corporations to their apparent personal benefit. Transparency International (2006) recorded rising corruption in Russia after 2004, while corruption fell in most of the region. Despite hugely increased expenditures on law enforcement, Russia's murder rate was higher under Putin than under Yeltsin. It is difficult to escape the impression that a major goal of the Putin system was the enrichment of the top state officials. Rising political repression and declining transparency facilitated their corruption. The increasingly aggressive foreign policy was also helpful for this policy of corruption. Unlike most of the other former Soviet republics, which seemed steeped in market economic reforms, Russia appeared to have fallen victim to the oil curse.

The ultimate outcome of the Putin system became majority-state-owned "national champions," such as Gazprom, the Russian Railways, and the arms export agency Rosoboronexport. Each of them was chaired and managed by a Putin crony, usually from the KGB in St. Petersburg. Ideally, a national champion was a monopoly. These state corporations were as a rule less transparent than private, publicly traded companies. They tended to purchase more assets rather than invest in their prior assets. Asset-stripping by state officials was perceived as legitimate. As a consequence, the formation of national champions reduced economic growth and aggravated corruption.

The post-Soviet space is the stage of a ferocious competition between democracy, oligarchy, and authoritarianism. In Putin's second term, Russia became a police state, serving the interests of that very police. As the bureaucrats were let loose, progressive reforms were precluded. Only Russia recorded a major renationalization (European Bank for Reconstruction and Development 2006) and a sharp rise in corruption (Transparency International 2006). In the language of Mancur Olson (2000), Putin may be described as a "rowing bandit," the lowest level of state formation. Kazakhstan, by contrast, could make a claim to be a modernizing authoritarian state, like Singapore or South Korea at an earlier stage. Olson would call Kazakhstan's President Nazarbayev a "stationary bandit," thinking of the value of his booty in the long term. A similar point could be made about Armenia and Azerbaijan. Ukraine, by contrast, is far more open and competitive. It is an oligarchy about to break down into a competitive democracy. The same might be true of Moldova. From this perspective, competition and pluralism as well as privatization and deregulation are welcome developments unlike authoritarian order and centralization.

Joseph Stiglitz (2006, p. 43), on the contrary, sympathized with Putin and his renationalization: "when Vladimir Putin succeeded Yeltsin, he understood that such concentration of wealth was a threat to him and to Russian democracy, such as it was. . . . it was not hard for Putin to figure out how to use the power of the state – within the rules of the game – to recapture significant amounts of assets." He went on to laud Putin's confiscation of Yukos. In the same vein, Marshall Goldman (2003, p. 238) wrote, admittedly much earlier, sympathetically about Putin, advocating renationalization: "the Russian government should consider creating a state-run mutual fund which would take over ownership of the remaining shares." The fundamental dividing line in post-Soviet economic analysis remains whether privatization or the state is perceived as the greatest problem. Those who are not too worried about the excessive power of the state are not likely to be very upset about the demise of democracy either.

Regardless of Putin's overcentralized dictatorship having produced a high economic growth rate during its construction, the full-fledged model does not appear to be a very viable system in the long run. It may prove self-destructing, as it kills the golden geese that lay its eggs. The evil Soviet state has been revived under the auspices of the KGB. It pampers those in power with privileges, but it does not provide the citizens with law and order. KGB alumni exploit state companies to enhance their control and wealth.

Russia's current problems lie in the incompleteness of its reforms. The KGB should have been abolished and condemned after the abortive coup in August 1991, and full democratization should have been Yeltsin's focus in 1991. The mass privatization was no mistake but rather the greatest achievement, but it should have gone further. Gazprom and the railways should have been broken up and privatized as the oil companies and the coalmines were. Then these sectors could have been deregulated. And, of course, a former KGB officer should have been disqualified from the post of president as being professionally too deformed to be able to guarantee democracy.

At the end of 2006, Russia looked frail because of its overcentralization of state power. Despite its high growth and large financial reserves, the state is petrified, possessing little ability to handle social crisis. Institutional comparisons are made with Leonid Brezhnev's stagnation. All institutions but those preserving macroeconomic stability have been undermined. Political competition has been eliminated. No checks or balances remain. Economic reforms have ended, and property rights are in limbo. Although President Putin insists that he will resign in 2008 after his second term as president, it is difficult to see how he can do so in a state based on extra-legal rules, with his popularity as the only source of legitimacy.

11

The Impact of the Outside World

The collapse of communism and the Soviet bloc dominated public discussion all over the world in 1989. Among the questions raised were the following: What relation would the postcommunist countries have to the West? What assistance did they need? What could and should the West do for them? Which organizations should be used? How much financing was needed, and was the West ready?

The West's desire for the postcommunist countries' success as democracies and market economies is often taken for granted, but Western opinion was divided. A broad Western opinion favored democracy and market economies, even though most protagonists were tacitly doubtful about the prospects for democracy in the former Soviet Union. The West saw little threat from the former Soviet Union but also little gain. An important countercurrent argued that Russia was a patent menace best kept down and out. There was no consensus about what the West could or should do. In effect, the West as a whole adopted Central Europe, and Scandinavia adopted the Baltics. Southeast Europe was left in a limbo, and Russia with the rest of the CIS were left out in the cold.

Most opposed large-scale Western financial support for the postcommunist East for a variety of reasons. At this time, development aid to the Third World was approaching a nadir, because it had been widely discredited as corrupting rather than helping. The old development aid community looked on the volume of total Western assistance as a zero-sum game, and they worried that large resources would be diverted from the Third World to the somewhat wealthier transition countries. Much of the free-market right, especially in the United States, opposed all government assistance. In Europe, the left advocated large government transfers both at home and abroad, but they objected to the right-wing project of building capitalism. The fallen rulers were, after all, fellow socialists. Economists of various convictions doubted the absorptive capacity of the postcommunist countries. The obvious compromise was to minimize public spending on postcommunist transition. A Marshall Plan for Eastern Europe was never an option.

Economically, the opening of new countries to capitalism with new exchanges of goods, services, capital, and labor offered both opportunities and threats. Initially, many West European countries were most afraid of receiving large numbers of refugees, as had been the case after previous upheavals in Eastern Europe – Hungary in 1956, Czechoslovakia in 1968, and Poland in 1968 and 1981. The collapse of the German Democratic Republic had started with a mass exodus to West Germany, and the low standard of living in the East was evident. West Europeans did not welcome immigration because of their own unemployment and nationalism. Their fear of immigration inspired a two-pronged approach. The West Europeans wanted to assist their closest neighbors in their economic development to convince their people to stay at home, while they desired to keep more distant people away through strict visa regulations.

In this chapter, section one examines the international role in the successful return of East-Central Europe to Europe. Section two turns to the much less successful international policy on the CIS countries. Section three scrutinizes trade policy, which reflected the same gulf between EU accession countries and the CIS. The chapter concludes with some judgment on international assistance.

The Dream of Europe

To Central Europe, the Baltics, and Southeast Europe, the European Union offered the dream of "a return to Europe," or full membership of the EU. This was a time of European revival. The European Union had just decided to accept Austria, Sweden, and Finland as full members, and they acceded in 1995. The question was not if but how and when the EU would expand. Central Europe and the Baltics were widely perceived as constituent parts of "Europe," and they appeared manageable.

Germany had just seen its dream of reunification fulfilled, and under Chancellor Helmut Kohl, it was the driving force for Eastern expansion of the EU. For centuries, it had been the dominant cultural, economic, and political power in Central Europe, with Poland, Czechoslovakia, and Hungary forming Germany's natural sphere of interest. Predominantly, its Eastern neighbors saw this as an opportunity for integration in Europe, and Germany served as their peer country.

The four Nordic countries – Finland, Sweden, Denmark, and Norway – felt a great affinity to the three Baltic states – Estonia, Latvia, and Lithuania – for historical, geographic, and cultural reasons. They were all small neighboring countries. During the Baltic independence in the interwar period, regional cooperation in the Baltic Sea had been extensive. Although Lithuania's history was connected with Poland, it joined the Nordic-Baltic sphere. Because only 8 million people lived in the three Baltic countries, the Nordic countries with about 22 million cared for them as little brothers. A strong peer relation developed, and the Nordic and Baltic countries came to share executive directors in the International Monetary Fund (IMF) and the World Bank.

Geographically, Bulgaria and Romania belonged to Europe, but they attracted little outside interest. Romania was culturally close to France, but France was scarcely engaged. Besides, Bulgaria and Romania were parts of the volatile Balkans, where Yugoslavia was exploding in bloody separatist wars, which further limited external interest. Finally, as their old communist parties stayed in power, the West felt politically alienated and doubted their interest in market reforms for good reasons. For years, Bulgaria and Romania were hanging loose, but after considerable EU hesitation, they became candidates for EU enlargement, and their course was set.

The East-Central European countries were determined to "return to Europe," and from 1992 to 1993 the EU concluded so-called Europe Agreements with the Central and Southeast European countries (see Table 11.1). The EU concluded free trade agreements with the Baltic states in 1994 and Europe Agreements in 1995. The Europe Agreements aimed at a broad integration of these countries into the EU, not only lowering barriers to trade but also establishing a framework for political dialogue and the harmonization of legislation. The Europe Agreements provided free trade in industrial goods within ten years, although the EU agricultural market remained closed until the Central European and Baltic countries became full EU members in May 2004.

All the East-Central European countries applied for membership of the EU early on, and in July 1997, Poland, the Czech Republic, Hungary, and Estonia were invited to negotiate terms for membership. In 1999, this offer was extended also to Latvia, Lithuania, Slovakia, Romania, and Bulgaria. Their conviction of their future EU membership came to dominate their outlook. For East-Central Europe, the EU was by far the most important international community, and its vast market drove the export-oriented growth of this region. Radical trade liberalization helped the East-Central European countries to reorient their trade at an extraordinary speed to

Table 11.1. *EU agreement policy and EU accession*

	EU association agreement	EU partnership and cooperation agreements	EU accession
Central Europe			
Poland	March 1992	–	May 2004
Czech Republic	March 1992	–	May 2004
Slovakia	March 1992	–	May 2004
Hungary	March 1992	–	May 2004
Southeast Europe			
Romania	March 1993	–	Jan. 2007
Bulgaria	Jan. 1994	–	Jan. 2007
Baltics			
Estonia	June 1995	–	May 2004
Latvia	June 1995	–	May 2004
Lithuania	June 1995	–	May 2004
CIS			
Russia	–	June 1994	–
Belarus	–	March 1995	–
Ukraine	–	June 1995	–
Moldova	–	Nov. 1994	–
Armenia	–	April 1996	–
Azerbaijan	–	April 1996	–
Georgia	–	April 1996	–
Kazakhstan	–	Jan. 1995	–
Kyrgyzstan	–	Feb. 1995	–
Tajikistan	–	–	–
Turkmenistan	–	Nov. 1997	–
Uzbekistan	–	June 1996	–

Source: European Bank for Reconstruction and Development (1997, p. 88).

the European Union, which soon accounted for two-thirds of their trade (Baldwin 1994; Mizsei and Rudka 1995; Messerlin 2001).

The EU played an all-dominant role in the transition of its future members. Its contributions were many and great. It functioned as peer countries for the applicants, substantiating the dream of a "return to Europe." The EU offered considerable, early market access that greatly helped the accession countries to undertake their market reforms and return to economic growth. Its technical assistance was substantial. It did deliver EU membership after 14 years for the most reformist postcommunist countries. The EU transferred its market economic model by setting legal and administrative standards. All EU candidate members had to adopt *acquis communautaire,* the common EU body of law of 170,000 pages. Thus, the accession countries adopted most institutions characteristic of the EU countries, which resolved many problems of their postcommunist transition, supported by substantial technical assistance. The EU demanded democracy and assisted in building it, which might have been its most important contribution, considering that democracy failed in all the twelve CIS countries. The same is true of the rule of law. The EU also provided the new members with national security.

A problem, however, was that the EU exported its model of social welfare with high taxes, large social transfers, and overregulated labor and agricultural markets, which has delivered little growth both in the old EU and Central Europe. Although visa regulations were eased, the old EU members were reluctant to open their labor market to the applicants. Even when the Central European and Baltic countries became full members of the EU in 2004, only three old EU members – the United Kingdom, Ireland, and Sweden – opened their labor markets to the new members immediately, while the other twelve old EU members insisted on transition periods of varying length. The resources the EU transferred were not large until the accession countries actually joined the EU, but considering the poor fate of East Germany, that may be seen as an advantage.[1]

Ironically, East Germany stands out as one of the least successful transition countries. After an initial spurt, its growth rate has lingered around 2 percent a year (World Bank 2002). Of all the postcommunist countries, it recorded the highest unemployment peaking early at 35 percent. Although it has fallen, it has only halved and remains the highest in Europe (Siebert 1992). Some blame the East German predicament on shock therapy. Over night, it received the West German mark, *acquis communautaire*, and the West German court system. Inflation never became a problem, and West Germany took care of its oversize national debt.

East Germany's problems, however, were not connected with shock therapy but the choice of economic model and policy. Although inflation was low, East Germany suffered from poor macroeconomic policies. The fundamental problem was that East Germany was priced out of the market and rendered totally noncompetitive. Two mechanisms reinforced this greatest social welfare trap of all time. One cause was that West Germany flooded its new Eastern *Laender* with money, arising from a new "solidarity tax" on

---

[1] One of the most balanced and informative eastern assessments of the advantages and drawbacks of the EU for Russia has been made by two Russian liberals (Mau and Novikov 2002).

all German incomes. In the years 1991–7 East Germany received a mind-boggling average annual transfer of $82 billion, 40 to 60 percent of East Germany's GDP. By comparison, total World Bank loans and grants to the transition countries amounted to $19 billion in 1991–2000 and IMF disbursements to $38 billion in 1990–9. The inter-German transfer was almost twice as large as total North-South development assistance, and it received many times more grant assistance than all other transition countries taken together (World Bank 2002, pp. 37–8; Åslund 2002, p. 426). East Germany suffered from a "Dutch disease" as the windfall priced it out of all markets. Strangely, this costly and harmful transfer remains around $80 billion a year. Another mechanism that made sure that East Germany was overpriced was that the West German trade unions and employers' associations agreed on high wages for East German workers, which rendered them noncompetitive. The West German trade unions negotiated for the East Germans, but they cared only about their own workers, and the West German employers' association had no interest in the competitiveness of East Germany either (Pickel and Wisenthal 1997).

As if to add insult to injury, East Germans were deprived of any role in the privatization; enterprises were effectively given away as corporate welfare to West German corporations in the most expensive of all privatizations, and real estate was given back to West German émigrés through restitution (Brada 1996). As a revenge on the West Germans, East Germans have voted for the maintenance of excessive social welfare and high taxes to finance it. The poor performance of the East German economy illustrates the futility of some good institutions, such as West German courts, if macroeconomic policies are patently flawed. The gigantic West German transfer to East Germany appears one of the greatest public financial follies of all times.

Western Failure to Act in the East

No country in Eurasia was more important than Russia. Peacefully, it had let the Eastern European countries and all the Soviet republics become independent, and it was devastated by economic crisis. Despite its benign behavior and its economic hardship, fear of Russian expansion lingered. Until recently, the Soviet Union had sparred with the United States as the other superpower, and it still possessed 30,000 nuclear warheads. Others worried about its implosion, but few were comfortable with Russia.

Traditionally, the Soviet Union had seen the United States as its competitor and peer, but the gaping economic chasm between the two countries made this perception implausible. Both the George H. W. Bush and the Clinton administrations tried to maintain special bilateral relations with Russia, as if it were still a superpower.[2] It was difficult to endow this "strategic partnership" with content, however, considering that the official Russian GDP in 1999 corresponded to as little as 2 percent of the U.S. GDP at the contemporary exchange rate. To Europeans, Russia was too big and frightening, with its population of 145 million, nearly twice as large as united Germany, although the Russian GDP shrank below that of Switzerland at current exchange rates. An instant European consensus declared that Russia could never become a member of the European Union, rendering it an outsider without peer.

A small but influential group of American policy thinkers, notably "realist" geopoliticians Henry Kissinger and Zbigniew Brzezinski, regarded Russia as outside of Western civilization and wanted to keep it down and out. They still considered Russia a threat to its neighbors, so the weaker Russia was, the feebler this threat. Kissinger (1994, p. 815) commented on the brief post-Soviet period: "But the dominant geopolitical thrust has been Russia's attempt to restore its pre-eminence in all the territories formerly controlled from Moscow." Kissinger (2000) reiterated his fear of the success of Russian economic reform: "But if the strengthening of Russia as a result of reform produces gradual encroachment – as, in effect, all its neighbors fear – Russia's quest for domination sooner or later will evoke Cold War reactions." Similarly, Brzezinski (1997) saw as the geopolitical task in the post-Soviet region to strengthen every state, including China, against Russia. "On balance, it is probable that neither the disappointment nor the weakening of the Russian westernizers could have been avoided" (p. 102). Kissinger discounted the possibility of Russia becoming a democracy. Yet nobody advocated open aggression against Russia.

A broader Western apprehension was that their markets would be flooded with cheap Eastern goods. Exports of steel and agricultural produce from Russia, Ukraine, and Kazakhstan threatened moribund steelworks and overprotected agriculture in the West. The EU and the United States repeatedly imposed antidumping sanctions against steel and chemical exports from Russia and Ukraine, and little agricultural produce was allowed to enter. The East Europeans were defenseless against these protectionist measures (Messerlin 2001).

To the other CIS countries Russia was the standard bearer, on which they remained dependent. They enjoyed little international support, and none

---

[2] The outstanding source on U.S. policy on Russia in the 1990s is Goldgeier and McFaul (2003).

of them could even hope to be successful if Russia were not. Asia played no significant role. Turkey was ambitious, trying to develop multiple links with the Turkic nations in the region – Azerbaijan, Turkmenistan, Kazakhstan, Kyrgyzstan, and Uzbekistan, but distances were long, and Turkey's finances were poor. China was passive, preoccupied with the maintenance of stability in Central Asia out of concern for potential uprisings among its Turkic minorities in Sinkiang.

When the Soviet Union dissolved in December 1991, postcommunist transition was well established. Radical market reform had set the tone for Eastern Europe's transition. The international community had long focused on market transition in the Soviet Union. The highly political G-7 (composed of the seven big, Western, industrialized countries – the United States, Japan, Germany, France, the United Kingdom, Italy, and Canada) replaced the more economically oriented G-24 that handled the financing of the transition programs in Central Europe and the Baltics. At the request of the G-7, four international economic organizations – the IMF, the World Bank, the Organization for Economic Cooperation and Development (OECD), and the European Bank for Reconstruction and Development (EBRD) – undertook a major study of the Soviet economy, its reform and criteria for Western market economic assistance in 1990. Because of the novel Soviet openness, the resulting three-volume study contained lots of new information. It advocated a radical and comprehensive reform of the Polish type (IMF et al. 1991).

In June and July 1991, a group of prominent Harvard social scientists and Russian economists pursued a private project, called "the Grand Bargain," on how to reform the Soviet economy. It advocated a radical economic reform supported by large Western assistance just before the G-7 meeting in London in July 1991 (Allison and Yavlinsky 1991). However, in the Soviet Union, this proposal was never taken seriously or even earnestly promoted, and President Mikhail Gorbachev failed to make any plausible proposal, given that his political control was on the wane. The West had no substantive basis for action. The Grand Bargain attracted considerable Western media sympathy, but the Western leaders were not interested in offering any financial support for Russia (Goldgeier and McFaul 2003).

The leading advocate of international assistance for Russia was Harvard Professor Jeffrey Sachs. Proposals of early large-scale international assistance were primarily connected with the radical reform program (Lipton and Sachs 1990a; Sachs 1993, 1994). Sachs emphasized that foreign assistance could be useful only if a country made serious attempts at economic reform: "Of course, foreign aid is not the main factor in economic success. The reforms themselves were the key. My argument is that foreign aid is critical to helping the reforms themselves take hold" (Sachs 1994, p. 504). Most of the postcommunist countries started from a position of depleted international reserves, excessive debt service, and, in some cases, overwhelming foreign debt. To give financial stabilization a chance, a country needed replenishment of its reserves and possibly some international assistance with its foreign debt service. Sachs (1994, p. 504) argued: "The market cannot do it all by itself; international help is critical."

Sachs's advocacy (1994, p. 504) was also political: "Aid is crucial because reforms are inherently very fragile at the outset. There is typically little consensus on what should be done, pessimism is rife, and the reformers' hold on power and on policy is tenuous." He refuted the idea that reformers succeed by constructing a "social consensus," and he underlined the degree of confusion, anxiety, and conflicting opinions at the time of any major reform. In Poland in 1989, as in Germany in 1948, there was no consensus, and consensus was no precondition of successful reform. On the contrary, it arose out of successful reforms. In a similar vein, Andrei Shleifer and Robert Vishny (1998, p. 13) argued: "Foreign aid, if used politically, can come to the aid of these reformers, and offer them resources that help them to stay in power and pursue their goals." These ideas never became a Western consensus but remained controversial.

The Europeans looked to America on such a big policy issue, and only the U.S. president could act, but he did nothing. The Bush administration was tardy in realizing that the Soviet Union was breaking up and wanted to shore it up until its very end. As late as August 1991, President Bush made his infamous "chicken Kiev speech," admonishing the Ukrainians to stay in the Soviet Union. Two weeks later, the abortive August 1991 coup in Moscow sounded the death-knell for the Soviet Union, leaving reform to the soon-to-be independent states. Russia opted for democracy, with Boris Yeltsin as democratically elected president. On October 28, 1991, Yeltsin (1991) made the greatest speech of his life to the Russian parliament, unveiling a comprehensive radical economic reform proposal. He also appealed at length for substantial and manifold Western support, although he was somewhat vague and refrained from specifying the amount:

We appeal officially to the International Monetary Fund, the World Bank, and the European Bank for Reconstruction and Development, inviting them to work out a detailed plan for cooperation and participation in the economic reforms. We appeal to the developed countries and to international organizations for technical help and assistance first and foremost in training of cadres and in the analysis and working out of recommendations for the key economic, ecological, and regional issues. . . . Russia confirms its intention to observe the international obligations of the USSR.

His reform speech was overwhelmingly approved in a vote by the Russian parliament. A week later, President Yeltsin undertook a fundamental government reform, abolishing dozens of branch ministries and cutting government staff drastically. He appointed a new cabinet, consisting of young economic reformers, with Yegor Gaidar as deputy prime minister and reform leader. Rarely has such a great historical opportunity arisen, and seldom has its coming been so evident. Yeltsin's young reform government was working night and day to prepare their reforms, and a strong informed Western opinion urged their governments to support Russian reform. The *New York Times* (November 12, 1991) editorialized: "The challenge for the West is to encourage Mr. Yeltsin's real, radical program by giving attentive assistance now." On December 17, 1991, the *Financial Times* concurred: "Now is the first and, perhaps, the last chance for the west to promote radical economic reform in the former Soviet Union." How right they were!

But the leading Western governments revealed no intention to support Russia's market reforms. In mid-November 1991, the new Russian reform administration received the deputy ministers of finance of the G-7. During four days of negotiations, they discussed only one issue, "the joint and several responsibility" of the soon-to-be former Soviet republics for the Soviet debt. Although the G-7 representatives were aware of the impending breakup of the Soviet Union, their only interest was to secure their claims. The young Russian reformers were shocked and dismayed by the G-7's complete disinterest in any discussion of their reform plans but kindly signed the Western proposals.

The next Western initiative was a sheer diversion. A high-level international conference on humanitarian aid to the former Soviet Union was convened by the U.S. government in Washington, D.C., in late January 1992, just after Russia had launched its daring reforms. The U.S. administration organized this meeting to show that it thought about the former Soviet Union, but it designed the conference to discuss only humanitarian assistance and avoided all discussion of support for reform. Nobody from the former Soviet Union was even invited. The West noisily wasted time (Åslund 1995).

The prospect of U.S. presidential elections in November 1992 stalemated the Bush administration, because it thought international assistance was unpopular with the voters. The Soviet collapse was so peaceful and democratic that no action seemed needed. Personally, President Bush favored Soviet President Mikhail Gorbachev over Russian President Yeltsin, evidently not concerned that only Yeltsin had been democratically elected. Gorbachev's aide Grigory Yavlinsky was preferred over Yeltsin's reform

Table 11.2. *U.S. peace dividend, 1992–9*

	Percentage of GDP	Current dollars (billions)
1992	1.1	69
1993	1.5	98
1994	1.9	132
1995	2.2	160
1996	2.5	192
1997	2.6	211
1998	2.8	238
1999	2.8	259
Total		**1,359**

Source: U.S. Census Bureau (1999, p. 368; 2000, p. 360).

leader Yegor Gaidar, who was not known in Washington. In February 1992, the well-informed *Washington Post* columnist Jim Hoagland concluded that the United States did not provide any support to Russia because President George Bush reckoned Boris Yeltsin was a transitional figure (*Washington Post*, February 11, 1992). This was the only big chance for the West to support reform in Russia, and the responsibility for missing it rests squarely with President George H. W. Bush.

On April 1, 1992, five months after his dramatic appeal to the Western governments, President Yeltsin received an answer of sorts. U.S. President George Bush and German Chancellor Helmut Kohl declared their intent to mobilize a $24 billion Western aid package for Russia. However, their April fool's claim was never substantiated (Åslund 1995). In early April, the Russian reformers faced an onslaught by the semidemocratic, and by now antireformist, parliament. By June 1992, President Yeltsin effectively gave up on reform and appointed three old-style industrialists, including Viktor Chernomyrdin, as deputy prime ministers. The spectacular absence of Western support contributed to the fall of the Russian reform government.

The amounts discussed were minor in comparison with the potential benefits. The total request for financial assistance to Russian economic reform in 1992 was about $25 billion, of which $6 billion was intended for a stabilization fund. Almost all the "assistance" would have been in the form of credits. A reasonable bilateral U.S. contribution would have been $3 billion, yet the United States reaped $69 billion in peace dividend that very year (see Table 11.2). In comparison, the Marshall Plan comprised 2 percent of the U.S. GDP at the end of the 1940s, which would have meant $125 billion for the United States in 1992 (Milward 1984; U.S. Census Bureau 1999, p. 459). The West did give Russia credits of more than $12 billion in 1992, but they were commodity credits, which actually blocked reform because they became rents to commodity traders and their corrupt conduits. They were bilateral loans, not conditional on any reform measures and not coordinated with international financial institutions (Åslund 1995).

The heart of the matter was that the Soviet military threat was gone. The West had already cashed in on the collapse of the Soviet Union. It had won the Cold War and wanted to "go home," by radically reducing its military expenditures. All Western countries slashed their defense budgets, especially the United States. The Reagan administration spent 6.0 percent of U.S. GDP on defense from 1982 to 1989. In 1998 and 1999, the U.S. defense budget had plummeted to 3.2 percent of GDP. I define the peace dividend as the difference between the Cold War standard defense cost (6.0 percent of GDP) and the later defense cost as a share of GDP. By this definition, the United States benefited from a peace dividend of no less than 2.8 percent of GDP, or $242 billion in current U.S. dollars, in 1999 because the Soviet military threat had evaporated. The cumulative U.S. peace dividend from 1992 to 1999 amounted to an enormous $1.4 trillion current U.S. dollars (see Table 11.2). As the U.S. budget deficit used to be approximately 3 percent of GDP, the elimination of the Soviet military threat alone eliminated the U.S. budget deficit. This huge gain went largely unnoticed because nobody claimed it. The Republicans wanted more defense expenditures, and the Democrats alleged the eradication of the budget deficit was a result their sophisticated economic policy. For the Western governments, the peace dividend was free, giving them no reason to act. Gratitude is no force in world politics.

Trade Policy: A Gulf Between the EU and the CIS

The liberalization of foreign trade has been considerable, but from the very beginning, a chasm erupted between the EU accession countries, including the Baltic states, and the CIS countries. The dividing line was EU policy. The EU became the savior of East-Central Europe, locking the accession countries into a standard Western trading system early on.

All countries in East-Central Europe undertook early and radical liberalization of their foreign trade regimes. The liberalization of their exports was complete, nearly all the quantitative barriers to trade were abolished, and import tariffs were reduced dramatically to the single digits (EBRD 1994). The Council of Mutual Economic Assistance (CMEA) state trading system was eliminated on January 1, 1991. A liberal foreign trade system was firmly established. Their trade liberalization was cemented by multiple international agreements. The Central European countries and Romania were already members of the General Agreement on Tariffs and Trade (GATT), which became the World Trade Organization (WTO). They had adopted the international legal norms for trade, and they could turn to the WTO for protection in international trade disputes. Bulgaria joined the WTO in 1996, and the three Baltic countries were admitted in 1998–2000.

The CIS countries, on the contrary, had nowhere to turn but to one another, and weak states make weak partners. The EU was quite protectionist to the CIS countries. Foreign trade developed very differently in the CIS. In early 1992, all CIS countries were shocked by financial collapse and acute shortages of most goods. Producers' desire to secure supplies dominated trade policy. Governments were preoccupied with state building and short-term crisis management, having little time for trade policy.

In this vacuum, bureaucrats of the old state planning system seized control over intra-CIS trade, turning it into a Soviet theme park. The old state supply organizations were transformed into monopolies for CIS trade. Although free trade was evolving domestically, state trade prevailed between the CIS states. The first CIS trade agreements were reminiscent of old Soviet trade agreements within the CMEA, with compulsory deliveries at fixed prices for major products. Old state enterprises continued to deliver unsalable goods to other CIS countries in exchange for Russian state credit, while valuable commodities sold to CIS countries at low regulated prices were often reexported illicitly at an enormous cost to the Russian state. The main trade barrier was the discretionary regulation of exports. CIS exporting companies had to sell their commodities through a state trading organization, as in the Soviet Union, at a price far below the world price. Commodity exports required export licenses and quotas, issued by the national Ministry of External Economic Relations, which naturally became a pinnacle of corruption (IMF 1994b; Michalopoulos and Tarr 1994, 1996; Michalopoulos and Drebentsov 1997; Olcott et al. 1999).

Nor had the CIS countries locked in foreign trade liberalization through any international agreements. In 1993, the first CIS countries submitted their applications to join GATT, soon to become the WTO, but it took years before anything happened. Unlike the IMF and the World Bank, the WTO has little staff and does little to facilitate membership applications, which take six years on average to reach completion. Another peculiarity of the WTO is that it is easier for small countries with little trade to join than for big countries whose exports have a greater impact on foreign markets. The first to join the WTO were four small CIS countries: Kyrgyzstan in 1998,

Georgia in 2000, Moldova in 2001, and Armenia in 2003. Unfortunately, they did not see major changes in their trade conditions as a result of their accession to the WTO because their big neighbors stayed outside of the WTO, and WTO rules did not apply to them. A major change is under way as the three big CIS economies – Ukraine, Russia, and Kazakhstan – are about to join the WTO. After their accession, WTO membership should have greater impact on trade conditions.

The twelve-member Commonwealth of Independent States, which was set up in December 1991 to replace the Soviet Union, was ambiguous in its nature. On one hand, it was a means to abolish the Soviet Union. On the other, it embodied Russian imperial dreams of restoring the Soviet Union. This ambivalence rendered the CIS pretty dysfunctional, because Russia pushed for greater integration than any other CIS member desired. Several countries (Belarus, Kazakhstan, Kyrgyzstan, Tajikistan, and Armenia) wanted close relations with Russia, but others (Ukraine, Moldova, Georgia, Azerbaijan, Turkmenistan, and Uzbekistan) reckoned that distance lends enchantment. The CIS concluded a large number of agreements on various topics. The countries close to Russia signed many such agreements, whereas the others usually refused. Even those countries that signed CIS agreements rarely ratified them, leaving the CIS littered with hundreds of agreements that never came into force.

The most important CIS agreement was an Agreement on the Creation of a Free Trade Zone in 1994, which formed the basis for trade between the CIS countries. Yet this trade has not been very free. When a company or industry in one CIS country successfully exported to another CIS country, the importing country often clamped down with a sudden quota or prohibitive import tariff without any impediment. Because the CIS lacks any conflict-solving mechanism, its members have to settle all trade disputes in bilateral negotiations. As a consequence of this lack of principles, many trade conflicts are not resolved. Free trade is likely to arise only when most CIS countries become members of the WTO, because the WTO does possess such a conflict-solving mechanism with its many trade conventions, an arbitration mechanism, and the option of substantial penalties (Olcott et al. 1999).

Rather than accepting its need for WTO membership and speed up its accession, Russia has invented one new intergovernmental organization after another. A first attempt at deeper integration was a Russian-Belarusian Union launched in 1993 to renew the ruble zone. In 1994, it was supposed to become not only a monetary union but also lead to a merger of the two countries. Nothing more than a partial customs union has resulted, however. In 1995, disappointed with the malfunctioning free trade zone, Russia, Belarus, and Kazakhstan launched a Customs Union, which Kyrgyzstan and Tajikistan later joined. Again, it never came into fruition because Russia demanded that the other countries adopted its comparatively high tariffs (Olcott et al. 1999). After several years of failure, the Customs Union was renamed the Eurasian Economic Community in 2000, which did not reinvigorate it, even if Uzbekistan joined for political reasons in 2006. Undiscouraged by these remarkable failures, in 2003 President Putin proposed a new Single Economic Space of Russia, Belarus, Kazakhstan, and Ukraine. It was supposed to be a free trade area, a customs union, and a currency union, although Putin's real purpose was presumably to tie Ukraine more closely to Russia before the Ukrainian presidential elections in 2004. The Single Economic Space became as unsuccessful as other CIS trade initiatives, but as all the other failed intergovernmental CIS organizations, it lingers on.

Meanwhile, the CIS state trading system gradually fell apart because Russia was no longer prepared to subsidize it. As a consequence, intra-CIS trade plunged by some 70 percent from 1991 to 1994, and little new trade could evolve. Only by 1995 had most CIS countries (apart from Belarus, Uzbekistan, and Turkmenistan) liberalized most exports, and intra-CIS trade was reasonably free, so that new foreign trade could finally evolve (Michalopoulos and Tarr 1997). Soon, new protectionism gained momentum. Although formal tariffs remained low, nontariff barriers, such as the certification of produce and quotas, proliferated. Increasingly, CIS countries undertook unilateral sanctions against one another. For instance, Russia introduced strict quotas on imports of vodka and sugar from Ukraine in 1996, and Kazakhstan levied 200 percent import tariffs on some imports from Kyrgyzstan and Uzbekistan in 1999 (Olcott et al. 1999). The usual cause was a successful expansion of exports, often unleashed by abrupt changes in real exchange rates.

Remarkably, the CIS countries closest to the EU exported the least to the EU. The explanation is that especially Ukraine and Moldova primarily exported so-called sensitive products, subject to particularly severe protectionism. Two-thirds of the exports of Ukraine, consisting of metals, agricultural produce, chemicals, and textiles, are deemed "sensitive" by the EU. Moldova faces severe protectionism both from the EU and CIS countries, its traditional markets, because it exports overwhelmingly agricultural goods, and it has failed miserably in breaking through these trade barriers. This protectionism is probably the main reason for Moldova having suffered the greatest decline in output and standards of living of all postcommunist countries. Today, it is by far the poorest country in Europe (Messerlin 2001; Åslund and Warner 2004).

The EU has meant little to the CIS countries. It concluded bilateral Partnership and Cooperation Agreements with all the CIS countries apart from Tajikistan from 1994 to 1997 (see Table 11.1). These agreements contained little of substance, however. It also concluded individual trade agreements with the CIS countries, but these grant them only limited market access because most of them are not WTO members. Although the exports of the East-Central European countries to the EU market skyrocketed from about half in 1989 to two-thirds of their total exports in 2003, the share of former Soviet exports going to the EU was stable at about one-third. The absence of any legal multilateral framework has made the CIS countries suffer from both each other's unilateral sanctions and the absence of legal defense against antidumping actions in the rest of the world.

In 2003, the EU came up with a new concept, the European Neighborhood Policy, which was designed for Western CIS and North African countries. Russia was greatly insulted and turned down the offer, whereas Belarus was excluded because of its dictatorship. Ukraine and Moldova, however, accepted the offer and concluded action plans with the EU in 2005. The three Transcaucasian countries, Georgia, Armenia, and Azerbaijan, also wanted to become part of the European Neighborhood Policy, which the EU accepted (Milcher et al., 2007). The EU is trying to offer a framework that can facilitate closer cooperation with CIS countries. It also contains a proposal of bilateral free trade agreements with the respective CIS countries. The European Neighborhood Policy may lead to a certain bridging between some CIS countries, but the chasm between the EU and the CIS countries remains remarkably deep.

Early on, a number of estimates of future trade were made with the gravity model, which predicts the volumes of trade a country will have with other countries on the basis of GDP and mutual distance. They foresaw a drastic reorientation of the postcommunist countries' trade to the West, primarily to the EU (Collins and Rodrik 1991; Hamilton and Winters 1992). Oleh Havrylyshyn and Hassan Al-Atrash (1998) found that East-Central Europe had undertaken such a reorientation of its commerce as early as 1992, but the CIS countries continued to trade irrationally too much with one another. Yet by 2000, only Belarus, Tajikistan, and Moldova pursued most of their trade with transition countries, reflecting considerable structural change.

The differences between the two regions in trade deregulation and policy are also evident from their total trade volume as a ratio of their GDP

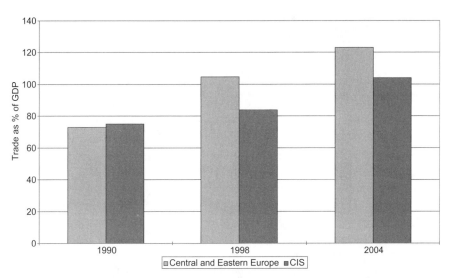

Figure 11.1. Openness of the Economy, 1990, 1998, and 2004. *Source:* World Bank (2006).

(see Figure 11.1). At the outset of transition, East-Central Europe and the CIS countries were approximately equally integrated in world trade. From 1990 to 1998, exports of Central and Eastern Europe took off, whereas trade in the CIS countries lingered. After 1998, exports of both regions have surged impressively, being the most dynamic exporters in the world, and the expansion continues (World Bank 2005a, p. 2). Central Europe remains the most integrated, but even the nonreformers have become highly integrated, which is likely to force them all to focus on achieving greater competitiveness (cf. Figure 3.6).

International Assistance: Insufficient but Crucial

The West cannot be described as enthusiastic about helping postcommunist transformation. It cared about the success of Central Europe and the Baltics, which it soundly assisted. For the rest, Western support was tardy and hesitant, encouraging slowness and indecision also among decision makers in those transition countries.

The dearth of international institutional development is illustrative. The end of World War II generated the United Nations, the Bretton Woods institutions, the Marshall Plan, and the OECD. The conclusion of the Cold War gave birth only to the European Bank of Reconstruction and Development. It was not an ordinary regional development bank but an investment bank,

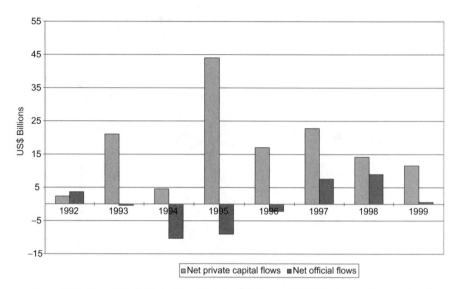

Figure 11.2. Countries in Transition: Net Capital Flows, 1992–99. *Source:* International Monitary Fund (2000, p. 62).

designed to service big private corporations, which did not exist in the early transition. First, enterprises had to be privatized or grow large. Next, they needed to have three years of audited accounts by an internationally recognized auditing company. Therefore, the EBRD could not play any role in the early transition, only after a country already had well-functioning, creditworthy companies, and then international assistance was much less of a need. As a result of this unfortunate design, the EBRD became useful in a country only after its transition had already succeeded. Instead, the IMF and the World Bank became the leading international organizations assisting countries in their actual transition. The Western government funding that went to the EBRD would have made a much greater contribution to transition if it had been used for the cofinancing of IMF programs in the first underfinanced IMF stabilization programs.

Considering that postcommunist transition was the dominant international policy issue in the 1990s, large-scale international assistance could have been expected, but Western financial support was tiny, and most of it consisted of credits. Figure 11.2 presents IMF estimates of net capital flows to countries in transition from 1992 to 1999. Incredibly, "net official flows," that is, all governmental or intergovernmental financing to the transition countries, were negative from 1993 to 1996. At the height of the hyperinflation and the ensuing stabilization in the CIS, the transition countries actually

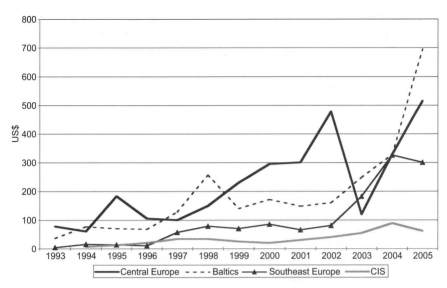

Figure 11.3. Foreign Direct Investment Inflow per Capita, 1993–2005. *Source:* EBRD (various years).

paid more to Western governmental organizations in principal and interest on old loans to communist governments than they received in credits and grants. Private inflows, by contrast, were substantial already by 1993, as private portfolio investments flew into treasury bills and stocks. Surprisingly, they stayed positive even during the Russian financial crisis.

Foreign direct investment, which is the true indicator of success, gained momentum in 1995 and has grown persistently in throughout the region (see Figure 11.3). Initially, foreign direct investment was concentrated to Central Europe and the Baltics, but the oil-rich CIS countries Kazakhstan and Azerbaijan also caught up. Surprisingly, transition has been financed by the private sector; foreign governments did not even make a positive contribution. However, international public financing was vital until 1993 because private finance was not available amid rampant macroeconomic crisis, and that was when countries most needed international financial support. The timing of the financing was more important than the volume of finance.

The most important task of Western assistance was to introduce a new market economic paradigm. Whenever a country needs new thinking, it turns to outsiders both at home and abroad, because much of the knowledge that is new to an isolated establishment already exists among domestic dissidents or international scholars. Every reforming country utilized substantial foreign advice. Chief issues for foreign advice were liberalization, macroeconomic stabilization, privatization, and the drafting of new laws. The most prominent economic advisors were independent academics. The most famous was Professor Jeffrey D. Sachs of Harvard University, who worked primarily in Poland and Russia.[3] Countries and international organizations were happy to share their knowledge and values, particularly through their own consultants, because key advisors at the summit of government can be highly influential. Considering that only a limited number of foreign advisors can be effective, such assistance is cheap. Macroeconomics required only a few senior advisors, whereas privatization called for numerous technical experts. All conceivable bilateral and international organizations have provided technical assistance. Even so the main technical assistance agencies, the EU's PHARE (EU technical assistance program for EU accession countries) and TACIS (Technical Assistance for the CIS) and the USAID (United States Agency for International Development) disbursed annually less than $2 billion altogether (Åslund 2002, tables 10.5 and 10.6). Advice to governments through thousands of consultants was abundant, but it had extraordinary impact. The whole economic thinking of the region changed toward normal market economic ideas in a few years, and the international contribution was significant. An amazing volume of legal texts was drafted by foreign experts – literally hundreds of laws in every post-Soviet country.

International advisors to top government officials are usually controversial. They are accused of being demons or ineffective, or both. In a completely new situation, policy makers needed to gain easy access to serious advice. Given that the old regime had prohibited the study of most of the relevant questions, foreign advisors were badly needed. Top policy makers in a time of crisis have extremely little time, so they could not handle more than a few advisors, whose messages had to be brief and clear. There was neither time nor need for nuance. Key decisions had to be taken fast to avoid disaster. Naturally, such advisors must be loyal to the policy maker in question and chosen by him or her rather than by a foreign government. Often, top advisors were financed by nongovernmental organizations (NGOs). The IMF and the World Bank were the dominant policy-advising organizations, and they fulfilled many of these functions, but governments usually wanted to have their own reliable counterparts to respond to those organizations. Foreign advice was controversial because it was effective.

---

[3] Jeffrey Sachs and I worked together as economic advisors to the Russian government from November 1991 until January 1994.

The most urgent and financially demanding economic task was macroeconomic stabilization, which is a standard IMF assignment. The IMF concludes an agreement with a country in dire financial straights, usually a one-year standby agreement. The IMF commits itself to provide certain loans, which are paid out in tranches, to expand a country's international reserves. In return, the recipient country has to commit itself to fulfill certain fiscal and monetary conditions, primarily to reduce its budget deficit. The IMF received so much public criticism that a cursory newspaper reader might have got the impression that the IMF is a global government in charge of postcommunist transformation. This critical publicity reflected how active and effective the IMF was under the leadership of Michel Camdessus and Stanley Fischer. It acted much faster and more aggressively than any other international organization. It had highly qualified staff, and its centralized hierarchy worked swiftly like an army. The IMF also possessed sufficient funds to make a difference. With its total disbursements of credits to the transition countries of $38 billion from 1990 to 1999, the IMF was by far the most important provider of financial support to transition countries, and it offered large credits early when countries were in their deepest crises. Of this amount $22 billion went to Russia (Åslund 2002, Table 10.7). A problematic feature of the IMF, however, is that anonymous officials have great power over economic policy. One midranking mission chief for a country can make or break an IMF stabilization program, and few even know about it. The prominence of the IMF was the choice of the United States and the other G-7 countries, because the IMF has embodied the Washington Consensus of conservative fiscal and monetary policy as well as a pathos of free markets, and it was widely considered the most competent and professional international organization, closely followed by the World Bank (Gould-Davies and Woods 1999).

Initially, the outcome of the IMF's work in the region was mixed with early successes in Central Europe and the Baltics, but failure in the CIS. The big black mark on the IMF's work in the transition countries remains its failure to call for an early breakup of the ruble zone, but ultimately this was a political decision taken by its leading member governments. One decade after transition, however, the record looked much more impressive. All transition countries had inflation under control, and all but the three intransigent nonreformers had undertaken their stabilizations under the supervision of the IMF. Today most of these credits have been paid back. In many programs, the IMF stalled disbursements for some time, for example, in Poland in 1991 and in Russia in 1998. These controversial decisions showed that the IMF took its conditions seriously, yet the many renewed IMF agreements proved that most countries were anxious to continue their cooperation with the IMF. It has accomplished its chief aim of bringing inflation down, and the question is only whether this could have been accomplished earlier and at a lower social cost.

The most important and disputed structural change was privatization because it determined whether an economy would become capitalist or not. However privatization was carried out, it was technically complex and required innovation as well as many skills that had not existed in the socialist economies. More foreign consultants were needed for privatization than for any other reform. The two agencies that assisted the most in privatization were the World Bank and the USAID. Although privatization inevitably aroused scandals everywhere, about 65 percent of the economy in the region was privatized, indicating the impressive impact of Western assistance to privatization.

Thus, the three fundamental tasks of building a market economy – the paradigm itself, macroeconomic stabilization, and privatization – were accomplished with great focus and targeted assistance from the international community. The criticism these acts aroused are little but evidence of their importance and the efficacy of the assistance. Organizations that did nothing of significance were not criticized, because they were not taken seriously.

A novelty in postcommunist transformation was the substantial role played by international NGOs. The foundations created in the region by billionaire philanthropist George Soros became the pioneers in international support in building civil society.[4] Inspired by philosopher Karl Popper, George Soros (1991) aimed at building an open society. Preceding the fall of communism, he gave grants from his personal fortune to many new NGOs, starting in Hungary and Poland. He financed photocopiers and international exchanges, stimulating the development of local NGOs. As communism collapsed, Soros expanded the scope of his activities to all postcommunist countries. His foundations became role models for other organizations and governments, which seemed to be playing "follow George." The Soros approach had many advantages. He was personally deeply involved, traveling extensively in the region with an entrepreneurial outlook. Using his own money, Soros could offer substantial gifts instantly. His total funding rose

---

[4]   As a matter of disclosure: From August 1994 to the end of 1997, I was advising the Ukrainian government on economic reform financed by the Open Society Institute (the main Soros foundation). I am also cochairing the board of trustees of the Kyiv School of Economics, initiated and supported by George Soros.

to more than $400 million a year by the late 1990s, making his foundations the greatest donors to the region after USAID and the EU. By being fast and nonbureaucratic, Soros responded to the enthusiasm of activists, paying lower salaries but mobilizing more motivated collaborators than consulting firms. Spending most of his money on local activism, Soros stimulated the evolution of permanent local NGOs. He ventured into multiple sensible activities beyond the pale of others. Increasingly, he has spent his money on education and democratization. His role has been so great that the history of postcommunist transformation is to a considerable extent the history of the Soros foundations.

Many tasks received little or poor international support, notably the building of democracy and legal systems, the combat of corruption, and the reform of medical care and education. Usually, several causes were combined. First of all, if no prominent policy maker in a country demanded reform and external support for a particular cause, nothing could be done. In most transition countries, the judicial system and the whole social sector were notoriously conservative, demanding more resources, but rarely attempting to use them more efficiently. Without domestic reformers in key positions, foreign aid to that sector would inevitably be wasted and often was. The World Bank has persistently advocated reforms in health care and education but encountered little policy interest in most countries. In 1998, the World Bank (1998) published the book *Assessing Aid: What Works, What Doesn't and Why*. One of its main conclusions was that a government could not be forced to reform against its will through conditionality, and this assessment was confirmed by the postcommunist experiences. Another problem was that in many cases, Western theory was poor, and no useful set of policy advice was at hand. Moreover, if no international organization was in charge of an issue, as the IMF was for macroeconomic stabilization, international coordination was often lacking, and a multitude of foreign consultants with different foreign employers contradicted one another. By and large, numerous international donors have provided a quite sufficient number of consultants of multiple skills. Still much could have been done in the private sector, but government tended to be oriented to government-to-government cooperation. Foreign governments have done little to build new, good, private, educational institutions in the region for the development of good education in new capitalist skills, such as economics and other social sciences, business administration, and law. Similarly, little international assistance has been devoted to long-term scholarships abroad.

Even if the crucial stages of postcommunist transformation are now over, our future view of it, especially of the role of the outside world, is still on hold because it will be determined by the eventual outcome. If peace, democracy, and sustained economic growth prevail, many will claim the success. If the outcome is meager or worse, the judgment will be harsh because much more could have been done in the initial transition. Yet although the West cannot take too much pride in its assistance to the postcommunist world, it has been reasonably open and positive, and it has not intimidated these countries. The main sins were those of omission – a lack of interest, financing, and understanding.

Conclusions: A World Transformed

The changes that have taken place in East-Central Europe and the former Soviet Union are nothing but extraordinary. At the same time, it is striking how uneven progress has been. Some countries appear to have done it all, but others have barely taken the first steps. Market economic reforms have been highly successful, whereas democratization has been only partially auspicious, and the introduction of the rule of law even less so.

To assess how far the region has proceeded, these countries are first summarized as five models. Next, major developments in the region are recapitulated, and finally, I try to suggest why certain policies succeeded in certain countries and not in others.

Five Models

The outcomes of the postcommunist transformation have been remarkably different. Today these 21 countries that were once so similar have become rather diverse. Eighteen have become market economies, but three (Belarus, Turkmenistan, and Uzbekistan) have not (see Table C.1). The same eighteen countries have privatized more than half of their economies, but the other three have not. East-Central Europe has become fully democratic, whereas the CIS reformers are at best partially democratic but mostly mildly authoritarian. The nonreformers are all tyrannies. Corruption and the weakness of the rule of law are worrisome, and the situation is worse where less other reforms have occurred. Inflation has been brought under control throughout the region in, or close to, single digits. The growth rates were generally low or negative in the 1990s, but growth has been splendid since 1999, apart from in Central Europe, where it has been moderate. The main explanation for the poor growth performance of Central Europe appears to be the large public expenditures. The clearest dividing line runs between the nine countries

Table C.1. *Success of transition, 2005*

	Baltics	CE	SEE	CIS-9	CIS-3
Market economy[1]	Yes	Yes	Yes	Yes	No
Private share,% of GDP[2]	75	79	73	64	32
Democracy[3]	Free	Free	Free	Partially free	Not free
Corruption[4]	5	4	4	3	2
Inflation[5]	4	3	7	7	9
Unemployment rate,%	8	12	9	7[6]	NA
Average GDP growth,%, 2001–5	8	4	5	9	8
Public expenditures,% of GDP, 2004	35	46	42	27	35
EU membership	Yes	Yes	Soon	No	No

1. At least 0.70 on the structural reforms index 2005 (see Figure C.1).
2. European Bank of Reconstruction and Development (EBRD 2005) assessment.
3. Freedom House (2006) assessment.
4. Transparency International (2005) (from 0 = highly corrupt to 10 = highly clean).
5. Average consumer price index, year end.
6. CIS-9 countries with plausible statistics (Armenia, Kazakhstan, Moldova, Russia, and Ukraine).
Sources: EBRD (2005), Freedom House (2006), Transparency International (2005), United Nations Economic Commission for Europe (2006), and World Bank (2006).

that are, or are about to become, members of the European Union and the twelve CIS countries. Putting these assessments together, we arrive at five groups of countries with different economic, political, and social models.

1. The Baltic states: market economies with private ownership and democracy, low corruption, and high growth thanks to small governments. The three Baltic states – Estonia, Latvia, and Lithuania – are the star performers. They are full democracies with normal market economies and predominant private ownership. They have a steady, high growth rate of around 8 percent a year. Their corruption is the least. Their inflation is low, and their budgets are close to balance. The Baltic governments are small and well run.

2. Central Europe: democratic market economies but social democratic welfare traps. The four Central European Countries – Poland, the Czech Republic, Slovakia, and Hungary – are still richer than the Baltic states, and they have even larger private shares and lower inflation. They are also full democracies with normal market economies, but their growth rate is only 4 percent a year, half of the Baltic level, and their corruption is somewhat higher. Their crucial shortfalls are high public expenditures, high taxes, large social transfers, and considerable budget deficits. Overregulated labor markets have caused high unemployment. Slovakia might have broken out of this social welfare trap, but populist politics render swift improvement unlikely in Poland, the Czech Republic, and Hungary.

3. Southeast Europe: following Central Europe or the Baltics? The Southeast European countries Bulgaria and Romania became EU members in January 1997, and they are democracies and market economies. In most regards, they are similar to the Central Europeans, but they have slightly higher inflation and less private enterprise, although more growth and less unemployment. At present, they are close to the social welfare trap of Central Europe but they may be steering in the more liberal Baltic direction.

4. The CIS-9: corrupt, partially free market economies with high growth thanks to low taxes. With some delay, the nine reformist CIS countries have become market economies based on private enterprise. Unlike the East-Central European countries, they are partially free or mildly authoritarian, and their corruption is considerable. Their saving grace is a stellar growth rate of no less than an average 9 percent from 2000 to 2005, thanks to their slashing of public expenditures, which are staggeringly 19 percentage units of GDP lower than in Central Europe. The "colored revolutions" have underlined the political instability of these oligarchic states. Some countries have recently consolidated authoritarian rule (Russia, Kazakhstan, and Azerbaijan), whereas others are democratizing (especially Ukraine). This is the most diverse group in terms of political system and level of economic development.

5. The CIS-3: Soviet-type tyrannies. The three unreformed CIS countries – Belarus, Turkmenistan, and Uzbekistan – are harsh dictatorships with no market economies. Their private sector remains marginal, and the state is large and highly corrupt. Even so, these restored Soviet economies have limited inflation and impressive annual growth rates, although their statistics are subject to considerable doubt. Little can shake these regimes but a violent overthrow of the despot.

The foremost problems for Central Europe are excessive taxes, large social transfers, and overregulation, leading to low growth and high unemployment. The key threat to the CIS reformers is authoritarianism and corruption, which undermine property rights. The Baltic countries are threatened by little but overheating.

Achievements and Revelations

Today it is difficult to imagine how great the intellectual confusion was in the early transition (see Chapter 2). After more than a decade and a half of transition, most answers are evident. We can list major achievements and revelations during the postcommunist transformation.

A market economy could be built, and the radical market reform program worked. All its major components were necessary for success. The three countries that failed to marketize proved that the success of marketization was not a given.

No country suffered from too radical or early market reform. Slower reforms caused greater and more long-lasting output decline, higher inflation, greater income differentials, more corruption, and less democracy.

The crucial problem was to overcome the extraordinary initial rent seeking. It was like a seven-headed hydra, and rent seeking abated only after all the heads had been cut off. Yet rents dissipated over time. The sooner rent seeking was brought under control, the less harm was done to the economy and society.

Almost all postcommunist countries saw a sharp initial output slump, although much of it was a statistical illusion. Wars and hyperinflation caused the greatest damage. The abolition of direct and indirect trade subsidies also had significant impact. Value detraction and structural distortions had to go, resulting in both real and illusory output decline.

A radical initial deregulation was vital for economic success and the combat of corruption. The earlier, the more comprehensive, and the more abrupt the deregulation, the fewer the opportunities to develop rents through arbitrage.

The inflationary pressures were great and manifold. The more rigorous a macroeconomic stabilization was, the more successful it became. Fiscal adjustment was key. No stabilization attempt was too severe.

The earlier and faster privatization was, the better its quality and economic performance. Any privatization was better than none. The most important aspect of privatization was political acceptance, so that the resulting property rights were respected. Private enterprise has been crucial to economic recovery and structural reforms.

The building of democracies has been mediocre. The only successful democratization has been the wholesale imitation of European Union institutions. The dominant political theory was flawed, and no relevant set of policy advice was at hand. Nor did any international organization focus on the building of democracy. The dearth of input resulted in poor outcomes.

The shortfalls in the building of a legal system were the greatest. Few lawyers engaged in reforms. No relevant legal theory was apparent. Reform attempts were partial. No international organization was preoccupied with legal reform. Little was attempted, and consequently little has been accomplished. Corruption has become the bane of the CIS countries because of their excessive state powers together with very limited state capacity and their failure to develop a normal legal system. Corruption is best combated with freedom, transparency, and democracy. Some harm caused by corruption has been mitigated by sharp cuts in public expenditures, flat and low taxes, and reduced contact between state officials and individuals.

The most outstanding rent seekers became oligarchs. They responded rationally to the existing legal and economic conditions. As long as rent seeking prevailed, they sought its prolongation. After the establishment of a normal market economy, they turned highly productive, successfully reviving big old Soviet factories and driving economic growth. Politically, oligarchic regimes have proved unstable. Ideally, their competition can breed normal democracies and market economies, as is happening in Southeast Europe and possibly in Ukraine. The alternative is the consolidation of authoritarian state power in the hands of a unified political elite, whether a family as in the Central Asian countries and Azerbaijan or a branch of the security police as in Russia.

Ironically, the weakest part of the communist state turned out to be the state. Private enterprises have bred all postcommunist successes. State capacity has proved far smaller than anybody but true libertarians presumed, and especially the post-Soviet states are predatory. After one and a half decades of transition, market failure is no longer a big topic. Most of the time, market failures could be resolved through privatization. State failures, by contrast, abound, as reforms of the state have turned out to be the most difficult, and its corruption is the blemish of postcommunist transition. All the region's greatest shortfalls today are related to state failure: lack of democracy, a weak judicial system, poor law enforcement, corruption, slow public health care reform, and tardy public education reform. Either our knowledge of how to reform the state is too limited or the task is not solvable on this scale. Whatever the explanation, the obvious conclusion is that a greater reliance on private enterprise is the best way forward.

Paradoxically, although the state has failed to fulfill its positive roles, it has come back faster than anybody could believe in the early transition as a power. State security has beaten both the mafia and the oligarchs in the course of a few years and reestablished its monopoly on violence. The problem is that most of the CIS countries do not use this monopoly for the public good but rather for the personal benefits of the ruling elite. Given the evidently mean-spirited nature of the post-Soviet state, post-Soviet people do not believe in its potential benevolence. Because social democracy is nurtured by such a belief, social democratic parties of significance exist only in the four Central European countries and in Lithuania.

The European Union has played a great and multifaceted role in postcommunist transformation. In the East, the EU stood for civility, normalcy, the rule of law, democracy, and wealth. Early on, the EU offered great market access to East-Central Europe, but not to the CIS countries. The EU's finest achievement was to induce East-Central Europe to emulate democracy through institution building as well as systematic peer pressure. The EU reproduced its own legal and institutional model in East-Central Europe. The drawback is that Central Europe has fallen into a West European social welfare trap with high taxes, large social transfers, and overregulation, especially of labor and agricultural markets, which limits economic growth. Because this is a European dilemma, the EU possesses no solution. The new EU members have adopted two contrasting attitudes to economic policy. Central Europe behaves like Greece did as a new EU member in the 1980s, maintaining large budget deficits, while minimizing structural reforms, trusting that the EU will bail them out. The Baltic states, by contrast, maintain economic policies as stringent as before. Presumably, the explanation is that the Baltic states, as small, newly independent states, neighboring on their previous occupier, remain wary.[1] Arguably, Russia's hostility to the Baltic states salvages them from the complacency of the Central Europeans.

Membership in the CIS has led to much poorer initial economic, political, and other institutional reforms. Until 1999, CIS economic performance was miserable. The great covariance between several factors complicates an analysis of causality, and many alternative explanations have been offered. My preferred explanation is the devastating effect of hyperinflation, aggravated by the maintenance of the ruble zone, which explains why the Baltics could escape the early CIS doldrums. Another important reason is the combination of the communist legacy and Gorbachev's naïve reforms, which built one of the most formidable rent-seeking machines the world has ever seen (Åslund 1991). The standard suggestion is greater distortions because of longer time under communism. Richard Pipes (2005) emphasized the great cultural and historical legacy of tsarist Russia. The oil windfall may also be a curse for Russia, Kazakhstan, Azerbaijan, and Turkmenistan (Arendh 2005; Gaddy and Ickes 2005; Tompson 2005), with Russia and Kazakhstan being less democratic than typical of countries at their level of economic development. The CIS countries also suffered from poor access to external markets (Åslund and Warner 2004). The problems were so monumental that it would have been unrealistic to expect any reformers, however strong their popular mandate and intellectual prowess, to solve them within less than several years.

In the early transition, left-wing Western intellectuals complained that 1989 did not produce any new ideas. East Europeans were tired of all original

---

[1] A similar argument could be made for Slovenia.

socialist ideas and aspired to the boring normality of Western Europe, but nor did the left-wingers like what they heard. Novelties have been forthcoming. The greatest innovation of postcommunism is mass privatization, and, belatedly, it works. In the aftermath of the mass privatization, a large new empirical literature on corporate governance, property rights, and law and finance has evolved. Another innovation has been flat personal income taxes that might be about to revolutionize the world. The new systematic study of corruption is to a considerable degree a result of the great problems it caused in transition. Postcommunist transition has exposed Western thinking to serious tests. At present, we seem to understand how to build a market economy, whereas the ignorance of democracy building and the construction of a legal system are all the more striking. It might be true that the liberal revolutionaries of 1989 did not want to be original, but by keeping their eyes and minds open, they have produced new original insights.

Many ideas were not confirmed by experiences in the transition. It is difficult to find any empirical support for gradualism, that is, deliberately undertaking reforms more slowly than is possible. In deregulation or macroeconomic stabilization, the greater the rigor and speed, the better it was for other reforms and economic growth. Specifically, there is no long-term evidence that slow privatization leads to any higher quality of privatization. Nor did gradual reforms lead to more institutional and legal reform. All the pillars of a market economy could be built – and they were.

Why Certain Policies Worked and Others Did Not

Finally, we come to the fundamental question of why some policies worked and others did not. No chain is stronger than its weakest link. A clear chain goes from idea, through operative policy formulation, political breakthrough, political leadership, expertise, and parliamentary support to measurement. In addition, international standard setting and assistance proved useful.

First, little can be accomplished without lucid *ideas*, a tenable theory. John Maynard Keynes's (1936/1973, pp. 383–4) concluding words in his *General Theory* remain true:

the ideas of economists and political philosophers, both when they are right and when they are wrong, are more powerful than is commonly understood. Indeed the world is ruled by little else. Practical men, who believe themselves to be quite exempt from any intellectual influences, are usually the slaves of some defunct economist.... I am sure that the power of vested interests is vastly exaggerated compared with the gradual encroachment of ideas.

New ideas are always controversial, rendering a consensus impossible. To search for an early consensus means refraining from using the best ideas at hand. The ideas of radical market economic reform stood the test of time, whereas transitology proved not very helpful for democratization, and no theory for the building of legal institutions was present. As Václav Klaus so well showed in the Czech Republic, ideology could be of great help, but it was used too little (Appel 2004).

Second, to be relevant, a theory has to be formulated as a set of *operative policy advice*. The success of the economists lay in their preparedness to formulate simplified policy advice for radical market economic reform. Academics of many other disciplines considered such simplifications inappropriate or even disqualifying for serious scholars. Reform requires simplicity and lucidity rather than nuance.

Third, a *political breakthrough* or discontinuity is needed. The best option is a regime change leading to democracy, but a financial crisis that merely changes the government can also help, as in Bulgaria and Romania in 1997 or in Russia in 1998. Political windows of opportunity or periods of "extraordinary politics" are as crucial as brief. Path-breaking market reforms occurred either immediately after democratization or after rent seeking had been brought under control several years later.

Fourth, *political leadership* is vital for reform. A top policy maker has to focus on a problem to solve it. The greatest sins were those of omission.

Fifth, to get anything done, *expertise* is needed. It can be domestic or foreign. In the midst of a crisis, surprisingly few politicians accomplish amazingly much. Many reforms were rightly named after one single policy maker who stubbornly dragged through a reform (the Balcerowicz, Klaus, and Gaidar reforms, the Chubais privatization, etc.).

Sixth, *parliamentary support* is also necessary. Many reformers thought reforms were best imposed through presidential decrees, but this idea was disproved. An ordinary parliamentary process, with its checks and balances, enhances the quality of law, whereas presidential decrees tend to be haphazard, contradictory, short-lived, and disrespected. In the legislative process, an elite group is formed in support of the new legislation. As a consequence, early parliamentary elections after democratization were important for the success of reform.

Seventh, *measurement* is vital for policy focus. Whatever is measured can be accomplished. Macroeconomic stability benefited from ample measures, and it was achieved rather soon. For years, corruption was not measured, but as soon as measurement started, multiple methods were found to reduce corruption, and it has started declining in numerous countries.

Eighth, *international organizations* played a major role in the transition. They set standards, provided relevant policy advice, and evaluated outcomes. The International Monetary Fund (IMF) imposed macroeconomic standards with great success, and the EU spread democracy. The World Bank and USAID (United States Agency for International Development) have greatly contributed to privatization. No international organization focused on democracy building or the building the rule of law, and little progress occurred.

Ninth, *international financing* was very limited, but two major positive effects were achieved. Multiple agencies financed economic policy advice, which enlivened the market economic paradigm. The IMF successfully imposed its standards through conditional aid. Financial stabilization and subsequent growth are linked to conditional IMF assistance. One single territory, East Germany, received gigantic international financing, and this excessive aid had no positive consequences.

It did not matter whether an idea was foreign or domestic, but it had to make sense. Initially, most ideas came from abroad because the intellectual world is global. Good foreign ideas worked, whereas bad ideas repeatedly failed until they were abandoned and replaced by better domestic ideas. One forceful idea of domestic origin has been low flat income taxes. For years, they were resisted by the IMF, which argued that a country had to improve its tax administration first, but that could only be done after the tax system had been made more rational. The sooner a sensible and viable idea is found, the better, and the search for new ideas usually starts abroad. Models have been successfully transplanted from one country to another when they have been intelligible and viable. The victorious reformers listened to international advice and made appropriate choices themselves. By necessity, most reforms started from above, but to become sustainable, they had to be accepted and supported from below. No reforms were carried out in consensus, although majority support was a great advantage for a reform so that vested interests could be steamrolled.

Bibliography

Abalkin, Leonid I. (1992) "Ekonomicheskaya reforma: rezultaty i perspektivy (Economic Reform: Results and Perspectives)," *Ekonomicheskaya gazeta* (no. 21, May), pp. 14–15.

Acemoglu, Daron (2003) "The Form of Property Rights: Oligarchic vs. Democratic Societies," NBER Working Paper 10037, Cambridge, MA: National Bureau of Economic Research.

———— (2005) "Constitutions, Politics, and Economics: A Review Essay on Persson and Tabellini's *The Economic Effects of Constitutions*," *Journal of Economic Literature*, **43** (4): 1025–48.

————, and Simon Johnson (2005) "Unbundling Institutions," *Journal of Political Economy*, **113** (October): pp. 949–95.

Aghion, Phillipe, and Olivier Blanchard (1994) "On the Speed of Transition in Central Europe," in Stanley Fischer and Julio Rotemberg, eds., *NBER Macroeconomic Annual 1994*. Cambridge, MA: MIT Press, pp. 283–320.

Akaev, Askar A. (2000) *Perekhodnaya ekonomika glazami fizika* [The Transition Economy in the Eyes of a Physicist]. Bishkek: Uchkun.

Akerlof, George A., Andrew K. Rose, Janet L. Yellen, and Helga Hessenius (1991) "East Germany in from the Cold: The Economic Aftermath of Currency Union," *Brookings Papers on Economic Activity* **21** (1): 1–105.

Allison, Christine, and Dena Ringold (1996) "Labor Markets in Central and Eastern Europe, 1989–1995," World Bank Technical Paper 352.

Allison, Graham, and Grigoriy Yavlinsky (1991) "Window of Opportunity: Joint Program for Western Cooperation in the Soviet Transition to Democracy and the Market Economy," mimeo, Cambridge, MA: Harvard University, and Moscow: Center for Economic and Political Research, June 29.

Altstadt, Audrey L. (1997) "Azerbaijan's Struggle toward Democracy," in Karen Dawisha and Bruce Parrott, eds., *Conflict, Cleavage, and Chance in Central Asia and the Caucasus*. New York: Cambridge University Press, pp. 110–55.

Amsden, Alice H., Jacek Kochanowicz, and Lance Taylor (1994) *The Market Meets Its Match: Restructuring the Economies of Eastern Europe*. Cambridge, MA: Harvard University Press.

Anderson, James H., David S. Bernstein, and Cheryl W. Gray (2005) *Judicial Systems in Transition Economies: Assessing the Past, Looking to the Future*. Washington, DC: World Bank.

Anderson, James H., and Cheryl W. Gray (2006) *Anticorruption in Transition 3: Who Is Succeeding... and Why?* Washington, DC: World Bank.

Appel, Hilary (2004) *A New Capitalist Order: Privatization and Ideology in Russia and Eastern Europe*. Pittsburgh, PA: University of Pittsburgh Press.

Arbatov, Georgi (1992) "Kuda poshli den'gi?" [Where Did the Money Go?], *Nezavisimaya gazeta*, April 3, p. 4.

Arendh, Rudiger (2005) "Can Russia Break the 'Resource Curse'?" *Eurasian Geography and Economics*, **46** (8): 584–609.

Aron, Leon (2000) *Yeltsin: A Revolutionary Life*. New York: St. Martin's Press.

Ash, Timothy Garton (1983) *The Polish Revolution: Solidarity 1980–82*. London: Jonathan Cape.

———— (1990) *We the People: The Revolution of '89 Witnessed in Warsaw, Budapest, Berlin & Prague*. Cambridge: Granta Books.

Åslund, Anders (1985) *Private Enterprise in Eastern Europe: The Non-Agricultural Sector in Poland and the GDR*. New York: St. Martin's Press.

———— (1989) "Soviet and Chinese Reforms – Why They Must Be Different," *The World Today* **45** (11): 188–91.

———— (1990) "How Small Is the Soviet National Income?" in Henry S. Rowen and Charles Wolf, Jr., eds., *The Impoverished Superpower: Perestroika and the Soviet Military Burden*. San Francisco: Institute for Contemporary Studies, pp. 13–61, 288–305.

———— (1991) *Gorbachev's Struggle for Economic Reform*, 2nd ed. Ithaca, NY: Cornell University Press.

———— (1992) *Post Communist Economic Revolutions: How Big a Bang?* Washington, DC: The Center for Strategic and International Studies.

———— (1995) *How Russia Became a Market Economy*. Washington, DC: Brookings Institution.

———— (1996) "Reform vs. 'Rent-Seeking' in Russia's Economic Transformation," *Transition (OMRI)* (January 26): 12–16.

———— (1997a) "Economic Causes of Crime in Russia," in Jeffrey D. Sachs and Katharina Pistor, eds., *The Rule of Law and Economic Reform in Russia*. Boulder, CO: Westview Press, pp. 79–94.

———— (1997b) "Observations on the Development of Small Private Enterprises in Russia," *Post-Soviet Geography and Economics* **38** (4): 191–205.

———— (1998) "Russia's Financial Crisis: Causes and Possible Remedies," *Post-Soviet Geography and Economics*, **39** (6): 309–28.

———— (1999) "Why Has Russia's Economic Transformation Been So Arduous?" Annual Bank Conference on Development Economics, April 28–30, Washington, DC: World Bank.

———— (2000) "Why Has Ukraine Failed to Achieve Economic Growth?" in Anders Åslund and Georges de Ménil, eds., *Economic Reform in Ukraine: The Unfinished Agenda*. Armonk, NY: M. E. Sharpe, pp. 255–77.

———— (2001) "Ukraine's Return to Economic Growth," *Post-Soviet Geography and Economics*, **42** (5): 313–28.

——— (2002) *Building Capitalism: The Transformation of the Former Soviet Bloc.* New York: Cambridge University Press.

——— (2004a) "Russia's Economic Transformation under Putin," *Eurasian Geography and Economics,* **45** (6): 397–420.

——— (2004b) "Ukraine Whole and Free: What I saw at the Orange Revolution," *The Weekly Standard,* December 27, pp. 11–12.

——— (2006) "The Ancien Régime: Kuchma and the Oligarchs," in Anders Åslund and Michael McFaul, eds., *Revolution in Orange.* Washington, DC: Carnegie Endowment for International Peace, pp. 9–28.

Åslund, Anders, Peter Boone, and Simon Johnson (1996) "How to Stabilize: Lessons from Post Communist Countries," *Brookings Papers on Economic Activity* **26** (1): 217–313.

——— (2001) "Escaping the Under-Reform Trap," IMF Staff Papers, Special Issue, **48** (4): 88–108, Washington, DC: International Monetary Fund.

Åslund, Anders, and Mikhail Dmitriev, eds. (1996) *Sotsialnaya politika v period perekhoda k rynku: problemy i resheniya* [Social Policy in the Transition to a Market Economy: Problems and Solutions]. Moscow: Carnegie Endowment for International Peace.

Åslund, Anders, and Nazgul Jenish (2006) "The Eurasian Growth Paradox," Working Paper 06–5. Washington, DC: Institute for International Economics.

Åslund, Anders, and Simon Johnson (2004) "Small Enterprises and Economic Policy," Working Paper 43. Washington, DC: Carnegie Endowment for International Peace.

Åslund, Anders, and Michael McFaul, eds. (2006) *Revolution in Orange: The Origins of Ukraine's Democratic Breakthrough.* Washington, DC: Carnegie Endowment for International Peace.

———, and Georges de Ménil, eds. (2000) *Ukrainian Economic Reform: The Unfinished Agenda.* Armonk, NY: M. E. Sharpe.

Åslund, Anders, and Andrew Warner (2004) "The EU Enlargement: Consequences for the CIS Countries," in Marek Dąbrowski, Ben Slay, and Jaroslaw Neneman, eds., *Beyond Transition: Development Perspectives and Dilemmas.* Aldershot: Ashgate, pp. 231–52.

Aukutsionek, S. (1998) "Barter v rossiiskoi promyshlennosti" [Barter in Russian Industry], *Voprosy ekonomiki* **70** (2): 51–60.

Aven, Petr O. (1994) "Problems in Foreign Trade Regulation in the Russian Economy," in Anders Åslund, ed., *Economic Transformation in Russia.* New York: St. Martin's Press, pp. 80–93.

——— (2000) "Ekonomichesky rost i obshchestvennaya moral'" [Economic Growth and Public Morality], *Kommersant Daily,* February 29.

Balcerowicz, Leszek (1992) *800 dni skontrolowanego szoku* [800 Days of Controlled Shock]. Warsaw: Polska Oficyna Wydawnicza "BGW."

——— (1994) "Understanding Postcommunist Transitions," *Journal of Democracy,* **5** (4): 75–89.

——— (1995) *Socialism, Capitalism, Transformation.* Budapest: Central European University Press.

Balcerowicz, Leszek, Cheryl W. Gray, and Iraj Hashi (1997) *Exit Processes in Economies in Transition,* Budapest: Central European University Press.

Baldwin, Richard E. (1994) *Towards an Integrated Europe.* London: Centre for Economic Policy Research.

Banarjee, Biswajit, Vincent Koen, Thomas Krueger, Mark S. Lutz, Michael Marrese, and Tapio O. Saavalainen (1995) "Road Maps of the Transition: The Baltics, the Czech Republic, Hungary, and Russia," International Monetary Fund Occasional Paper 127.

Barro, Robert J. (1989) "Economic Growth in a Cross Section of Countries," NBER Working Paper 3120, Cambridge, MA: National Bureau of Economic Research.

_____ (1996) "Democracy and Growth," *Journal of Economic Growth* **1** (1): 1–27.

Barro, Robert J. and Xavier Sala-i-Martin (2004) *Economic Growth.* Cambridge, MA: MIT Press.

Begg, David (1996) "Monetary Policy in Central and Eastern Europe: Lessons after Half a Decade of Transition," International Monetary Fund Working Paper 108.

_____ (1998) "Pegging Out: Lessons from the Czech Exchange Rate Crisis," *Journal of Comparative Economics* **26** (4): 669–90.

Bel, Germà (2006) "The Coining of 'Privatization' and Germany's National Socialist Party," *Journal of Economic Perspectives* **20** (3): 187–94.

Bell, John D. (1997) "Democratization and Political Participation in 'Postcommunist' Bulgaria," in Karen Dawisha and Bruce Parrott, eds., *Politics, Power, and the Struggle for Democracy in South-East Europe.* Cambridge: Cambridge University Press, pp. 353–402.

Bennett, John, Saul Estrin, and Giovanni Urga (2005) "Methods of Privatization and Economic Growth in Transition Economies," WIDER Jubilee Conference, Helsinki, Finland, June 17–18, 2005. Available: http://www.wider.unu.edu (accessed June 19, 2006).

Berengaut, Julian, Augusto Lopez-Laros, Francoise Le Gall, Dennis Jones, Richard Stern, Ann-Margaret Westin, Effie Psalida, and Pietro Garribaldi (1998) "The Baltic Countries: From Economic Stabilization to EU Accession," International Monetary Fund Occasional Paper 173.

Berg, Andrew (1994) "Supply and Demand Factors in the Output Decline in East and Central Europe," *Empirica* **21**: 3–36.

_____, Eduardo Borensztein, Ratna Sahay, and Jeronim Zettelmeyer (1999) "The Evolution of Output in Transition Economies: Explaining the Differences," International Monetary Fund Working Paper 73.

Berg, Andrew and Jeffrey D. Sachs (1992) "Structural Adjustment and International Trade in Eastern Europe: The Case of Poland," *Economic Policy* **7** (14): 117–73.

Bergson, Abram (1961) *The Real National Income of Soviet Russia since 1928.* Cambridge, MA: Harvard University Press.

_____ (1997) "How Big Was Soviet GDP?" *Comparative Economic Studies* **39** (1): 1–14.

Berkowitz, Daniel M., Joseph S. Berliner, Paul R. Gregory, Susan J. Linz, and James R. Millar (1993) "An Evaluation of the CIS's Analysis of Soviet Economic Performance, 1970–90," *Comparative Economic Studies* **35** (2): 33–57.

Black, Bernard, Reiner Krakkman, and Anna Tarassova (2000) "Russian Privatization and Corporate Governance: What Went Wrong?" *Stanford Law Review* **52** (6): 1731–805.

Blanchard, Olivier (1997) *The Economics of Transition in Eastern Europe.* Oxford: Clarendon Press.

Blanchard, Olivier, Rudiger Dornbusch, Paul Krugman, Richard Layard, Lawrence Summers (1991) *Reform in Eastern Europe.* Cambridge, MA: MIT Press.

Blanchard, Olivier, and Michael Kremer (1997) "Disorganization," *Quarterly Journal of Economics*, **112** (4): 1091–126.

Blasi, Joseph R., Maya Kroumova, and Douglas Kruse (1997) *Kremlin Capitalism: Privatizing the Russian Economy*. Ithaca, NY: Cornell University Press.

Boeri, Tito, and Katherine Terrell (2002) "Institutional Determinants of Labor Reallocation in Transition," *Journal of Economic Perspectives* **16** (1): 51–76.

Boettke, Peter J. (1993) *Why Perestroika Failed: The Politics and Economics of Socialist Transformation*. New York: Palgrave.

Bogomolov, Oleg T. (1992) "Net ni vremeni, ni effektivnoi vlasti" [There is neither time, nor effective power], *Nezavisimaya gazeta*, February 7, p. 4.

———, ed. (1996) *Reformy glazami amerikanskikh i rossiiskikh uchenykh* [Reforms in the Eyes of American and Russian Scholars]. Moscow: Rossiisky ekonomichesky zhurnal.

Bolotin, Boris (1988) "A More Complete Picture: New Findings from the USSR State Committee for Statistics," *Moscow News*, no. 11.

Bonin, John P., and Mark E. Schaffer (1995) "Banks, Firms, Bad Debts and Bankruptcy in Hungary 1991–94," Centre for Economic Performance, London School of Economics, Discussion Paper 234, April.

Boone, Peter, and Jakob Hørder (1998) "Inflation: Causes, Consequences, and Cures" in Peter Boone, Stanisław Gomułka, and Richard Layard, eds., *Emerging from Communism: Lessons from Russia, China and Eastern Europe*. Cambridge, MA: MIT Press, pp. 43–71.

Borish, Michael S., and Michel Noël (1996) "Private Sector Development during Transition: The Visegrad Countries," World Bank Discussion Paper no. 318.

Boycko, Maxim (1991) "Price Decontrol: The Microeconomic Case for the 'Big Bang' Approach," *Oxford Review of Economic Policy* **7** (4): 35–45.

Boycko, Maxim, Andrei Shleifer, and Robert W. Vishny (1995) *Privatizing Russia*. Cambridge, MA: MIT Press.

BP (2006) *Quantifying Energy: BP Statistical Review of World Energy*. London: BP. Available: http://www.bp.com/sectiongenericarticle.do?categoryId=9009511&contentId=7017940 (accessed July 2, 2006).

Brada, Josef C. (1993) "The Transformation from Communism to Capitalism: How Far? How Fast?" *Post-Soviet Affairs* **9** (1): 87–110.

——— (1996) "Privatization Is Transition – Or Is It?" *Journal of Economic Perspectives* **10** (2): 67–86.

Brady, Rose (1999) *Kapitalizm: Russia's Struggle to Free Its Economy*. New Haven, CT: Yale University Press.

Braguinsky, Serguey, and Grigory Yavlinsky (2000) *Incentives and Institutions: The Transition to a Market Economy in Russia*. Princeton, NJ: Princeton University Press.

Brainerd, Elizabeth (1998) "Market Reform and Mortality in Transition Economies," *World Development* **26** (11): 2013–27.

Brealey, Richard A., and Stewart C. Myers (2000) *Principles of Corporate Finance*. New York: McGraw-Hill.

Broadman, Harry G., ed. (1999) "Russian Enterprise Reform: Policies to Further the Transition," World Bank Discussion Paper 400.

Brown, Annette N., Barry W. Ickes, and Randi Ryterman (1994) "The Myth of Monopoly: A New View of Industrial Structure in Russia," World Bank Policy Research Working Paper 1331.

Brown, Archie (1996) *The Gorbachev Factor*. Oxford: Oxford University Press.

Brown, J. David, John S. Earle, and Álmos Telegdy (2005) "The Productivity Effects of Privatization: Longitudinal Estimates from Hungary, Romania, Russia, and Ukraine," Upjohn Institute Staff Working Paper 05–121, October.

Brucan, Silviu (1992) "Democracy and Odds with the Market in Post-Communist Societies," in Michael Keren and Gur Ofer, eds., *Trials of Transition: Economic Reform in the Former Communist Bloc*. Boulder, CO: Westview Press, pp. 19–25.

Bruno, Michael, and William Easterly (1998) "Inflation Crises and Long-Run Growth" *Journal of Monetary Economics* **41**: 3–26.

Bruno, Michael, Guido di Tella, Rudiger Dornbusch, and Stanley Fischer, eds. (1988) *Inflation Stabilization: The Experiences of Israel, Argentina, Brazil, Bolivia, and Mexico*. Cambridge, MA: MIT Press.

Brzezinski, Zbigniew (1997) *The Grand Chessboard: American Primacy and Its Geostrategic Imperatives*. New York: Basic Books.

Bunce, Valerie (1999a) "The Political Economy of Postsocialism," *Slavic Review* **58** (4): 756–93.

———— (1999b) *Subversive Institutions: The Design and the Destruction of Socialism and the State*. Cambridge: Cambridge University Press.

Cagan, Phillip (1956) "The Monetary Dynamics of Hyperinflation" in Milton Friedman, ed., *Studies in the Quantity Theory of Money*. Chicago: University of Chicago Press, pp. 25–117.

Calvo, Guillermo A., and Carlos A. Végh (1999) "Inflation Stabilization and BOP Crises in Developing Countries," NBER Working Paper 6925.

Calvo, Guillermo A., and Fabrizio Coricelli (1992) "Stabilizing a Previously Centrally Planned Economy: Poland 1990," *Economic Policy* 14: 175–226.

Calvo, Guillermo A., and Fabrizio Coricelli (1993) "Output Collapse in Eastern Europe: The Role of Credit," *IMF Staff Papers* **40** (1): 32–52.

Campos, Nauro F., and Fabrizio Coricelli (2002) "Growth in Transition: What We Know, What We Don't, and What We Should," *Journal of Economic Literature* **40** (3): 793–836.

Cangiano, Marco, Carlo Cottarelli, and Luis Cubeddu (1998) "Pension Developments and Reforms in Transition Economies," International Monetary Fund Working Paper 151.

Capelik, Vladimir (1992) "The Development of Antimonopoly Policy in Russia," *RFE/RL Research Report* **1** (34): 66–70.

———— (1994) "Should Monopoly Be Regulated in Russia?" *Communist Economies and Economic Transformation* **6** (1): 19–32.

Carothers, Thomas (2000) *Aiding Democracy Abroad: The Learning Curve*. Washington, DC: Carnegie Endowment for International Peace.

Chernichovsky, D., H. Barnum, and E. Potapchik (1996) "Health System Reform in Russia: The Finance and Organization Perspectives," *Economics of Transition* **4** (1): 113–34.

Christoffersen, Peter, and Peter Doyle (2000) "From Inflation to Growth: Eight Years of Transition," *Economics of Transition* **8** (2): 421–51.

Chu, Ke-Young, and Sanjeev Gupta (1993) "Protecting the Poor: Social Safety Nets during Transition," *Finance & Development* (June): 24–7.

Chubais, Anatoly B., ed. (1999) *Privatizatsiya po-rossiiski* [Privatization the Russian Way]. Moscow: Vagrius.

Cienski, Jan (2006) "Poland Digs Deep to Make a Case for Coal," *Financial Times*, May 31, p. 14.

Citrin, Daniel A., and Ashok K. Lahiri, eds. (1995) "Policy Experiences and Issues in the Baltics, Russia, and Other Countries of the Former Soviet Union," International Monetary Fund Occasional Paper 133.

Claessens, Stijin, and Simeon Djankov (1997) "Politicians and Firms: Evidence from Eastern Europe," mimeo, World Bank.

Coase, Ronald H. (1988) *The Firm, the Market, and the Law*. Chicago: University of Chicago Press.

Cohen, Stephen F. (2000) *Failed Crusade: American and the Tragedy of Post-Communist Russia*. New York and London: Norton.

Collins, Susan M., and Dani Rodrik (1991) *Eastern Europe and the Soviet Union in the World Economy*. Washington, DC: Institute for International Economics.

Commander, Simon, and Fabrizio Coricelli, eds. (1995) *Unemployment, Restructuring and the Labor Market in East Europe and Russia*. Washington, DC: World Bank.

Commander, Simon, and John McHale (1996) "Unemployment and the Labor Market in Transition: A Review of Experience in East Europe and Russia," in Bartolomiej Kaminski, ed., *Economic Transition in Russia and the New States of Eurasia*. Armond, NY: M. E. Sharpe, pp. 277–314.

Commander, Simon, and Christian Mumssen (1998) "Understanding Barter in Russia," EBRD Working Paper 37.

Commander, Simon, and Mark Schankerman (1997) "Enterprise Restructuring and Social Benefits," *Economics of Transition* 5 (1): 1–24.

Crowther, William (1997) "The Politics of Democratization in Postcommunist Moldova," in Karen Dawisha and Bruce Parrott, eds., *Democratic Changes and Authoritarian Reactions in Russia, Ukraine, Belarus and Moldova*. Cambridge: Cambridge University Press, pp. 282–329.

Dąbrowski, Marek (1996) "Fiscal Crisis in the Transformation Period: Trends, Stylized Facts and Some Conceptual Problems," Warsaw: Center for Social and Economic Research, Studies and Analyses 72.

Dąbrowski, Marek, Stanisław Gomułka, and Jacek Rostowski (2001) "Whence Reform? A Critique of the Stiglitz Perspective," *Policy Reform* 4: 291–324.

Dąbrowski, Marek, Marcin Luczyński, and Malgorzata Markiewicz (2000) "Fiscal Policy, 1991–1999," in Anders Åslund and Georges de Ménil, eds., *Ukrainian Economic Reform: The Unfinished Agenda*. Armonk, N.Y: M. E. Sharpe, pp. 113–43.

Dąbrowski, Marek, Marcin Swiecicki, Stefan Kawalec, Janusz Lewandowski, Jan Szomburg, Janusz Beksiak, and Ryszard Bugaj (1989) *Propozycie Przekształcenie Polskiej Gospodarki* [Proposals for the Transformation of the Polish Economy]. Warsaw: PTE.

Dahrendorf, Ralf (1990) *Reflections on the Revolution in Europe*. London: Chatto & Windus.

Davis, Christopher (2001) "The Health Sector: Illness, Medical Care, and Mortality," in Brigitte Granville and Peter Oppenheimer, eds., *Russia's Post-Communist Economy*. New York: Oxford University Press, pp. 475–538.

DeLong, Bradford (2002) "Robber Barons" in Anders Åslund and Tatyana Maleva, eds., *Ocherki o mirovoi ekonomiki: Vydayushchiesya ekonomisty mira v Moskovskom Tsentre Karnegie* [Series of Lectures on Economics: Leading World Experts at the Carnegie Moscow Center]. Moscow: Carnegie Endowment for International Peace, pp. 179–208.

De Melo, Martha, and Cevdet Denizer (1999) "Monetary Policy during Transition: An Overview," in Mario I. Blejer and Marko Skreb, eds., *Financial Sector Transformation: Lessons from Economies in Transition.* Cambridge: Cambridge University Press, pp. 19–92.

De Melo, Martha, Cevdet Denizer, and Alan Gelb (1997a) "From Plan to Market: Patterns of Transition," in Mario I. Blejer and Marko Skreb, eds., *Macroeconomic Stabilization in Transition Economies.* Cambridge: Cambridge University Press, pp. 17–72.

De Melo, Martha, Cevdet Denizer, Alan Gelb, and Stoyan Tenev (1997b) *Circumstance and Choice: The Role of Initial Conditions and Policies in Transition Economies,* World Bank Policy Research Working Paper 1866.

De Melo, Martha and Alan Gelb (1996) "A Comparative Analysis of Twenty-eight Transition Economies in Europe and Asia," *Post-Soviet Geography and Economics* **37** (5): 265–85.

―――― (1997) "Transitions to Date: A Comparative Overview," in Salvatore Zecchini, ed., *Lessons from the Economic Transition: Central and Eastern Europe in the 1990s.* Norwell, MA: Kluwer, pp. 59–78.

de Soto, Hernando (2000) *The Mystery of Capital: Why Capitalism Triumphs in the West and Fails Everywhere Else.* New York: Basic Books.

de Tocqueville, Alexis [1856] (1955) *The Old Regime and the French Revolution.* New York: Doubleday.

Deutsches Institut für Wirtschaftsforschung (DIW) (1977) *Handbuch DDR-Wirschaft* (Manual of the GDR Economy). Reinbek at Hamburg: Rowohlt.

Dewatripont, Mathias, and Gérard Roland (1992a) "The Virtues of Gradualism and Legitimacy in the Transition to a Market Economy," *Economic Journal* **102**: 291–300.

―――― (1992b) "Economic Reform and Dynamic Political Constraints," *Review of Economic Studies* **59**: 703–30.

Diamond, Larry (1995) "Democracy and Economic Reform: Tensions, Compatibilities, and Strategies for Reconciliation," in Edward P. Lazear, ed., *Economic Transition in Eastern Europe and Russia.* Stanford, CA: Hoover Institution Press, pp. 107–58.

―――― (1999) *Developing Democracy: Towards Consolidation.* Baltimore, MD: John Hopkins University Press.

Djankov, Simeon (1999) "Ownership Structure and Enterprise Restructuring in Six Newly Independent States," Social Science Research Networking Paper Series.

Djankov, Simeon and Peter Murrell (2002) "Enterprise Restructuring in Transition: A Quantitative Survey," *Journal of Economic Literature* **40** (3): 739–92.

Dmitriev, Mikhail E. (1996) "Sotsial'nye problemy i byudzhetny krizis v Rossiiskoi Federatsii" [Social Problems and Budgetary Crisis in the Russian Federation], in Åslund and Dmitriev (1996) *Sotsialnaya politika v period perekhoda k rynku: problemy i resheniya* [Social Policy in the Transition to a Market Economy: Problems and Solutions]. Moscow: Carnegie Endowment for International Peace, pp. 105–28.

―――― (1997) *Byudzhetnaya politika sovremennoi Rossii* (Budgetary Policy in Contemporary Russia). Moscow: Carnegie Endowment for International Peace.

―――― (1999) "Sotsialnaya sfera v usloviyakh finansovogo krizisa: problemy adaptatsii (The Social Sphere during a Financial Crisis: Problems of Adaptation)," *Voprosy ekonomiki* **71** (2): 53–64.

Dmitriev, Mikhail E. and Nikolai Kartsev (1996) "Fiscal Policy of CIS Countries in 1993–1995," Center for Social and Economic Research, Studies and Analyses no. 84, May.

Dmitriev, Mikhail E. and Tatyana Maleva (1997) "Russian Labor Market in Transition: Trends, Specific Features, and State Policy," *Social Research* **64** (4): 1499–529.

Dmitriev, Mikhail E. M. Y. Matovnikov, L. V. Mikhailov, L. I. Sycheva, E. V. Timofeev, and A. Warner (1996) *Rossiiskie banki nakanune finansovoi stabilizatsii* [Russian Banks on the Eve of Financial Stabilization]. St. Petersburg: Norma.

Dobbs, Michael (1997) *Down with Big Brother: The End of the Soviet Empire.* New York: Knopf.

Dornbusch, Rudiger (1992) "Monetary Problems of Post Communism: Lessons from the End of the Austro-Hungarian Empire," *Weltwirtschaftliches Archiv* **128** (3): 391–424.

Dornbusch, Rudiger and Sebastian Edwards, eds. (1991) *The Macroeconomics of Populism in Latin America.* Chicago: University of Chicago Press.

Drazen, Allen, and Vittorio Grilli (1993) "The Benefit of Crises for Economic Reforms," *American Economic Review* **83** (3): 598–607.

Drèze, Jean, and Amartya Sen (1989) *Hunger and Public Action.* New York: Oxford University Press.

Dudwick, Nora (1997) "Political Transformation in Postcommunist Armenia: Images and Realities," in Karen Dawisha and Bruce Parrott, eds., *Conflict, Cleavage, and Chance in Central Asia and the Caucasus.* Cambridge: Cambridge University Press, pp. 69–109.

Dunlop, John (1993) *The Rise of Russia and the Fall of the Soviet Empire.* Princeton, NJ: Princeton University Press.

Dynkin, Aleksandr, and Aleksei Sokolov (2002) "Integrirovannye biznes-gruppy v rossi-iskoi ekonomike" [Integrated Business Groups in the Russian Economy], *Voprosy ekonomiki* **74** (4): 78–95.

Earle, John S., and Saul Estrin (1996) "Worker Ownership in Transition," in Roman Frydman, Cheryl Gray, and Andrzej Rapaczynski, eds., *Corporate Governance in Central Europe and Russia,* vol. 2. Budapest: Central European University Press, pp. 1–61.

―――― (1997) "After Voucher Privatization: The Structure of Corporate Ownership in Russian Manufacturing Industry," Centre for Economic Policy Research Discussion Paper 1736.

Earle, John S., Roman Frydman, and Andrzej Rapaczynski, eds. (1993) *Privatization in the Transition to a Market Economy.* Budapest: Central European University Press.

Earle, John S., Roman Frydman, Andrzej Rapaczynski, and Joel Turkewitz (1994) *Small Privatization.* Budapest: Central European University Press.

Ebrill, Liam, Oleh Havrylyshyn, et al. (1999) "Reforms of Tax Policy and Tax Administration in the CIS Countries and the Baltics," International Monetary Fund Occasional Paper 175.

Ellerman, David (2003) "On the Russian Privatization Debate," *Challenge* **46** (3): 6–28.

Elster, Jon (1990) "The Necessity and Impossibility of Simultaneous Economic and Political Reform," in Piotr Ploszajski, ed., *Philosophy of Social Choice.* Warsaw: IfiS Publishers, pp. 309–16.

Elster, Jon, Claus Offe, and Ulrich K. Preuss (1998) *Institutional Design in Post Communist Societies.* Cambridge: Cambridge University Press.

Emerson, Michael (1992) "The CIS on the Maastricht Road?" *Ekonomicheskaya gazeta,* no. 51, December.

European Bank for Reconstruction and Development (EBRD) (1994) *Transition Report 1994*. London: EBRD.

———— (1996) *Transition Report 1996*. London: EBRD.

———— (1997) *Transition Report 1997*. London: EBRD.

———— (1998) *Transition Report 1998*. London: EBRD.

———— (1999) *Transition Report 1999*. London: EBRD.

———— (2000) *Transition Report 2000*. London: EBRD.

———— (2002) *Transition Report 2002*. London: EBRD.

———— (2004) *Transition Report 2004*. London: EBRD.

———— (2005) *Transition Report 2005*. London: EBRD.

———— (2006) *Transition Report 2006*. London: EBRD.

———— and World Bank (2002) *Business Environment and Enterprise Performance Survey* (BEEPS). Available: http://www.worldbank.org/ (accessed May 10, 2006).

———— (2005) *Business Environment and Enterprise Performance Survey* (BEEPS). Available: http://www.worldbank.org/ (accessed June 22, 2006).

European Commission (various years) *Central and Eastern Eurobarometer. Public Opinion and the European Union.*

Fedorenko, Nikolai, Nikolai Petrakov, Vladlen Perlamutrov, V. Dadayan, and Dmitri Lvov (1992) "Shturm rynochnykh redutov poka ne udalsya" [The Storm of Market Redoubts Has Not Succeeded So Far], *Izvestiya* (March 18): p. 3.

Fedorov, Boris G. (1994) "Russian Finances in 1993" *Voprosy ekonomiki* **66** (1): 4–85.

Fischer, Stanley (1993) "The Role of Macroeconomic Factors in Growth," *Journal of Monetary Economics* **32**: 458–512.

———— (2005) *IMF Essays from a Time of Crisis: The International Financial System, Stabilization and Development*. Cambridge, MA: MIT Press.

Fischer, Stanley and Alan Gelb (1991) "The Process of Socialist Economic Transformation," *Journal of Economic Perspectives* **5** (4): 91–105.

Fischer, Stanley and Ratna Sahay (2000) "The Transition Economies after Ten Years," International Monetary Fund Working Paper 30.

Fischer, Stanley, Ratna Sahay, and Carlos A. Végh (1996a) "Stabilization and Growth in Transition Economies: The Early Experience," *Journal of Economic Perspectives* **10** (2): 45–66.

———— (1996b) "Economies in Transition: The Beginnings of Growth," *American Economic Review* **86** (2): 229–33.

———— (1997) "From Transition to Market: Evidence and Growth Prospects," in Salvatore Zecchini, ed., *Lessons from the Economic Transition: Central and Eastern Europe in the 1990s*. Norwell, MA: Kluwer, pp. 79–101.

Fish, M. Steven (2005) *Democracy Derailed in Russia: The Failure of Open Politics*. Cambridge: Cambridge University Press.

Freedom House (1999) "Freedom in the World: The Annual Survey of Political Rights and Civil Liberties, 1998–1999." Available: http://www.freedomhouse.org/survey99/ (accessed July 3, 2006).

———— (2006) "Freedom in the World 2006: Selected Data from Freedom House's Annual Global Survey on Political Rights and Civil Liberties," Available: http://www.freedomhouse.org/uploads/pdf/Charts2006.pdf (accessed July 3, 2006).

Freeland, Chrystia (2000) *Sale of the Century: Russia's Wild Ride from Communism to Capitalism*. New York: Crown Business.

Frydman, Roman, Cheryl Gray, Marek Hessel, and Andrzej Rapaczynski (1997) "Private Ownership and Corporate Performance: Some Lessons From Transition Economies," World Bank Policy Research Paper 1830.

Frydman, Roman, Marek Hessel, and Andrzej Rapaczynski (1998) "When Does Privatization Work? The Impact of Private Ownership on Corporate Performance in Transition Economies," Economic Research Report 32, C. V. Starr Center for Applied Economics, New York University.

Frydman, Roman and Andrzej Rapaczynski (1994) *Privatization in Eastern Europe: Is the State Withering Away?* Budapest: Central European University Press.

Frydman, Roman, Andrzej Rapaczynski, John S. Earle, et al. (1993a) *The Privatization Process in Central Europe.* Budapest: Central European University Press.

———— (1993b) *The Privatization Process in Russia, Ukraine, and the Baltic States.* Budapest: Central European University Press.

Frye, Timothy (2000) *Brokers and Bureaucrats: Building Market Institutions in Russia.* Ann Arbor: University of Michigan Press.

———— (2001) "Keeping Shop: The Value of the Rule of Law in Warsaw and Moscow," in Peter Murrell, ed., *Assessing the Value of Law in Transition Economies.* Ann Arbor: University of Michigan Press, pp. 229–48.

Gács, János (1995) "The Effects of the Demise of the CME and the USSR on Output in Hungary," in Robert Holzmann, Georg Winckler, and János Gács, eds., *Output Decline in Eastern Europe: Unavoidable, External Influence or Homemade?* Boston: Kluwer, pp. 161–80.

Gaddy, Clifford G., and Barry W. Ickes (1998) "Russia's Virtual Economy," *Foreign Affairs* **77** (5): 53–67.

Gaddy, Clifford G., and Barry W. Ickes (2005) "Resource Rents and the Russian Economy," *Eurasian Geography and Economics* **46** (8): 559–83.

Gaidar, Yegor (1993) "Inflationary Pressures and Economic Reform in the Soviet Union," in P. H. Admiraal, ed., *Economic Transition in Eastern Europe.* Oxford: Blackwell, pp. 63–90.

———— (1998) "Taktika reform i uroven' gosudarstvennoi nagruzki na ekonomiku" [Tactics of Reform and the Level of State Burden on the Economy], *Voprosy ekonomiki* **70** (4): 4–13.

———— (2000) *Days of Defeat and Victory.* Seattle: University of Washington Press.

———— (2003) *State and Evolution: Russia's Search for a Free Market,* Seattle: University of Washington Press.

———— (2005) *Dolgoe vremya* [The Long Term]. Moscow: Delo.

Gambetta, Diego (1993) *The Sicilian Mafia.* Cambridge, MA: Harvard University Press.

Garibaldi, Pietro, and Zuzana Brixiova (1997) "Labor Market Institutions and Unemployment Dynamics in Transition Economies," International Monetary Fund Working Paper 137.

Geddes, Barbara (1994a) "Challenging the Conventional Wisdom," *Journal of Democracy* **5** (4): 104–18.

———— (1994b) *Politician's Dilemma: Building State Capacity in Latin America.* Berkeley and Los Angeles: University of California Press.

Gerashchenko, Viktor V. (Interview with) (1992) "Tseny, den'gi, kredity" [Prices, Money and Credits], *Ekonomika i zhizn* **46** (November): pp. 1, 5.

Glaziev, Sergei Yu. (1996) "Ob otkrytosti i razumnoi zashchite rossiiskoi ekonomiki" [On the Openness and Sensible Protection on the Russian Economy], in Bogomolov, Oleg T., ed., *Reformy glazami amerikaskikh i rossiskikh uchenykh* [Reforms in the eyes of American and Russian scholars]. Moscow: Rossisky ekonomichesky zhurnal, pp. 223–36.

Glinski, Dmitri, and Peter Reddaway (1999) "The Ravages of 'Market Bolshevism,'" *Journal of Democracy* **10** (2): 19–34.

Goldgeier, James M., and Michael McFaul (2003) *Power and Purpose: U.S. Policy Toward Russia after the Cold War*. Washington, DC: Brookings Institution.

Goldman, Marshall I. (1991) *What Went Wrong with Perestroika*. New York: Norton.

———— (1996) *Lost Opportunity: What Has Made Economic Reform in Russia So Difficult?* New York: Norton.

———— (2003) *The Piratization of Russia: Russian Reform Goes Awry*. London, New York: Routledge.

Goleniowska, Stanisława (1997) "Delayed Reforms of the Social Policy," in *Economic Scenarios for Poland*. Warsaw: Center for Social and Economic Research, pp. 31–42.

Gomułka, Stanisław (1989) "Shock Needed for Polish Economy," *The Guardian*, August 19.

Gorbachev, Mikhail S. (1987a) *Izbrannye rechi i stati* [Selected Speeches and Articles], vol. 2. Moscow: Politizdat.

———— (1987b) *Perestroika: New Thinking for Our Country and the World*. New York: Harper & Row.

Goskomstat SSSR (1991) *Narodnoe Khoziaistvo SSSR v 1990 g* [The National Economy of the USSR in 1990). Moscow: Finansy i statistika.

Goskomstat (1997) *Rossiisky statistichesky yezhegodnik* [Russian Statistical Yearbook]. Moscow: Goskomstat.

Gould-Davies, Nigel, and Ngaire Woods (1999) "Russia and the IMF," *International Affairs* **75** (1): 1–21.

Granville, Brigitte (1990) "Convertibility and Exchange Rates in Poland: 1957–1990." London: Royal Institute of International Affairs, Discussion Paper 33.

———— (1995a) *The Success of Russian Economic Reforms*. London: Royal Institute for International Affairs.

———— (1995b) "So Farewell Then Rouble Zone," in Anders Åslund, ed., *Russian Economic Reform at Risk*. New York: St. Martin's Press, pp. 65–88.

————(2002) "The IMF and The Rouble Zone, Response to Odling-Smee and Pastor,"*Comparative Economic Studies*, **44** (4): 59–80.

Gray, Cheryl W., and Arnold Holle (1997) "Bank-Led Restructuring in Poland (II): Bankruptcy and Its Alternatives," *Economics of Transition* **5** (1): 25–44.

Gray, Dale F. (1998) "Evaluation of Taxes and Revenues from the Energy Sector in the Baltics, Russia, and Former Soviet Union Countries," International Monetary Fund Working Paper 34, March.

Grosfeld, Irena, and Jean-François Nivet (1997) "Wage and Investment Behaviour in Transition: Evidence for a Polish Panel Data Set," Centre for Economic Policy Research Discussion Paper 1726.

Grosfeld, Irena and Paul Hare (1991) "Privatization in Hungary, Poland and Czechoslovakia," *European Economy*, special edition, no. 2: 129–56.

Grosfeld, Irena and Gérard Roland (1995) "Defensive and Strategic Restructuring in Central European Enterprises," Centre for Economic Policy Research Discussion Paper 1135.

Grygorenko, Yegor, Yuriy Gorodnichenko, and Dmytro Ostanin (2006) "Relative Property Rights in Transition Economies: Can the Oligarchs Be Productive?" Economics Education and Research Consortium Working Paper no. 4, Moscow.

Gwartney, James, and Robert Lawson (2006) *Economic Freedom of the World: 2006 Annual Report*. Vancouver: The Fraser Institute.

Hall, Robert, and Charles Jones (1999) "Why Do Some Countries Produce So Much More Output per Worker than Others?" *Quarterly Journal of Economics* **114** (1): 83–116.

Halpern, László (1996) "Real Exchange Rate and Exchange Rate Policy," *Economics of Transition* **4** (1): 211–28.

Halpern, László and Charles Wyplosz (1996) "Equilibrium Exchange Rates in Transition Economies," International Monetary Fund Working Paper 125.

Hamilton, Carl B., and L. Alan Winters (1992) "Trade with Eastern Europe," *Economic Policy* **7** (14): 77–116.

Hanke, Steve H., Lars Jonung, and Kurt Schuler (1992) *Monetary Reform for a Free Estonia: A Currency Board Solution*. Stockholm: SNS Förlag.

Hansson, Ardo H. (1993) "The Trouble with the Rouble: Monetary Reform in the Former Soviet Union," in Anders Åslund and Richard Layard, eds., *Changing the Economic System in Russia*. New York: St. Martin's Press, pp. 163–82.

———— (1997) "Macroeconomic Stabilization in the Baltic States," in Mario I. Blejer and Marko Skreb, eds., *Macroeconomic Stabilization in Transition Countries*. New York: Cambridge University Press, pp. 256–80.

Hansson, Ardo H. and Jeffrey D. Sachs (1992) "Crowning the Estonian Kroon," *Transition* (World Bank) **3** (9): 1–3.

Hansson, Ardo H. and Triinu Tombak (1999) "Banking Crises in the Baltic States: Causes, Solutions, and Lessons," in Mario I. Blejer and Marko Skreb, eds., *Financial Sector Transformation: Lessons from Economies in Transition*. New York: Cambridge University Press, pp. 195–236.

Harding, April L. (1995) "Commercial Real Estate Market Development in Russia," World Bank CDFS Discussion Paper 109.

Hardy, Daniel C., and Ashok K. Lahiri (1994) "Cash Shortage in the Former Soviet Union," International Monetary Fund Working Paper 67.

Hausmann, Ricardo, and Liliana Rojas-Suarez, eds. (1996) *Banking Crises in Latin America*. Washington, DC: Inter-American Development Bank.

Havrylyshyn, Oleh (2006) *Diverging Paths in Post-Communist Transformation: Capitalism for All or Capitalism for the Few?* Basingstoke, England; New York: Palgrave Macmillan.

Havrylyshyn, Oleh and Hassan Al-Atrash (1998) "Opening Up and Geographic Diversification of Trade in Transition Economies," International Monetary Fund Working Paper 22.

Havrylyshyn, Oleh and Donald McGettigan (2000) "Privatization in Transition Countries," *Post-Soviet Affairs* **16** (3): 257–286.

Havrylyshyn, Oleh and Thomas Wolf (2001) "Growth in Transition Countries, 1990–1998: The Main Lessons," in Oleh Havrylyshyn and Saleh M. Nsouli, eds., *A Decade of Transition: Achievements and Challenges*. Washington, DC: International Monetary Fund, pp. 83–128.

Hay, Jonathan R., and Andrei Shleifer (1998) "Private Enforcement of Public Laws: A Theory of Legal Reform," *American Economic Review* **88** (2): 398–403.

Hayek, Friedrich A. [1944] (1986) *Road to Serfdom.* Chicago: University of Chicago Press.

——— (1960) *The Constitution of Liberty.* London: Routledge & Kegan Paul.

Healy, Judith, and Martin McKee (2001) "Hospitals in Transition in Central and Eastern Europe and Central Asia," *Euro health,* **7** (3): 1.

Hellman, Joel S. (1998) "Winners Take All: The Politics of Partial Reform in Postcommunist Transitions," *World Politics* **50** (2): 203–34.

Hellman, Joel S., Geraint Jones, Daniel Kaufmann, and Mark Schankermann (2000) "Measuring Governance and State Capture: The Role of Bureaucrats and Firms in Shaping the Business Environment," mimeo, the European Bank for Reconstruction and Development and World Bank.

Hendley, Kathryn, Barry W. Ickes, Peter Murrell, and Randi Ryterman (1997) "Observations on the Use of Law by Russian Enterprises," *Post-Soviet Affairs* **13** (1): 19–41.

Hernandez-Cata, Ernesto (1997) "Liberalization and the Behavior of Output during the Transition from Plan to Market," *IMF Staff Papers* **44** (4): 405–29.

Hewett, Edward A. (1974) *Foreign Trade Prices in the Council for Mutual Economic Assistance.* Cambridge: Cambridge University Press.

——— (1988) *Reforming the Soviet Economy.* Washington, DC: Brookings Institution.

Heybey, Berta, and Peter Murrell (1999) "The Relationship between Economic Growth and the Speed of Liberalization during Transition," *Journal of Policy Reform* **3**: 121–37.

Hobbes, Thomas [1651] (1968) *Leviathan.* London: Penguin.

Hoffman, David (2002) *The Oligarchs.* New York: Public Affairs.

Holzmann, Robert (1997a) "Starting over in Pensions: The Challenges Facing Central and Eastern Europe," *Journal of Public Policy* **17** (3): 195–222.

——— (1997b) "Pension Reform in Central and Eastern Europe: Necessity, Approaches and Open Questions," *Serie Financiamiento del Desarrollo,* no. 45, United Nations: Economic Commission for Latin American and the Caribbean, Santiago, Chile, April.

Huntington, Samuel P. (1991) *The Third Wave: Democratization in the Late Twentieth Century.* Norman: University of Oklahoma Press.

——— (1992–93) "What Cost Freedom? Democracy and/or Economic Reform," *Harvard International Review* **15** (2): 8–13.

Illarionov, Andrei N. (1998a) "Kak byl organizovan rossiisky finansovy krizis (1)" [How the Russian Economic Crisis Was Organized, part 1], *Voprosy ekonomiki* **70** (11): 20–35.

——— (1998b) "Kak byl organizovan rossiisky finansovy krizis (2)" [How the Russian Economic Crisis Was Organized, part 2], *Voprosy ekonomiki* **70** (12): 12–31.

Impavido, Gregorio (1997) "Pension Reform and the Development of Pension Funds and Stock Markets in Eastern Europe," *Most* **7** (3): 101–35.

International Monetary Fund (IMF) (1992) "The Coordination of Monetary Policy in the Ruble Area," mimeo, April 29.

——— (1993) *Economic Review: Russian Federation.* Washington, DC: IMF.

——— (1994a) *Economic Review: Financial Relations among Countries of the Former Soviet Union.* Washington DC: IMF.

——— (1994b) *Economic Review: Trade Policy Reform in Countries of the Former Soviet Union.* Washington, DC: IMF.

_____ (1994c) "Fund Policies with Regard to Currency Stabilization Funds: Preliminary Considerations." Washington, DC: IMF.

_____ (2000) *World Economic Outlook*. Washington, DC: IMF, April.

_____ (2006) IMF World Economic Outlook database, April 2006 (accessed June 14, 2006).

_____ (2007) IMF World Economic Outlook database, April 2007 (accessed April 19, 2007).

International Monetary Fund (IMF), IBRD, Organization for Economic Cooperation and Development, and EBRD (1991) *A Study of the Soviet Economy*. Paris: February.

Inter-Parliamentary Union (2000) (www.ipu.org) (accessed May 18, 2000).

Isham, Jonathan, Daniel Kaufmann, and Lant H. Pritchett (1997) "Civil Liberties, Democracy, and the Performance of Government Projects," *World Bank Economic Review* **11** (2): 219–42.

Ježek, Tomáš (1997) "The Czechoslovak Experience with Privatization," *Journal of International Affairs* **50** (2): 477–88.

Johnson, Juliet (2000) *A Fistful of Rubles: The Rise and Fall of the Russian Banking System*. Ithaca, NY: Cornell University Press.

Johnson, Simon (1994) "Private Business in Eastern Europe," in Olivier Jean Blanchard, Kenneth A. Froot, and Jeffrey D. Sachs, eds., *The Transition in Eastern Europe*. Chicago: University of Chicago Press, pp. 245–90.

_____, Daniel Kaufmann, and Andrei Shleifer (1997a) "The Unofficial Economy in Transition," *Brookings Papers on Economic Activity* **27** (2): 159–239.

_____ (1997b) "Politics and Entrepreneurship in Transition Economies," Working Paper no. 57, The William Davidson Institute, University of Michigan.

_____, and Heidi Kroll (1991) "Managerial Strategies for Spontaneous Privatization," *Soviet Economy* **7** (4): 281–316.

_____, Heidi Kroll, and Mark Horton (1993) "New Banks in the Former Soviet Union: How Do They Operate?" in Anders Åslund and Richard Layard, eds., *Changing the Economic System in Russia*. New York: St. Martin's Press, pp. 183–209.

_____, and Gary W. Loveman (1995) *Starting Over in Eastern Europe: Entrepreneurship and Economic Renewal*. Boston: Harvard Business School Press.

Johnson, Simon, John McMillan, and Christopher Woodruff (2000) "Entrepreneurs and the Ordering of Institutional Reform: Poland, Slovakia, Romania, Russia and Ukraine Compared," *Economics of Transition* **8** (1): 1–36.

Karatnycky, Adrian, Alexander Motyl, and Charles Graybow, eds. (1999) *Nations in Transit 1998*. New Brunswick, N.J.: Transaction Publishers.

Karl, Terry Lynn, and Phillipe Schmitter (1991) "Modes of Transition in Latin America, Southern and Eastern Europe," *International Social Science Journal* **128**: 269–84.

Kaser, Michael (1996) "Post Communist Privatization: Flaws in the Treuhand Model," Discussion Papers in German Studies, University of Birmingham.

Katz, Barbara G., and Joel Owen (2000) "Choosing between Big Bang and Gradual Reform: An Option Price Approach," *Journal of Comparative Economics* **28** (1): 95–107.

Kaufmann, Daniel (1997) "Corruption: Some Myths and Facts," *Foreign Policy*, no. 107, pp. 114–31.

Kaufmann, Daniel and Aleksander Kaliberda (1996) "Integrating the Unofficial Economy into the Dynamics of Post-Socialist Economies: A Framework of Analysis and

Evidence," in Bartlomiej Kaminski, ed., *Economic Transition in Russia and the New States of Eurasia.* Armonk, NY: M. E. Sharpe, pp. 81–120.

Kaufmann, Daniel and Paul Siegelbaum (1996) "Privatization and Corruption in Transition Economies," *Journal of International Affairs* **50** (2): 419–58.

Keane, Michael P., and Eswar S. Prasad (2000) "Inequality, Transfers and Growth: New Evidence from the Economic Transition in Poland," IMF Working Paper no. 117, Washington, DC: International Monetary Fund.

Keen, Michael, Yitae Kim, and Ricardo Varsano (2006) "The 'Flat Tax(es)': Principles and Evidence," IMF Working Paper no. 218, Washington, DC: International Monetary Fund.

Keynes, John Maynard [1936] (1973) *The General Theory of Employment, Interest, and Money.* London: Macmillan.

Khanna, Tarun, and Jan W. Rivkin (2001) "Estimating the Performance Effects of Business Groups in Emerging Markets," *Strategic Management Journal* **22** (1): 45–74.

Kharas, Homi, Brian Pinto, and Sergei Ulatov (2001) "An Analysis of Russia's 1998 Meltdown: Fundamentals and Market Signals," *Brookings Papers on Economic Activity* 1: 1–50.

Khasbulatov, Ruslan (1992) "Programma dlya Khasbulatova" [Program for Khasbulatov], *Nezavisimaya gazeta*, April 3, p. 5.

Kissinger, Henry (1994) *Diplomacy.* New York: Simon & Schuster.

———— (2000) "Mission to Moscow," *Washington Post*, May 15, p. A15.

Kitschelt, Herbert, Zdenka Mansfeldova, Radoslaw Markowski, and Gábor Tóka (1999) *Post Communist Party Systems: Competition, Representation, and Inter-Party Cooperation.* Cambridge: Cambridge University Press.

Klaus, Václav (1992) *Dismantling Socialism: A Preliminary Report.* Prague: Top Agency.

———— (1994) *Rebirth of a Country: Five Years After.* Prague: Ringier.

Klebnikov, Paul (2000) *Godfather of the Kremlin: The Decline of Russia in the Age of Gangster Capitalism.* Orlando, FL: Harcourt.

Klein, Lawrence R., and Marshall Pomer, eds. (2001) *The New Russia: Transition Gone Awry.* Stanford, CA: Stanford University Press.

Knack, Stephen, and Philip Keefer (1995) "Institutions and Economic Performance: Cross-Country Tests Using Alternative Institutional Measures," *Economics and Politics* **7** (3): 207–27.

Kołodko, Grzegorz W. (2000) *From Shock to Therapy: The Political Economy of Postsocialist Transformation.* Oxford: Oxford University Press.

Komulainen, Tuomas, and Iikka Korhonen, eds. (2000) *Russian Crisis and Its Effects.* Helsinki: Kikimora.

Kornai, János (1980) *Economics of Shortage.* Amsterdam: North Holland.

———— (1986) "The Hungarian Reform Process: Visions, Hopes, and Reality," *Journal of Economic Literature* **24**: 1687–737.

———— (1990) *The Road to a Free Economy. Shifting from a Socialist System: The Example of Hungary.* New York: Norton.

———— (1992a) *The Socialist System. The Political Economy of Communism.* Princeton, NJ: Princeton University Press.

———— (1992b) "The Postsocialist Transition and the State: Reflections in Light of Hungarian Fiscal Problems," *American Economic Review* **82** (2): 1–21.

_____ (1994) "Transformational Recession: The Main Causes," *Journal of Comparative Economics* **19** (1): 39–63.

"Korrespondent Journal's List of 30 Richest Ukrainians," Ukrainian News Agency, June 30, 2006.

Kramer, Mark (1997) "Social Protection Policies and Safety Nets in East-Central Europe: Dilemmas of the Postcommunist Transformation," in Ethan B. Kapstein and Michael Mandelbaum, eds., *Sustaining the Transition: The Social Safety Net in Postcommunist Europe*. New York: Council on Foreign Relations, pp. 46–123.

Krastev, Ivan (2000) "The Strange (Re)Discovery of Corruption" in Ralf Dahrendorf, Yehuda Elkana, Aryen Neier, William Newton-Smith, and Istvan Rev, eds., *The Paradoxes of Unintended Consequences*. Budapest: Central European University Press.

Kravchuk, Robert S. (1999) "The Quest for Balance: Regional Self-Government and Subnational Fiscal Policy in Ukraine" in Taras Kuzio, Robert S. Kravchuk, and Paul D'Anieri, eds., *State and Institution-Building in Ukraine*. New York: St. Martin's Press, pp. 155–211.

Kroll, Luisa and Allison Fass, eds. (2006) "The World Billionaires," *Forbes*, March 9. Available: http://www.forbes.com/billionaires/ (accessed on August 1, 2006).

Kroll, Luisa and Lea Goldman, eds. (2005) "The World Billionaires," *Forbes*, March 10 Available: http://www.forbes.com/lists/2005/03/09/bill05land.html (accessed on June 2, 2005).

Krueger, Anne O. (1974) "The Political Economy of the Rent-Seeking Society," *American Economic Review* **64** (3): 291–303.

_____ (2002) "Why Crony Capitalism Is Bad for Economic Growth," in Stephen Haber, ed. *Crony Capitalism and Economic Growth in Latin America: Theory and Evidence*. Stanford, CA: Hoover Institution Press, pp. 1–23.

Krueger, Gary, and Marek Ciolko (1998) "A Note on Initial Conditions and Liberalization during Transition," *Journal of Comparative Economics* **26**: 718–34.

Kunicova, Jana, and Susan Rose-Ackerman (2001) "Electoral Rules as Constraints on Corruption: The Risks of Closed-List Proportional Representation." Mimeo, Yale University.

La Porta, Rafael, Florencio Lopez-de-Silanes, and Andrei Shleifer (1999a) "Corporate Ownership around the World," *Journal of Finance* **54** (2): 471–517.

La Porta, Rafael, Florencio Lopez-de-Silanes, Andrei Shleifer, and Robert Vishny (1998) "Law and Finance," *Journal of Political Economy* **106**: 1113–55.

_____ (1999b) "The Quality of Government," *Journal of Law, Economics and Organization* **15** (1): 222–79.

Laar, Mart (2002) *Little Country That Could*. London: Centre for Research into Post-Communist Economies.

Lackó, Mária (2000) "Hidden Economy – an Unknown Quantity?" *Economic of Transition* **8** (1): 117–49.

Lainela, Seija, and Pekka Sutela (1994) *The Baltic Economies in Transition*. Helsinki: Bank of Finland.

Lavigne, Marie (2000) "The Economics of the Transition Process: What Have We Learned?" *Problems of Post Communism* **47** (4): 16–23.

Layard, Richard, and John Parker (1996) *The Coming Russian Boom*. New York: Free Press.

Layard, Richard and Andrea Richter (1995) "Labour Market Adjustment – the Russian Way," in Anders Åslund, ed., *Russian Economic Reform at Risk*. New York: St. Martin's Press, pp. 119–47.

Levine, Ross (2005) "Law, Endowments and Property Rights," *Journal of Economic Perspectives* **19** (3): 61–88.

Levine, Ross and David Renelt (1992) "A Sensitivity Analysis of Cross-Country Growth Regressions," *American Economic Review* **82** (4): 942–63.

Lewandowski, Janusz, and Jan Szomburg (1989) "Property Reform as a Basis for Social and Economic Reform," *Communist Economies* **1** (3): 257–68.

Lieberman, Ira W., Stilpon S. Nestor, and Raj M. Desai, eds. (1997) *Between State and Market: Mass Privatization in Transition Economies*. Washington, DC: World Bank and Organization for Economic Cooperation and Development.

Lieven, Anatol (1993) *The Baltic Revolution: Estonia, Latvia, Lithuania, and the Path to Independence*. New Haven, CT: Yale University Press.

Lieven, Dominic (2000) *Empire: The Russian Empire and Its Rivals*. New Haven, CT: Yale University Press.

Lindblom, Charles E. (1977) *Politics and Markets*. New York: Basic Books.

Linz, Juan J., and Alfred Stepan (1992) "Political Identities and Electoral Sequences: Spain, the Soviet Union, and Yugoslavia," *Daedalus* **121** (2): 123–40.

Lipset, Seymour Martin (1959) "Some Social Requisites of Democracy: Economic Development and Political Legitimacy," *The American Political Science Review* **53** (1): 69–105.

Lipton, David, and Jeffrey D. Sachs (1990a) "Creating a Market in Eastern Europe: The Case of Poland," *Brookings Papers on Economic Activity* **20** (1): 75–147.

———— (1990b) "Privatization in Eastern Europe: The Case of Poland," *Brookings Papers on Economic Activity* **20** (2): 293–341.

Lloyd, John (1998) "Who Lost Russia?" *New York Times*, August 15.

Lougani, Prakash, and Nathan Sheets (1997) "Central Bank Independence, Inflation and Growth in Transition Economies," *Journal of Money, Credit and Banking* **29** (3): 381–99.

Lovei, Laszlo (1998) "Gas Reform in Ukraine: Monopolies, Markets, and Corruption," *Viewpoint*, note no. 169, World Bank.

Lvov, Dmitri S. (1996) "Obnovlennye orientiry ekonomicheskoi politiki" [Renewed Directions for Economic Policy], in Bogomolov, Oleg T., ed., *Reformy glazami amerikanskikh i rossiiskikh uchenykh* [Reforms in the Eyes of American and Russian Scholars]. Moscow: Rossiisky ekonomichesky zhurnal, pp. 163–84.

Maleva, Tatyana, ed. (1998) *Gosudarstvennaya i korporativnaya politika zanyatosti* [The State and Corporate Employment Policy]. Moscow: Carnegie Endowment for International Peace.

Maravall, José María (1994) "The Myth of Authoritarian Advantage," *Journal of Democracy* **5** (4): 17–31.

Marcinèin, Anton, and Sweder van Wijnbergen (1997) "The Impact of Czech Privatization Methods on Enterprise Performance Incorporating Initial Selection-Bias Correction," *Economics of Transition* **5** (2): 289–304.

Marer, Paul (1985) *Dollar GNPs of the U.S.S.R. and Eastern Europe*. Baltimore, MD: Johns Hopkins University Press.

Marsh, Peter (2006) "Sector Comes in from the Cold," *Financial Times*, June 14, 2006, p. 4.

Matyukhin, Georgy G. (1993) *Ya byl glavnym bankirom Rossii* [I Was Russia's Main Banker]. Moscow: Vysshaya shkola.

Mau, Vladimir (1999) "Rossiiskie ekonomicheskie reformy glazami zapadnykh kritikov" [Russian Economic Reforms in the Eyes of Western Critics], *Voprosy ekonomiki* **71** (11): 4–23.

Mau, Vladimir and Irina Starodubrovskaya (2001) *The Challenge of Revolution: Contemporary Russia in Historical Perspective*. Oxford: Oxford University Press.

Mau, Vladimir and V. Novikov (2002) "Otnoshenia Rossii i ES: prostranstvo vybora ili vybor prostranstva?" [The Relationship between Russia and the EU: Space of Choice or Choice of Space?] *Voprosy ekonomiki* 6: 133–43.

Mauro, Paulo (1995) "Corruption and Growth," *Quarterly Journal of Economics* **110** (3): 681–712.

———— (1998) "Corruption and the Composition of Government Expenditures," *Journal of Public Economics* **69** (2): 263–79.

McFaul, Michael (1997) *Russia's 1996 Presidential Elections: The End of Polarized Politics*. Stanford, CA: Hoover Press.

———— (1999) "The Political Economy of Social Policy Reform in Russia: Ideas, Institutions, and Interests," in Linda J. Cook, Mitchell A. Orenstein, and Marilyn Rueschmeyer, eds., *Left Parties and Social Policy in Postcommunist Europe*. Boulder, CO: Westview Press, pp. 207–34.

———— (2000) "Russia's 1999 Parliamentary Elections: Party Consolidation and Fragmentation," *Demokratizatsiya* **8** (1): 5–23.

———— (2001) *Russia's Unfinished Revolution: Political Change from Gorbachev to Putin*. Ithaca, NY: Cornell University Press.

———— (2006) "Conclusion: The Orange Revolution in a Comparative Perspective," in Anders Åslund and Michael McFaul, eds., *Revolution in Orange*. Washington, DC: Carnegie Endowment for International Peace, pp. 165–95.

McKinsey Global Institute (1999) *Unlocking Economic Growth in Russia*. Moscow: McKinsey & Company.

Megginson, William L., and Jeffry M. Netter (2001) "From State to Market: A Survey of Empirical Studies on Privatization," *Journal of Economic Literature* **39** (2): 321–89.

Megginson, William L., Robert C. Nash, and Matthias van Randenborgh (1994) "The Financial and Operating Performance of Newly Privatized Firms: An International Empirical Analysis," *Journal of Finance* **49** (2): 403–52.

Mercedes Balmaceda, Margarita (1998) "Gas, Oil and the Linkages between Domestic and Foreign Policies: The Case of Ukraine," *Europe-Asia Studies* **50** (2): 257–86.

Messerlin, Patrick A. (2001) *Measuring the Costs of Protection in Europe: European Commercial Policy in the 2000s*. Washington, DC: Institute for International Economics.

Michalopoulos, Constantine, and Vladimir Drebentsov (1997) "Observations on State Trading in the Russian Economy," *Post-Soviet Geography and Economics* **38** (5): 264–75.

————, Michalopoulos, Constantine and David G. Tarr (1996) *Trade Performance and Policy in the New Independent States*. Washington, DC: World Bank.

———— (1997) "The Economics of Customs Union in the Commonwealth of Independent States," *Post-Soviet Geography and Economics* **38** (3): 125–43.

Michalopoulos, Constantine and David G. Tarr, eds. (1994) *Trade in the New Independent States*. Washington, DC: World Bank.

Mihalisko, Kathleen J. (1997) "Belarus: Retreat to Authoritarianism," in Karen Dawisha and Bruce Parrott, eds., *Democratic Changes and Authoritarian Reactions in Russia, Ukraine, Belarus and Moldova*. Cambridge: Cambridge University Press, pp. 223–81.

Mikhailsovkaya, Inga B. (1994) "Crime and Statistics: Do the Figures Reflect the Real Situation?" *Demokratizatsiya* **2** (3): 412–25.

Milanovic, Branko (1998) *Income, Inequality, and Poverty during the Transition from Planned to Market Economy*. Washington, DC: World Bank.

Milcher, Susanne, Ben Slay, and Mark Collins (2007) "The Economic Rationale of the 'European Neighborhood Policy,'" in Anders Åslund and Marek Dąbrowski, eds., *Europe after Enlargement*. New York: Cambridge University Press, pp. 165–88.

Miles, Mark A., Mary Anastasia O'Grady, and Kim R. Holmes (2006) *2006 Index of Economic Freedom: The Link Between Economic Opportunity and Prosperity*. Washington, DC: The Heritage Foundation.

Mill, John Stuart [1859] (1975) *On Liberty*, New York: Norton.

Milward, Alan S. (1984) *The Reconstruction of Western Europe 1945–51*. London: Methuen.

Minassian, Girabed (1998) "The Road to Economic Disaster in Bulgaria," *Europe-Asia Studies* **50** (2): 331–49.

Misikhina, S. (1999) "Sotsialnye vyplaty i lgoty v Rossiiskoi Federatsii: raspredelenie po gruppam s razlichnym urovnem dokhoda" [Social Benefits in the Russian Federation: Distribution according to Income Levels], *Voprosy ekonomiki* **71** (2): 85–90.

Mizsei, Kálmán (1993) *Bankruptcy and the Post Communist Economies of East-Central Europe*. New York: Institute for East-West Studies.

Mizsei, Kálmán and Andrzej Rudka, eds. (1995) *From Association to Accession: The Impact of the Association Agreements on Central Europe's Trade and Integration with the European Union*. New York: Institute for East-West Studies.

Montesquieu, Charles de Secondat [1748] (1977) *The Spirit of Laws*. Berkeley: University of California Press.

Morck, Randall, Daniel Wolfenzon, and Bernard Yeung (2005) "Corporate Governance, Economic Entrenchment, and Growth," *Journal of Economic Literature* **43** (3): 655–720.

Morris, Charles R. (2005) *The Tycoons: How Andrew Carnegie, John D. Rockefeller, Jay Gould, and J. P. Morgan Invented the American Supereconomy*. New York: Times Books.

Murphy, Kevin A., Andrei Shleifer, and Robert W. Vishny (1992) "The Transition to a Market Economy: Pitfalls of Partial Reform," *Quarterly Journal of Economics* **57** (3): 889–903.

———— (1993) "Why Is Rent-Seeking So Costly to Growth?" *American Economic Review* **83** (2): 409–14.

Murrell, Peter (1992a) "Conservative Political Philosophy and the Strategy of Economic Transition," *East European Politics and Societies* **6** (1): 3–16.

———— (1992b) "Evolutionary and Radical Approaches to Economic Reform," *Economics of Planning* **25** (1): 79–95.

_____ (1992c) "Evolution in Economics and in the Economic Reform of the Centrally Planned Economies," in Christopher Clague and Gordon C. Rausser, eds., *The Emergence of Market Economies in Eastern Europe*. Cambridge, MA: Blackwell, pp. 35–53.

_____, ed. (2001) *Assessing the Value of Law in Transition Economies*. Ann Arbor: University of Michigan Press.

Murrell, Peter and Mancur Olson (1991) "The Devolution of Centrally Planned Economies," *Journal of Comparative Economics* **15** (2): 239–65.

Murrell, Peter and Yijang Wang (1993) "When Privatization Should Be Delayed: The Effect of Communist Legacies on Organizational and Institutional Reforms," *Journal of Comparative Economics* **17** (2): 385–406.

Myrdal, Gunnar (1968) *Asian Drama: An Inquiry into the Poverty of Nations*, vol. 2. New York: Twentieth Century Fund.

Nellis, John (1994) "Privatization in Estonia," World Bank FPD Note 19.

_____ (2001) "Time to Rethink Privatization in Transition Economies?" in Oleh Havrylyshyn and Saleh M. Nsouli, eds., *A Decade of Transition: Achievements and Challenges*. Washington, DC: International Monetary Fund, pp. 160–193.

Nicholls, Ana (1999) "Health and Wealth," *Business Central Europe*, June, pp. 12–17.

Nolan, Peter (1995) *China's Rise, Russia's Fall: Politics, Economics and Planning in the Transition from Stalinism*. New York: St. Martin's Press.

North, Douglass C. (1981) *Structure and Change in Economic History*. New York: Norton.

_____ (1994) "Economic Performance through Time," *American Economic Review* **84** (3): 359–68.

Nove, Alec (1969) *An Economic History of the U.S.S.R.* Harmondsworth: Penguin.

_____ (1977) *The Soviet Economic System*. London: George Allen & Unwin.

Novoprudsky, Semen (2000) "Vozbuzhdenie ot protsedury" [Excitement over Procedures], *Izvestiya*, February 19, p. 5.

Nuti, Domenico Mario (1996) "Inflation, Interest and Exchange Rates in the Transition," *Economics of Transition* **4** (1): 137–58.

Odling-Smee, John (2004) "The IMF and Russia in the 1990s," IMF Working Paper no. 155. Washington, DC: International Monetary Fund.

Odling-Smee, John, and Gonzalo Pastor (2002) "The IMF and the Ruble Area, 1991–93," *Comparative Economic Studies*, **44** (4): 3–29.

O'Donnell, Guillermo, and Philippe Schmitter (1986) *Transitions from Authoritarian Rule: Tentative Conclusions about Uncertain Democracies*. Baltimore, MD: Johns Hopkins University Press.

Ofer, Gur, and Aaron Vinokur (1992) *The Soviet Household under the Old Regime. Economic Conditions and Behaviour in the 1970s*. Cambridge: Cambridge University Press.

Offe, Claus (1997) *Varieties of Transition. The East European and East German Experience*. Cambridge, MA: MIT Press.

Olcott, Martha Brill (1996) *Central Asia's New States: Independence, Foreign Policy, and Regional Security*. Washington, DC: United States Institute of Peace Press.

Olcott, Martha Brill, Anders Åslund, and Sherman Garnett (1999) *Getting It Wrong*. Washington, DC: Carnegie Endowment for International Peace.

Olson, Mancur (1971) *The Logic of Collective Action. Public Goods and the Theory of Groups*. Cambridge, MA: Harvard University Press.

_____ (1982) *The Rise and Decline of Nations. Economic Growth, Stagnation, and Social Rigidities*. New Haven, CT: Yale University Press.

——— (2000) *Power and Prosperity. Outgrowing Communist and Capitalist Dictatorships.* New York: Basic Books.

Organization for Economic Cooperation and Development (OECD) (1996) *The Changing Social Benefits in Russian Enterprises.* Paris: OECD.

——— (2000a) *OECD Economic Surveys: Russian Federation.* Paris: OECD.

——— (2000b) *OECD Economic Surveys: The Baltic States.* Paris: OECD.

Orlowski, Lucjan (1993) "Indirect Transfers in Trade among Former Soviet Union Republics: Sources, Patterns and Policy Responses in the Post-Soviet Period," *Europe-Asia Studies* **45** (6): 1001–24.

——— (1995) "Direct Transfers between the Former Soviet Union Central Budget and the Republics: Past Evidence and Current Implications," *Economics of Planning* **28** (1): 59–73.

Owen, David, and David O. Robinson, eds. (2003) *Russia Rebounds.* Washington, DC: International Monetary Fund.

Paeglis, Imants (1996) "Latvia: Privatization Accelerates, Boosts Economic Reform," *Transition* (World Bank), December 13, pp. 37–40

Parkhomenko, Sergei (1992) "Volsky sozdaet partiyu pragmatikov" [Volsky Creates a Party of Pragmatists], *Nezavisimaya gazeta*, May 13, p. 2.

Pasvolsky, Leo (1928) *Economic Nationalism of the Danubian States.* London: George Allen & Unwin.

Perotti, Enrico C., and Stanislav Gelfer (2001) "Red Barons or Robber Barons? Governance and Investment in Russian Financial-Industrial Groups," *European Economic Review* **45**: 1601–17.

Persson, Torsten, Gerard Roland, and Guido Tabellini (2000) "Comparative Politics and Public Finance," *Journal of Political Economy* **108** (6): 1121–161.

Persson, Torsten and Guido Tabellini (2000) *Political Economics: Explaining Economic Policy.* Cambridge, MA: MIT Press.

——— (2003) *Economic Effects of Constitutions.* Cambridge, MA: MIT Press.

——— (2004) "Constitutions and Economic Policy," *Journal of Economic Perspectives* **18** (1): 75–98.

Persson, Torsten, Guido Tabellini, and Francesco Trebbi (2003) "Electoral Rules and Corruption," *Journal of the European Economic Association* **1** (1): 958–89.

Petrakov, Nikolai, Vladlen Perlamutrov, Yuri Borozdin, and V. Manevich (1992) "Pravitelstvo utratilo kontrol nad eckonomicheskimi protsessami" [The Government Has Lost Control over the Economic Processes], *Nezavisimaya gazeta*, March 6, p. 4.

Pickel, Andreas, and Helmut Wiesenthal (1997) *The Grand Experiment.* Boulder, CO: Westview Press.

Pinto, Brian, Marek Belka, and Stefan Krajewski (1993) "Transforming State Enterprises in Poland: Evidence on Adjustment by Manufacturing Firms," *Brookings Papers on Economic Activity* **23** (1): 213–71.

Pinto, Brian, Vladimir Drebentsov, and Alexander Morozov (1999) "Dismantling Russia's Nonpayments System: Creating Conditions for Growth," report by the World Bank, Moscow, September.

Pipes, Richard (1990) *The Russian Revolution.* New York: Vintage Books.

——— (2005) *Russian Conservatism and Its Critics: A Study in Political Culture.* New Haven, CT: Yale University Press.

Pistor, Katharina, Martin Raiser, and Stanisław Gelfer (2000) "Law and Finance in Transition Economies," *Economics of Transition* **8** (2): 325–68.

Pistor, Katharina, and Andrew Spicer (1996) "Investment Funds in Mass Privatization and Beyond: Evidence from the Czech Republic and Russia," Harvard Institute for International Development, Cambridge, MA, Development Discussion Paper no. 565.

Pleskovic, Boris (1994) "Financial Policies in Socialist Countries in Transition," World Bank Policy Research Working Paper 1242.

Pleskovic, Boris, Anders Åslund, William Bader, and Robert Campbell (2000) "State of the Art in Economics Education and Research in Transition Economies," *Comparative Economic Studies* **42** (2): 65–108.

Popov, Vladimir (2000) "Shock Therapy Versus Gradualism: The End of the Debate," *Comparative Economic Studies* **42** (1): 1–57.

Prizel, Ilya (1997) "Ukraine between Proto-Democracy and 'Soft' Authoritarianism," in Karen Dawisha, and Bruce Parrott, eds., *Democratic Changes and Authoritarian Reactions in Russia, Ukraine, Belarus and Moldova.* Cambridge: Cambridge University Press, pp. 330–69.

Prytula, Olena (2006) "The Ukrainian Media Rebellion," in Anders Åslund and Michael McFaul, eds., *Revolution in Orange.* Washington, DC: Carnegie Endowment for International Peace, pp. 103–24.

Przeworski, Adam (1991) *Democracy and the Market.* Cambridge: Cambridge University Press.

_____ (1995) *Sustainable Democracy.* Cambridge: Cambridge University Press.

Puglisi, Rosaria (2003) "The Rise of the Ukrainian Oligarchs," *Democratization,* **10** (3): 99–123.

Rajan, Raghuram G., and Luigi Zingales (2003) "The Great Reversals: The Politics of Financial Development in the Twentieth Century," *Journal of Financial Economics* **69** (1): 5–50.

Reddaway, Peter, and Dmitri Glinski (2001) *The Tragedy of Russia's Reforms: Market Bolshevism against Democracy.* Washington, DC: United States Institute of Peace Press.

Rodrik, Dani (1992) "Making Sense of the Soviet Trade Shock in Eastern Europe: A Framework and Some Estimates," in Mario Blejer, Guillermo A. Calvo, Fabrizio Coricelli, and Alan H. Gelb, eds., *Eastern Europe in Transition: From Recession to Growth?* World Bank Discussion Paper 196.

Roland, Gérard (1993) "Political Economy of Restructuring and Privatization in Eastern Europe," *European Economic Review* **37** (2–3): 533–40.

_____ (1994) "On the Speed and Sequencing of Privatisation and Restructuring," *Economic Journal* **104** (426): 1158–68.

_____ (2000) "Corporate Governance Systems and Restructuring: The Lessons from the Transition Experience," Washington, DC: World Bank, Annual Bank Conference on Development Economics, April 18–20.

Rosati, Dariusz K. (1995) "The Impact of the Soviet Trade Shock on Central and East European Economies," in Robert Holzmann, Georg Winckler, and Janos Gács, eds., *Output Decline in Eastern Europe: Unavoidable, External Influence or Homemade?* Boston: Kluwer, pp. 131–59.

_____ (1996) "Exchange Rates Policies during Transition from Plan to Market," *Economics of Transition* **4** (1): 159–84.

Rose-Ackerman, Susan (1999) *Corruption and Government: Causes, Consequences, and Reform.* Cambridge: Cambridge University Press.

Rostowski, Jacek (1993) "The Inter-Enterprise Debt Explosion in the Former Soviet Union: Causes, Consequences, Cures," *Communist Economies and Economic Transformation* **5** (2): 131–59.

———— (1994) "Interenterprise Arrears in Post Communist Economies," International Monetary Fund Working Paper, April.

———— (1998) *Macroeconomic Instability in Post Communist Countries.* Oxford: Clarendon Press.

Russian Academy of Sciences (RAN), Economic Department, and the International Foundation "Reform" (1994) "Sotsialno-ekonomicheskie preobrazovaniya v Rossii: sovremennaya situatsiya i novye podkhody" [Social-Economic Transformations in Russia: The Contemporary Situation and New Approaches], mimeo, Moscow, January.

Russian Economic Barometer (2000) III Quarter.

Russian European Centre for Economic Policy (RECEP) (1999) *Russian Economic Trends,* various issues.

Rustow, Dankwart (1970) "Transitions to Democracy: Toward a Dynamic Model," *Comparative Politics* **2** (3): 337–64.

Rutskoi, Aleksandr (1992) "Est' li vykhod iz krizisa? (Is There a Way out of the Crisis?)" *Pravda,* February 8, p. 3.

Sachs, Jeffrey D. (1990) "What Is to Be Done?" *The Economist,* January 13, pp. 19–24.

———— (1991) "Crossing the Valley of Tears in East European Reform," *Challenge* **34** (5): 26–34.

———— (1992) "The Economic Transformation of Eastern Europe: The Case of Poland," *Economics of Planning* **25**: 5–19.

———— (1993) *Poland's Jump to the Market Economy.* Cambridge, MA: MIT Press.

———— (1994) "Life in the Economic Emergency Room," in John Williamson, ed., *The Political Economy of Policy Reform.* Washington, DC: Institute for International Economics, pp. 501–23.

———— (1995a) "Why Russia Has Failed to Stabilize," in Anders Åslund, ed., *Russian Economic Reform at Risk.* New York: St. Martin's Press, pp. 53–64.

———— (1995b) "Postcommunist Parties and the Politics of Entitlements," *Transition* (World Bank) **6** (3): 1–4.

———— (1996) "The Transition at Mid Decade," *American Economic Association Papers and Proceedings* **86** (2): 128–33.

Sachs, Jeffrey D. and David A. Lipton (1990) "Poland's Economic Reform," *Foreign Affairs* **63** (3): 47–66.

———— (1993) "Remaining Steps to a Market-based Monetary System," in Anders Åslund, and Richard Layard, eds., *Changing the Economic System in Russia.* New York: St. Martin's Press, pp. 127–62.

Sachs, Jeffrey D. and Andrew Warner (1995) "Economic Reform and the Process of Global Integration," *Brookings Papers on Economic Activity* **25** (1): 1–118.

———— (1996a) "Natural Resource Abundance and Economic Growth," mimeo, Harvard Institute for International Development, Cambridge, MA.

———— (1996b) "Achieving Rapid Growth in the Transition Economies of Central Europe," Harvard Institute for International Development, Development Discussion Paper no. 544.

Sachs, Jeffrey D. and Wing Thye Woo (1994) "Reform in China and Russia," *Economic Policy,* no. 18: 101–45.

Sala-i-Martin, Xavier (1997) "I Just Ran Two Million Regressions," *American Economic Review* **87** (2): 178–83.

Sargent, Thomas J. (1986) "The Ends of Four Big Inflations," in Thomas J. Sargent, ed., *Rational Expectations and Inflation*. New York: Harper and Row, pp. 40–109.

Schaffer, Mark (1998) "Do Firms in Transition Have Soft Budget Constraints? A Reconsideration of Concepts and Evidence," *Journal of Comparative Economics* **26** (1): 157–79.

Schumpeter, Joseph A. [1943] (1976) *Capitalism, Socialism and Democracy*. London: George Allen & Unwin.

Selowsky, Marcelo, and Ricardo Martin (1996) "Policy Performance and Output Growth in the Transition Economies," *American Economic Review* **87** (2): 349–53.

Selyunin, Vasili, and Grigori I. Khanin (1987) "Lukovaya tsifra" [Cunning Number], *Novy mir* **63** (2): 181–201.

Shapiro, Judith (1995) "The Rising Mortality Crisis and its Causes," in Anders Åslund, ed., *Russian Economic Reform at Risk*. New York: St. Martin's Press, pp. 149–78.

Shkolnikov, V. M., E. M. Andreev, and T. M. Maleva (2000) *Neravenstvo pered litsom smerti v Rossii* [Inequality Facing Death in Russia]. Moscow: Carnegie Moscow Center.

Shleifer, Andrei (1997) "Government in Transition," *European Economic Review* **41** (3–5): 385–410.

⸻ (2005) *A Normal Country: Russia after Communism*. Cambridge, MA: Harvard University Press.

Shleifer, Andrei and Daniel Treisman (2000) *Without a Map: Political Tactics and Economic Reform in Russia*. Cambridge, MA: MIT Press.

⸻ (2004) "A Normal Country," *Foreign Affairs* **83** (2): 20–38.

Shleifer, Andrei and Dmitry Vasiliev (1996) "Management Ownership and Russian Privatization" in Roman Frydman, Cheryl Gray, and Andrzej Rapaczynski, eds., *Corporate Governance in Central Europe and Russia*, vol. 2. Budapest: Central European University Press, pp. 62–77.

Shleifer, Andrei and Robert W. Vishny (1993) "Corruption," *Quarterly Journal of Economics* **108** (3): 599–617.

⸻ (1998) *The Grabbing Hand: Government Pathologies and Their Cures*. Cambridge, MA: Harvard University Press.

Shmelev, Nikolai P. (1987) "Avansy i dolgi" [Advances and Debts], *Novy mir* **63** (6): 142–58.

Siebert, Horst (1992) *Das Wagnis der Einheit* [The Daring of Unity]. Stuttgart: Deutsche Verlags-Anstalt.

Slay, Ben (1996) "Post Communist Competition Policy: Conclusions and Suggestions," in Ben Slay, ed., *De-Monopolization and Competititon Policy in Post Communist Economies*. Boulder, CO: Westview Press, pp. 229–37.

Slay, Ben and Vladimir Capelik (1997) "The Struggle for Natural Monopoly Reform in Russia," *Post-Soviet Geography and Economics* **38** (7): 396–429.

Slider, Darrell (1997) "Democratization in Georgia," in Karen Dawisha and Bruce Parrott, eds., *Conflict, Cleavage, and Chance in Central Asia and the Caucasus*. Cambridge: Cambridge University Press, pp. 156–98.

Sonin, Konstantin (2003) "Why the Rich May Favor Poor Protection of Property Rights," *Journal of Comparative Economics* **31**:715–31.

Soros, George (1991) *Underwriting Democracy*. New York: Free Press.

Stark, David, and László Bruszt (1998) *Postsocialist Pathways: Transforming Politics and Property in East Central Europe.* Cambridge: Cambridge University Press.

Steele Gordon, John (2004) *An Empire of Wealth: The Epic History of American Economic Power.* New York: HarperCollins.

Stiglitz, Joseph E. (1999a) "Whither Reform? Ten Years of Transition," presented at the Annual Bank Conference on Development Economics, Washington, DC, April 28–30.

——— (1999b) "Quis Custociet Ipsos Custodes? Corporate Governance Failures in the Transition," presented at the Annual Bank Conference on Development Economics – Europe, Paris, June 21–3.

——— (2000) "The Insider: What I Learned at the World Economic Crisis," *New Republic,* April 17 and 24, pp. 56–60.

——— (2002) *Globalization and Its Discontents.* New York: Norton.

——— (2006) *Making Globalization Work.* New York: Norton.

Sutela, Pekka (1998) *The Road to the Russian Market Economy, 1993–1998.* Saarijärvi: Kikimora.

Swinnen, Johan F. M. (1999) "The Political Economy of Land Reform Choices in Central and Eastern Europe," *Economics of Transition* 7 (3): 637–64.

Székely, István P., and David M. G. Newberry, eds. (1993) *Hungary: An Economy in Transition.* Cambridge: Cambridge University Press.

Tait, Alan A., and S. Nuri Erbas (1995) "Excess Wages Tax," International Monetary Fund Working Paper no. 17, February.

Tanzi, Vito, ed. (1992) *Fiscal Policies in Economies in Transition.* Washington, DC: International Monetary Fund.

Tanzi, Vito and Hamid Davoodi (1997) "Corruption, Public Investment, and Growth," International Monetary Fund Working Paper no. 139.

Tanzi, Vito and Ludger Schuknecht (2000) *Public Spending in the 20th Century.* Cambridge: Cambridge University Press.

Tanzi, Vito and George Tsibouris (2000) "Fiscal Reform over Ten Years of Transition," IMF Working Paper no. 113. Washington, DC: International Monetary Fund.

Tarr, David G. (1994) "The Terms-of-Trade Effects of Moving to World Prices on Countries of the Former Soviet Union," *Journal of Comparative Economics* 18 (1): 1–24.

Timoshenko, Viktor (1998) "Vse bogatye lyudi Ukrainy zarabotali svoi kapitaly na rossiiskom gaze" [All Rich People in Ukraine Made Their Money on Russian Gas], *Nezavisimaya gazeta,* October 16.

Tismaneanu, Vladimir (1997) "Romanian Exceptionalism? Democracy, Ethnocracy, and Uncertain Pluralism in Post-Ceauşescu Romania," in Karen Dawisha and Bruce Parrott, eds., *Politics, Power, and the Struggle for Democracy in South-East Europe.* Cambridge: Cambridge University Press, pp. 403–51.

Tompson, William (2005) "The Political Implications of Russia's Resource-Based Economy," *Post-Soviet Affairs* 21 (4): 335–59.

Tornell, Aaron, and Andrés Velasco (1995) "Money-Based versus Exchange Rate-Based Stabilization with Endogenous Fiscal Policy," NBER Working Paper no. 5300.

TransMONEE database (2006) UNICEF Innocenti Research Center, Florence. Available: http://www.unicef-icdc.org/resources/transmonee.html (accessed June 14, 2006).

Transparency International (2005) "Corruption Perceptions Index." Available http://transparency.org/policy_research/surveys_indices/cpi/2005 (accessed May 22, 2006).

——— (2006) "Corruption Perceptions Index." Available: http://transparency.org/ policy_research/surveys_indices/cpi/2006 (accessed May 23, 2006).

Treisman, Daniel S. (1998) "Fighting Inflation in a Transitional Regime: Russia's Anomalous Stabilization," *World Politics* **50**: 235–65.

——— (2000) "The Causes of Corruption: A Cross-National Study," *Journal of Public Economics* **76**: 399–457.

United Nations Development Program (1998) *Poverty in Transition?* New York: United Nations.

United Nations Economic Commission for Europe (1990) *Economic Survey of Europe in 1989–1990.* New York: United Nations.

——— (1991) *Economic Survey of Europe in 1990–1991.* New York: United Nations.

——— (1992) *Economic Survey of Europe in 1991–1992.* New York: United Nations.

——— (2000) *Economic Survey of Europe,* no. 2/3, New York: United Nations.

——— (2003) *Economic Survey of Europe,* no. 2, New York: United Nations.

——— (2004) *Economic Survey of Europe,* no. 2, New York: United Nations.

——— (2006) Statistical Database. http://www.unece.org/stats/data.htm (accessed various dates April-July 2006).

United Nations University World Institute for Development Economics Research (UNU-WIDER) (2006) World Income Inequality Database, version 2.0a. (accessed May 2, 2006).

U.S. Census Bureau (1999) *Statistical Abstract of the United States.* Available: http://www. census.gov/prod/www/statistical-abstract-us.html (accessed July 12, 2006).

——— (2006) International Database. http://www.census.gov/ipc/www/idbnew.html (accessed July 10, 2006).

Uvalic, Milica, and Daniel Vaughan-Whitehead, eds. (1997) *Privatization Surprises in Transition Economies: Employee-Ownership in Central and Eastern Europe.* Cheltenham: Edward Elgar.

Veblen, Thorstein [1899] (1994) *The Theory of the Leisure Class.* New York: Penguin.

Volkov, Vadim (2002) *Violent Entrepreneurs: The Use of Force in the Making of Russian Capitalism.* Ithaca, NY: Cornell University Press.

Von Mises, Ludwig [1920] (1972) "Economic Calculation in the Socialist Commonwealth," in Alec Nove and D. Mario Nuti, eds., *Socialist Economics.* Harmondsworth: Penguin, pp. 75–91.

Voslenskii, Mikhail S. (1984) *Nomenklatura.* Garden City, NY: Doubleday.

Westin, Peter (2005) "'What If?' Russia 2015 at $50/bbl and $100/bbl," Aton Capital, Moscow, October 3.

Williamson, John (1990) *Latin American Adjustment: How Much Has Happened?* Washington, DC: Institute for International Economics.

——— (1995) *What Role for Currency Boards?* Washington, DC: Institute for International Economics.

Williamson, Oliver E. (1975) *Markets and Hierarchies.* New York: Free Press.

Wilson, Andrew (2006) *Ukraine's Orange Revolution.* New Haven, CT: Yale University Press.

Wilson, Dominic, and Roopa Purushothaman (2003) "Dreaming with BRICs: The Path of 2050," Golman Sachs, Global Economics Paper 99.

Winiecki, Jan (1988) *The Distorted World of Soviet-Type Economies.* London: Routledge.

——— (1991a) *Resistance to Change in the Soviet Economic System.* New York: Routledge.

———— (1991b) "The Inevitability of a Fall in Output in the Early Stages of Transition to the Market: Theoretical Underpinnings," *Soviet Studies* **43** (4): 669–76.

World Bank (1994a) *Averting the Old Age Crisis: Policies to Protect the Old And Promote Growth*. Oxford: Oxford University Press.

———— (1994b) *World Development Report 1994: An Infrastructure for Development*. Oxford: Oxford University Press.

———— (1996a) *World Development Report 1996: From Plan to Market*. Oxford: Oxford University Press.

———— (1996b) *Fiscal Management in Russia*. Washington, DC: World Bank.

———— (1998) *Assessing Aid: What Works, What Doesn't and Why*. New York: Oxford University Press.

———— (2000a) World Development Indicators, CD-ROM.

———— (2000b) *Making Transition Work for Everyone: Poverty and Inequality in Europe and Central Asia*. Washington, DC: World Bank.

———— (2002) *Transition The First Ten Years: Analysis and Lessons for Eastern Europe and the Former Soviet Union*. Washington, DC: World Bank.

———— (2004) *Social Protection in ECE during the Transition: An Unfinished Agenda*. Washington, DC: World Bank.

———— (2005a) *From Disintegration to Reintegration: Eastern Europe and the Former Soviet Union in International Trade*. Washington, DC: World Bank.

———— (2005b) *Growth, Poverty, and Inequality: Eastern Europe and the Former Soviet Union*, Washington, DC: World Bank.

———— (2005c) *Current Issues in Fiscal Reform in Central Europe and the Baltic States 2005*, Washington, DC: World Bank.

———— (2006) *World Development Indicators*, online database. Available: http://worldbank.org/ (accessed various dates April-July, 2006).

World Bank and International Finance Corporation (2006) *Doing Business in 2006: Creating Jobs*, Washington, DC: World Bank. Available: http://www.doingbusiness.org/ (accessed June 20, 2006).

Wyplosz, Charles (1999) "Ten Years of Transformation: Macroeconomic Lessons." World Bank, Annual Bank Conference on Development Economics, Washington, DC, April 28–30.

Yaremenko, Yuri, Viktor Ivanter, Aleksandr Nekrasov, Marat Yzyakov, and Vyacheslav Panfilov (1992) "Nado li otpuskat' tseny na toplivo?" [Is It Necessary to Let the Prices of Fuel Free?], *Nezavisimaya gazeta*, April 1, p. 4.

Yavlinsky, Grigory, and Serguey Braguinsky (1994) "The Inefficiency of *Laissez-Faire* in Russia: Hysteresis Effects and the Need for Policy-Led Transformation," *Journal of Comparative Economics* **19** (1): 88–116.

Yekhanurov, Yuri I. (2000) "The Progress of Privatization," in Anders Åslund and Georges de Ménil, eds., *Ukrainian Economic Reform: The Unfinished Agenda*. Armonk, NY: M. E. Sharpe, pp. 189–214.

Yeltsin, Boris N. (1991) "B. N. Yeltsin's Speech," *Sovetskaya Rossiya*, October 29.

Yevstigneev, Ruben, and Liudmila Yevstigneeva (1999) "Kuda zhe vedut reformy?" [Where Do the Reforms Lead?], *Voprosy ekonomiki* **71** (9): 4–18.

Index

education issues, 303
election monitoring, 239
electoral rules, 224–225, 230
Elster, Jon, 211–213
employee privatization, 158, 161–162
Engels, Friedrich, 11
enterprise development, 165–168
entrepreneurial banking systems, 121–123
Estonia
  banking crisis of, 122
  corruption reduction in, 251, 255
  demand barriers in, 68
  democratization/reform attempts, 25
  EU membership application, 283–284
  and exchange rates, 34
  governmental reform success, 231
  and HIV/AIDS, 194
  liberalization/stabilization programs, 111,
    128–129
  multi-party coalitions, 228
  population decline, 193
  radical structural reforms, 84–86
  return of growth, 60–61
  structured parliaments, 225
  WTO membership, 293
EU. *See* European Union (EU)
Eural Trans Gaz trading company,
  99
Eurasian Economic Community, 294–
  295
Europe
  demise of Communism, 20–23, 29
  fear of Russia, 287
  revolutions of 1848
European Bank for Reconstruction and
    Development (EBRD)
  birth of, 297
  Soviet economy study, 288
  Structural Reform Index, 84
  transition index, 83
European Commission, 233
European Monetary Union, 127
European Neighborhood Policy (EU),
  296
European Union (EU), 30
  antidumping sanctions against
    Russia/Ukraine, 287
  defense of ruble zone, 108–109
  disbursement of financial aid, 300
  Europe Agreements
  labor market paradigm, 92

and legal system reform, 246, 247
multifaceted transitional role, 309–310
and pension reform, 202
pressure for raising tariffs, 90
reunification of Germany, 282
social welfare paradigm advocacy, 96
transitional role of, 284–285
exchange rates, 123–127
  in Baltic states, 125–126
  in Czechoslovakia, 34, 124–125
  in Hungary, 125
  influence of Russian financial crash,
    127
  in Poland, 34, 100–101
  unification of, 89
external liberalization, 72, 88, 89

Federov, Boris, 110
finance ministry, reinforcement of, 112
financial stabilization, 111, 127–142. *See also*
    Russian financial crash
  arrears crisis, 132–133
  of Bulgaria, 131–132
  of Estonia, 111, 128–129
  of Poland, 111, 127–128
  postcommunist stabilization lessons,
    138–142
  of Russia, 129–131
Fischer, Stanley, 31, 71
Fish, Steven, 211
five-year plan, of Stalin, 11
foreign investments, ongoing growth of,
  299
foreign trade, liberalization of, 89–92,
  292–297
Fraser Institute, index of economic freedom,
  83
free economic zones, 91–92
Freedom House index, 215, 217, 239
Friedman, Milton, 149

Gaddy, Clifford, 133, 136
Gaidar, Yegor, 25, 31, 88, 146, 234, 290–291
  radical economic reform ideas, 44
Gambetta, Diego, 243
Gamsakhurdia, Zviad, 26
Gazprom gas monopoly (Russia), 98–99, 246,
  262
Geddes, Barbara, 210
General Agreement on Tariffs and Trade
    (GATT). *See* World Trade Organization

Moldova, 25–26
Communist Party power consolidation, 221
constitutional conflicts, 226
corruption in, 251
declining male life expectancy, 188–189
electoral path, 219–220
frozen conflict in, 236
influence of war, 236
output declines, 60
population decline, 193
poverty levels, 186–187
public health expenditures, 190
Soviet social welfare model, 199–200
state of democracy/market economic transformation, 215
strengthening parliamentary system, 227
unemployment rates, 96
voucher privatization, 157
WTO membership, 293–294
monetary policy, 119–123
capital flight, 123
entrepreneurial banking systems, 121–123
monopolies, 87–89. *See also* antimonopoly policies; coal monopoly; Gazprom gas monopoly; transportation monopoly
Nemtsov's attack on, 99
Russian break up of, 96–101
World Bank regulation of, 97
Morck, Randall, 257
Murphy, Kevin A., 102
Murrell, Peter, 39–40, 43
Myrdal, Gunnar, 208

Nagorny Karabakh conflict, in Azerbaijan, 26, 236
Naishul, Vitaly, 149
National Democratic Institute, 239
National Salvation Front, in Romania, 23
NATO. *See* North Atlantic Treaty Organization
Nazarbayev, Nursultan, 27, 279
Nemtsov, Boris, 99
Nicholas I (Tsar), 237
Niyazov, Saparmurat, 27, 101
Nomenklatura system
and Brezhnev, 17–18
as collective dictator, 17
of Communist Party, 12
vs. democratization, 207, 209
gradual economic transitions, 38

Kazakhstan/Turkmenistan/Uzbekistan rule through, 27
kleptocratic nature of, 241–242
and rent seeking, 39
retention of power, 25
splitting of, 206
nongovernmental organizations (NGOs), 239, 302–303
North, Douglass C., 43
North Atlantic Treaty Organization (NATO), 30

Offe, Claus, 211–213
oligarchies
in CIS countries, 274
economics of, 259–264
instability of, 275–276
politics of, 264–267
vs. state companies, 261–262
oligarchs
complaints/criticisms of, 267–272
cooperation with communists, 220–221
definition, 256–257
economic entrenchment by, 264
as *homo oeconomicus*, 265
identification of, 257–259
Kremlin extortion of, 265
organized crime *vs.*, 243–244
Putin *vs.*, 265, 273, 276, 280
and rent seeking, 309
state enterprises *vs.*, 261–262
usefulness of, 275
weakening of, 221
Olivera-Tanzi effect, 114
Olson, Mancur, 39–40, 236, 279
Open Society Institute, 239
Orange Revolution, 222, 223, 269, 271
Organization for Economic Cooperation and Development (OECD)
Soviet economy study, 288
and pension reform, 202
Organization for Security and Cooperation in Europe (OSCE), 239
Orlowski, Lucjan, 66
"Orthodoxy, Autocracy, Nationality" (Uvarov), 237
Ostanin, Dmytro, 262–263
Otpor student organization, Serbia, 223
output
decline and recovery, 59–61
exaggeration of slump, 63–69